Herbaceous Perennials

F. A. GILES
REBECCA McINTOSH KEITH
DONALD C. SAUPE

Illustrated by F. A. Giles

RESTON PUBLISHING COMPANY
A Prentice-Hall Company • Reston, Virginia

Herbaceous Perennials

Library of Congress Cataloging in Publication Data

GILES, FLOYD.
    Herbaceous perennials.

    1. Perennials. I. Keith, Rebecca, joint author.
II. Saupe, Donald, joint author. III. Title.
SB434.G54   635.9'32   80–11830
ISBN 0–8359–2822–5

Herbaceous Perennials,
by Floyd Giles, Rebecca Keith, and Donald Saupe
© 1980 by Reston Publishing Company, Reston, Virginia

All rights reserved.
No part of this book may be reproduced
in any way or by any means
without permission in writing from the publisher.

10 9 8 7 6 5 4 3 2 1

PRINTED IN THE UNITED STATES OF AMERICA

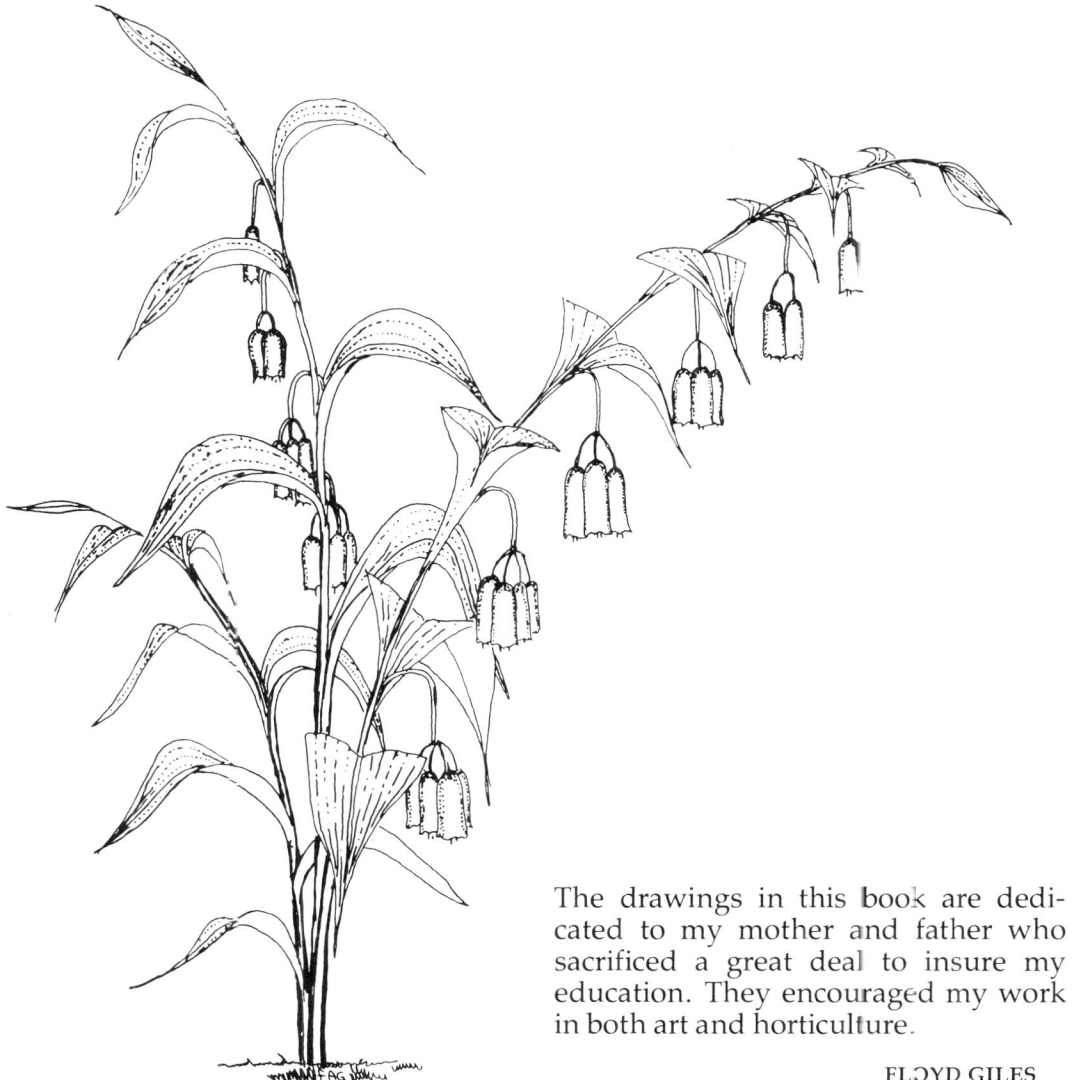

The drawings in this book are dedicated to my mother and father who sacrificed a great deal to insure my education. They encouraged my work in both art and horticulture.

FLOYD GILES

Preface

We would like to acknowledge a debt of gratitude to three classic reference works in the field:

BAILEY, L.H., *The Standard Cyclopedia of Horticulture* (New York: Macmillan, 1941)

THE STAFF OF THE L.H. BAILEY HORTORIUM, Cornell University, *Hortus Third: A Concise Dictionary of Plants Cultivated in the United States and Canada;* initially compiled by LIBERTY HYDE BAILEY and ETHEL ZOE BAILEY, revised and expanded by the staff of the L.H. Bailey Hortorium (New York: Macmillan, 1976)

CUMMING, RODERICK W., and ROBERT E. LEE, *Contemporary Perennials* (New York: Macmillan, 1960)

Contents

HERBACEOUS PERENNIALS 1

Acanthus, 2
Achillea, 4
Aconitum, 8
Aegopodium, 12
Ajuga, 14
Alcea, 16
Alchemilla, 18
Anaphalis, 20
Anchusa, 22
Anthemis, 24
Aquilegia, 26
Arabis, 30
Armeria, 32
Artemisia, 34
Asarum, 36
Asclepias, 38
Aster, 40

Astilbe, 46
Aubrieta, 50
Aurinia, 52

Baptisia, 54
Belamcanda, 58
Bellis, 60
Bergenia, 62

Campanula, 64
Centaurea, 70
Cerastium, 72
Chrysanthemum, 74
Cimicifuga, 82
Clematis, 84
Convallaria, 88
Coreopsis, 90

Delphinium, 92
Dianthus, 96
Dicentra, 102
Dictamnus, 106
Digitalis, 108
Dodecatheon, 110
Doronicum, 112

Echinacea, 114
Echinops, 116
Epimedium, 118
Eremurus, 120
Erigeron, 122
Eryngium, 124
Euphorbia, 126

Gaillardia, 130
Galium, 132
Geranium, 134
Gypsophilia, 136

Helenium, 140

Helianthemum, 14
Helianthus, 144
Heliopsis, 146
Helleborus, 148
Hemerocallis, 150
Hesperis, 154
Heuchera, 156
Hibiscus, 158
Hosta, 160

Iberis, 164
Iris, 166

Kniphofia, 170

Lathyrus, 172
Lavandula, 174
Liatris, 176
Limonium, 178
Linum, 180
Liriope, 182
Lobelia, 184

Lunaria, 188
Lupinus, 190
Lychnis, 192
Lysimachia, 196
Lythrum, 198

Macleaya, 200
Mertensia, 202
Monarda, 204
Myosotis, 206

Oenothera, 208

Paeonia, 210
Papaver, 216
Phlox, 220
Physalis, 226
Physostegia, 228
Platycodon, 230
Polemonium, 232
Polygonatum, 234
Primula, 236

Pulmonaria, 238

Rudbeckia, 240

Saponaria, 242
Scabiosa, 244
Sedum, 246
Sempervivum, 250
Stachys, 252

Thalictrum, 254
Thermopsis, 256
Thymus, 258
Tradescantia, 260
Trollius, 262

Verbena, 264
Veronica, 266
Viola, 270

Waldsteinia, 274

Yucca, 276

BULBS   279

Allium, 280
Anemone, 286

Colchicum, 292
Crocus, 294

Eranthus, 298

Fritillaria, 300

Galanthis, 302

Hyacinthus, 304

Leucojum, 306

Lilium, 308
Lycoris, 314

Muscari, 316

Narcissus, 318

Ornithogalum, 322

Puschkinia, 324

Scilla, 326

Tulipa, 328

Herbaceous Perennials

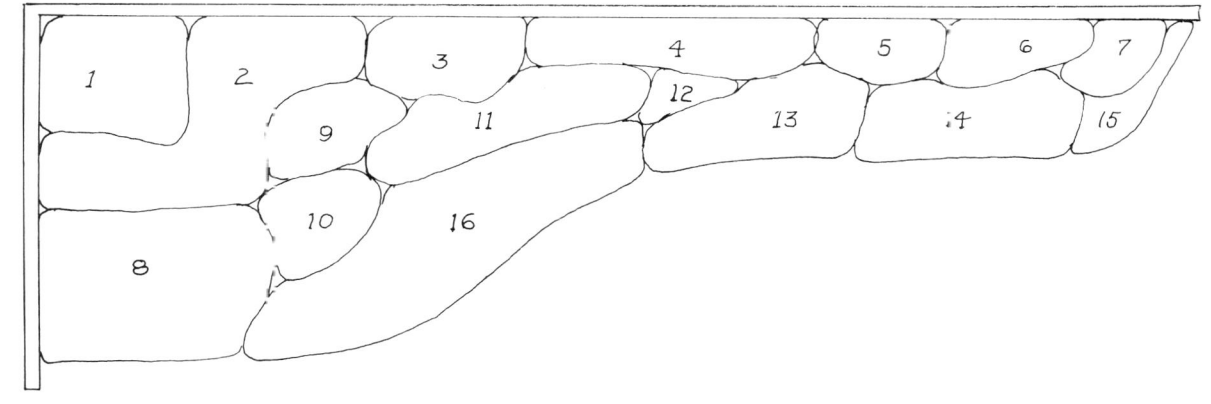

Perennials

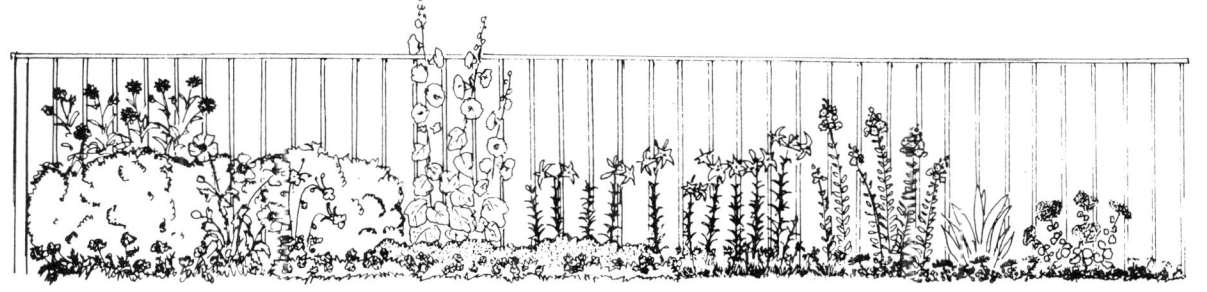

1. HELIOPSIS
2. CHRYSANTHEMUM
3. ALCEA ROSEA
4. LILIUM
5. PHLOX
6. IRIS
7. SEDUM SPECTABILE
8. VERBENA CANADENSIS
9. AQUILEGIA X HYBRIDA
10. PAPAVER ORIENTALE
11. AURINIA SAXATILIA
12. LYCORIS SQUAMIGERA
13. DIANTHUS BARBATUS
14. SEDUM SPURIUM 'SCHORBUSSER BLUT'
15. SEDUM ACRE 'GOLD CAP'
16. AUBRIETA DELTOIDEA

Acanthaceae
(Acanthus family)

Acanthus spinosissimus (Acanthus spinosus)
Spiny Bear's-breeches

FLOWERS: The purple flowers are borne in long erect spikes atop 2- to 4-foot flower stalks. Each flower is 1 inch across and is subtended by large, leaflike, shiny green, often fringed purple bracts tipped with recurved spines. The irregular, broadly flaring, tubular flowers have a 4-lobed calyx with 2 lobes smaller than the other 2, a corolla with a short tube, an expanded 3-lobed lower lip, no upper lip, and 4 stamens. The flowers are single- or double-lipped and are borne sessile in July and August for a 2-month-long flowering season.

LEAVES: The attractive, bold foliage is mostly basal, deeply and irregularly pinnatifid, with each lobe ending in rigid, glistening white spines. The shiny dark green leaves are rigid and leathery and are up to 2 feet long and 1 foot across. The leaves must be handled with gloves.

PLANT CHARACTERISTICS: This impressive 3- to 4-foot-high plant grows vigorously. Once planted, it is difficult to eradicate because each broken root is capable of growing.

GARDEN VALUE: *Acanthus spinosissimus* is a stately perennial. Although the flowers are handsome, the plants are often grown solely for their distinctive foliage, with the flower stalks being removed as soon as they appear. It is an excellent anchor plant for the pe-

Acanthus

consists of 20 or more species of perennial herbs and subshrubs found mostly in the Mediterranean region but extending to tropical and subtropical Asia and Africa. The genus name comes from the Greek word *akanthos*, meaning "thorn."

rennial garden; the foliage can also be displayed effectively in narrow or individual beds. Subtropical in appearance, it is sometimes grown in permanent landscape containers on the terrace or patio.

The flower spikes may be cut for flower arrangement; they last weeks in water. Although the original colors tend to fade, the flowers are often dried for winter bouquets.

CULTURE: *Acanthus* is a very adaptable plant. It will grow in sun or shade; however, flowering is best in sun. This plant grows best in a warm, rich, light, well-drained soil.

This plant's wide-ranging roots make it a good selection for dry areas.

Plant in spring or fall. Space plants 3 feet apart. Too much water can be fatal, especially in winter or spring. Because the plants need protection in the northern states, you should mulch them heavily in fall. Those planted in the fall need extra protection. Feed regularly with a balanced fertilizer during the growing season.

After flowering for 3 to 5 years, they can be dug up and divided in either spring or fall.

Acanthus can be divided in spring or propagated by seed sown in spring. Seedlings take 3 years to flower. Root cuttings taken in fall require two years to produce a flowering-sized plant.

ADDITIONAL NOTES: This plant was a favorite of the Greeks and Romans of the 5th century B.C. The leaf and scroll (which acts as a stalk) form the principal adornment of the Corinthian capital.

NATIVE HABITAT: Southern Europe. ◇

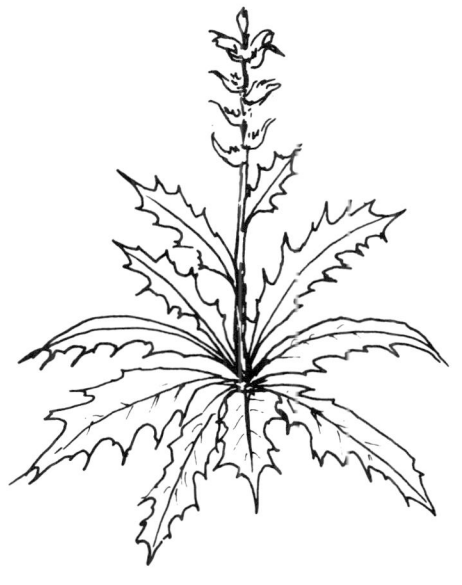

Achillea

contains nearly 100 species of usually aromatic perennial herbs native to the Northern Temperate Zone of the Old World.

The name *Achillea* refers to Achilles, who, according to legend, was supposed to have healed his wounds with the plant.

Compositae—Anthemis tribe (Composite family)

Achillea filipendulina (Achillea eupatorium)
Fern-leaf Yarrow

FLOWERS: The many small, yellow flowers are $\frac{3}{16}$ inch across and are borne in flower heads from June to September. The dense, convex corymbs are nearly 5 inches across. The disc flowers are tubular, bisexual, and fertile. The ray flowers are female and fertile.

LEAVES: The aromatic gray-green leaves are alternate or in a basal rosette, simple, 1- or 2- pinnatifid, linear-lanceolate, up to 10 inches long, and hairy.

PLANT CHARACTERISTICS: This perennial grows up to 4 feet high. The stiff, erect stems are furrowed and glandular-spotted, almost hairy.

GARDEN VALUE: The plant provides brilliant midsummer color in the perennial border, mixed border, or wild flower garden or a naturalized area. The flowers are excellent for cut flowers or dried for winter bouquets. If the lower leaves are stripped off when the stem is cut, the fresh flowers will last longer.

CULTURE: The plant requires a sunny site in a well-drained, fertile soil. Plant in spring. Space plants about 2 feet apart. Scatter a handful of bonemeal about the base of the plants each spring. Although the plants tolerate dryness, they produce better flowers when kept fairly moist. Taller varieties usually need staking when grown in a rich soil under ideal conditions. Flower heads turn brown and ugly and should be removed. Clumps should be divided after 3 or 4 years of flowering to maintain vigor.

It is most easily propagated by dividing the plant in spring. Seeds may be sown in the spring and will flower the following year.

NATIVE HABITAT: Asia Minor, the Caucasus.

SELECTED CULTIVARS AND VARIETIES: ◊ 'Coronation Gold': Abundant 3-inch-wide, mustard-yellow flowers, borne from June through August; gray-green foliage. ◊ 'Gold Plate': Butter-yellow flower heads up to 6 inches across. ◊ 'Parker's Variety': Deep yellow flowers 3 to 4 inches across. ◊ var. *alba*: White flowers. ◊

Compositae—Anthemis tribe
(Composite family)

Achillea millefolium
Common Yarrow
Also known as Milfoil, Sanguinary, Thousandseal, Nose-bleed, Soldier's Wound-wort, Knyghten Milfoil, Old Man's Pepper

FLOWERS: Many small flowers, about $\frac{1}{4}$ inch across and usually muddy white, are borne, in terminal, flat, dense corymbs 2 to 3 inches across, from mid-July to mid-September. The involucral bracts are oblong and somewhat hairy. The disc flowers are tubular, bisexual, fertile, and yellow. The ray flowers are either absent or female and fertile.

LEAVES: The strongly aromatic leaves are alternate or in a basal rosette. They are simple, finely 2- or 3-pinnately dissected, and tomentose or nearly glabrous. The lower leaves are lanceolate to oblanceolate, long-petioled—up to 8 inches long—and $\frac{1}{2}$ inch across. The upper leaves are lanceolate to linear and sessile.

PLANT CHARACTERISTICS: This weedy perennial grows up to 3 feet high and is rhizomatous. The flowering stems are simple or corymbosely branched above and pubescent or nearly glabrous.

GARDEN VALUE: *Achillea millefolium* is best reserved for the wild flower garden or a naturalized area. It can be grown in very poor, dry soil where grass cannot grow and can be mowed to keep it low. Only the cultivars should be grown in the perennial border. The flowers are excellent for fresh flower arrangements or dried for winter bouquets.

CULTURE: The plant requires a sunny site in a well-drained, fertile soil. Plant in spring. Space plants about 12 inches apart. Scatter a handful of bonemeal about the base of the plants annually. Although the plants tolerate dry conditions, they produce better flowers when kept fairly moist.

They are propagated by division of the plants or by seed sown in spring.

NATIVE HABITAT: Dry soils in Europe and western Asia; it has been naturalized in North America, New Zealand, and Australia.

ADDITIONAL NOTES: The dried leaves have medicinal properties. The flowers are used in Sweden as a hop substitute in brewing beer.

SELECTED CULTIVARS: The cultivars are superior to the species. ◊ 'Crimson Beauty': Bright red flowers 2 to 3 inches across. ◊ 'Fire King': Bright rosy-red flowers 2 to 3 inches across atop 18-inch stems, with silvery foliage. ◊ 'Kelwayi': Magenta-red flowers. ◊ 'Rosea': Pink flowers. ◊ 'Rubra': Deep pink flowers.

RELATED SPECIES:

Achillea nana: Dwarf Yarrow. Dull white flowers $\frac{3}{8}$ inch across are borne in dense, rounded corymbs atop 6-inch-high stems throughout most of the summer. The leaves are strongly aromatic, finely dissected, and about 1 inch long. This stoloniferous perennial is tufted and about 8 inches high. Its native habitat is Southern Europe. The primary use is in a rock garden, as an evergreen carpet, and between flagstones in walks. It is an excellent plant for hot, dry, sandy sites. The plant will not exceed 4 inches in height when grown in sandy soil.

Achillea ptarmica. Sneezewort, Sneezeweed, White Tansy. Flowers up to $\frac{3}{4}$ inch across are borne in loose, rounded corymbs 3 to 6 inches across from July to September. The disc flowers are greenish-white; the ray flowers are white. The dark green, shiny leaves are alternate or in a basal rosette; they are sessile and simple, range from linear to lanceolate, grow 1 to 4 inches long and $1\frac{1}{2}$ to 3 inches across, and are finely serrate, essentially glabrous, and slightly clasping at the base. This rhizomatous perennial grows 1 to 2 feet high. The stems are glabrous or slightly pubescent. The foliage is fine-textured; the plant is grown for its cut flowers. All parts of *Achillea millefolium* have a pungent flavor and, when dried, excite sneezing. For best performance, the plant should be divided annually. Cultivars are propagated by division. Its native habitat is Europe and Western Asia, and it has been naturalized in Eastern North America. The root was dried, ground, and used for homemade snuff in colonial times.

⋄ 'Angel's Breath': Profuse, pure white flowers. ⋄ 'The Pearl': White flowers atop a 15-inch-high plant. This plant was known as "the great cemetery plant" in the late 1800s. ⋄ 'Perry's White': Double white flowers. ⋄ 'Snowball': Double white flowers.

Achillea tomentosa: Woolly Yarrow. Bright yellow flowers $\frac{1}{8}$ inch across are borne, in dense $1\frac{1}{2}$- to 2-inch-wide flat-topped corymbs, from June to September. The gray-woolly rosette is almost evergreen at the base and is aromatic when crushed. This mat-forming perennial grows 6 to 12 inches high. It requires full sun and light sandy soil. Use in a rock garden, between flagstones, and as a ground cover in sunny areas, especially if the top is cut off to reveal the gray matlike basal foliage. This plant can be maintained as a low ground cover by mowing. Light foot traffic usually causes little damage. The plant spreads rapidly unless growing in very poor soil. It should be divided annually for best performance. Its native habitat is Europe and Western Asia.

⋄ 'Aurea': Darker yellow flowers. ⋄ 'Moonlight': Pale yellow flowers atop a 1-foot-high stem. ⋄ 'Nana': Dwarf form. ⋄

Aconitum

comprises over 100 species of summer- or autumn-flowering perennials with tuberous roots and stems that are erect, trailing, or somewhat climbing. The plants are native to the Northern Temperate Zone.

The roots, leaves, and seeds of the plants in the *Aconitum* genus are poisonous—as are the flowers of some species—not when touched but when consumed or when the sap enters the bloodstream through scratches or wounds. *Aconitum* roots could be mistaken for horseradish. Some species are a source of drugs. The poison used on arrows in India came from one Himalayan species.

According to legend, Theophrastus named the plants *Aconitum* because he had observed large colonies of them growing around Acona, Greece. The common name Monkshood refers to the hood-shaped flowers.

Ranunculaceae
(Crowfoot or Buttercup family)

Aconitum carmichaelii (Aconitum fischeri)
Azure Monkshood

FLOWERS: Numerous showy, deep purple flowers about $1\frac{1}{2}$ inches high are borne in August and September on pubescent pedicels in a dense panicle. The center raceme is 1 to 8 inches long. The unusual flowers are irregularly symmetrical and bisexual and have many stamens. The showy part of the flower consists of the 5 petaloid sepals. The upper sepal is large and helmet-shaped; the lateral edge of the opening is almost straight. There are from 2 to 5 small petals. The upper 2 are spurlike and are included in the helmet; others are minute or absent.

LEAVES: The handsome, leathery, dark green leaves are alternate, single, palmately cleft, and 2 to 6 inches across. The leaves remain attractive throughout the season.

PLANT CHARACTERISTICS: This sturdy, erect perennial grows $2\frac{1}{2}$ to 4 feet high, and in some sites it may attain a height of 6 feet or more. The roots are tuberous and turnip-shaped.

GARDEN VALUE: *Aconitum carmichaelii* has been popular for a long time in European gardens but has never achieved extensive popularity in America. The tall, dignified spikes are handsome in the middle and back of the perennial border, in the shrub border, as a specimen clump, or in a naturalized wooded area. The plant contrasts beautifully with many perennials of different color and form: the white, red, or purple flowers of *Phlox paniculata* and *Lilium*; the white flowers of *Chrysanthemum maximum*; and the yellow flowers of the late-flowering *Helenium* and *Achillea filipendulina*. It is also attractive with *Anemone japonica*, *Helianthus*, and *Aster* 'Harrington's Pink'. Planted with *Delphinium*, the vertical background effect of the perennial border extends into late summer. This plant provides excellent, unusual, cut flowers.

CULTURE: *Aconitum carmichaelii* grows best in a cool, moist, well-drained soil with abundant amounts of leaf mold or organic matter. It prefers partial shade, where the flowers last for a longer time, but will grow in full sun if sufficient moisture is available. *Aconitum* thrives in cool, mountainous regions with cool nights; it is difficult to grow in climates with hot summers.

Plant in fall or early spring. Place

tuberous roots 2 inches deep and at least 2 feet from other plants. If planting in spring, place the plants in their permanent location before extensive foliage develops. Soil should not be allowed to dry out; keep it moist with a leaf mold or well-decomposed compost mulch and add supplemental water during drought periods in the growing season. Apply a well-balanced fertilizer each spring. Tall, slender forms may need staking. The plants usually require 1 or more seasons to become established; once established, they should not be disturbed. The plants increase so slowly that they do not require division. Protection is necessary during the first winter.

Plants may be propagated by division, but they are severely disturbed when the roots are divided and replanted. The seeds, which should be sown immediately after ripening, do not germinate readily or produce uniform plants. Seedlings will produce flowers in 2 or 3 years.

ADDITIONAL NOTES: *Aconitum carmichaelii* is one of the most popular *Aconitum*; it is often cultivated under the name *Aconitum fischeri*.

NATIVE HABITAT: Eastern Asia. ◇

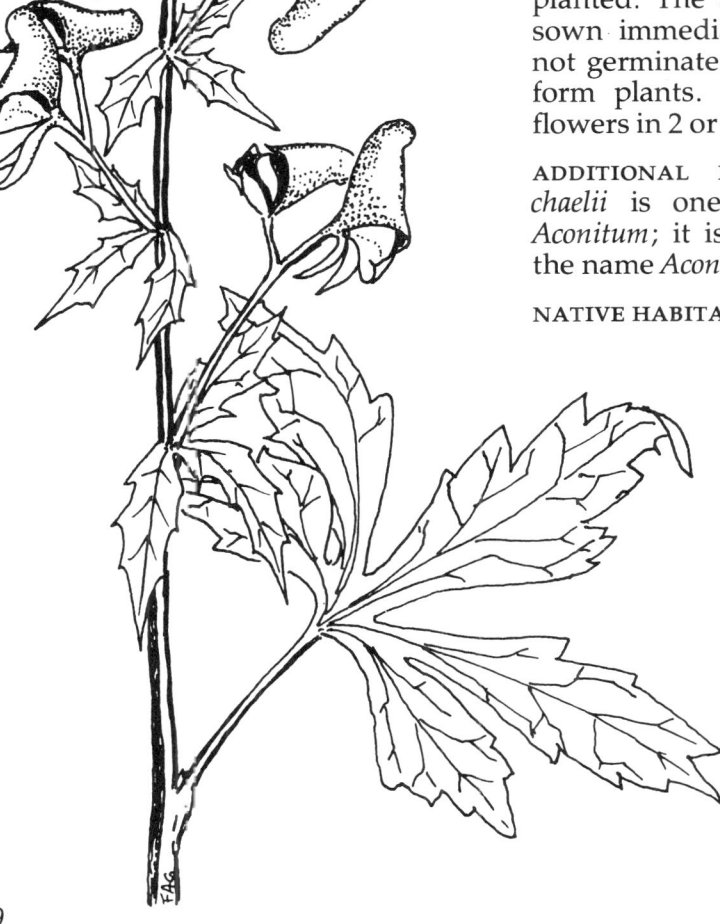

FLOWERS: The violet flowers are 1¼ to 1½ inches high and are borne in 2- to 8-inch-long, dense racemes in July and August. The pedicels are erect and pubescent. The flowers are showy and large, irregularly symmetrical and bisexual. The showy part of the flower consists of the 5 petaloid sepals. The upper sepal is larger, ¾ inch high, and is helmet-shaped with a short beak-like visor; the lateral edge of the opening is almost straight. There are from 2 to 5 small petals; the upper 2 are spur-like and are included in the helmet; the others are minute or absent.

LEAVES: The leaves are alternate, 2 to 4 inches across, and 3-cleft; each lateral segment is cut again, almost to the base, into linear lobes.

PLANT CHARACTERISTICS: This erect, narrow plant is rather leafy and grows up to 3 or 4 feet high. The tuberous roots are shaped like turnips.

GARDEN VALUE: *Aconitum napellus* is the Common Monkshood of the English perennial gardens. Like the *Aconitum carmichaelii*, its tall, dignified spikes can be handsomely displayed in the middle and back of the perennial border. Planted with *Delphinium*, it allows the vertical background effect of the perennial border to continue into late summer. It is also used in the shrub border, as a specimen clump, or in a naturalized woodland area. The plant contrasts handsomely with perennials of different colors and forms: *Phlox paniculata*; *Lilium*; *Anemone japonica*; *Helianthus*; *Helinium*; *Aster* 'Harrington's Pink'; *Achillea filipendulina*; and *Chrysanthemum maximum*. It provides interesting and unusual cut flowers.

Ranunculaceae
(Crowfoot or butter-cup family)

Aconitum napellus
English Monkshood
Also known as True Monkshood, Common Monkshood, Garden Monkshood, Helmet flower, Garden Wolfsbane, Bear's-foot, Turk's Cap, Friar's-cap, Soldier's-cap, Officinal Aconite.

CULTURE: *Aconitum napellus* grows best in a cool, moist, well-drained soil with abundant amounts of leaf mold or organic matter. It prefers partial shade but will tolerate full sun if sufficient moisture is available. The flowers will survive longer in a partially shaded site. *Aconitum* thrives in cool mountainous regions with cool nights; it is difficult to grow in climates with hot summers.

Plant in early spring or fall; if in spring, place the plants in their permanent location before extensive foliage develops. Place the tuberous roots 2 inches deep and at least 2 feet apart. Do not allow the soil to dry out; keep it moist with a leaf mold or compost mulch, and add supplementary water during dry periods in the growing season. Apply a well-balanced fertilizer each spring. The tall, slender forms may need staking. The plants usually require one or more seasons to become established; once this is accomplished, any disturbance of the roots will cause them to suffer severely. The plants increase so slowly that they do not require division. Winter protection is necessary during the first winter.

Plants may be propagated by division, but they are severely disturbed by the process of dividing and replanting the roots. The seeds, which should be sown immediately after ripening, do not germinate easily or provide uniform results. Seedlings will produce flowers in 2 or 3 years.

ADDITIONAL NOTES: *Aconitum napellus* is a variable species. Many varieties differ in the shades of colors of the flowers, which are often mottled or lined with white. Much material known under this name in the trade is *Aconitum henryi* or *Aconitum pyramidale*.

This plant (especially the roots) is the most poisonous species of *Aconitum*. The dried leaves and roots provide the medicinal drug aconite, a heart sedative.

NATIVE HABITAT: Northern Europe and Asia.

SELECTED CULTIVARS AND VARIETIES: ◇ 'Newry Blue': Very deep blue flowers. ◇ 'Spark's Variety': Very large, deep violet-blue flowers produced in August and September. ◇ var. *album*: Nearly white flowers, grows 4 to 5 feet high. ◇

Aegopodium

consists of 5 species of coarse herbs with creeping rootstocks, native to Europe and Asia.

Aegopodium is derived from the Greek words *aix,* meaning "goat," and *podion,* meaning "little foot"; the name probably refers to the shape of the leaves. The species and its cultivar have become known popularly as Goutweed because the plant supposedly was used as an antidote for gout.

Umbelliferae
(Parsley or Carrot Family)

Aegopodium podagraria 'Variegatum'
Silveredge Goutweed
Also known as Silveredge Bishop's-weed

FLOWERS: The small, insignificant flowers are borne in June, in long-peduncled compound umbels, about $1\frac{1}{2}$ to $2\frac{1}{2}$ inches across, atop 18 to 24 inch stalks. The flower consists of a 5-lobed calyx, 5 petals, and 5 stamens.

LEAVES: The biternate leaves are green-margined with irregular white patterns. The basal and lower leaves are long-petioled, with the petiole expanded at the base. The leaflets are ovate, acute or acuminate at the apex; rounded or cordate, and often oblique, at the base; they are sharply serrate and are about $1\frac{1}{2}$ inches long. The upper leaves are similar but smaller; they are usually simply ternate with short, broadly-expanding petioles.

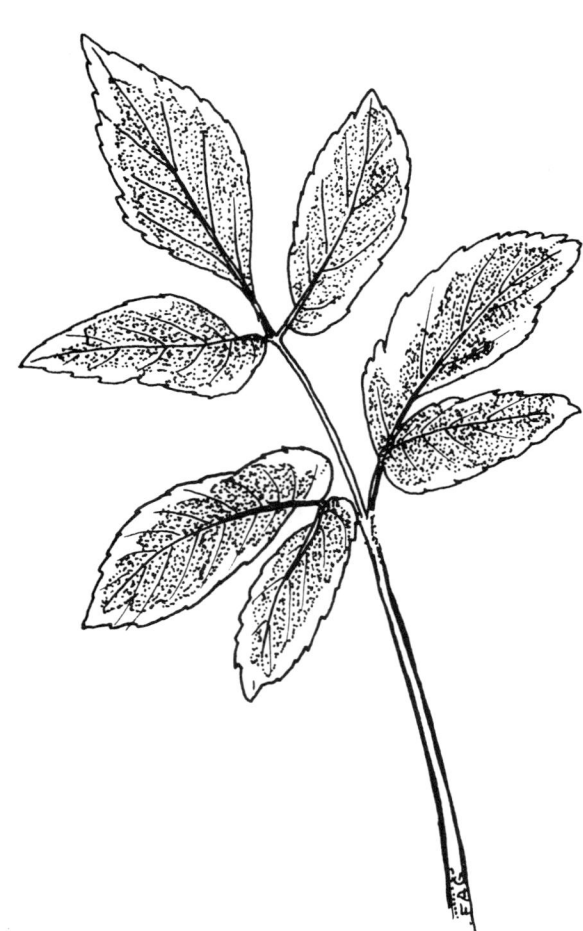

PLANT CHARACTERISTICS: This low-growing, rhizomatous, rapidly spreading perennial grows 6 to 14 inches high. A rather coarse, hardy, weedy plant, it dies to the ground in winter.

GARDEN VALUE: The plant is grown primarily for its attractive foliage, which brightens dark areas. Often used as a ground cover or edging, it tends to spread rapidly, especially in shaded areas that have fertile soil. Using the plant in sites with poor, dry soils or in confined areas reduces its prolific nature.

CULTURE: The plant thrives in any soil and withstands wet conditions as well as drought. It tolerates sun or shade; however, the variegated foliage will burn slightly in full sun.

Plant in spring or fall. *Aegopodium* is easily transplanted; any small portion of the rhizome will root and grow. Supplemental fertilizer is not needed. It can be cut low with a lawn mower 2 or 3 times a year and survive. Remove flowers when they fade to enhance the appearance of the plant.

It is usually propagated by division of the clump. Seeds readily germinate wherever they land.

ADDITIONAL NOTES: The variegated cultivar is more common and is not as vigorous as the species. Common names for the species include Herb Gerard, Ashweed, Ground Ash, and Ground Elder.

NATIVE HABITAT: Europe, but has been naturalized in North America.

Ajuga

includes about 40 species of annual or perennial herbs in the temperate areas of Europe.

The botanical name *Ajuga* is said to be a corruption of *Abiga*, a closely related plant.

Labiatae
(Mint family)

Ajuga reptans
Carpet Bugle, Bugleweed

FLOWERS: The blue or purple flowers are borne in May and June, in crowded verticillasters, which are usually 6-flowered and which are arranged in 6-inch terminal spikes. The subtending bracts are often tinged blue. The compact upright spike is held rigidly above the flat leaves. The calyx is campanulate, with 5 teeth roughly as long as the tube (which is larger than the calyx), a ring of hairs inside, and a 2-lipped limb. The upper lip is very short; the lower is 3-lobed and spreading.

LEAVES: The large, shiny, dark green leaves are usually evergreen and opposite; they are ovate or obovate, and entire or sinuate. The basal leaves are crenate or undulate, $2\frac{1}{2}$ inches long and 1 inch wide. The stem leaves are ovate, smaller, and usually nearly sessile. The leaves of the stolons are usually petioled. Some leaves remain colored and effective throughout the winter.

PLANT CHARACTERISTICS: This pubescent, fast-spreading perennial usually grows 4 to 5 inches high. It forms a low, dense, flat mat of foliage that is tolerant of light foot traffic. The roots are shallow; the flower stems are erect, stout, and square in cross-section. The slender, fast-creeping stolons from a single plant can cover a 3-square-foot area in a single year. The plant sometimes invades the lawn.

GARDEN VALUE: The stoloniferous nature of *Ajuga reptans* makes it desirable as a ground cover, an edging, or a substitute for grass.

CULTURE: This plant, which grows in

sun or heavy shade and tolerates almost any well-drained soil, is easily grown.

Plant in spring or fall about 10 to 12 inches apart. Because they are shallow-rooted, the plants must be watered well during drought periods. Keep them moderately moist, and feed with a balanced fertilizer once during the growing season.

The easiest method of propagation is to sever and transplant the rooted stolons. The plants may also be started by dividing the clumps in spring or by sowing seed at any time of year.

DISEASE PESTS: *Ajuga reptans* suffers from winter crown rot and root nematode.

ADDITIONAL NOTES: There are many different forms of *Ajuga reptans*. It readily hybridizes with *Ajuga genevensis* and *Ajuga pyramidalis*.

NATIVE HABITAT: Europe.

SELECTED CULTIVARS: ◊ 'Alba': Creamy-white flowers. ◊ 'Bronze Beauty': Deep blue flowers and purplish-bronze foliage. ◊ 'Burgundy Glow': Foliage is tricolor; the new growth is bright burgundy; as the leaves age, they become creamy white and dark pink. ◊ 'Gaiety': Blue flowers and striking bronze-purple foliage. ◊ 'Giant Bronze': Large metallic-bronze leaves. ◊ 'Giant Green': Bright green leaves. ◊ 'Jungle Green': Crisped, green, roundish leaves. ◊ 'Multicoloris': Leaves are mottled red, white, and yellow on green. ◊ 'Purpurea': Medium and dark purple leaves. ◊ 'Rosea': Rose-pink flowers. ◊ 'Silver Beauty': Light cream and dark green leaves. ◊ 'Tottenhami': Purple flowers and leaves that turn bronze-purple in autumn. ◊ 'Variegata' (cv. 'Albovariegata', probably *Ajuga variegata*): Mottled creamy-yellow leaves that burn when grown in the sun; a less vigorous plant.

RELATED SPECIES: *Ajuga genevensis*. Geneva Bugle, Erect Bugle. The blue or violet flowers are borne in May and June, in 6- or more-flowered verticillasters. The bracts are obovate, blue- or violet-tinged, and coarsely toothed. Basal leaves are petiolate, oblong-spatulate, and pubescent; they grow up to 4½ inches long and 2 inches wide and are sparingly toothed or entire. The stem leaves are much smaller; they are sessile, oblong-elliptic or obovate, narrowed at the base, and usually coarsely dentated. The stems are erect and pubescent, ranging from nearly glabrous to densely hairy, and are 4 to 16 inches high. Several stems usually arise from a crown. The plant is rhizomatous and tends to grow in an upright clump about 6 to 9 inches high. Its native habitat is Eurasia. ◊ 'Pink Spires': Pink flowers and evergreen foliage. ◊ 'Rosea': Pink flowers.

RELATED CULTIVARS: *Ajuga pyramidalis* 'Metallica Crispa' (*Ajuga metallica crispa*). The flowers are a metallic, glossy blue; the leaf margin is crisped. Leaf color is purplish-brown in summer, red in autumn. This plant grows up to 5 inches high. ◊

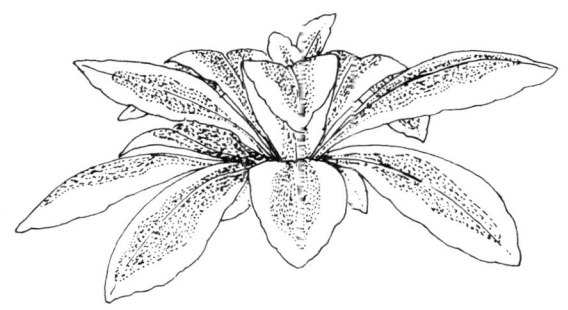

Alcea

consists of 60 species of mostly biennial or short-lived perennial herbs that are found from the Eastern Mediterranean region to Central Asia.

Malvaceae
(Mallow family)

Alcea rosea (Althaea rosea)
Hollyhock

FLOWERS: The showy flowers are borne on an elongated raceme or spike. Each plant flowers over a long period from July to August. The flowers are regularly symmetrical and bisexual and are subtended by involucral bracts that are united basally and are triangular to lanceolate. The calyx is 5-lobed, and the stamens are united in a tubular, 5-angled, glabrous, staminal column. The corolla, which is single or double, is 3 to 5 inches across. The 5 petals are usually 2 or more inches long and obovate; they are united at the base to the staminal column and usually overlap one another. The petals are white, pink, purple, and occasionally yellow. The raceme is produced the second year; flowering begins at its bottom and moves upward so that 1½ to 2 feet of the stem are covered with flowers throughout the flowering season.

LEAVES: The coarse leaves are alternate, simple, shallowly and palmately 7-lobed; they are rugose, 5 to 8 inches across, and suborbicular.

PLANT CHARACTERISTICS: This tall, vertical, pubescent plant grows 5 to 9 feet high. Each rosette produces from 3 to 6 flowering stems.

GARDEN VALUE: These tall spires are

known as an old-fashioned garden plant. It is an excellent background plant for the perennial border and may also be used along a fence or wall as a screen. The plant combines well with other so-called "cottage plants"—*Lilium*, *Rosmarinus officinalis* (Rosemary), *Linum perenne*, *Salvia X superba*, *Aster*, and *Macleaya*.

CULTURE: The plant requires full sun, moist, well-drained soil, and good air circulation. Plant in spring. Place the crowns slightly below soil surface. Give supplemental water during drought periods and fertilize with a balanced fertilizer in early spring.

Alcea rosea is a short-lived perennial that should be treated as a biennial. Although it may live and flower for several years (especially if its faded flowering stalks are cut off immediately after flowering has ceased), an old plant rarely flowers as much as a new plant started from seed. Once established, *Alcea rosea* often grows spontaneously from the seeds dropped.

Sow seeds in July or August to produce flowering plants the next season.

INSECT AND DISEASE PESTS: *Alcea rosea* is often seriously affected by red spider, rust, and mildew.

ADDITIONAL NOTES: This plant was propagated in the fifth or sixth century but was not introduced into England until nearly 1000 years later. It is associated with English gardens and cottages of the Elizabethan period and with early colonial gardens.

NATIVE HABITAT: China.

SELECTED CULTIVARS: ◇ 'Fire King': Scarlet flowers. ◇ 'Golden Drop': Sulphur-yellow flowers. ◇ 'Newport': Pink flowers. ◇ 'Powder Puffs': Double flowers, up to 5 inches across, in mixed pastel colors, atop 6- to 8-foot-high plants in July. The plants need abundant water and a rich soil. ◇

Alchemilla

consists of about 200 species of annual or perennial herbs that are hardy and particularly suited for the rock garden and front row border. The plants, which are primarily native to the Northern Temperate Zone, are usually difficult to classify because of an apomictic nature. The name *Alchemilla* has an Arabic origin.

Rosaceae
(Rose Family)

Alchemilla vulgaris
Common Lady's-mantle

FLOWERS: The small, greenish or yellowish flowers, borne in compound cymes, are produced in May and June. The flowers are $\frac{1}{8}$ inch across and are regularly symmetrical, bisexual, and apetalous, with 4 or 5 sepals.

LEAVES: The handsome, green, orbicular leaves reach 2 to 3 inches in width and are alternate, palmately lobed, with from 7 to 11 shallow-toothed lobes. They are predominantly radial.

PLANT CHARACTERISTICS: This perennial, which ranges from pubescent to nearly glabrous, grows 8 to 18 inches high.

GARDEN VALUE: This ground cover is an unusual addition to a partially shaded rock garden or the front row of a border. The delicate sprays provide excellent cut flowers, which can be dried for winter flower arrangements.

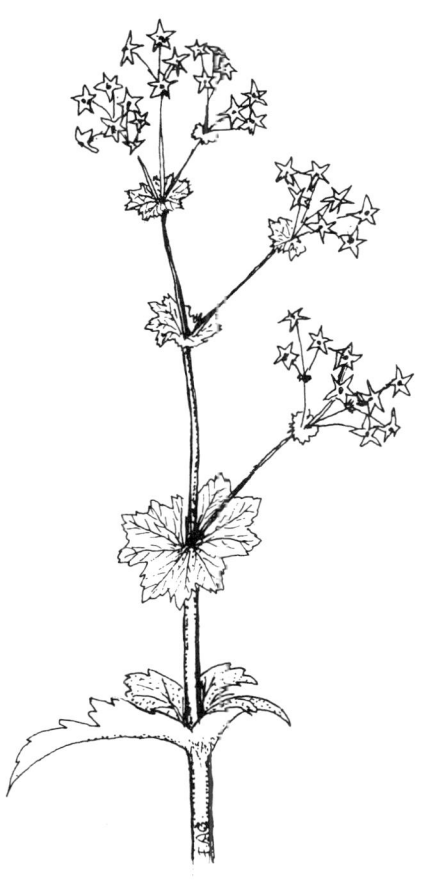

CULTURE: *Alchemilla vulgaris* is easily grown. It prefers partially shaded sites and an average soil with abundunt organic matter. It is easily propagated by division or seeds.

ADDITIONAL NOTES: *Alchemilla vulgaris*, according to ancient legend, contributed to the adornment of the Virgin Mary. It has been used for medicinal purposes.

NATIVE HABITAT: Europe. ◇

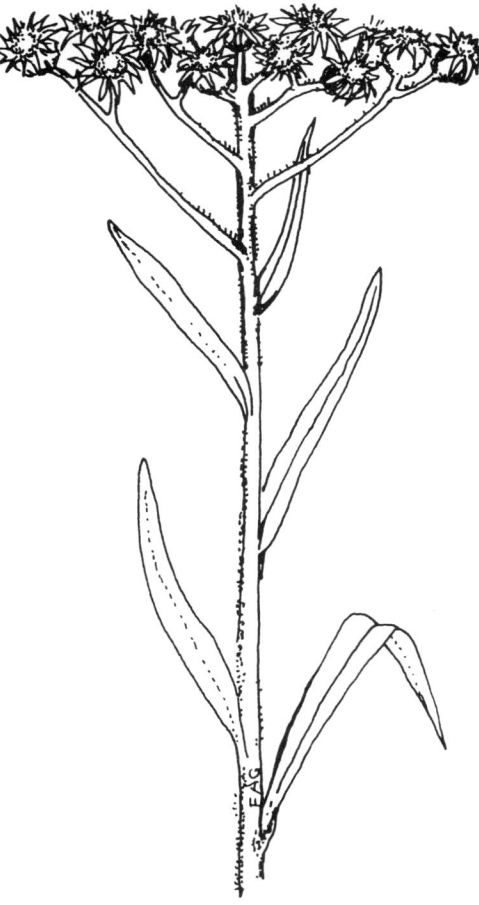

Anaphalis

includes 35 species of dioecious or polygamodioecious, gray or white woolly, leafy-stemmed perennial herbs native to Europe, Asia, and North America. The name is derived from the Greek name for a similar plant.

Compositae—Inula tribe
(Composite Family)

Anaphalis margaritacea
Common Pearly Everlasting
Also known as Large-flowered Everlasting, Immortelle, Life-everlasting.

FLOWERS: The numerous yellow flowers are tubular and $\frac{1}{4}$ inch across; they are borne in July and September, in terminal, discoid corymbs that are 2 to 4 inches across. The conspicuous involucral bracts are stiff, dry, and pearly white.

LEAVES: The sage-green leaves are alternate, ranging from linear-lanceolate to lanceolate, and narrowing to a sessile base; they are 3 to 5 inches long and 2 to 4 inches across, 1- or faintly 3-nerved, and white-tomentose.

PLANT CHARACTERISTICS: This rhizomatous perennial grows from 2 to 3 feet high. The stiffly erect stems are leafy, tomentose, and corymbosely branched at the top.

GARDEN VALUE: The white foliage and involucral bracts create an interesting white accent among the green-leafed plants and the bright autumn colors. Place in a wild flower garden or a naturalized area. The flowers are attractive in flower arrangements, especially when dried and dyed for winter bouquets.

CULTURE: The plant performs best in a dry, sunny site. It will grow in very poor soils. Plant in spring or fall. Set plants 12 to 15 inches apart.

Seeds sown in summer will flower the next season. Divide in spring or fall when clumps become overcrowded, usually after 3 or 4 years.

ADDITIONAL NOTES: The crushed foliage has a lemon-lime fragrance and can be used in sachets.

To collect the flowers for dried flower arrangements, pick them before they mature (while they are still white on the upper surface), and they will last for many years. If gathered early, they are whitish; if harvested later, the

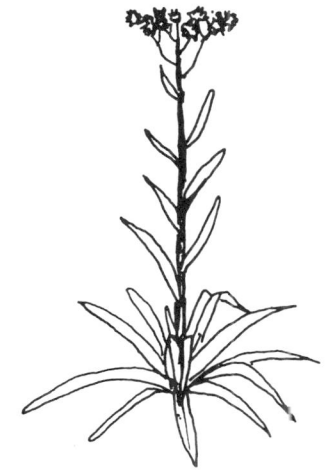

flowers turn cream-colored. Eventually the tiny seeds are dispersed by the wind and only the involucral bracts are left. Although they are still useful in dried flower arrangements, the flowers are not as full. Pick long-stemmed flowers, tie them into bundles, and hang them upside down in a dark, dry, airy spot until the flowers are completely dried, then store them indefinitely.

NATIVE HABITAT: *Anaphalis margaritacea* is widespread in North America and Eastern Asia. ◊

Anchusa

includes 40 species of coarse, hairy, erect herbs that are annual, biennial, and perennial. These blue- or purple-flowered plants are native to Europe, Asia Minor, and Africa. The genus name is derived from the Greek word *anchousa*, meaning "rouge" or "paint for the skin." Ancients produced a rouge from the roots of the plant. The common name, also of Greek origin, is *bu-gloss*, meaning "ox-tongue;" it refers to the shape and rough texture of the foliage.

Boraginaceae
(Borage family)

Anchusa azurea (Anchusa italica)
Italian Bugloss
Also called Italian Alkanet, Summer Forget-me-not

FLOWERS: The numerous blue flowers are tubular or funnelform and are borne in graceful, loose, leafy-bracted paniculate or racemose scorpioid cymes. The individual flowers are about ¾ inch across and are borne continuously from June to September, if not allowed to go to seed. The corolla is 5-lobed and the 5-parted calyx is parted almost to the base. The flowers resemble *Myosotis*, the true Forget-me-not.

LEAVES: The simple, alternate leaves are both basal and cauline. They are coarse, hispid, rough, and range from oblong to lanceolate and oblanceolate. The lower leaves may be 1 foot or more in length. The foliage becomes floppy and unattractive after the flowers fade.

PLANT CHARACTERISTICS: This strong-growing, erect perennial grows 3 to 5 feet high. A coarse plant, it has rough hispid stems and fleshy roots.

GARDEN VALUE: *Anchusa azurea* produces lovely blue flowers at a time when there are not many blue flowers in the garden. It is popularly used as a filler or showy background plant in the perennial border, mixed garden, or woodland garden and is an excellent companion to compliment *Chrysanthemum coccineum*, *Heuchera*, and *Anthemis*. The cultivars are superior to the straight species. *Anchusa azurea* does not, however, produce a good cut flower.

CULTURE: This plant performs best in full sun but tolerates light shade. It grows in moist soils but not wet soil; without good drainage, the plant rots in winter.

Spring planting is recommended. Space plants 1½ to 2 feet apart. *Anchusa* responds well if given a good, rich soil and fed occasionally to produce better plants and more flowers. Water the plants well; do not let them dry out. When flowering is finished, cut stalks back to encourage a second flowering. This can sometimes be repeated for a third, although less generous, flowering in late fall. The plants require staking in windy sites. Because they can die out in cold winters, a light mulch, such as evergreen boughs, should be placed around the plant crowns to prevent rot; or pot them in late fall and place in a cold frame during winter. Thin out volunteer seedlings annually to prevent overcrowding. Divide after every second or third season of flowering; the plants rarely flower for more than 2 seasons without being divided. Dig up, separate, and replant in either spring or fall.

The plants should be propagated annually, by root cuttings collected in spring, or by seed sown in the greenhouse or cold frame in spring or early summer. Seedlings will not be of the same quality as named varieties produced from root cuttings or clump division. Divide the clumps in spring or fall. Plants started by any method will flower the next season.

ADDITIONAL NOTES: *Anchusa azurea* is the most popular species of the genus. This lovely blue-flowering plant attracts bees.

NATIVE HABITAT: The plant is native to the Mediterranean region but has become naturalized in North America.

SELECTED CULTIVARS: ◇ 'Dropmore': Deep blue flowers in loose heads, borne in June and July; the plants grow up to 6 feet high and perform best in part shade. ◇ 'Feltham Pride': Bright blue flowers in dense clusters; a compact form. ◇ 'Loddon Royalist': A neat, 3-foot-tall plant. ◇ *'Myosotidiflora'*: Bears a cluster of flowers in May and June; grows well in semi-shade or full sun, reaches 12 inches of height; is well suited to the rock garden or the front of the border. ◇ 'Opal': Light blue flowers borne in June and July on 6-foot stalks. ◇ 'Pride of Dover': Deep sky-blue flowers on 4-foot stalks that require staking. ◇ 'Royal Blue': Triangular in shape and about 3 feet high; intensely royal-blue flowers very similar to 'Loddon Royalist'. ◇

Anthemis

consists of about 100 species of predominantly aromatic, annual or perennial herbs, primarily native to the Mediterranean region and Near East but also found in Europe, Western Asia, and Northern Africa.

The genus name *Anthemis* is derived from the Greek name for Chamomile.

Compositae—Anthemis tribe (Composite family)

Anthemis tinctoria
Golden Marguerite
Also known as Chamomile, Yellow Chamomile, Ox-eye Chamomile

FLOWERS: The numerous flowers, 1 to 2 inches across, are radiate and are borne, solitary and terminally on branches, from midsummer to frost. The receptacle is conical. The involucre is saucer-shaped; the involucral bracts are all nearly equal or imbricate in several rows, usually with dry margins and chaffy scales. The disc flowers are tubular, bisexual, and yellow. Ray flowers are usually present, female or neutral, and golden-yellow in color.

LEAVES: The aromatic leaves are alternate, incised-dentate, pinnately dissected, up to 3 inches long, and usually glabrous on the upper surface and white-tomentose on the lower surface.

PLANT CHARACTERISTICS: The plant is a bushy biennial or short-lived perennial that reaches from 2 to 3 feet in height. The stems range from erect to ascending and are angular, pubescent, and leafy. The plant is drought resistant.

GARDEN VALUE: This popular, hardy plant is a fine plant for a site that is hot and sandy. Use the cultivars in the perennial border; use the straight species in a naturalized area. It produces excellent flowers for cutting.

CULTURE: The plant prefers full sun but will flower in partial shade. Tolerant of any soil, it grows best in a dry sandy soil. If the soil is poorly drained in the winter, the plant usually succumbs. If the conditions are too ideal, it tends to become weedy and to spread rampantly.

Plant in spring, space the plants 12 to 18 inches apart. Water sparingly and do not apply fertilizer. The plant is difficult to stake. Remove faded flowers to prolong the flowering season and to reduce self-sowing. If it is not divided after every second year of flowering, *Anthemis tinctoria* tends to develop a dead spot in the crown.

Is easily propagated by division or by seed. Sow seeds in spring; divide in spring or early autumn. Stem cuttings collected in spring will flower later that season. Do not propagate cultivars from seed; they tend to revert to the straight species.

ADDITIONAL NOTES: *Anthemis tinctoria* is the best ornamental species of the genus. This heavy-scented plant, similar to Pyrethrum, is the source of today's cultivars. The genus contains 2 or 3 weedy species.

The flowers were collected by the French to extract a yellow dye.

NATIVE HABITAT: Central and Southern Europe and Western Asia; naturalized somewhat in the United States.

SELECTED CULTIVARS: ◇ 'Beauty of Grallagh': Larger, richer-colored flowers, $2\frac{1}{2}$ to 3 inches across, atop an upright, more compact plant. ◇ 'Grallagh Gold': One of the best: shiny, yellow flowers, 3 inches across, good for cut flowers. ◇ 'Kelwayi' (*Anthemis kelwayi*): Hardy Marguerite. Dark yellow flowers and more finely cut foliage. ◇ 'Moonlight': Pale yellow flowers. ◇ 'Perry's Variety': Large, bright golden flowers. ◇ 'Thora Perry': Orange-tinted flowers and gray foliage. ◇

Aquilegia

consists of about 70 species of variable, perennial herbs that are hardy, mostly erect, and prominently branched. The plants are native to the Northern Temperate Zone.

The botanical name *Aquilegia* is of uncertain origin. Some botanists say it is derived from the Latin word *aquila*, meaning "eagle-like", because the spurs resemble the beak of an eagle; others say the name is derived from *aquilegus*, meaning "water-drawer." The common name Columbine was attached to this plant because the spurred flowers resemble a dove.

Hummingbirds are attracted to the plants in this genus; they seek nectar in the spurs.

Ranunculaceae
(Crowfoot or Butter-cup family)

Aquilegia X *Hybrida*
(Long-spurred and short-spurred hybrid)
Columbine

FLOWERS: The dainty, showy, nodding flowers are 3 to 4 inches across and are borne in May and June, on upright spikes which terminate the branches. There are 5 purplish sepals which are petaloid, regular, and set on top of the whitish petals. The white petals are concave and have a short, broad lip or lamina; they usually produce a long, hollow, backward-projecting spur that is hooked or knobbed at the end and contains nectar. The buds and the flowers hang inverted, but after pollination has occurred they slowly rise so that the ripened fruits are borne erect.

LEAVES: The lacy leaves are 2- or 3-ternate. The leaflets are roundish and obtusely lobed.

PLANT CHARACTERISTICS: These hardy perennials grow from 1½ to 3 feet high; they are erect with prominent paniculate branches and produce large clumps.

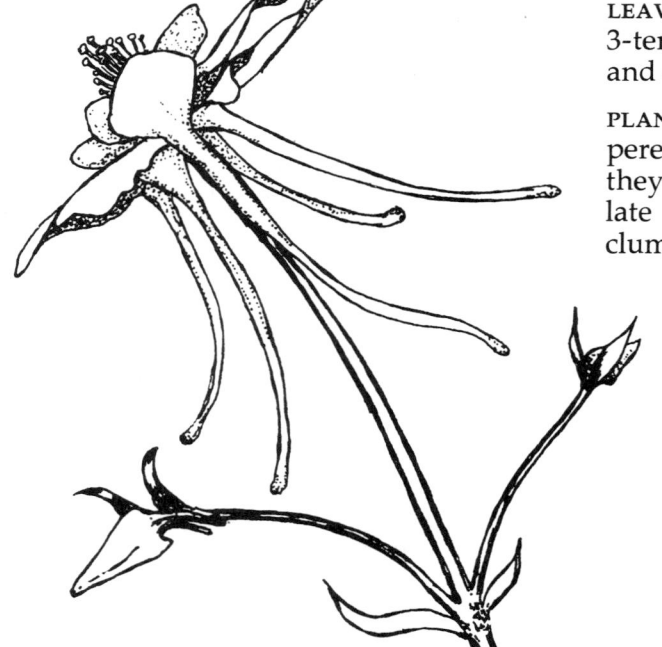

GARDEN VALUE: *Aquilegia* X *hybrida* is a beautiful, delicate, and elegant plant for the perennial border. One of the most popular perennials, it is grown for its exquisite flowers and lacy foliage. Place it in the front or middle position in the perennial border or the wild flower garden. The plant is most effective when grouped or massed in informal sites. The long-spurred types are attractive when grown with *Doronicum* and *Iris*. Because the flowering season ends early and the leaves tend to fade, the plants should be placed where the foliage can be camouflaged by the developing foliage of other plants such as *Phlox*, *Lilium*, *Iris siberica*, *Thalictrum*, *Polygonatum*, *Campanula persicifolia*, *Trollius*, and ferns. The dainty, graceful flowers provide interest to fresh flower arrangements.

CULTURE: The plants prefer a light, moist, well-drained, and fertile soil. Select a partially shaded or sunny site where the plants are protected from the wind. Partial shade prolongs the flowering season and encourages naturalizing.

Plant *Aquilegia* in early spring or late summer. Space plants 10 to 15 inches apart. Shade the young plants at first, then briefly expose them to partial sun before exposing them to full sun. Supply additional moisture during dry periods in the growing season. Feed regularly with a balanced fertilizer. Remove faded flowers to prevent seed development. Because the plants tend to live only 4 to 6 years, then deteriorate, replace them after a few years with new plants. In northern areas, provide a light mulch in late fall to prevent the plants from heaving out of the ground during periods of alternate freezing and thawing.

Division of roots or offshoots may be made in late fall or early spring and will produce flowers the following spring. Seedlings may be sown in the greenhouse or hotbed in March, or in the open ground in April. They may be set out after the danger of frost has passed and will produce flowers the following season. Because seeds from the garden tend to revert to less desirable plants, the best results are obtained when seeds are purchased from a commercial seed house.

INSECT AND DISEASE PESTS: *Aquilegia* may suffer occasionally from light attacks of mildew and leaf miner. Leaf miners usually disfigure the leaves. Their presence is easily detected by the irregular, white, winding trails of the pest as it feeds on the inner tissues of the leaves. The clump may be treated with an insecticide.

ADDITIONAL NOTES: The most common *Aquilegia* are the hybrids, not the individual species. *Aquilegia* X *hybrida* is a cross between *Aquilegia canadensis* and *Aquilegia vulgaris*.

The plants in the genus tend to interhybridize and self-sow when located in a suitable site. In time, the seedlings usually revert to less desirable types. Thus, occasional renewal is needed.

SELECTED CULTIVARS: ◊ 'Biedermeier': Grows up to 12 inches high. ◊ 'Crimson Star': A free-flowering plant about 18 to 30 inches high, with long, bright crimson spurs and a white center tinted red. ◊ 'McKana's Giant': Grows from 2 to 3 feet high and has flowers in mixed bold colors. ◊ 'McKana's Improved'. ◊ 'Mrs. Scott Elliot Hybrids': Crimson, purple, blue, and pink long-spurred flowers. ◊ 'Rose

Queen': Bears long-lasting, profuse flowers in shades of soft rose with a white corolla. ◇ 'Silver Queen': Bears pure white flowers, atop stems 24 to 30 inches high, over a long flowering season.

RELATED SPECIES:

Aquilegia alpina: Alpine Columbine. The delicately nodding, bright blue flowers are $1\frac{1}{2}$ to 2 inches across and are borne in July and August atop 2- to 5-flowered stems. The sepals are $1\frac{1}{4}$ inches long and acute. The limb of the petals is oblong, usually white, and $\frac{5}{8}$ inch long. The short spurs are rather coarse, $\frac{5}{8}$ to 1 inch long, and range from straight to incurved. The leaves are large and 3-lobed. Stem leaves are petioled and biternate; basal leaves are biternate, 1 to 2 inches long, and partially petioled. The dwarf plant is densely pubescent in the upper parts and grows to about 1 foot high. This native of the Swiss Alps is a valuable plant for the rockery.
◇ 'Alba': White flowers. ◇ 'Atro-violacea': Dark violet-purple flowers. ◇ 'Hensol Harebell': Deeper blue flowers; usually grows from 20 to 24 inches high. ◇ 'Superba': Similar to the species above but does not come true to seed.

Aquilegia caerulea: Colorado Columbine. The 2-inch-wide flowers are borne in May and June on several-flowered stems. The light-to-deep blue sepals are oblong, spreading, and 1 to $1\frac{1}{2}$ inches long. The petal-limb is white and $\frac{5}{8}$ to 1 inch in length. The long slender spurs are $1\frac{1}{4}$ to 2 inches long, outward-curving, and knobbed at the end. The basal leaves are thin and biternate; the stem leaves are simple. The stems are finely pubescent on the upper parts. The plant grows 1 to $1\frac{1}{2}$ feet high, and is a short-lived perennial in hotter climates. This popular species is grown in the perennial border, rock garden and wild flower garden, and in a naturalized area. Native to the Rocky Mountains, it is the state flower of Colorado and a parent of the long-spurred hybrids.
◇ 'Alba': Pure white flowers; does not breed true from seed. ◇ 'Candidissima': White flowers; does not breed true from seed. ◇ 'Citrina': Citron-yellow flowers. ◇ 'Cuprea': Copper-red flowers. ◇ 'Helenae': Blue and white flowers on a robust 15-inch-high plant; a cross between *Aquilegia caerulea* and *Aquilegia flabellata*. ◇ 'Mrs. Nichols': Long-spurred blue flowers; grows up to 30 inches high. ◇ 'Rosea': Pink or red flowers that are often double. ◇ var. *alpina*: A low-growing plant with blue sepals up to $\frac{3}{4}$ inch in length; it is native to the Northwestern part of Wyoming. ◇ var. *daileyae*: Blue flowers with no spurs and with sepals up to $1\frac{1}{2}$ inches long; it is native to Colorado. ◇ var. *ochroleuca* (var. *albiflora*): White sepals; it is native to the Western Rocky Mountain areas.

Aquilegia canadensis: American Columbine; also known as Wild Columbine, Meeting-house. Nodding flowers 2 to 3 inches across are borne, in several-flowered stems, in May and June. The sepals are yellowish or tinted red on the back; they are somewhat divergent, ovate, glandular pubescent, and about $\frac{1}{2}$ inch long. The limb of the petal is yellow, shorter, and truncate. The short, bright red spurs are hollow, straight, $\frac{3}{4}$ to 1 inch long, and they narrow to a knob at the end. The leaves are finely textured. The plant grows 12 to 30 inches in height, and it may reach 3 feet in wooded areas. It prefers a dry sandy site that ranges

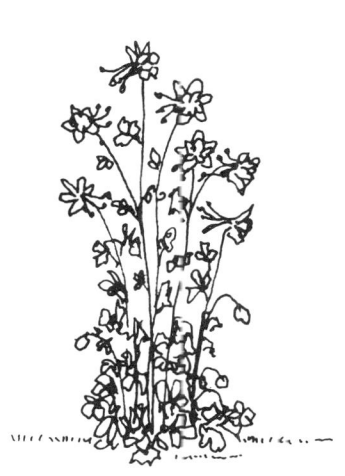

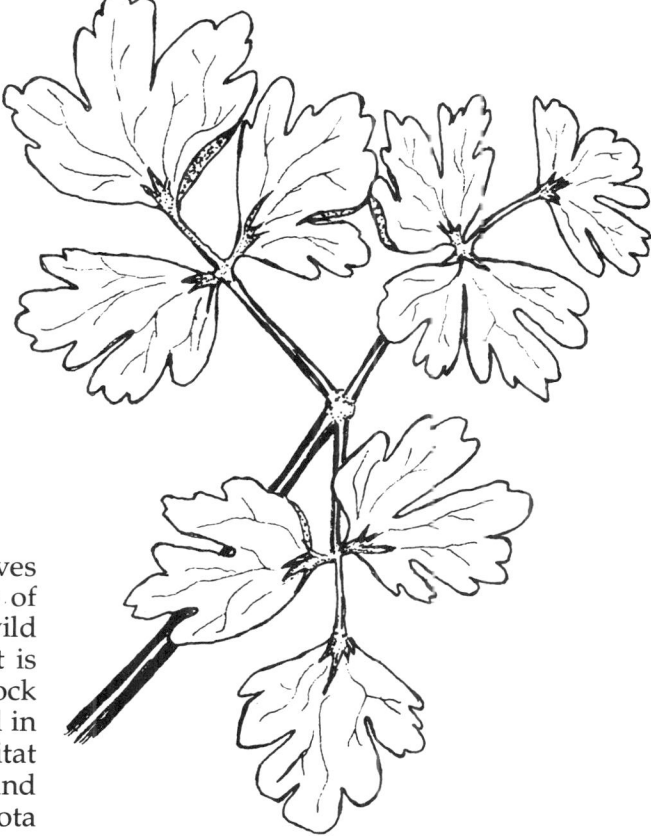

from sunny to semi-shaded and thrives on a sunny gravel ledge. It is one of the most graceful and attractive wild flowers native to North America. It is ideal for the perennial garden, rock garden, and wild flower garden and in a naturalized area. Its native habitat ranges from Nova Scotia to Florida, and from the East Coast west to Minnesota and Tennessee. It is one of the parents of the modern hybrids. ◊ 'Nana': Dwarf form.

Aquilegia flabellata: Fan Columbine. The waxy, nodding flowers are 2 inches across and are borne, on 1- or 2- flowered stems, from July to August. The sepals range in color from blue-purple to lilac and are about 1 inch long and obtuse. The petals range from lilac to pale yellow at the top; they are oblong and about $\frac{1}{2}$ inch long. The spurs are lilac, $\frac{5}{16}$ to $\frac{5}{8}$ inch long and are strongly hooked at the end. The stamens do not protrude beyond the limb of the petals. The leaves are steel-blue/green in color. This plant, which grows 12 to 18 inches high, is excellent for the rock garden. Its native habitat is Japan.

Aquilegia longissima: Long-spurred Columbine. The pale yellow flowers are erect and are borne from July to October. The spurs are filiform, pendent, and range from $3\frac{1}{2}$ to 6 inches in length. The sepals are spreading, acuminate, and 1 inch long. The limb of petals is spreading and is $\frac{5}{8}$ to 1 inch long. The thin basal leaves are triternate. The plant is loosely branched and from 2 to 3 feet high; it is beautiful in the perennial border. Its native habitat ranges from Western Texas to New Mexico. Because of its long spurs, this species is one of the parents of the long-spurred hybrids. *Aquilegia chrysantha* is occasionally sold as *Aquilegia longissima*. ◊

Arabis

comprises more than 100 species of predominantly low, annual, biennial, and perennial herbs native to North America and Eurasia. The name may be derived from Arabia, which might refer to the preference of the plants for dry soil.

Cruciferae
(Mustard family)

Arabis caucasica (Arabis albida)
Wall Rock Cress, Wall Cress

FLOWERS: The fragrant white flowers are about $\frac{1}{2}$ inch across and are produced freely, in loose, terminal racemes, for a short period from April to early May. The bisexual, regularly symmetrical flowers have 4 sepals and 4 petals with spreading, oval, obtuse limbs that form a cross. The flowers are borne atop 6- to 8-inch stems.

LEAVES: The attractive gray leaves are alternate, and either entire, lobed, or pinnately toothed; they are usually soft whitish-pubescent, 1 to 3 inches long, and tend to be evergreen. The basal leaves are usually obovate, tapering to the base. The stem leaves are auricle to sagittate at the base.

PLANT CHARACTERISTICS: This attractive, low-growing, spreading, softly pubescent perennial grows 6 to 10 inches high, forming tufted mats with many rosettes.

GARDEN VALUE: Use this excellent garden plant to edge, to cover steep banks, or in front of the flower border. In the rock garden or rock wall, confine it so that it cannot overtake neighboring plants. *Arabis* provides good, short-stemmed cut flowers.

CULTURE: *Arabis caucasica* is an extremely hardy plant and fairly easy to grow. Although it grows well in poor soil, a sandy soil with good drainage is best. It prefers full sun but will grow in partial shade; heavy shade results in more abundant foliage.

Plant in early spring. They may be transplanted when plants are in full flower if a ball of soil is kept around the roots. Do not apply a quick-acting fertilizer, but use compost, bone meal, or well-rotted manure. Keep plants on the dry side; their performance is only mediocre in wet seasons. After flowering, prune them back to 1 to 3 inches from the clump to increase branching and to rejuvenate the plants. During the winter months, cover with evergreen boughs to protect against low temperatures and winter wind. Do not mulch with leaves, because wet leaves become compacted and smother the plants. Divide the plants every third spring.

They are easily propagated by division in early spring or in September. Sow seeds of the species in spring; take cuttings of the cultivars.

ADDITIONAL NOTES: *Arabis caucasica* is very similar to *Arabis alpina*.

SELECTED CULTIVARS: ◊ 'Flore Pleno': A pure white double-flowered form with 12-inch racemes. The flowers survive longer and are better as cut flowers than those of the straight species. The woolly gray clumps usually spread to 18 inches in width. ◊ 'Variegata': Leaves with conspicuous, irregular, creamy-white patches that tend to revert to the normal foliage color of the species. ◊

Armeria

consists of about 35 species of perennial, evergreen, low-growing, tufted herbs or subshrubs. It is primarily native to the mountains and seashores of Europe, Western Asia, and Northern Africa, as well as the extreme Northeast and the Pacific Coast of North America.

The genus name *Armeria* is Latin in origin. Many nurseries once listed the plants in the genus as *Statice*.

Plumbaginaceae
(Plumbago or Leadwort Family)

Armeria maritima (Armeria vulgaris)
Common Thrift, Sea Pink

FLOWERS: The pink or white flowers are borne in compact, globular heads up to 1 inch across. The flower scapes are glabrous or pubescent, 2 to 12 inches high, and each bears a solitary terminal flower head subtended by involucral bracts. The outermost bracts are united and form a sheath surrounding and enclosing the upper part of the scape. The flowers are bisexual, regularly symmetrical, and 5-merous. The calyx is 5-lobed, funnelform, single-ribbed, scarious, and colored; its base is sometimes prolonged into a spur. The 5 petals, united only at the base, taper toward it; the 5 stamens are opposite the corolla lobes. Flowering begins in April and continues sporadically throughout the summer.

LEAVES: A rich bluish color, the evergreen leaves are borne in a neat, dense basal rosette. The leaves are thin, narrow, linear, single-nerved, and somewhat obtuse; they grow up to 4 inches or more in length.

PLANT CHARACTERISTICS: This hardy evergreen grows up to 12 inches high. It is a low-growing, tufted, compact plant.

GARDEN VALUE: Its symmetrical tufts of foliage make it a superior edging. *Armeria maritima* is ideal as a ground cover, growing between stepping stones or flagstones in the terrace and along garden paths, as well as in a rock garden or in front of a mixed or perennial border. The plant also thrives in seacoast gardens. It provides splendid cut flowers.

CULTURE: *Armeria maritima* is extremely hardy and easy to grow. Although it will grow in moist soils, it requires perfect drainage, and grows better in light, sandy soils in sunny sites.

Plant in spring or fall, and space plants 9 to 12 inches apart. Because excessive moisture and fertility reduce flower production, keep plants dry and do not apply fertilizer. Remove faded flowers to encourage sporadic flowering into September. Because plants tend to rot in the center, they must be lifted, separated, and replanted after 3 years or when centers begin to deteriorate.

Sow fresh seeds in August, after soaking them in water for several hours; do not allow them to dry out. Cultivars do not reproduce true-to-type from seeds. Divide cultivars or the straight species in early spring or early fall. Cuttings are not easily rooted.

NATIVE HABITAT: Southern Greenland, Iceland, and Northwestern Europe.

ADDITIONAL NOTES: *Armeria maritima* is the most common species of the genus. Its flowers are used medicinally for urinary problems. Many of the species of *Armeria* and their varieties hybridize freely.

SELECTED CULTIVARS AND VARIETIES: ◇ 'Alba': White flowers. ◇ 'Vindictive': Fine, deep pink flowers. ◇ var. *laucheana*: Deep crimson flowers in dense heads atop 6-inch-high plants. ◇

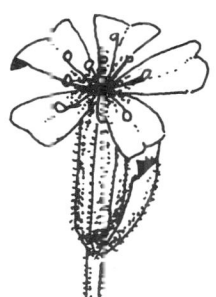

Artemisia

includes about 200 species of annual, biennial, and perennial herbs or shrubs that are usually aromatic and are primarily native to the dry areas of the Northern Hemisphere.

The generic name *Artemisia* honors Artemisia, the mythological wife of Mausolus.

Compositae -Anthemis tribe
(Composite family)

Artemisia schmidtiana
Satiny Wormwood, Silvermound Artemisia

FLOWERS: The flower heads are radiate or discoid, up to $\frac{3}{16}$ inch across, and are borne in pyramidal panicles from August to September. The flowers are not spectacular. The involucre is cylindrical to globose; the involucral bracts are imbricate in several rows, dry, (at least the inner row), and scarious or scarious-margined. The receptacle is hemispherical and either naked or bearing long, white hairs. The disc flowers are small, white or yellow; the ray flowers are either female and fertile or absent.

LEAVES: The attractive leaves are aromatic and bitter-tasting; they are alternate, up to 2 inches long, and twice palmately divided. The segments are linear and have silvery-white, silky hairs. The upper leaves are linear.

PLANT CHARACTERISTICS: This rhizomatous perennial forms a tuft 8 to 12 inches high and 18 to 24 inches across.

GARDEN VALUE: *Artemisia* is grown primarily for its foliage and its aromatic qualities. *Artemisia schmidtiana* is used for carpet bedding, in the front of the perennial border, in dry rock gardens, and as a edging plant.

CULTURE: The plant grows best under full sun and in dry conditions. It prefers poor soils but will not tolerate a wet soil during winter.

Plant in spring and space about 12 to 18 inches apart. Fertilizer is not necessary. Apply additional water during dry periods in the summer. Usually, the unattractive flowers are removed. When used for carpet bedding or as an edging, the plants will require pruning; however, the clumps rarely spread and usually do not require division.

It is usually propagated by division in spring; stem cuttings are most easily rooted then as well.

NATIVE HABITAT: Japan.

SELECTED CULTIVARS: ◊ 'Nana': Angel's-hair. Gray hummock with finely-cut, silky foliage; a novelty in the rock garden, grows only 2 to 4 inches high. ◊ 'Silver Mound': Attractive silvery-gray, finely-cut aromatic foliage with slender stems; grows 6 to 12 inches high and 12 or more inches across; excellent for edging, in a rock garden, or as a ground cover; foliage (which wilts at first, but is erect after several hours) often used in fresh flower arrangements.

RELATED SPECIES:

Artemisia dracunculus (*Artemisia redowskii*): Tarragon, Estragon. Rounded, whitish-green flowers up to $\frac{1}{8}$ inch across are borne in loosely spreading panicles. The green leaves are entire or 2- to 5-cleft, glabrous, and 4 to 6 inches long. The stem leaves are linear or lanceolate; the lower leaves are usually deciduous; the basal leaves are 3-cleft at the top. This rhizomatous perennial grows up to 2 feet high and varies from nearly scentless to strongly aromatic. The stems are erect, branched, and range from glabrous to hairy. Seeds are rarely produced; propagation is primarily by division. The leaves are used to flavor salads, fish, sauces, and confectioneries, as well as in perfumes and toilet water. The plant's native habitat is Southern Europe, Asia, and the United States, west of the Mississippi River.

Artemisia ludoviciana: Western Mugwort, Cudweed, White Sage. The tiny brown or white flower heads are $\frac{1}{8}$ inch across and are usually borne in rather dense panicles. The leaves range from linear to oblong, are entire or lobed, up to 4 inches long, and white-tomentose on the underside, becoming nearly glabrous on the upper side when old. The upper leaves are entire; the lower leaves are toothed or parted. This aromatic perennial grows from 2 to 3 feet high and is quite rhizomatous. The stems are erect or ascending. This plant is best when used in naturalized settings. Its native habitat extends from Michigan and Washington in the North to Arkansas and Mexico in the South. In the East, it is sometimes found as a weed. It is grown for its silvery-white foliage rather than its flowers.

◊ var. *albula* (Silver King Artemisia): The leaves are lanceolate, about $\frac{3}{4}$ inch long, and white-tomentose on both surfaces. Its native habitat is the Western United States. ◊

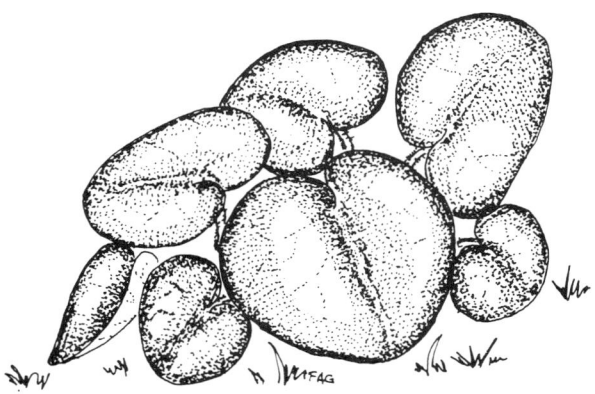

Asarum

Asarum consists of about 75 species that are native to the Northern Temperate Zone. The common name for these low, rhizomatous, stemless perennials is Wild Ginger or Asarabacca.

The derivation of the name *Asarum* is unknown. The common name, Wild Ginger, refers to the pungent aroma of the cut rhizomes.

Aristolochiaceae
(Birthwort family)

Asarum europaeum
European Wild Ginger

FLOWERS: The $\frac{1}{2}$-inch-wide, greenish-purple or brown flowers are borne singly in April and May, near the surface of the ground below the foliage. The corolla is rudimentary or lacking. The calyx is corolla-like, campanulate, and three-parted.

LEAVES: The evergreen leaves are stemless, cordate, leathery, and of a uniformly glossy dark green; they grow 2 to 3 inches wide on petioles up to 5 inches long.

PLANT CHARACTERISTICS: This evergreen perennial is 5 inches tall and spreads slowly by rhizomes.

GARDEN VALUE: *Asarum europaeum* is an attractive woodland plant that is very useful singly or in groups. It is one of the best choices for a ground cover in a deeply shaded area. The plant is also well-suited for use in shady rock gardens or wild flower gardens, in a naturalistic area, in shaded woodlands, or as an edging plant.

CULTURE: *Asarum* is easily cultured. It grows best in deep shade but tolerates half-shade. It is most successfully grown in moist, acid soils rich in organic matter supplied by leaf mold, compost, or other organic material.

Plant in spring. Supply additional water during drought periods. The plants may require some time to become established. It is propagated by cuttings or by simple division in early spring, before new growth begins. Seeds may be sown outside as soon as ripe, but they will not germinate until the following year.

ADDITIONAL NOTES: Although not as well known as it should be, *Asarum europaeum* is the outstanding species of the genus.

NATIVE HABITAT: Europe; rich, shady, mountain woods.

RELATED SPECIES: *Asarum canadense*: Wild Ginger, Canada Snakeroot. The large, apetalous flowers arise from ground level on a short, solitary stem borne in the fork of two leaves. The inconspicuous flowers, which are borne in April and May, are 1 inch across with a campanulate calyx opening into three pointed lobes, purplish green on the outside and a rich maroon on the inside. The pubescent, green, deciduous leaves are 2 to 7 inches across, coarsely textured, on hairy petioles up to 1 foot long. The leaves are kidney-shaped, pointed, and not mottled, with a deep and open sinus. The plant forms a carpet about 6 to 8 inches tall; it spreads rapidly from brown or greenish-brown rhizomes. Easily transplanted, it loves shade and prefers a rich soil that ranges from slightly acid to calcareous. It is usually propagated by means of division of the plant in spring. *Asarum canadense* is native to an area that extends from New Brunswick in the North to North Carolina in the South and to Missouri in the West. The rhizomes, when bruised or cut, smell strongly like ginger and in past generations were collected, dried, and used as a substitute for ginger. The leaves may cause dermatitis to susceptible persons. ◇

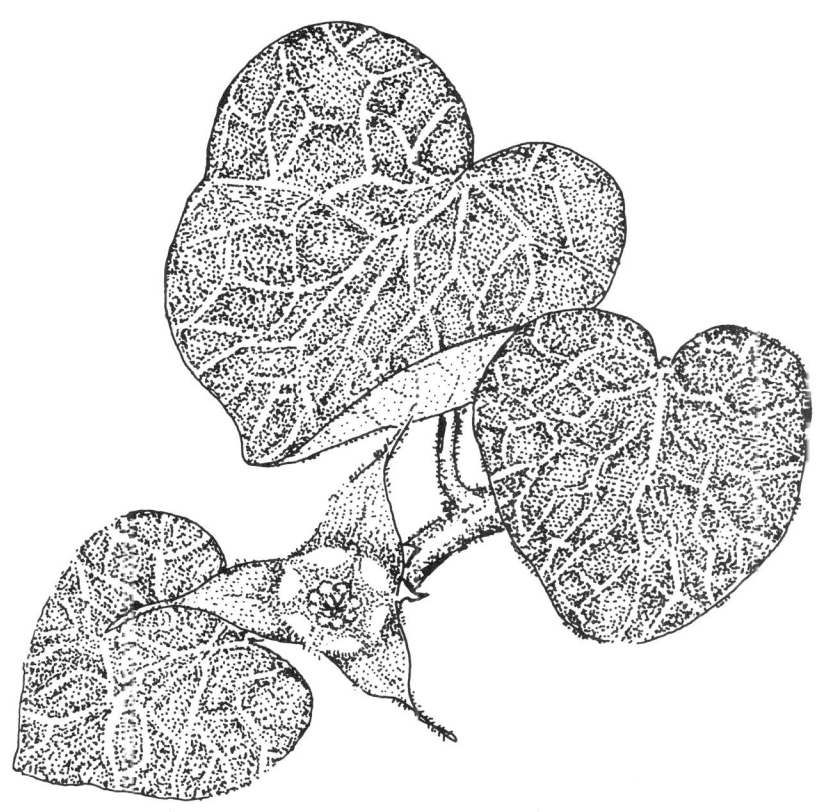

Asclepiadaceae
(Milkweed family)

Asclepias tuberosa
Butterfly Weed
Also known as Butterfly Milkweed, Pleurisy Root, Yellow Milkweed, Tuberroot, Indian Paintbrush, Chigger Flower.

FLOWERS: The extremely showy, bright orange (rarely red or yellow), fragrant flowers are beautifully and curiously shaped. The flowers are $\frac{1}{2}$ to $\frac{3}{4}$ inch across, radially symmetrical, and are borne, in axillary or terminal umbellate cymes 2 inches across, in July and August. The calyx is deeply 5-lobed. The greenish-orange corolla is rotate, 5-lobed, valvate, $\frac{1}{4}$ inch long, and generally reflexed, hiding the calyx. The bright orange (occasionally yellow) corona has slender horns and 5 hood-like lobes. The corona is stalked, lanceolate, about $\frac{1}{4}$ inch long, and has a short tooth on each lateral margin.

FRUIT: The white, pubescent, follicles are usually paired, narrowly fusiform, and 2 to 3 inches long on deflexed or erect pedicels. In fall the fruits open along one side to dispel seeds, usually with tufts of silky hairs that are collectively called a coma.

LEAVES: The pubescent leaves are alternate, simple, entire, narrowly lanceolate to oblanceolate, and 2 to $4\frac{1}{2}$ inches long.

PLANT CHARACTERISTICS: This hardy, erect, hispid perennial has many stout, erect stems and grows $1\frac{1}{2}$ to 3 feet high, in a broadly domed, bushy clump. The tap roots are deep and woody, yet never rampant. Once a good root system is established, the plant is practi-

Asclepias

consists of about 200 species of perennial herbs, usually with milky sap, that are widely distributed throughout North America and Africa. This genus contains many ornamental weedy species naturalized in wastelands in this country. Its name refers to Aesculapius, a Graeco-Roman god of medicine.

38

cally indestructible. The plant usually sends up 5 to 10 flower stalks.

GARDEN VALUE: This fine perennial enlivens the summer garden. It is especially useful in sunny, dry spots, particularly on sunbaked sites or along the seacoast. Use it singly or in groups of three in the perennial border or naturalize it in the wild flower garden or on a sunny bank. The brilliant orange-colored flowers seldom clash with the colors of other garden perennials.

When cut, the extraordinary orange flowers are long-lasting. They may be pressed or dried and will retain their brilliance. The ornamental seed pods may be used in dried arrangements.

CULTURE: *Asclepias tuberosa* tolerates any well-drained garden soil but usually rots in wet soils. Full sun and a dry, poor, sandy soil produce the best plants.

Plant in spring or fall, 8 to 12 inches apart. Because large sizes do not transplant well, purchase plants in small sizes. Because the plants die back to the ground each fall and new growth begins late in the spring, you should cultivate carefully around the site. If the crowns are inadvertently cut off, new eyes are usually formed in time. First year seedling roots are susceptible to heaving, so mulch well before winter begins and check frequently. An occasional feeding of a balanced fertilizer is beneficial but not necessary. The plants usually grow taller in good garden soil than in the wild, but seldom require staking. The clumps increase slowly and need no attention for a long time. Once the plants are established, the long tap root makes it difficult to divide or transplant.

Although seeds do not germinate well, seed propagation is usually the easiest for the homeowner. Sow seeds outside in spring or summer to produce a flowering-sized plant in two years. Do not disturb the young plants for the first year. Root cuttings can be taken in very early spring.

ADDITIONAL NOTES: *Asclepias tuberosa* is the most beautiful and most popular species of the genus and grows wild in dry fields, on hillsides, and along roadsides. It is closely related to many weedy species, among which is the common milkweed; both attract butterflies. The plants in the genus usually have milky sap; however, it is not abundant in *Asclepias tuberosa*.

This plant reportedly supplied American Indians with medicine and food; the root was used in the treatment of pleurisy, the green fruit was added in the cooking of buffalo meat, and the flowers yielded a crude sugar. Dried, its fruit has medicinal properties, and the root is occasionally used in medicines as an emetic or to induce perspiration. The leaves and stems are supposed to be poisonous to animals.

NATIVE HABITAT: North America; from Maine west to North Dakota and south to Florida, Arizona, and New Mexico. ◊

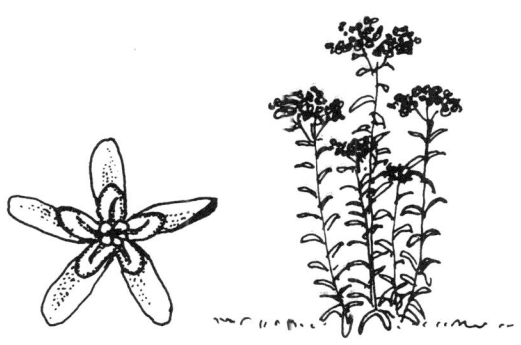

Aster

includes between 250 and 500 species of predominantly perennial herbs, native to broad areas of North and South America, Asia, Africa, and Europe.

The genus name *Aster* is Latin for "star"; it refers to the star-like appearance of the flowers.

Compositae - Aster tribe
(Composite family)

Aster alpinus
Alpine Aster, Rock Aster

FLOWERS: The flower heads are usually radiate, solitary, and 1½ to 2 inches across. The flowers are borne in May and June, atop 10-inch stems. The involucral bracts are unequal or imbricate in several or many rows. The receptacle is flat, pitted, and naked. The yellow disc flowers are bisexual. The flat ray flowers are female or neutral, blue to violet, and borne in a single row.

LEAVES: The pale green leaves are evergreen, alternate, simple, and entire; they are mostly basal, 2 to 3 inches long, narrow, and spatulate. The stem leaves are smaller and linear.

PLANT CHARACTERISTICS: This perennial forms a neat, rounded clump up to 10 inches high.

GARDEN VALUE: These lovely plants are usually used in bold clumps in the front of the border, in the rock garden, or in the alpine garden. They are the earliest Aster to flower and provide acceptable cut flowers.

CULTURE: The plants like an open site in full sun but will tolerate partial shade. Requiring perfect drainage, they grow best in a light, rich, rather dry, alkaline soil; they usually will not survive wet soils in winter.

Plant in spring, spacing plants about 8 inches apart. They prefer only a moderate amount of moisture during the growing season. Mulch carefully during the winter with pine boughs or straw because the evergreen leaves tend to rot under a heavy leaf mulch. Under ideal conditions, the plants usually require division of the clump after every 3 years of flowering.

Aster alpinus is usually propagated by division of the clump in spring or fall. The plants sow seeds freely, or seeds may be sown in spring, which will flower the following year. Named cultivars, however, should be propagated by divisions or cuttings, because the seeds do not reproduce true to type.

DISEASE PESTS: *Aster*, particularly the late-fall flowering types, can be seriously infected by mildew, Aster yellows, and rust.

NATIVE HABITAT: Mountains of North America, Europe, and Asia.

SELECTED CULTIVARS: ◇ 'Albus': Cloudy white flowers. ◇ 'Caeruleus': Blue ray flowers atop 10-inch stems. ◇ 'Dark Beauty': Rich, deep violet flowers atop a taller, more robust plant. ◇ 'Goliath': Lavender-blue flowers $2\frac{1}{2}$ inches across. ◇ 'Roseus': Pink flowers atop 6-inch stems. ◇ 'Rubra': Rosy-purple ray flowers. ◇ 'Superbus': Purple ray flowers on larger, showier heads. ◇

Compositae—Aster tribe
(Composite family)

Aster novae-angliae
New England Aster

FLOWERS: The flower heads are freely borne from August into October. Up to 2 inches across, they are usually radiate, rarely solitary, and are usually borne crowded in corymbose clusters toward the ends of the branches. The involucral bracts are equal or imbricate in many rows, herbaceous or scarious; they are linear-awl-shaped, green, pubescent, glandular, and sticky. The receptacle is flat, pitted, and naked. The disc flowers are yellow and bisexual. The 40- to 50-ray flowers, which are borne in a single row, are variable; they are usually purple, blue, or violet in the wild and are either female or neutral.

LEAVES: The thin, gray-green leaves are alternate, simple, and entire, and oblong-lanceolate; they are 2 to 5 inches long and 1 inch across, and scabrous or with stiff hairs on the upper surface and softer hairs on the under. The lower leaves are early deciduous; the others are sessile and auriculate-clasping.

PLANT CHARACTERISTICS: The long, graceful stems, arising from a woody crown or thick rhizome, are stout, hairy, very leafy, and branch near the top. The height of the plant varies greatly, ranging from 3 feet to 6 feet.

GARDEN VALUE: *Aster novae-angliae* is a very showy plant, suitable for a naturalized area or wild flower garden and as a background plant in the perennial border. It produces long-lasting cut flowers. The hybrids produce better plants for a prominent display in the perennial border.

CULTURE: The plant prefers a sunny site that has a rich, moist, well-drained soil. Plant in spring, spacing about 3 or 4 feet apart. Apply a balanced fertilizer in spring and fall to encourage the most intense flower coloring. Water well and cultivate regularly. Pinching the growing tips of the plants, once in late spring and once again 4 weeks later, encourages branching, shortens the tall varieties enough so that staking is usually unnecessary, and stimulates flower production. Because the plant self-sows freely, the faded flowers should be removed to reduce self-seeding. After every second year of flowering, the plants should be divided and reset in fall or spring.

The plant is usually propagated by division in fall or spring or by sowing seeds in spring, which flower the following year. Because the seeds do not reproduce true to type, named cultivars are usually increased by division or through the use of cuttings.

DISEASE PROBLEMS: *Aster novae-angliae* may be affected by rust, Aster yellows, or mildew.

ADDITIONAL NOTES: *Aster novae-angliae* is a very common wild flower, and one of the largest and most beautiful species of the genus.

NATIVE HABITAT: Eastern North America.

SELECTED CULTIVARS: There are many varieties of this species—although they are less popular than those of *Aster novi-belgii*. Millard Harrington, a farmer in Williamsburg, Iowa, collected the seeds from the best pink plants he could find and eventually selected an outstanding cultivar 'Harrington's Pink', which led to the development of more cultivars. ◊ 'Albus': White ray flowers. ◊ 'Barr's Blue': Purple-blue flowers. ◊ 'Barr's Pink': Bright, rose-purple ray flowers with golden disc flowers; the plant attracts butterflies. ◊ 'Harrington's Pink': Pink flowers. ◊ 'Incomparabilis': Fuchsia-purple ray flowers atop a dwarf plant. ◊ 'Mt. Rainier': White ray flowers. ◊ 'Red Star': Dark carmine-rose flowers.

◊ 'Roseus': Rose-pink ray flowers. ◊ 'September Glow': Ruby-red ray flowers. ◊ 'Survivor': Rose-red flowers atop a 2½-foot-high plant.

RELATED HYBRID: *Aster X frikartii* 'Wonder of stäfa'. Single, fragrant, violet-blue flowers with yellow centers, 3 to 4 inches across, are borne from July until frost. The gray foliage is clean. The plant grows 18 to 24 inches high in a loose tumbling growth habit; it needs staking when grown in rich soil and requires protection during the winter in northern areas. This plant compliments *Papaver orientale*, *Lilium candidum*, and *Dicentra eximia* by concealing their lack of summer foliage; it also provides superb cutting flowers. Divide after every third year of flowering. Carl Frikart, a nurseryman of Stäfa, Switzerland, named this plant; it is a cross of *Aster thomsonii* and *Aster amellus*, and is usually listed commercially as *Aster frikartii*. ◊

Compositae—Aster tribe
(Composite family)

Aster novi-belgii
New York Aster

FLOWERS: Numerous flower heads about 1 inch across are borne in a corymbose-paniculate inflorescence in August and September. The involucral bracts are herbaceous or scarious and are unequal or imbricate in several or many rows. The receptacle is flat, pitted, and naked. The disc flowers are yellow and bisexual. The 15 to 25 ray flowers, which are borne in a single row, are rich blue-violet and are either female or neutral.

LEAVES: The firm, thick leaves are alternate, simple, entire, and smooth. They range from oblong-lanceolate to lanceolate and are sessile, more or less auriculate, rough-margined, narrow, and grow $2\frac{1}{2}$ to 5 inches long. The lower leaves are smaller and early deciduous.

PLANT CHARACTERISTICS: This rhizomatous perennial grows 3 to $4\frac{1}{2}$ feet high. It varies in growth from small and slender to large and stout. Its stems are slender and either glabrous or with lines or hairs.

GARDEN VALUE: Use *Aster novi-belgii* as a background plant in the wild garden, in a naturalized area, and in the perennial border. It compliments the fall-flowering *Chrysanthemum*. Its flowers remain attractive for only a short time in fresh flower arrangements.

CULTURE: The plant grows best in full sun and will not tolerate heavy shade. It requires a moist well-drained fertile soil.

Plant in the spring, spacing at least 2 feet apart to prevent leaf diseases promoted by crowding and poor air circulation. Apply a balanced fertilizer in spring and autumn to encourage the most intense flower colors. Water well during dry periods in the growing season and cultivate when necessary. To encourage heavier flower production, to stimulate branching, and to shorten the stem so that staking is generally unnecessary, pinch off the growing tips of the plants, once in late spring and once again 4 weeks later. Division in the spring or fall of every year or every second year produces neater growth habits.

The plant self-sows freely, but because seeds do not reproduce true to type cultivars are usually increased by division or by use of cuttings. Divide in spring or fall. Sow seeds in spring for flowers the following year.

DISEASE PESTS: *Aster novi-belgii* can be seriously affected by rust, Aster yellows, or mildew.

ADDITIONAL NOTES: *Aster novi-belgii* received great acclaim in England upon its arrival there in or around 1700. Yet, after its initial popularity had passed, it was rarely grown until this century. After 1900, however, English hybridizers began to develop finer and more diverse types. Ernest Ballard, who died in 1952, became the leading breeder with his unusually large-flowered cultivars, 'Eventide' in particular. These cultivars are very popular in England, where they are usually called Michaelmas Daisies because the flowers reach their peak around September 29, St. Michael's Day.

NATIVE HABITAT: North America, from Newfoundland south to Georgia.

SELECTED CULTIVARS: There are hundreds of cultivars of this Aster, and new ones are listed every year. ◊ 'Ada Ballard': Large mauve-blue flowers. ◊ 'Autumn Glory': Claret-red flowers. ◊ 'Clarity': Spotlessly white flowers. ◊ 'Crimson Brocade': Bright red flowers that appear double when opening and later reveal yellow centers. ◊ 'Ernest Ballard': Large, 2-inch-wide, semidouble, mulberry-crimson flowers. ◊ 'Eventide': Large, gentian-blue, semi-double flowers; the 3- to 4-foot-high plant requires staking. ◊ 'Glorious': Carmine-pink flowers. ◊ 'Marie Ballard': Large, soft, powdery blue flowers that are fully doubled when opening and later reveal golden disc flowers. ◊ 'Patricia Ballard': Pink flowers. ◊ 'White Lady': White flowers. ◊ 'Winston Churchill': Beetroot-purple flowers with yellow centers, 1½ inches across, borne on a very compact, bushy plant 2 feet high. ◊

Astilbe

consists of about 14 species of perennial herbs native to Eastern Asia and North America.

The genus name is believed to be derived from 2 Greek words: *a*, meaning "without," and *stilbe*, meaning "brilliance". The foliage is similar to that of *Aruncus,* for which it is often mistaken. The plants also resemble *Spireae* and are occasionally listed under that name in the trade.

Saxifragaceae
(Saxifrage family)

Astilbe X arendsii
Hybrid Astilbe
Also known as False Spirea, Goatsbeard, Meadowsweet

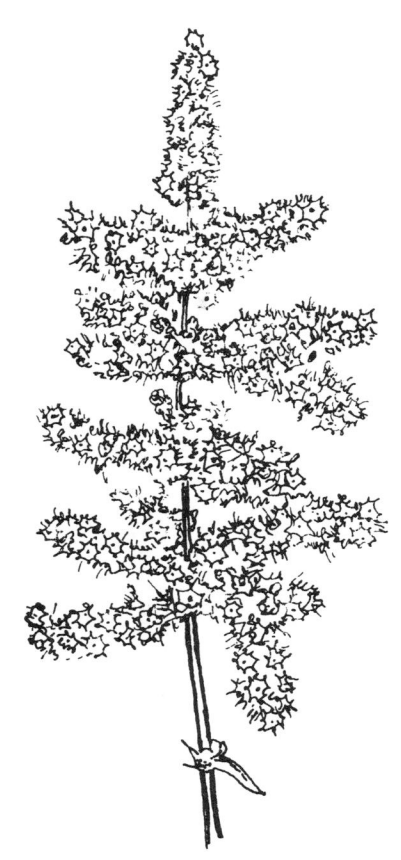

FLOWERS: The minute, white, pink, purplish, or red flowers are borne in spectacular, fluffy, dense panicles 8 to 12 inches long atop 2- to 3½-foot-tall stems. The flowers are perfect and regularly symmetrical. The small calyx is usually 4- or 5-parted, with 4 or 5 petals. There are as many or twice as many stamens as petals.

LEAVES: The leaves range from dark green to bronze and are alternate and 2- or 3-ternately compound. The leaflets are toothed or cut.

PLANT CHARACTERISTICS: The mounds of foliage are 12 to 18 inches high. The flower stalks are from 2 to 3½ feet high, depending upon the cultivar.

GARDEN VALUE: Plant *Astilbe X arendsii* in the perennial border or mixed border, in woodland settings, or near water. The plant combines well with *Chrysanthemum maximum, Stachys lantana, Artemisia stellerana, Hosta, Primula,* moisture-loving *Iris, Monarda didyma,* and ferns. The panicles provide excellent fresh cut flowers if allowed to open fully before being picked. After opening, the spikes can be dried for dried flower arrangements.

CULTURE: The plant tolerates a sunny site but prefers a partly shaded site. It

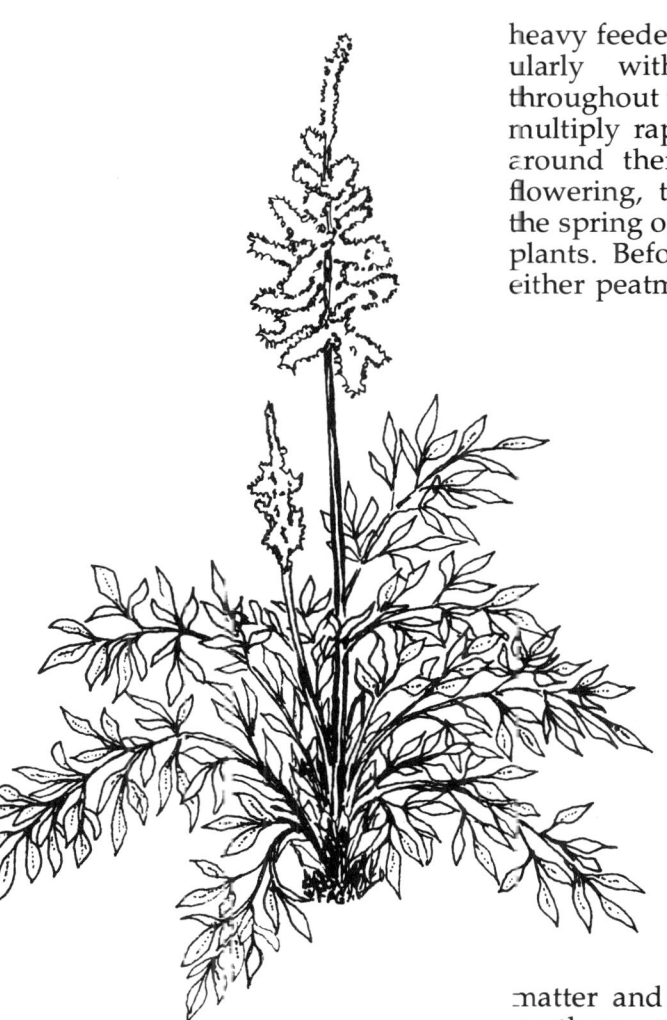

heavy feeders, they should be fed regularly with a balanced fertilizer throughout the growing season. *Astilbe* multiply rapidly and exhaust the soil around them; after 3 or 4 years of flowering, they should be divided in the spring or autumn to rejuvenate the plants. Before replanting, incorporate either peatmoss or composted organic matter and fertilizer into the soil. In northern areas, provide a light mulch during the winter months.

It is most easily propagated by division of the plants during the dormant period in fall or spring. Seeds should be sown in spring and require 2 years to produce flowering-sized plants.

INSECT PESTS: *Astilbe* can be severely damaged by red spider during hot dry periods in the summer. The minute pest feeds on the leaves, causing gray spots on their undersides and gradually causing them to yellow.

grows best in a rich, moist, well-drained soil that has generous amounts of humus to retain moisture in summer, yet is well-drained in winter.

Plant in early spring or autumn, and space plants 15 to 18 inches apart. They are easily transplanted, even when in flower. Keep plants moist during the growing season. Because the plants are shallow-rooted and

ADDITIONAL NOTES: *Astilbe X arendsii* names a series of hybrids. George Arends of Ronsdorf, Germany, interbred *Astilbe japonica*, *Astilbe thunbergii*, *Astilbe astilboides*, and *Astilbe davidii* to produce many of the excellent cultivars under this name.

SELECTED CULTIVARS: ◊ 'Avalanche': Pure white flowers on slightly arching, 30-inch stems. ◊ 'Bremen': Deep carmen-rose flowers. ◊ 'Bridal Veil': White flowers. ◊ 'Catalya Pink': Light pink flowers. ◊ 'Deutschland': Pure white flowers atop 2-foot-high flower stems; vigorous and compact, one of the best white-flowering cultivars. ◇ 'Diamond': White flowers. ◇ 'Etna': Crimson flowers. ◇ 'Europa': Clear pink flowers in 18- to 24-inch panicles above dark green foliage. ◇ 'Fanal': Bright garnet-red flowers borne, in narrow panicles atop 18- to 24-inch stems, in July and August; the leaves are bronze. ◇ 'Federsee': Crimson flowers borne atop 2½-foot stems in July and August; a compact plant, it is more drought tolerant than the other cultivars. ◇ 'Fire': Carmine-red flowers. ◇ 'Gladstone': Pure white flowers. ◇ 'Gloria': Dark pink flowers. ◇ 'Ostrich Plume': Bright salmon-pink flowers on 40-inch stems. ◇ 'Peach Blossom': Peach-blossom-pink flowers in dense panicles. ◇ 'Pink Curtsy': Soft pink flower spikes borne nearly horizontally above the foliage, giving a pleasing lacy effect. ◇ 'Professor Weilen': Cream-colored flowers on 48-inch stems. ◇ 'Queen Alexander': Carmine-pink flowers. ◇ "Red Sentinel": Carmine- to purplish-red, loose, feathery panicles; the leaves are reddish-green and finely cut. ◇ 'Rheinland': Carmine-pink flowers. ◇ 'Simplicity Rosea': Bright pink flowers.

RELATED SPECIES:

Astilbe chinensis: Chinese Astilbe. White, rose, or purplish flowers are borne in July, sessile in narrowly-branched panicles. The axis of the infloresence is densely woolly. The petals are linear-spatulate and longer than the yellowish-white or pink calyx. The leaves are 2- or 3-ternately pinnate; the leaflets are ovate-oblong, doubly serrate, hairy, and 2 to 3½ inches long. The plant grows 1½ to 2 feet high and is native to China.

var. *davidii* (*Astilbe davidii*): David Astilbe. Rose-purple flowers are borne in 2-foot-high panicles. The leaves are 2- or 3-ternately pinnate; the leaflets are ovate, coarsely and unequally serrate, and about 1½ inches in length. The flower stems are 4 to 6 feet high. *Astilbe chinensis* var. *davidii* is one of the parents of such hybrid plants as *Astilbe* X *arendsii*.

◇ 'Pumila': The 8-inch-high plant bears mauve flowers in late summer. It is outstanding for the rock garden. ◇

Aubrieta

comprises about 12 species of mat-forming, mountain perennial herbs with stellate or simple hairs (rarely glabrous). These plants, grown for their colorful spring flowers, are native to the area between Southern Europe and Iran.

Sometimes spelled *Aubrietia*, this genus was named after Claude Aubriet, the French natural-history painter of the early 18th century.

Cruciferae
(Mustard family)

Aubrieta deltoidea
Purple Rock-cress

FLOWERS: The numerous mauve/deep-purple flowers are $\frac{3}{4}$ inch across and are borne, from April to June, in short, terminal racemes just above the dense mat of foliage. The usually bisexual, regularly symmetrical flowers have 4 sepals with a cylindrical calyx $\frac{1}{2}$ the length of the petals. The 4 large petals are long-clawed, forming a cross with their spreading limbs. *Aubrieta* flowers are similar to those of *Arabis*.

LEAVES: The attractive silver-green leaves are evergreen, alternate, simple, and range from rhombic to obovate-cuneate; they are pubescent, usually less than 1 inch long, and have 1 or 2 teeth on each side. The foliage is attractive throughout the growing season.

PLANT CHARACTERISTICS: This compact, mat-forming perennial is pubescent with stellate or simple hairs, rarely glabrous, and grows 3 to 6 inches, occasionally to 1 foot, in height.

GARDEN VALUE: *Aubrieta deltoidea* is an old favorite in the rock garden, but it is also suitable for a dry wall planting, porch boxes, an edging, the front of the perennial border or mixed border, or wherever a spreading plant is desired. It provides masses of flowers that combine well with *Aurinia* or *Arabis*.

CULTURE: The species prefers semi-shade and a light, porous, well-drained soil. When exposed to full sun or high temperature, its flowering period is reduced. The climate of the West Coast is perfect for *Aubrieta*, but it is usually grown only with difficulty elsewhere in the United States.

Plant in spring. Space plants about 10 inches apart. Shearing off flower spikes after they have faded may induce a fall flowering. Prune old plants drastically when they spread too rampantly.

The plant is easily propagated by division of the clump in spring. Seeds sown in spring will germinate easily and flower the second season. Take cuttings in midsummer or layer from trailing shoots.

ADDITIONAL NOTES: Although closely related to *Arabis*, *Aubrieta* is a neater, more compact plant and is somewhat more difficult to grow. It thrives in England.

Several varieties are offered in the trade, with flowers varying only slightly in color. Single, semi-double, and double flowered forms are available.

NATIVE HABITAT: Greece, Sicily, Asia Minor.

SELECTED CULTIVARS: ◇ 'Bougainvillei': Light violet flowers; a dwarf compact plant. ◇ 'Campbellii': Large purple flowers; a large plant. ◇ Cardinal Richelieu': Brilliant royal-purple flowers. ◇ 'Dawn': Large, semi-double, clear pink flowers. ◇ 'Eyrise Strain': Long, large, deep violet flowers. ◇ 'Graeca': Large, light blue flowers; one of the best cultivars. ◇ 'Lavender': Large, wide-petaled lavender flowers. ◇ 'Leichtlinii': Bright reddish-crimson flowers; a profusely-flowering dwarf. ◇ 'Moerheimii': Large mauve flowers; flowers all summer. ◇ 'Purple Cascade': Purple flowers. ◇ 'Red Cascade': Red flowers. ◇ 'Variegata': Variegated leaves. ◇

Aurinia

consists of about 7 species of biennial or perennial herbs native to Central and Southern Europe and Turkey. Included until recently in *Alyssum*, these plants were separated on the basis of morphological differences of the foliage.

The common name Madwort and the botanical name *Alyssum* sprang from a mythological belief that these plants had powers to calm the troubled mind; *Alyssum* is of Greek origin, meaning "allaying of rage".

Cruciferae
(Mustard family)

Aurinia saxatilis (Alyssum arduini, Alyssum orientale, Alyssum saxatile)
Basket-of-gold, Golden Alyssum
Also known as Goldentuft, Goldentuft Alyssum, Madwort, Rock Madwort

FLOWERS: Pale golden-yellow flowers are borne, profusely in dense panicles on 12-inch stems, in April and May. The flowers are regularly symmetrical and have 4 sepals and 4 petals which spread to form a cross.

LEAVES: The soft, stellate-hairy, silvery-gray leaves are alternate and have long and deeply grooved petioles. The numerous basal leaves grow in tufted rosettes; they are spatulate and range from sinuate to repand-denate. Stem leaves are smaller and linear-oblanceolate. The foliage may persist to some extent over the winter, but occasionally suffers from winterburn. The plant will not tolerate foot traffic.

PLANT CHARACTERISTICS: Growing 6 to 12 inches high, this stellate-hairy, prostrate perennial sprawls, forming coarse, dense mats with woody roots.

GARDEN VALUE: *Aurinia saxatilis* is one of the most popular rock garden plants. Forming cascades of bright yellow flowers to signal the arrival of spring, this popular plant is used in dry walls, the rock garden, and the perennial and mixed border; it is also used as an edging and in hanging baskets and porch boxes. It contrasts pleasantly with *Phlox divaricata*, *Phlox subulata*, *Arabis*, dwarf forms of *Aquilegia*, *Daphne cneorum*, and spring-flowering bulbs.

CULTURE: *Aurinia saxatilis* is easy to grow. To produce masses of flowers, the plant requires a sunny site. It prefers a well-drained soil that ranges from neutral to slightly acid and is of average fertility; however, it is tolerant of most soils, as well as dry conditions.

Plant in the spring. Feed occasionally with a balanced fertilizer to promote growth and profuse flowering. Remove seed heads after flowering to enhance its appearance. Prune to shape and rejuvenate. Divide every third spring to rejuvenate old clumps and to curb excessive spreading.

Sow seeds in August. Propagate cultivars from cuttings taken in midsummer. Divide roots in early spring.

ADDITIONAL NOTES: *Aurinia saxatilis* is reputedly used to cure hydrophobia.

NATIVE HABITAT: Southern and Central Europe and Turkey.

SELECTED CULTIVARS: ◇ 'Citrina': Abundant, light yellow flowers. ◇ 'Compacta': Light yellow flowers, growing more densely and neatly than the straight species. ◇ 'Dudley Neville': Flowers ranging from peachbuff to chrome yellow; smaller leaves, and shorter flower stems; seedlings vary considerably. ◇ 'Floraplena': A rare double-flowering form that flowers for a longer period than the straight species and does not set seed. ◇ 'Nana': A compact form. ◇ 'Plena': Double yellow flowers ◇ 'Variegatum': Attractive variegated foliage. ◇ 'Basket-of-Gold' ◇

Baptisia

comprises about 30 to 35 species of erect perennial herbs native to North America.

The name *Baptisia* is derived from the Greek word *bapto*, meaning "to dip", and refers to the indigo-blue-like dye that is obtained from the flowers of some of the species.

Fabaceae (Leguminosae)
(Pea family)

Baptisia australis
Blue False Indigo
Also known as Blue Wild Indigo, Plains False Indigo, Wild Blue Indigo

FLOWERS: The indigo-blue flowers are up to 1 inch across and are borne, in loosely-flowered terminal racemes 9 to 12 inches long, in May and June. The corolla is papilionaceous. In the *Baptisia australis* flower, the standard is not larger than the wings. The calyx is campanulate and has 5 teeth.

FRUITS: The inflated pod containing the seeds is short, plump, black, and 2 to 3 inches long. It develops in late summer and splits along both margins to release the seeds.

LEAVES: The clean, handsome, richly bluish-green leaves are alternate, usually trifoliate, entire, obtuse, and have stipules. The leaflets range from oblanceolate to ovate and are $2\frac{1}{2}$ inches long. The graceful, arching foliage remains attractive until blackened by severe frosts.

PLANT CHARACTERISTICS: This attractive, glabrous, erect perennial is hardy, slow-growing, and long-lived and forms huge clumps 3 to 5 feet high and 2 to 3 feet across. The stems are killed with the first hard frost, but stems and pods remain.

GARDEN VALUE: The long sprays of the flowers are interesting, but the plant can also be grown for its foliage. It makes an excellent summertime hedge and is used in the background of the perennial border and mixed beds, as a specimen plant, and in a wild flower garden and a naturalized area. The species is excellent for holding soil on banks because of its extensive root system.

Its flowers are long-lasting when cut and used in bouquets. The foliage is attractive in fresh flower arrangements, and the fat seed pods are often dried for winter arrangements.

CULTURE: The plant requires full sunlight to produce the best flowers. When grown in partial shade it flowers less and develops excessive foliage. A dry location is ideal. It grows well in poor, dry soils.

Plant in very early spring. Space plants 18 to 30 inches apart. Water sparingly, and feed occasionally with a balanced fertilizer. The plants may require staking. Pinch off faded flowers to encourage the development of more flowers. The plant seldom needs dividing; older clumps become deep-rooted and do not transplant well.

Division is not easy, but it is the only way to perpetuate unusual traits; divide before or after the flowering season. Seeds sown in open ground in spring germinate well. The plant is difficult to transplant when young; for best results, transplant seedlings into a permanent location the second spring. 2 or 3 years are required to develop flowering-sized plants from seed.

ADDITIONAL NOTES: To prepare seed pods for winter arrangements, cut long-stems in early autumn, before they have become too weathered. Place the stems upright in a dry, airy spot until dried, and store until needed.

NATIVE HABITAT: From Pennsylvania south to Georgia and Tennessee.

SELECTED CULTIVARS:

'Old Orchard Hybrids'. A strain with flowers of tawny violet, buff, blue, and intermediate combinations of colors. Seedlings of these hybrids vary widely but are usually under 3 feet in height.

RELATED SPECIES:

Baptisia bracteata. The creamy white or soft yellow flowers are borne, on axillary racemes, in May and June. The leaves are compound and softly pubescent. The leaflets range from oblanceolate to obovate and are about 4 inches long. The plant grows 2 to 2 ½ feet high. The unique foliage and soft flower colors make this plant valuable in the perennial border or the wild flower garden. It is native to the area from North Carolina south to Georgia and Alabama.

Baptisia leucantha: Prairie False Indigo, White False Indigo. The white flowers are nearly 1 inch long and are borne in loose lateral racemes in June and July. The compound leaves are stalked and very obtuse; the leaflets are 2 inches long and range from obovate to cuneate. The plant grows up to 4 feet tall. It requires partial shade and does not tolerate droughts; water regularly. The leaves turn black when dried. Its native habitat is the area from Ohio to Minnesota and south to Mississippi and Texas. The plant has been used for medicinal purposes.

Baptisia tinctoria: Horsefly; also known as Horsefly Weed, Rattleweed, Wild Indigo, Clover Broom, Shoofly. The bright yellow flowers are about $\frac{1}{2}$ inch long and are borne on numerous few-flowered terminal racemes in June and July. The compound leaves resemble clover leaves. The leaves are petioled; the leaflets range from obovate to oblanceolate and are nearly or quite sessile, entire, and about 1 inch long. This glabrous, bushy plant grows 2 to 4 feet high. It requires little attention and tolerates drought conditions. It is most often used in a wild flower garden or in a naturalized area. A blue dye (which is an inferior substitute for indigo) can be extracted from the stems. The root is used in medications. The species turns black when it dries. Its native habitat is the area from Massachusetts south to Florida and west to Minnesota. ◇

Belamcanda

consists of 2 species of hardy monocotyledon perennial herbs native to China and Japan.

The genus name is of East Asian origin. The common name, Blackberry Lily, refers to the persistent, shiny, black seeds that resemble blackberries; another common name, Leopard Flower, was attached to the plant because of the dark-spotted orange flowers.

Iridaceae
(Iris family)

Belamcanda chinensis (Pardanthus chinensis)
Blackberry Lily
Also known as Leopard Flower, Leopard Lily

FLOWERS: Numerous, exotic, deep orange, red-dotted flowers $1\frac{1}{2}$ to 2 inches across, are borne in loose corymbs from July through September. Although the stem usually bears 15 to 20 flowers, only 3 or 4 flowers are open at any one time. Each lasts 4 or 5 days, twists spirally, and dries before dropping from the stem. They are bisexual and regularly symmetrical. There are 6 separate, oblong, and acute perianth segments; the 3 inner segments are slightly shorter. The filaments are reddish-purple.

PLANT CHARACTERISTICS: The stem is vertical and grows 2 to 3 feet high. The short, stout rhizomes are orange-yellow. The clump-forming rhizomes and long, narrow foliage somewhat resemble those of *Iris germanica*.

GARDEN VALUE: *Belamcanda chinensis* is used in the perennial border or the mixed border. The flowers are suitable for fresh flower arrangements, and the seed clusters provide unusual interest in dried arrangements.

CULTURE: The plant, which is easy to grow, prefers a rich, light, sandy soil in full sun. Plant when dormant, in early spring or fall. Place the rhizome $1\frac{1}{2}$ inches deep; space plants 1 foot apart. They may occasionally die out but are easily replaced by seeds sown in spring.

The plant can be propagated without difficulty by division of the rhizomes in spring. It produces flowers from seed the first or following year.

NATIVE HABITAT: China and Japan.

ADDITIONAL NOTES: The plant has been used medicinally by the Chinese. ◊

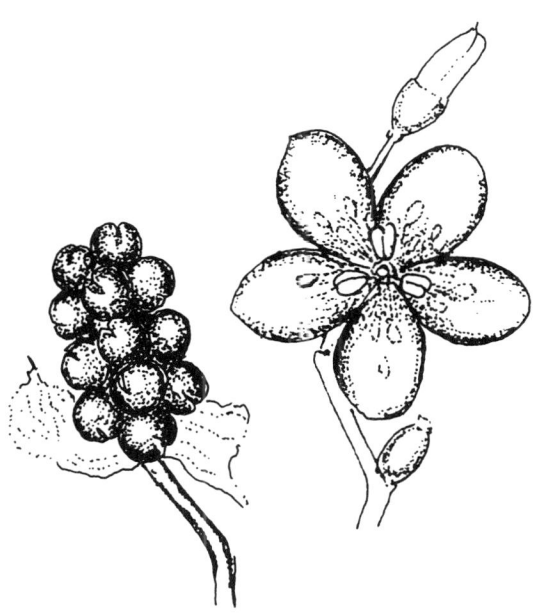

FRUITS: The fruit is a capsule. When ripe in autumn, the valves reflex to expose a column densely covered with round, glossy, black seeds. The seeds, which resemble blackberries, are persistent.

LEAVES: The linear leaves are basal and cauline and are 12 to 18 inches long and 1 inch wide.

Bellis

consists of about 15 species of annual or perennial herbs whose native habitat centers around the European and Mediterranean regions.

Bellis is derived from the Latin word *bellus*, meaning "pretty".

Compositae—Aster tribe
(Composite family)

Bellis perennis
English Daisy, True Daisy

FLOWERS: The flower heads are radiate and 1 to 2 inches wide; they are borne in 3- to 6-inch pubescent scapes, from April to June and scattered throughout the summer until fall. The involucre is hemispherical or campanulate; the involucral bracts are leaf-like and either equal or unequal in 2 rows. The naked receptacle ranges from convex to conical. The disc flowers are bisexual and yellow; the numerous ray flowers, which are borne in a single row, are white or pink and female.

LEAVES: The dark green leaves, in a basal rosette, range from spatulate to obovate, from glabrous to pubescent, and are usually 1 to 2 inches long and crenate.

PLANT CHARACTERISTICS: This small, tufted plant is usually grown as a biennial or an annual. The foliage grows 3 to 6 inches high, but the plant reaches 6 to 8 inches when in flower.

GARDEN VALUE: This is a fine ornamental plant when well-grown. Use it for mass effects, edging, and in the wild flower garden as well as in the rockery or a permanent landscape container. Use it also in the front part of the perennial border; it combines well with spring-flowering bulbs. However, in areas where conditions are conducive to its growth, it tends to colonize in the lawn area.

CULTURE: The plant likes warm sun; however, the North American midsummer sun is often detrimental to it. The ideal site is a cool, moist, fertile soil with abundant humus, in full sun or slightly shaded.

Plant in the spring, spacing about 8 or 9 inches apart. Feed regularly with a balanced fertilizer. Keep the plant well-watered; it does not tolerate drought conditions during the growing season. Cultivate regularly to eliminate smothering weeds. The plant does not winter well; in northern areas, it needs a light mulch 4 to 6 inches deep, applied after the ground freezes, during winter months, or it can be set into a cold frame. Where self-sowing occurs, the plantings must be kept in check; however, *Bellis perennis* does not reseed itself in the American Midwest. Volunteer seedlings from doubled flowering forms revert to the less desirable common single form, which should be eliminated.

The plant is easily propagated by sowing seeds in late August in a cold frame; if set out in early spring, the seedlings will then produce flowers that season. After flowering, divide each plant into single crowns and replant. Cultivars do not come true to type from seed.

DISEASE PESTS: *Bellis* is susceptible to mildew.

ADDITIONAL NOTES: *Bellis* is the true daisy immortalized by poets. The double flowering forms are the most popular.

NATIVE HABITAT: Western Europe; probably introduced to America in early Colonial days.

SELECTED CULTIVARS AND VARIETIES: ◇ 'Dresden China' ◇ 'Giant Rose' ◇ 'Monstrosa': Dark red, double flowers, large flower heads. ◇ 'Prolifera' ◇ 'Rosea': Rose-pink ray flowers. ◇ 'Snow Ball' ◇ 'Tuberosa': Rose-colored quilled ray flowers. ◇ var. *ranunculiflora*: Double flowers. ◇

Bergenia

consists of about 12 species of perennial herbs that have thick rhizomes and develop into large clumps or colonies. The plants are native to the temperate region of Asia.

The genus is named in honor of Karl August von Bergen, an 18th century botanist and physician of Frankfort, Germany. The plants may be listed in catalogs as *Saxifraga* or *Megasea*.

Saxifragaceae
(Saxifrage family)

Bergenia cordifolia (Saxifraga cordifolia)
Heartleaf Bergenia, Pig Squeak

FLOWERS: Large, waxy, clear rose flowers $\frac{1}{4}$ to $\frac{1}{2}$ inch across are borne, on short, thick pedicels in a densely nodding, scapose cyme up to 16 inches high, from late April through May. (It flowers during the winter months in California.) The flowers are bisexual and regularly symmetrical and have 5 short, broad sepals, 5 roundish petals, and 10 stamens.

LEAVES: The shiny, handsome leaves are large, fleshy, thickened, and have undulate-serrate margins. They are evergreen, alternate, orbiculate, and up to 10 inches long and 6 to 8 inches across; they are rounded or cordate at the base and have glandular pits. The petioles are long, thick, and sheathed at the base. The evergreen foliage remains attractive after the flowers fade and turns purplish-bronze during the winter.

PLANT CHARACTERISTICS: This dependable, long-lasting perennial grows 12 to 20 inches high. These plants are stout, with thick, short fleshy rhizomes; they form large clumps or colonies.

GARDEN VALUE: *Bergenia cordifolia* is grown for its showy, early flowers and ornamental foliage. Late frosts may damage the flower buds before they open. In northern areas the plant may not flower reliably; however, the foliage alone makes the plant worth growing. Use it as an accent plant in the perennial or mixed border or in a large rock garden. Mass it as a ground cover in a wet soil by a pool or along a stream. Place it along a path in a moist, shaded site. Its flowers and foliage are also attractive in flower arrangements.

CULTURE: *Bergenia cordifolia* grows well and colonies rapidly develop in wet soil, in partially shaded sites. If grown in a dry sunny site or in dense shade, the growth tends to be retarded.

Plant in spring or fall, spacing about 12 to 15 inches apart. Feed several times during the growing season with a balanced fertilizer. In the North, cover the plants with a light material such as pine boughs or straw during winter to protect the leaves from winter sun. After 3 or 4 years of flowering, the plants should be divided. Seeds can be sown in spring, or the plants can be divided in fall or spring.

NATIVE HABITAT: Siberia and Mongolia.

SELECTED CULTIVARS AND VARIETIES: There are white-flowered and purple flowered varieties. ◇

Campanula

Campanulaceae
(Bellflower family)

consists of about 300 species of annual, biennial, and perennial herbs, varying from small rosette or mat-forming plants to coarse, erect species. Many of these are prized ornamental plants; some are vigorously invasive. They are distributed throughout the swamps and moist-ground areas, as well as alpine and arboreal regions of the Northern Hemisphere, but are concentrated in the Caucasus, Balkan, and Mediterranean regions.

The name Campanula is of Latin origin, meaning "little bell"; it refers to the bell-shaped corolla characteristic of some species.

Campanula carpatica
Carpathian Harebell
Also known as Carpathian Bellflower, Tussock Bellflower

FLOWERS: The blue-lilac flowers are borne erect, either singly or in clusters, on 6- to 12-inch-long, slender, naked, axillary pedicels. The 5-lobed corollas are broadly campanulate, regularly symmetrical, and 1 to 2 inches across; the calyx has no appendages. The flowers are borne in July, but a few flowers often appear sporadically throughout the remainder of the summer.

LEAVES: The light green leaves are alternate, 2 inches or less in length, deeply serrate, and long-petioled, without stipules. The basal leaves are often longer, ovate-rotund, and much longer-petioled than the stem leaves, which are ovate-acuminate.

PLANT CHARACTERISTICS: This neat, glabrous, clump-forming perennial forms a mound 6 to 15 inches high and 12 to 18 inches across. The slender stems are leafy at the base, branching, and somewhat decumbent.

GARDEN VALUE: This is a useful and delightful species of *Campanula*. Valued for its flowers, and one of the leading rock garden members of the genus, it supplies color in middle and late summer. This plant, which is visually more impressive when massed, may also be used as an edging in a perennial garden, along a path, as a ground cover, or in a naturalized area. It also provides excellent cut flowers.

CULTURE: *Campanula carpatica* is unquestionably hardy when placed in a sunny site with a well-drained soil of average fertility.

Plant in the spring; do not crowd; space the plants about 8 inches apart. With care, the plants can be transplanted when in full flower. Feed in spring with well-rotted compost and bone meal worked into the soil around the base of the plants, then apply a well-balanced fertilizer 2 or 3 times during the growing season. A rich soil makes the plants more floriferous and the foliage more handsome. Keep the plants moist, and remove the faded flowers before seeds develop to prolong the flowering period. Provide winter protection in areas of severe winter climate. The plants are slow to spread but need renewal by division every 3 to 5 years, after flowering.

Propagate by seeds, division, or cuttings. Seeds germinate readily from spring sowing. Many varieties in the genus do not reproduce true to type, so they must be propagated by division in early spring or in August or by cuttings taken in the spring.

ADDITIONAL NOTES: Material offered as *Campanula raineri* is often a dwarf form of this species.

NATIVE HABITAT: The Carpathian Mountains of Austria.

SELECTED CULTIVARS: Many cultivars are in cultivation. ◇ 'Alba': White flowers. ◇ 'Blue Carpet': Medium clear blue flowers; a dwarf compact form. ◇ 'China Doll': Large mauve flowers. ◇ 'Cobalt': Deep blue flowers. ◇ 'Riverslea': Deep violet-blue, very open flowers. ◇ 'Turbinata': Solitary, deep purple-blue flowers, 2 inches across; smaller than the species, about 4 inches high; leaves are larger and the unbranched stems are prostrate. ◇ 'Wedgewood': Flat, pale blue-violet flowers. ◇ 'White Star': White flowers, better, although flat, than those of the older 'Alba'. ◇ 'White Wedgewood': White flowers. ◇

Campanulaceae
(Bellflower family)

Campanula persicifolia
Peach-leaved Bellflower
Also known as Willow Bellflower, Peach-bells, Paper Bellflower

FLOWERS: The flowers, which range in color from deep blue to white, are pedicelled and are borne solitary in June, terminal or axillary in a few-flowered raceme. The tubular calyx has no appendages; calyx lobes are acuminate, entire, wide at the base, and half as long as the corolla. The 5-lobed corolla is broadly campanulate and up to $1\frac{1}{2}$ inches long. The flowers appear stiff but have a delicate texture.

LEAVES: The simple, rigid leaves are alternate, without stipules; they are glabrous, crenulate, and 3 to 5 inches long. The rosette leaves are often longer, broader, and much longer-petioled than the stem leaves. They are oblong-lanceolate, up to 8 inches long, entire, serrulate, and smooth. The stem leaves are linear-lanceolate.

PLANT CHARACTERISTICS: This 3-foot, very durable, perennial forms an erect, leafy clump. The thin stems, usually unbranched, are graceful in appearance.

GARDEN VALUE: Grown for its flowers, *Campanula persicifolia* is a fine perennial more impressive in mass than as a single specimen. It is useful in the perennial border, wild flower garden, and a naturalized area. The flowers are excellent for fresh flower arrangements.

CULTURE: Growing in sun or semi-shade, this perennial tolerates a wide range of soils. However, it grows best in a well-drained soil with fertility ranging from average to rich. It tolerates dry, semi-shady spots.

Campanula persicifolia is easily grown. Plant in spring, spacing about 12 to 18 inches apart; do not crowd the plants. In spring, work well-rotted compost into the soil around the plants. Apply a well-balanced fertilizer 2 or 3 times during the growing season; a rich soil makes the plants more floriferous and the foliage more handsome. Keep plants moist; remove faded flowers to encourage flowering after July. Stake stems to prevent damage from wind and rain. Mulch in winter, both to protect plants from low temperatures and to provide support against heavy snows, which may break down the crowns and lead to decay. Dividing the basal tufts every second August usually improves flowering the following year. This species spreads slowly.

Seeds germinate readily from spring sowings, but some cultivars may not reproduce exactly true to type. Divide in early spring or August. Collect cuttings in spring.

ADDITIONAL NOTES: The native form of the species is quite scarce, as the seeds do not reproduce it true to type, leading to a quite variable species. *Persicifolia* means "peach-leaved".

NATIVE HABITAT: Europe and Northeastern Asia.

SELECTED CULTIVARS: ◇ 'Alba': Single white flowers. ◇ 'Alba Grandiflora': Large white flowers. ◇ 'Blue Gardenia': Deep blue, double flowers. ◇ 'Humosa': Double flowers. ◇ 'Moerheimei': Semi-double white flowers, 2 to 3 inches across. ◇ 'Mt. Hood': Double white flowers; the plant grows up to 30 inches high. ◇ 'Summer Skies': Double white flowers, flushed azure blue. ◇ 'Telham Beauty': Very large, powdery, porcelain blue flowers, 2 to 3 inches across, are borne, along the top half of the 4-foot flower stalk, from early to middle summer. The foliage is broader and heavier. Probably one of the best cultivars of the genus, this plant is easily grown from seed, and its number of chromosomes is doubled. ◇ 'Wiffral Belle': Double, steely blue-violet flowers.

RELATED SPECIES:

Campanula glomerata: Clustered Bellflower, Danes-blood Bellflower. The flowers are borne in dense terminal clusters of 15 to 20, fewer in axillary clusters. After the terminal head flowers, the axillary flowers begin to open. The upward-facing corolla is purple-blue, rarely white; it is ¾ to 1 inch long and narrowly campanulate. Flowering occurs primarily in June and July, with additional scattered flowers in August. The leaves range from cordate, ovate-oblong to lanceolate, and are minutely serrate, up to 5 inches long, with very short, stiff hairs. This 1- to 3-foot perennial is coarse and grows erectly.

Campanula glomerata is easily grown in any sunny or shady site and increases rapidly by rhizomes when growing in a fertile soil; spreading is reduced when growing in poor soils. Divide after 2 or 3 years of flowering; division is the usual method of propagation. The plant's native habitat is Europe and Asia. In some rural areas of England, this plant is known as 12 Apostles because the flower head sometimes has 12 flowers.

◇ 'Acaulis': Amethyst-violet flowers. ◇ 'Crown of Snow': White flowers and large leaves. ◇ 'Joan Elliott': Handsome deep violet flowers. ◇ 'Superba': Rich violet-blue flowers, showier than the straight species. ◇ var. *acaulis*: Small clusters of violet-blue flowers in June and July, on a dwarf plant 3 to 5 inches high. The sturdy little tuft makes an excellent rock garden plant. ◇ var. *dahurica*: Known as Danesblood in England, it bears deep, rich flowers freely in terminal clusters 3 inches across, on a 12- to 18-inch-high plant.

Campanula medium: Canterbury-bells. Flowers are borne 1 or 2 together, in long, heavy, showy, open racemes 1½ to 3 feet high, in June and July. The calyx is bristly ciliate with large ovate appendages. The large, upfacing corolla, ranging in color from blue to white, is campanulate, somewhat inflated at the base, and about 2 inches long. The leaves range from ovate to obovate and are about 10 inches long with winged petioles. This hardy biennial grows erect and reaches about 2 to 3 feet of height.

A popular garden plant, it combines effectively with *Delphinium, Alcae rosea,* and other similarly tall plants. The white-flowered form is especially highly-valued for use in flower arrangements for June weddings. This plant must be renewed each year by seeds sown in July or August, which produce flowering plants the next season. Do not smother seedlings with a mulch during winter. The native habitat of *Campanula medium* is Southern Europe.

Although usually biennial, an annual form has been developed, as well as several other interesting forms.

◇ 'Alba': White flowers. ◇ 'Caerulea': Blue flowers. ◇ 'Calycanthema' (var. *calycanthus*): Cup and Saucer. The calyx is petaloid, up to 3 inches across, flattened, and deeply or shallowly lobed; it resembles a saucer, with the inner corolla shaped like a cup. When one flower appears to be set within another, this is referred to as "hose-in-hose." ◇ 'Nana': Dwarf form. ◇ 'Rosea': Pink flowers.

Campanula portenschlagiana (Campanula muralis): Dalmatian Bellflower. The light bluish-purple flowers are borne, almost erect, several or many in racemes or narrow panicles on 3- to 4-inch stems, in May and June. The corolla is funnelform and up to 1 inch long. The tiny, shiny green leaves are petiolate, cordate, dentate, and somewhat evergreen. This perennial grows 6 to 8 inches high in a very tight little tuft with somewhat erect stems. It is a fine plant for the perennial garden, rock garden, or as a potted plant. When grown on dry walls, its cascading beauty can be delightfully displayed. It is native to Dalmatia and was named for an Austrian botanist.

Campanula poscharskyana: Serbian Bellflower. Masses of light lavender-blue flowers are borne in June, in racemes or narrow panicles. The broadly funnelform corolla is 1 to $1\frac{1}{4}$ inches long and has lanceolate calyx lobes. The sharp-pointed, kidney-shaped leaves are $1\frac{1}{2}$ inches long. This semi-prostrate perennial grows 4 inches high, forming large 3-foot clumps with long, trailing, weak, stems up to 2 feet in length. A rampant creeper, the stems trail over the ground and cling to dry walls. Use as a ground cover or on a sandy bank, and permit the stems to trail; it may also be planted between flagstones, although it will not tolerate much foot traffic. This plant prefers light shade but tolerates full sun and grows in any well-drained garden soil. It is drought resistant. Propagation is easily achieved. The plant, which is named after a Balkan botanist, is native to Dalmatia.

Campanula rapunculoides: Rover Bellflower, Creeping Bellflower, False Rampion. The large, simple, nodding flowers are borne in July and August, in an elongate, more or less naked, 1-sided terminal raceme. The calyx lacks appendages; the deep violet-blue corolla is funnelform and 1 inch or more across. The alternate, rough leaves grow 2 to 4 inches long. The basal leaves are very long-petioled, cordate-ovate, and serrate, the stem leaves are sessile and range from narrow-ovate to lanceolate. This erect perennial grows 3 to 4 feet high. A persistent species, it spreads by seeds and vigorous rhizomes to become an invasive weed; therefore do not grow it in the border, but restrict it to the wild flower garden or to a naturalized area. Its native habitat is Eurasia, although it has become naturalized throughout the United States. ◇

Centaurea

includes nearly 500 species of annual, biennial, and perennial herbs; they are primarily native to the Mediterranean region and the Near East, although 2 species are native to North America.

Centaurea, the genus name, is derived from the Greek word *centaur*, meaning "famous for healing." Legend claims that the centaur Chiron used this plant to heal his wounds and taught man the value of plants.

Compositae—Carduus tribe
(Composite family)

Centaurea montana
Perennial Bachelor's Button
Also known as Mountain Bluet, Mountain Knapweed

FLOWERS: The deep blue-violet flowers in heads are up to 3 inches across and are borne from May until July, solitary at the ends of slender 2-foot stems. The flowers are borne on long peduncles or sessile. The involucre is ovoid; the involucral bracts, which are imbricate in 4 or 5 rows, are entire or, more frequently, range from ciliate to pectinate, or have spiny appendages. The bracts have blue-fringed margins. The receptacle is flat and densely bristly. The flowers are tubular and bisexual, or the outer ones are enlarged, raylike, sterile, and up to 1 inch long.

LEAVES: The leaves range from lanceolate or elliptic to obovate-oblanceolate; they are entire and silvery tomentose. The basal leaves are petioled and up to $7\frac{1}{2}$ inches long. The stem leaves are alternate and successively reduced until sessile and decurrent. Young leaves are a silvery white color.

PLANT CHARACTERISTICS: This somewhat straggly perennial grows 12 to 18 inches high; it is hardy and drought resistant. Its stems are usually unbranched. Often stoloniferous, it spreads in fertile soil.

GARDEN VALUE: *Centaurea montana* is most effective when planted in groups. Use it in the perennial border or the mixed border. It provides excellent cut flowers.

CULTURE: Although it needs a sunny location, this perennial adapts to most conditions. It will grow in nearly any well-drained garden soil but spreads excessively in a rich soil.

Plant in spring, spacing about 12 inches apart. Provide the plant with a moderate amount of water, and feed it occasionally with a balanced fertilizer. Weak stems may need staking. After flowering, cut stems off at ground level to keep the plants from sprawling over neighboring plants and to induce fall flowering from new shoots. Divide the plants after every 2 or 3 years of flowering to prevent over-crowding.

Sow seeds or collect cuttings in September and leave the new plants in the greenhouse or hotbed over the winter to produce flowers the next season. Seeds may also be sown in spring and plants divided in early fall or spring.

ADDITIONAL NOTES: *Centaurea montana* is one of the most popular of the perennial *Centaurea*.

NATIVE HABITAT: Central Europe.

SELECTED CULTIVARS: ◇ 'Alba': White flowers. ◇ 'Caerulea': Blue flowers. ◇ 'Carnea': Flesh-colored flowers. ◇ 'Grandiflora': Blue flowers. ◇ 'Purpurea': Deep blue flowers. ◇

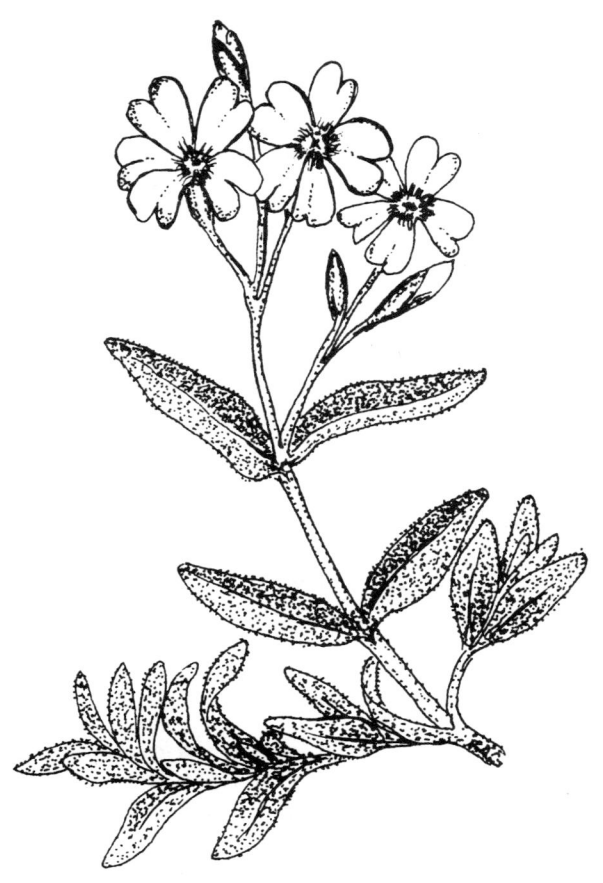

Cerastium

consists of about 60 species of annual and perennial herbs; distributed worldwide, these plants are predominantly mat-forming or cespitose, and hairy-stemmed, sometimes slightly woody basally. They are used in rockeries, beds, and borders. The name is derived from the Greek word *keras*, meaning "horn," and refers to the shape of the seed pods.

Caryophyllaceae
(Pink family)

Cerastium tomentosum
Snow-in-summer

FLOWERS: Masses of showy, small, pure white flowers are borne in loose, 3- to 15-flowered cymes, in May. The flowers, regularly symmetrical and $\frac{1}{2}$ to 1 inch across, consist of 5 (rarely 4) separate sepals, 5 (rarely 4) white petals, and from 5 to 10 stamens. The petals are notched, creating the illusion that there are 10 rather than 5.

LEAVES: The attractive, silvery-gray leaves are evergreen, simple, and opposite; they are entire, lanceolate, $\frac{3}{4}$ to 1 inch long and $\frac{1}{4}$ inch across, and white-woolly, with parallel veins.

PLANT CHARACTERISTICS: This prostrate

perennial grows 6 to 10 inches high. The branched stems are erect, white-woolly, and slightly woody basally. The strongly rhizomatous plant forms a heavy mat of growth, up to 9 square feet in area. A vigorous plant, it tends to spread rapidly under and around other plants; however, it withstands drought and is practically indestructible, even in difficult sites.

GARDEN VALUE: This common creeper, valued for its foliage, can be adapted from seacoast, desert, and mountain areas to use on level ground, in fills, or in rocky outcroppings. Use it as a ground cover or to edge a sunny path. *Cerastium tomentosum* is considered valuable for trailing over rock walls, in the rock garden, or between flagstones. Use it in the perennial or mixed border only where its rampant growth can be restrained by a structure such as a concrete walk.

CULTURE: *Cerastium tomentosum* is easily grown. It requires full sun and perfect drainage. Dry soils of low fertility are preferred; the less fertile the soil, the less the plants spread. However, it has been known to grow even in pure sand.

Purchase container-grown plants or divide old clumps. Keep them on the dry side, and feed once each spring; cultivation is not necessary. Divide the plants annually to restrain aggressive specimens.

The plants sow seeds freely. Seeds germinate easily in spring or late summer and remain viable in the soil for several years. After flowering has occurred, divide carefully to avoid damaging the roots. Take cuttings after flowering.

ADDITIONAL NOTES: *Cerastium* includes valuable decumbent plants that are very popular with home gardeners.

NATIVE HABITAT: From the mountains of Italy south to Sicily. ◇

Chrysanthemum

consists of up to 200 species; it is a diverse group of annual and perennial herbs and subshrubs that are often aromatic. Their native habitat is primarily in the Northern Hemisphere, particularly in Asia and Europe. *Chrysanthemum* has been grown in Chinese gardens since 550 B.C.

The genus name *Chrysanthemum* is derived from the Greek names *chrysos*, "gold", and *anthos,* "flower."

Compositae — Anthemis tribe (Composite family)

Chrysanthemum coccineum
Painted Daisy
Also known as Pyrethrum, Persian Insect Flower

FLOWER: The flower heads are usually

radiate, from 3 to 5 inches wide, single (sometimes double), and are borne, solitary at the ends of stems, in June and early July and sparsely throughout the summer until fall. The involucral bracts are more or less imbricate in 2 to 5 rows and have brown margins. The receptacle is naked and convex. The disc flowers are bisexual, fertile, and yellow. The ray flowers are female, fertile, and pink, red, or white.

LEAVES: The attractive, finely-textured, dark green leaves are alternate, sometimes in a basal rosette, entire, and 1- or 2-pinnatifid.

PLANT CHARACTERISTICS: This glabrous perennial grows 2 to 3 feet high. The long stems are usually unbranched. *Chrysanthemum coccineum* is a variable species and a short-lived perennial; it is somewhat drought resistant.

GARDEN VALUE: A popular summer-flowering plant, it is usually grown in the perennial garden. Group in 3s as specimen plants, or grow in combination with other perennials. This species and its cultivars provide excellent cut flowers.

CULTURE: The plant performs best in full sun but can tolerate light shade for part of the day. It requires a rich, well-drained soil with abundant organic matter; it will not survive in a soil that is continually wet during the winter.

Plant in spring. Space plants 10 inches apart. They are heavy feeders, and should be fed regularly and heavily with a balanced fertilizer. Cultivate around the base of the plants regularly, and keep them heavily mulched and well watered during the growing season. After the flowers have faded, cut back the shoots severely to encourage new growth at the base of the plant, which will flower a second time. Apply a mulch during the winter to protect against heaving during periods of alternate freezing and thawing. Divide the clumps every 3 or 4 years, preferably in late summer; cut the leaves in half to reduce wilting and mulch.

It is usually propagated by seeds sown in the spring. The plants can be divided in late summer or early spring.

INSECT PESTS: *Chrysanthemum coccineum* can be seriously affected by aphids.

ADDITIONAL NOTES: *Chrysanthemum coccineum* is the first species of the genus to flower.

NATIVE HABITAT: The Caucasus and Persia.

SELECTED CULTIVARS: The cultivars are far superior to the straight species. Some of the good single-flowered forms include: ◊ 'Crimson Giant': Large, velvety, crimson flowers 4 inches across. ◊ 'Eileen May Robinson': Single, salmon-pink flowers, excellent for cut flowers. ◊ 'Mrs. D. C. Bliss': Unusual coral-orange flowers. ◊ 'Scarlet Glow': Scarlet-crimson flowers. ◊ 'Victoria': Ruby-red flowers.

Some fine double-flowered forms include— ◊ 'Buckeye': Deep red flowers flecked with white. ◊ 'Helen': Soft, rose-pink flowers $2\frac{1}{2}$ inches across. ◊ 'Mrs. C. E. Beckwith': White flowers. ◊ 'Pink Bouquet': Pink flowers with silvery centers ◊ 'Rosary': Rose-pink flowers with silvery centers. ◊ 'Sensation': Small red flowers. ◊ 'Snowball': Large, double, white flowers with golden eyes and quilled centers. ◊

Composite—Anthemis tribe
(Composite family)

Chrysanthemum maximum
Shasta Daisy

FLOWERS: The large, flat, flower heads are usually radiate, about 2 to 4 inches across, and are freely borne, solitary on long stiff peduncles 20 to 30 inches high, from June until frost. The involucral bracts are more or less imbricate and are whitish transparent at the margin. The receptacle is naked and convex. The disc flowers are bisexual, fertile, and yellow. The ray flowers are female, fertile, and white.

LEAVES: The attractive leaves are alternate and in a basal rosette. The basal leaves, including the winged petiole, grow up to 1 foot long and are spatulate and serrate-dentate. The stem leaves are few, sessile, ranging from lanceolate to linear, and shorter than the lower rosette leaves.

PLANT CHARACTERISTICS: This glabrous perennial grows up to 2 to 4 feet high from a rosette. The stems are simple and rigid.

GARDEN VALUE: *Chrysanthemum maximum* cultivars are outstanding for the perennial border and are especially attractive when planted with *Astilbe*, *Delphinium*, *Echinops*, and *Heliopsis*. The single-flowering forms are graceful; the doubles often become too heavy and somewhat monstrous. The flowers are excellent and long-lasting when cut for use in fresh flower bouquets. Occasionally they are dyed by florists.

CULTURE: Most single-flowering cultivars require full sun and tolerate part shade; the double-flowering cultivars prefer part shade in sultry areas. These heavy feeders require a moist, rich, well-drained soil that is neutral in reaction and supplied with abundant humus. They do well in the hot Midwest but perform even better on the Pacific Coast and in the East.

Plant in spring or early fall, and space about 18 inches apart. During the growing season, apply a balanced fertilizer 3 or 4 times, keep well-watered during drought, mulch heavily, and cultivate well. The plants may require staking. Divide the clumps after every second year of flowering. Some plants may die if they become overcrowded or too exhausted from heavy flowering. Mulch lightly during the winter to protect against heaving during periods of alternate freezing and thawing.

It is propagated by division of the clumps in the fall, or by seeds sown in the spring.

DISEASE PROBLEMS: *Chrysanthemum maximum* is susceptible to crown rot, which is brought about by a lack of winter hardiness.

ADDITIONAL NOTES: This plant is a short-lived perennial but is often treated as a biennial because it tends to die out. Much of the material in the trade under this name actually describes the hybrid *Chrysanthemum* X *superbum*. The famous plant breeder Luther Burbank (1840–1926) is credited with producing the popular Shasta Daisy, so named because Mr. Burbank's work was performed near the white peaks of Mt. Shasta in California. He interbred *Chrysanthemum maximum* from the Pyrenees, *Chrysanthemum lacustre* from Portugal, *Chrysanthemum leucanthemum* (Ox-eye Daisy) from the United States, and *Chrysanthemum nipponicum* to produce this plant.

NATIVE HABITAT: The Pyrenees.

SELECTED CULTIVARS:
Among the popular single-flowering forms are: ◊ 'Alaska': Large white flowers with yellow centers. ◊ 'Edgebrook Giant': Large flowers, often 7 inches across. ◊ 'King Edward': Flowers in June and July, very hardy. ◊ 'Majestic': Large, 4-inch-wide flowers. ◊ 'Mark Riegel': 4- to 5-inch-wide flowers with 2 rows of ray flowers. ◊ 'May Queen' ◊ 'Polaris': Huge white flowers, 7 inches across. ◊ 'Stone Mountain': Large, 4-inch-wide flowers.

Popular semi-double flowering forms include — ◊ 'Little Miss Muffet': Dwarf plant. ◊ 'Thomas Killin': Anemone-centered flowers, up to 6 inches across.

Among the popular double-flowering forms are— ◊ 'Cobham's Gold': Creamy white flowers, up to 3 inches wide, with yellow anthers in the tubular disc flowers. ◊ 'Esther Read': Profusely flowering plant, 2 feet high. ◊ 'Horace Read': 4-inch-wide snowball-like flowers. ◊ 'Jennifer Read': Similar to 'Esther Read'. ◊ 'Snow Cloud': 3- to 4-inch-wide anemone-centered flowers. ◊ 'Wirral Supreme': 4-inch-wide flowers borne on strong plants in June and July.

Popular frilled selections include— ◊ 'Aglaya' ◊ 'Chiffon': Semi-double flowers. ◊ 'Beauté Nivelloise': Frilly white flowers with gold centers 3 inches across. ◊ 'Marconi': Fully 6-inch-wide flowers atop 2-foot stems, an excellent cut flower.

RELATED SPECIES: *Chrysanthemum parthenium:* Feverfew. Flower heads up to ¾ inch across are profusely borne, stalked in corymbs, in July and August. The disc flowers are yellow; ray flowers are either white or absent. There are single- and double-flowering forms. The aromatic leaves are oblong-ovate or ovate, 3 inches long, pinnatifid, and glabrous or lightly pubescent; the lower leaves are petioled. This perennial is bushy, erect, and grows 1 to 3 feet high. It has a short life span and is not reliably hardy in colder areas. It grows in sun or shade in a sandy, well-drained soil. Staking may be necessary. Remove faded flowers to prevent the plant from self-seeding. It grows readily from seed and flowers the second year. An old-fashioned plant, *Chrysanthemum parthenium* is popular for the perennial border. Its native habitat is Southeastern Europe and the Caucasus, but it has become naturalized in the United States. The whole plant is used in medicines for fevers and nervous ailments, and a tincture diluted with water and applied to the skin repels insects. The common name Feverfew is derived from the word *febrifuge*, which refers to its ability to reduce a fever. The specific epithet *parthenium*, according to Plutarch, was applied to the plant because it was used to save the life of a man who fell from the Parthenon while it was being constructed.

◊ 'Aureum': Gold Feather. Single, white flowers; chartreuse or yellowish green foliage that usually turns green later in the season, especially if the flowers are allowed to develop. This very hardy plant was commonly used for carpet bedding. ◊ 'Golden Ball': Bright yellow disc flowers, no ray flowers. ◊ 'Lemon Ball': Soft yellow disc flowers, no ray flowers. ◊ 'Selaginoides' (*Chrysanthemum selaginoides*): Leaves usually slashed, stems about 8 inches high. ◊ 'Silver Ball': White, fully double, rounded flowers. ◊

Compositae—Anthemis tribe
(Composite family)

Chrysanthemum X *morifolium*
Cultivars
Mum, Chrysanthemum

FLOWERS: The flower heads are radiate, of various colors, sizes, and shapes, and are usually borne in clusters from late August until November, depending upon the cultivar. The involucral bracts are usually scarious and imbricate in several rows. There are both disc and ray flowers in shades of yellow, bronze, pink, red, purple, lavender, and white.

The flowers are classified according to the arrangement of the petals: they are single, anemone, semi-double, and double. Individual florets are thread-, spoon-, quill-, and strap-shaped.

LEAVES: The leaves are usually thick and alternate, grayish-pubescent on the lower surface, and strongly aromatic. They range from lanceolate to ovate, grow 4 to 5 inches long, and have pinnatifid lobes ranging from entire to serrate.

PLANT CHARACTERISTICS: This stout perennial grows from 9 inches to over 3 feet high, depending upon the cultivar. The stems are erect or ascending. The plants are also classified according to their growth habit:

Cushion mum—Low, uniform mound spreading 2 or more feet and covered with small flowers.

Short—Compact, erect plants up to 9 inches high.

Medium—Upright plants 9 to 15 inches high with fewer and larger flowers.

Tall—Plants over 15 inches high with a loose erect growth habit; the few large flowers are borne at various heights and are the best for cut flowers.

GARDEN VALUE: With proper selection of the cultivars, an autumn garden of *Chrysanthemum* may be in flower from August until November, especially in frost-free areas. The low cushion types are used for the rock garden, for edging, and in the perennial or mixed border. Plant in groups of 3 or 5, or in masses. Place taller cultivars in the middle or back of the perennial garden or use as specimen plants. The flowers are excellent and long-lasting when cut.

CULTURE: The plant prefers full sun but will perform adequately with a minimum of 6 or 7 hours of direct sun daily. It grows best in a well-drained, fertile soil with abundant organic matter to ensure deep root growth. The plant requires a well-drained soil during the winter months.

Plant in spring after danger of frost has passed. Plants in full flower can be easily transplanted if they are moved with their roots in a ball of soil. They are usually purchased as small potted plants or rooted cuttings. Space plants 18 to 24 inches apart. Early establishment can lead to plants that are taller than desired.

When the plant reaches 6 to 8 inches in height, pinch the tip off each shoot to encourage bushy, floriferous clumps; this process should be repeated whenever new growth reaches this height, until about July 4. After that date, allow the flower buds to develop. Water deeply in dry periods during the growing season. Apply a balanced fertilizer in the spring. Tall plants may require staking when in flower.

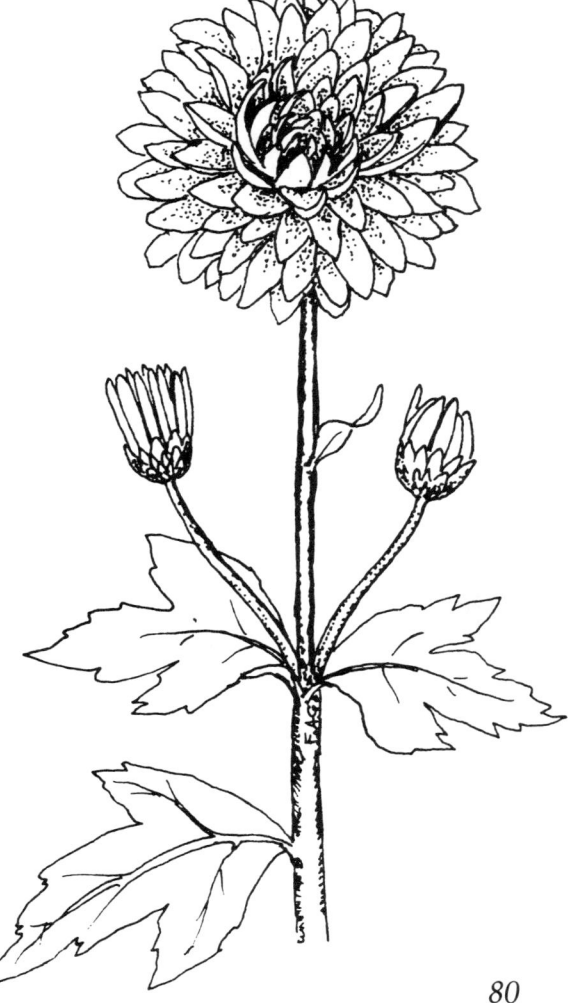

Disbudding is recommended for some cultivars; it is a technique in which large single flowers are produced. All the buds on the stem except one, the top or crown bud, is removed. Thus all the energy of the plant goes into producing a few superior flowers.

To keep the shallow roots from exposure to alternate periods of freezing and thawing, winter protection should be provided. Lightly apply 3 or 4 inches of loose mulch around the base of the plants after the ground has frozen solid. Remove gradually in spring after the danger of frost has passed. In colder areas, the plants must be lifted in late fall and placed in a cold frame during the winter. Each spring, the plant should be lifted, the crown discarded, and the side shoots replanted.

These plants are usually propagated by cuttings or division in the spring to maintain choice cultivars. Seeds are sometimes used to propagate these plants; however, the seedlings do not come true to type.

ADDITIONAL NOTES: *Chrysanthemum* X *morifolium* is a hybrid including *Chrysanthemum japonense*, *Chrysanthemum makinoi*, *Chrysanthemum indicum*, and *Chrysanthemum ornatum*, and maybe other species as well. Because many new hybrids are produced each year, no cultivars will be listed. ◇

These are "short-day" plants: they will set flower buds when exposed to a short (12 hours or less) period of daylight each day; therefore, they naturally flower in the autumn when the days are shorter.

Cimicifuga

consists of about 15 species of hardy, tall, erect, perennial herbs native to the Northern Temperate Zone.

The name *Cimicifuga* is derived from the Latin words *cimex*, meaning "bug," and *fugere*, meaning "to drive away," which literally means to drive away a bug—a reference to the unpleasant odor of the plants in the genus.

Ranunculaceae
(Buttercup or Crowfoot family)

Cimicifuga simplex
Kamchatka Bugbane

FLOWERS: The numerous small, white, flowers are borne, on short pedicels in dense, long racemes, which sometimes are panicles, from late September through October. Usually only 1 raceme (rarely 2) arises from a plant. There are from 2 to 5 petaloid, deciduous sepals; the petals, either absent or numbering from 1 to 8, are inconspicuous and are usually 2-lobed. The

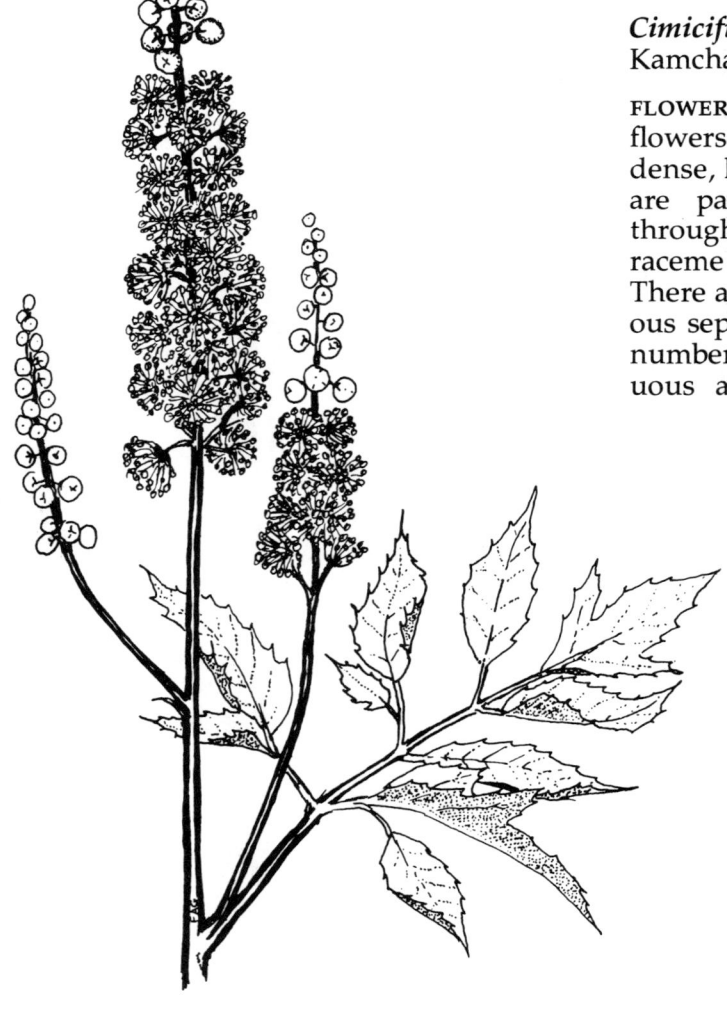

showy, attractive stamens are numerous and petaloid. Resembling white bottle brushes, the striking spires are held above the handsome foliage.

LEAVES: The large leaves are ternately decompound and grow from 4 to 12 inches in width and up to 2 feet in length.

PLANT CHARACTERISTICS: This excellent, simple-stemmed perennial grows vigorously and attains a height of 2 to 5 feet. An unpleasant odor, noticeable when at close quarters, emanates from the plant.

GARDEN VALUE: These statuesque plants have a delicate charm when properly located. Use the plant in a partially shaded wild garden or a woodland area, along the bank of a waterway, or in the middle or rear position of the perennial border. It provides good cut flowers if the arrangement is placed where the unpleasant odor is not a problem.

CULTURE: *Cimicifuga*, a woodland plant, prefers a partially shaded site and a rich, moist, acid soil with abundant organic matter. Although the plant survives in deep shade, it produces fewer flowers and more foliage when grown there. A rich soil will produce larger plants. The flowers are very unusual in their arrangement and texture.

Plant in early spring before new growth begins. For best results, water well during dry periods, and fertilize regularly. Established clumps may remain undisturbed for years.

It is usually propagated by division of the roots or by seed. Divide plants in early spring or in fall. Seeds should be sown soon after ripening.

NATIVE HABITAT: Rich woods in Japan, the Kamchatka Peninsula, Southeastern Siberia, and Manchuria.

SELECTED CULTIVARS: ◊ 'Armlechter': Larger flower spikes and a robust growth habit. ◊ 'White Pearl': Pure white flowers.

RELATED SPECIES: *Cimicifuga racemosa*: Cohosh Bugbane, Black Cohosh, Black Snakeroot. The flowers are borne, in erect racemes 1 to 3 feet high, in July and August. The flowering period is prolonged by the later flowering of the smaller lateral branches. The leaves are 2- or 3-ternate, then pinnate. The thin leaflets, which range from cuneate to cordate at the base, are 1 to 4 inches long and deeply toothed. The perennial grows from 3 to 8 feet high, depending on soil fertility and available moisture. It grows best in cool garden situations. The roots and rhizomes have medicinal properties. Its native habitat is in woods or along roads near the edges of forests, from Massachusetts to Ontario in the North to Georgia and Missouri in the South. ◊

Clematis

Clematis includes over 200 species of perennial herbs and woody climbing vines native to the Northern Temperate Zone.

The name *Clematis* is of Greek origin, meaning "slender vine."

Ranunculaceae
(Buttercup or Crowfoot family)

Clematis X *hybrida*
Hybrid Clematis

FLOWERS: The brightly colored, attractive flowers are borne solitary or in panicles. The flowers are bisexual, and urceolate, campanulate, or open flat. The conspicuous sepals are petaloid, usually numbering 4 or 5 (sometimes more), and valvate in bud. The apetalous flower has many stamens.

FRUIT: The seed is an achene with a long, feathery attachment.

LEAVES: The leaves are deciduous, opposite, and usually compound or simple. The slender petioles act as tendrils in climbing by clinging to the supports. The bright dark green foliage remains lush and lovely throughout the growing season.

PLANT CHARACTERISTICS: The plant has woody or semi-woody stems, depending upon the cultivar and the cultural conditions.

GARDEN VALUE: The large-flowering hybrids should be planted and trained to grow upward to cover walls, small buildings, trellises, or posts. The small-flowering ones are used on fences, arbors, porches, or to cover rocky areas. The bush-like forms grow well in the perennial or mixed border. Many of the cultivars supply good cut flowers.

CULTURE: The plants grow best in full sun or partial shade, in a rich, well-drained, alkaline soil. The hybrids succeed best when grown in partial shade. Keep the roots in a cool moist site.

Prepare the soil well before planting in the spring. If your soil is acid, incorporate lime. To determine the pH of your soil, take a soil sample and send it—along with a fee—for analysis to a soil testing laboratory or to your local county extension advisor or to the Agronomy or Horticulture department of your state land-grant university. Keep the plants reasonably moist. Apply an organic mulch in spring and fall to add nutrients and to keep the soil moist and cool. Protect the base of the stems from mechanical injury until the plants are well established. Those that flower on the current season's growth should be pruned immediately after flowering. Those that flower on old wood should be pruned in early spring before new growth is initiated.

The plant can be propagated by soft-wood cuttings. Some kinds can be propagated by division.

DISEASE PESTS: *Clematis* is affected by a leaf-spot and stem-rot disease, which varies according to the species or hybrid and according to the growing conditions. The leaf-spot first appears as a small water-soaked spot which becomes tan with a red margin. The fungus may grow down to the stem and form reddish lesions on the stem. Ultimately the plant dies unless the diseased tissues are removed.

SELECTED CULTIVARS: ◇ 'Comtesse de Bouchard': A *Clematis X jackmanii* hybrid with 6 satiny, rose-pink, curved petals on 5- to 6-inch flowers, which are borne on the current season's wood, from July to October. ◇ 'Duchess of Edinburgh': A *Clematis florida* hybrid; one of the best double, large, fragrant, pure white *Clematis*, the flowers are borne from May to June on old wood. ◇ 'Ernest Markham': A *Clematis vitifolia* hybrid with large red flowers, borne from July to September on the current season's wood. ◇ 'Henryi': A *Clematis lanuginosa* hybrid with creamy white flowers and dark stamens; the 6- to 8-inch-wide flowers appear on the current season's growth from June to July. ◇ 'Lord Neville': A *Clematis lanuginosa* hybrid; the rich plum-purple flowers have wavy edges and a deeper colored bar across each sepal; they are borne on the current season's wood, from June to August. ◇ 'Mme. Baron-Veillard': A *Clematis X jackmanii* hybrid; the large flowers, ranging in color from lilac-rose to dark lavender, have a long season of flowering. ◇ 'Mme. Edouard André': A *Clematis X jackmanii* hybrid; the slow-growing plant produces abundant, medium-sized purplish-red flowers during July and August, on the current season's wood. ◇ 'Mrs. Cholmondeley': A *Clematis lanuginosa* hybrid

with profusely-borne wisteria-blue flowers; the larger flowers have spaces between the sepals, are up to 8 inches across, and are freely produced from May until September on the current season's wood. ◇ 'Nelly Moser': A *Clematis patens* hybrid with 8 pale mauve-pink sepals, each with a deeper pink bar across the sepal; the flowers are borne on the previous year's growth in May and June and sometimes in September. ◇ 'Prins Hendrik': A *Clematis lanuginosa* hybrid; the large, 7-inch-wide flowers have rich, azure blue sepals which are slightly crumpled along the edges; the plant is a rapid grower and produces flowers profusely in July and August on the current season's growth. ◇ 'The President': A *Clematis patens* hybrid; the large flowers, ranging in color from deep blue to reddish-violet, have a paler-colored bar down the middle of each sepal; they are borne on old wood from June to October.

RELATED SPECIES:

Clematis integrifolia: Solitary Clematis. Indigo-blue flowers are borne, solitary and pendulous on long pedicels, from June to August. The flowers are urceolate and up to 1½ inches long. The 4 sepals are narrow, coriaceous, and 1 to 2 inches long. The fruits have styles up to 2 inches long. The handsome leaves are opposite, simple, and sessile; they are 2 to 4 inches long, entire, thin, and ovate-lanceolate. The plant grows erect, up to 2 feet high, and is colorful in the perennial border. The plant needs support. It grows best in partial shade or full sun in a rich, well-drained, neutral to alkaline soil. Once the plant has become established, do not disturb it. Its native habitat is Europe.
◇ 'Caerulea': Blue Solitary Clematis. The cultivar is more desirable than the species. If watered well during dry periods, large, porcelain blue, campanulate flowers are borne from June to August. The plant grows 16 to 24 inches high. It may require staking when grown in the perennial border. When placed in the rock garden or on the dry wall its trailing stems become quite attractive.

Clematis tangutica: Golden Clematis. Showy, bright yellow, campanulate flowers are borne, usually nodding and solitary, in June and occasionally in August; they may be up to 4 inches across. The sepals are glabrous except at the margins. The fruits are shining, silvery achenes that have very long plumose tails. The gray-green leaves are pinnate or bi-pinnate; the leaflets range from oblong-lanceolate to lanceolate, and are 3-lobed or 3-parted, irregularly serrate, and 1 to 3 inches long. The plant is a deciduous vine, climbing up to 10 feet high. The branchlets are slightly villous or nearly glabrous. *Clematis tangutica* is one of the best yellow-flowering species. It grows best in full sun or partial shade in a rich, well-drained, neutral or slightly alkaline soil. Once the plant has become established, do not disturb it. Its native habitat is Mongolia and Northwestern China.
◇ 'Farreri': Golden-yellow flowers. ◇

Convallaria

consists of 3 species of perennial, rhizomatous, monocot herbs native to the temperate regions of the Northern Hemisphere.

Convallaria is believed to have been derived from the Latin *Lilium convallium*, meaning "lily-of-the-valley"; *Lilium* is the Latin word for "lily," and *Convallis* is the Latin word for "valley."

Liliaceae
(Lily family)

Convallaria majalis
Lily-of-the-valley

FLOWERS: The dainty flowers are bell-shaped and nodding; they are white, fragrant, waxy, and about $\frac{1}{4}$ inch across. They are borne, in terminal, bracted, erect, 1-sided racemes, from mid-May to mid-June, above or among the foliage. The flowers are bisexual, regularly symmetrical, and have a globose-campanulate perianth with short, blunt, recurved lobes. The bracts are lanceolate and shorter than the pedicels.

LEAVES: The 2 or 3 green, basal leaves, arising from the rhizomes, are 8 inches long and 1 to 3 inches across, ranging from lanceolate-ovate to elliptic, entire, and glabrous. The foliage begins to appear less attractive in late summer and progressively deteriorates until it dies back to the ground, sometimes before the first killing frost.

PLANT CHARACTERISTICS: This hardy perennial grows up to 8 inches high from horizontal rhizomes that increase rapidly and tend to colonize. The upright buds on the horizontal rhizomes are called pips.

GARDEN VALUE: A popular plant, this old-fashioned perennial is an excellent ground cover in the shade, or may be used in perennial borders, mixed beds, and rock gardens. It is often effectively combined with low shrubs and ferns. Its cut flowers are valued for corsages or dainty bouquets.

CULTURE: The plant grows best in a partly shaded area in moderately rich, well-drained soil.

Plant in spring, spacing about 6 to 9 inches apart. The pips should be planted in groups of 5 or 6 to make a good clump. Keep the plants moist; they may burn somewhat if they lack moisture. An annual application of composted organic matter in the fall usually supplies all the necessary nutrients. Once established, a well-grown bed requires practically no attention. Because the roots become crowded in time, the beds should be replanted every few years, using vigorously growing clumps. If the plants spread too far, trim the rhizomes with a spade.

The plant is most easily propagated in the spring by division of the clumps or pips, which separate freely when dug.

ADDITIONAL NOTES: At one time, the roots and rhizomes were sold in drug stores for use in small doses as a heart tonic; the plant is poisonous in large doses.

NATIVE HABITAT: Europe; naturalized in the higher mountains of Eastern North America.

SELECTED CULTIVARS: The pink, flowering forms tend to lack color purity and fade under full sun. ◇ 'Aureo-variegata': Green leaves variegated with yellow. ◇ 'Florepleno': Double white flowers. ◇ 'Fortin's Giant': Larger than the straight species in every characteristic. ◇ 'Fortunei': Larger leaves and flowers than the straight species. ◇ 'Prolifican's': Double flowers. ◇ 'Rosea': Very light purplish-pink flowers. ◇

Coreopsis

includes over 100 species of annual and perennial herbs native to Africa and North and South America.

The genus name *Coreopsis* is derived from the Greek words *coris*, meaning "bug" and *opsis*, meaning "similar to," because the seeds resemble certain insects.

Compositae—Helianthus tribe (Composite family)

Coreopsis lanceolata
Perennial Coreopsis, Lance Coreopsis

FLOWERS: The masses of showy, golden, flower heads are borne in summer, in very long peduncles. The flowers are 1½ to 2½ inches across and radiate and are borne solitary or in loosely, corymbosely panicled inflorescense. The involucral bracts are in 2 rows. The disc flowers are yellow; the very showy ray flowers are yellow, notched or lobed, and sterile.

LEAVES: The few leaves are opposite, large, petioled, and predominantly simple; they are sometimes pinnately lobed and have blades or lobes that range from linear to oblanceolate. The upper leaves are entire; the lower leaves are usually pinnatrifid.

PLANT CHARACTERISTICS: The stems are erect or ascending and grow up to 18 to 24 or more inches in height. This clump-forming perennial is glabrous or nearly so, and is leafy towards the base.

GARDEN VALUE: This plant makes a showy addition to the perennial border, the mixed flower border, the wild flower garden, and a naturalized area. It is quite effective when planted near *Delphinium* and *Chrysanthemum maximum*. This *Coreopsis* is used extensively for cut flowers.

CULTURE: The plant is easily grown. It performs best in a sunny spot with a moist, well-drained, fertile soil that is especially well-drained during the winter months.

Plant in spring or fall. Space plants 12 inches apart. Feed plants regularly with a balanced fertilizer, and keep them cultivated. Apply a mulch during

the summer to keep the soil moist. Remove faded flowers to encourage flowering throughout the summer and to eliminate seedlings; the plant tends to self-sow. Divide clumps after 2 or 3 years of flowering.

Seeds sown early in the spring in the greenhouse or cold frame will provide a sparse flowering that season and a heavier one the second season. Divide plants in April or May.

INSECT PESTS: *Coreopsis lanceolata* is affected by aphids.

NATIVE HABITAT: From Ontario south to Florida and New Mexico.

SELECTED CULTIVARS: ◇ 'Baby Gold' ◇ 'Brown Eyes' ◇ 'Flore-pleno': Double-flowering cultivar. ◇ 'Gold Coin' ◇ 'Golden Wheel' ◇ 'Mayfield Giant'

RELATED SPECIES: *Coreopsis verticillata:* Threadleaf Coreopsis; also known as Whorled Tickseed and Pot-of-gold. Flower heads 1 or 2 inches across are borne in clusters on slender peduncles. The flowers are a pale, clear, yellow and are borne over a longer period of time (from June to September) than other *Coreopsis* species. The disc flowers are yellow; the ray flowers are sterile, notched, and yellow. The dainty, finely textured leaves are opposite, sessile, and palmately 3-parted, with 1- or 2-pinnate divisions; the ultimate segments are linear-filiform. This stocky, erect perennial grows 1 to 3 feet high and is corymbosely branched near the top; its flowers are used for fresh flower arrangements. Hardy and extremely weedy, it self-sows freely. It naturalizes well in difficult sites; it grows best in a dry, sunny one, and is quite drought resistant. The plant responds well to annual division. Its native habitat is from Maryland south to Florida and west to Arkansas. It is occasionally sold under the name 'Golden Shower'.

◇ 'Baby Sun' ◇ 'Gold fink': Bright yellow flowers, borne from late June to August, literally cover this 10- to 12-inch-high dwarf plant. ◇ 'Canarybird' ◇

Delphinium

includes approximately 300 species of annual, biennial, and perennial herbs primarily native to the Northern Temperate Zone.

The botanical name *Delphinium* stems from the Greek word *delphis*, meaning "dolphin," because before they expand the flower buds are thought to resemble dolphins. Generally, the annual forms are commonly called Larkspur, and the perennial forms, Delphinium.

Ranunculaceae
(Buttercup family)

Delphinium elatum
Common Delphinium
Also called Candle Larkspur, Bee Larkspur

FLOWERS: The beautiful, stately, racemes bear large, blue flowers, up to 2 to 3 inches across, from June to August. The racemes are dense and rigidly erect. The flowers, which have bracts that are entire, are usually bisexual and irregularly symmetical. The showy calyx consists of 5 petaloid sepals, one of which is spurred; they are blue, blunt, ovate, glabrous, and about $\frac{1}{2}$ inch long. There are from 2 to 3 smaller, dark or dull purple petals, often crowded in the throat (sometimes referred to as the "bee"). The upper pair of petals have spurs that project into the calyx; the lower 2 are yellow-bearded.

LEAVES: The large, handsome leaves are palmate and somewhat pubescent. They are 5- to 7-parted nearly to the base; the upper leaves, 3- to 5-parted. The leaf segments are over $\frac{1}{4}$ inch wide.

PLANT CHARACTERISTICS: The strong stems are upright, hollow, and brittle, and grow up to 4 to 6 feet high; they are borne from a knotty crown. *Delphinium elatum* may not be a long-lived perennial; it either dies or loses vigor after 2 or 3 years. It can be treated as an annual if seeds are sown early in the spring. The plant grows best where the growing season is cooler and withstands winter temperatures well below zero.

GARDEN VALUE: *Delphinium elatum* is one of the most beautiful perennials grown, a stately plant that is an integral part of the perennial border. Plant it in groups of 3 in a middle or back location in the perennial border, or use it as an accent flower in a mixed garden or a wild flower garden or against a fence. The plant blends well with *Lilium candidum*, *Heuchera*, *Chrysanthemum maximum*, *Hemerocallis*, *Campanula medium*, *Dianthus barbatus*, *Eremurus*, and *Kniphofia*. Its secondary flowering complements autumn flowers such as early *Chrysanthemum*. The plant also provides valuable, long-lasting cut flowers.

CULTURE: Although *Delphinium elatum* tolerates partial shade, full sun is ideal because it precludes the disease problems that are usually more prevalent in partial shade. A rich, well-drained, slightly alkaline, loose soil is best. Peatmoss, compost, or other forms of humus should be incorporated into the soil. (At the same time, if the soil is acid, sprinkle lime as recommended by the results of a soil test and thoroughly work it into the top 4 to 6 inches of

soil.) A wet soil promotes crown rot and root rot; plants can, however, be grown in raised beds if the soil is poorly drained.

Before planting, prepare the soil by spading deeply and incorporating the organic matter and lime. The plants can be set out from spring to early fall; they can even be moved when in full flower. Space 2 feet apart to insure good air circulation. The plants may rot if planted too deeply; keep their crowns level with the surface of the ground.

Delphiniums are heavy feeders and require plenty of nourishment to produce the healthy flowers and tall, beautiful flower stalks. Add a balanced fertilizer in early spring and several times during the growing season. Apply a small amount of lime to established plants early each spring. Supply abundant water during growing season by applying it directly to the roots; overhead watering (especially in the evening) can promote mildew on the foliage and can cause the heavy flower stalks to break. Keep plants mulched to retain the moisture in the soil

Stake the plants to prevent winds or heavy rains from toppling them. Set the stakes in place when the plants are about 1 foot high. Use a soft cord to tie and interlace the stems, which are hollow and easily broken, to each other and to the stakes at different heights.

Prune away the flower stalk below the last flower immediately after blooming. This will promote side shoots just below the cut that will give an extra bonus of flowers. As soon as these start to fade, cut the main stalks to the ground and allow the basal flower shoots to develop for fall flowers. These flowers are usually smaller in size, but their color is richer and deeper.

When cutting flowers for flower arrangements, leave 3 sets of leaves on the plant for food production.

Provide winter protection to prevent injury from periods of alternate freezing and thawing, which causes the plant roots to heave out of the ground. When the ground has frozen, apply coarse sand to the crown to help with drainage and to discourage snails. In northern areas, apply a light covering of hay or evergreen branches. Do not use leaves; they mat down when wet and suffocate the plant. To rejuvenate the clumps, divide them in spring after 3 or 4 years of flowering.

The plant is also easily propagated from seed. Sow seeds in a light soil in August or September and move to a permanent location in April. Seeds sown in February or March will flower the same season. Before sowing, apply a fungicide to the seed to prevent damping-off disease. Divide the clumps in early spring when new growth is just beginning. Take cuttings in the spring; dust the cut surfaces with a fungicide. Many gardeners start new plants every year to insure a supply of healthy flowering plants.

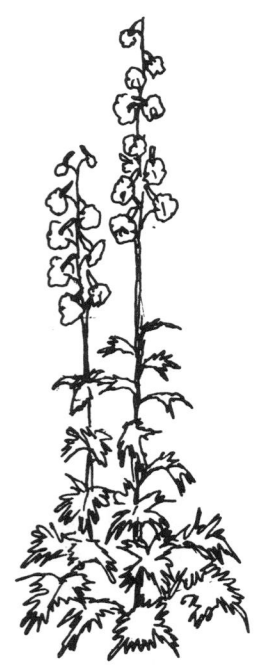

INSECT AND DISEASE PESTS: Disease pests which affect *Delphinium* include powdery mildew, bacterial leafspot, and bacterial bud rot. Cyclamen mites also injure the plants; the symptoms are blackened growth on the growing tips, also distorted or stunted leaves.

NATIVE HABITAT: Siberia.

ADDITIONAL NOTES: *Delphinium elatum* is a polymorphous and complex species. It is the common delphinium, bred for centuries, that has been popular in England since the 17th century. The straight species is seldom seen because modern hybrids are far superior.

Some species are poisonous to cattle.

Most plants cultivated as *Delphinium decorum* are *Delphinium elatum*.

SELECTED CULTIVARS: ◇ Blakmore and Langdon Series—Reportedly more perennial than the others; from England. ◇ The Connecticut Yankees—Bushy plants about 2½ feet high. The single flowers are 2½ inches across and flower from seed the first year. Three to 6 or more stems arise from each clump. ◇ Pacific Hybrids—Originated in America. These sturdy plants are usually 4 feet or more in height. The large, dense spikes are covered with florets up to 3 inches across. The flowers have rounded bees, are mostly double, and can be pastel blue, deep violet, lavender, indigo blue, or pure white in color. ◇ The Round Table Series—Named for the members of King Arthur's Court Astolate has pale pink flowers; King Arthur has dark blue flowers; Lancelot has clear lilac flowers; Galahad has white flowers without the traditional bee. ◇ The Wrexham Strain—Plants reach 6 feet or more in height, from England and Wales.

RELATED SPECIES:

Delphinium X belladonna (Delphinium bellamosum, Delphinium formosum): Garland Larkspur. The sepals are rich blue, light blue, or purple, petals are yellowish, and the spur is over 1 inch long. The plant is similar to *Delphinium elatum* but lacks a central raceme; the racemes are openly branched, shorter, and more numerous. The 3-to-4-foot-high plant produces lovely flowers for fresh flower arrangements. Because the plants are susceptible to mildew, good air circulation is required.

◇ 'Blue Bees': Blue flowers with a white eye. ◇ 'Clivedon Beauty': Sky blue flowers; about 3 feet high. ◇ 'Lamartime': Vivid purplish-blue flowers. ◇ 'Moerheimi': White flowers; discovered in 1906 in a Dutch nursery. ◇ 'Sapphire': Delicate, pale blue flowers. ◇

Dianthus

consists of about 300 species of annual, biennial, and perennial herbs, native chiefly to Eurasia but distributed throughout an area extending to South Africa. This genus provides many excellent rock garden plants—small, compact, and often pleasingly fragrant.

The name *Dianthus* is derived from the Greek words *dios*, "divine," and *anthos*, meaning "flower"; it signifies the high esteem in which the plant was held.

Caryophyllaceae
(Pink family)

Dianthus barbatus
Sweet William

FLOWERS: The brilliantly-colored flowers are borne, in May, on short pedicels in several- to many-flowered, dense, slightly rounded cymes 3 to 5 inches across. Regularly symmetrical, the flowers are sometimes double and may be white, pink, rose, red, purple, violet, or bicolored. The calyx, which is surrounded by 4 long-pointed bracts, is tubular, 5-toothed, many-nerved, and subtended by an epicalyx with aristate scales. The 5 petals, whose limbs often gradually taper into an elongated claw, range from toothed to fringed, are bearded inside and sometimes spotted.

LEAVES: The leaves are opposite, simple, and entire; they are parallel veined, short petioled, and lanceolate, with a conspicuous midrib. The leaf nodes are usually swollen. The opposite leaves often unite at the base, forming a sheath around the stem.

PLANT CHARACTERISTICS: This nearly glabrous plant grows $1\frac{1}{2}$ to 2 feet high,

in a close tuft that usually spreads out into a mat-forming clump. Some of the plants are biennial or short-lived perennials. The glabrous stems are 4-angled and simple or branched at the top.

GARDEN VALUE: *Dianthus barbatus* is a very popular, old-fashioned garden favorite for the front of the border or the rock garden, for massing, or as edging.

CULTURE: Full sun is best, and good air circulation is necessary. The plant prefers a warm, rich, well-drained, slightly alkaline soil. A poorly drained winter soil leads to the death of the plants. The hot, dry summers and wet winters of much of North America are not conducive to good growth; most plants in the genus grow best where the summers are cool and the winters mild.

Prepare the bed well before planting; if the soil pH is acid, incorporate lime. Plant in the spring, spacing about 12 to 15 inches apart. Water regularly, and feed each spring with a balanced fertilizer. Add lime 1 or 2 times during the summer to acid or neutral soils to keep the pH level high. Shear lightly after flowers have faded to encourage new growth and to prevent the formation of seeds; self-sowing is common but the seedlings usually revert to uninteresting colors. To maintain cultivars, seed must be sown each year for new plants the following year. In northern areas, cover the persistent foliage with evergreen boughs.

This species is readily grown from seed and flowers well the second year. Sow seeds in the cold frame in late summer and protect during the winter; the plants will flower the following season. Divide in spring.

ADDITIONAL NOTES: Some cultivars are only 6 inches high. As a result of this, their flowers can be easily splattered by rain, and their stems are too short for cut flowers. Some double forms are available.

NATIVE HABITAT: The Pyrenees, the Carpathian Mountains, the Balkan Peninsula; naturalized in China and North America.

SELECTED CULTIVARS: ◊ 'Albus': White flowers. ◊ 'Atrococcineus': Deep red flowers. ◊ 'Atrosanguineus': Deep blood-red flowers. ◊ 'Homeland': Red flowers. ◊ 'Indian Carpet': About 6 inches high. ◊ 'Midget': Mixed-colored flowers; about 4 inches tall. ◊ 'Newport Pink': An excellent salmon-pink form. ◊ 'Nigricans': Dark violet-purple flowers. ◊

Caryophyllaceae
(Pink family)

Dianthus deltoides
Maiden Pink
Also known as Meadow Pink, Pinks

FLOWERS: The colorful, fragrant flowers are ¾ to 1 inch across and are borne atop loose, wavy, flower stalks 4 to 15 inches high. Regularly symmetrical, the flower has a tubular calyx that is ¾ inch in length, pubescent, 5-toothed and many-nerved and is subtended by an epicalyx that usually has 2 (rarely 4) ovate pubescent scales. The 5-toothed petals, often gradually tapering into an elongated claw, are deep pink (rarely white), with a dark eye, and have an inverted V-shaped pocket at the base.

Dianthus deltoides blooms intermittently from the end of May until the end of June.

LEAVES: The striking bluish-green leaves are opposite, simple, and entire; they are parallel-veined, range from linear-oblanceolate to linear, have pubescent margins, and are often united in pairs at the base to form a sheath around the stem. The stem leaves are linear-lanceolate, 1 inch across, and sharply pointed. The nodes are usually swollen.

PLANT CHARACTERISTICS: This glaucous, densely tufted perennial, growing 6 to 15 inches high, has a trailing growth habit. Usually quick-spreading with its creeping rhizomes, the plant forms a neat mat of dense foliage but does not become weedy. Its stems are ascending, branching, and minutely pubescent.

GARDEN VALUE: With beautiful flowers, a delightful fragrance, and handsome foliage, *Dianthus deltoides*, one of the prettiest border pinks, has an old-fashioned charm that brightens any garden. Use it on low rock walls or ledges to display its trailing habit, in small groups in front of the perennial border or the rock garden, or in mass in the wild flower garden. As a ground cover or an edging, it is unexcelled. Its cheery colors and fragrance make it a source of fine cut flowers.

CULTURE: This species prefers a warm, rich, well-drained, slightly alkaline soil in full sun, with good air circulation. Poorly drained soils usually cause the plants to succumb in winter due to the ice.

Plant in spring. When preparing the bed for planting, incorporate lime into acid soils to enhance the growth of this plant. Add lime to acid or neutral soils again in the summer to maintain the good growth. Water regularly; feed annually with a balanced fertilizer. This species sows seeds freely; after flowers have faded, lightly shear the plant to discourage their formation and to promote new growth. If grown where winters are severe, place evergreen boughs over the persistent foliage to protect the plants after the ground freezes. The use of a light covering of evergreen boughs instead of a leaf mulch is recommended because a leaf mulch tends to become wet and compacted, causing the plant to rot. Some plants may last many years, others tend to die out after a few years.

Propagate by layering, by cuttings from vegetative shoots in midsummer, or by dividing the clumps in spring. If seeds are sown in the cold frame in late summer, and the seedlings are protected from low temperatures during the winter, the plants will flower the summer after the year in which they are sown.

ADDITIONAL INFORMATION: The ancient Britons called this plant "Sops-in-wine." The specific epithet, *deltoides*, stems from the inverted V-shaped pocket at the base of the petals.

NATIVE HABITAT: From Western Europe to Eastern Asia, naturalized in the United States.

SELECTED CULTIVARS: ◇ 'Albus': White flowers. ◇ 'Brilliant': Bright red flowers. ◇ 'Coccineus': Scarlet flowers. ◇ 'Compacta' (*Dianthus glaucus compactus*): A compact plant. ◇ 'Glaucus' (*Dianthus glaucus*): Glaucous leaves. ◇ 'Nanus' (*Dianthus glaucous nanus*): A dwarf plant. ◇ 'Roseus': Rose flowers. ◇ 'Ruber': Red flowers. ◇ 'Serpyllifolius': A mat-forming plant with leaves $\frac{1}{2}$ inch long. ◇

Caryophyllaceae
(Pink family)

Dianthus plumarius
Cottage Pink, Grass Pink
Also known as Common Grass Pink, Garden Pink, Pheasant's-eye Pink, Scotch Pink

FLOWERS: The very fragrant flowers are 1½ inch across and regularly symmetrical, and are borne, in 1- to 3-flowered inflorescence atop 18 inch stems, from May to July. The purplish calyx is tubular, up to 1 inch long, 5-toothed, many-nerved, and subtended by an epicalyx with 4 short, broad, spiny-tipped scales. The 5 petals are often fringed and up to ¾ inch long; the petal limb gradually tapers into an elongated claw. The petals are rose, purple, white, or multicolored.

LEAVES: The striking, distinctly glaucous blue, thickish leaves are opposite, simple, and entire; they are parallel-veined, 1-nerved, extremely narrow, keeled, and spread or bend backward. The paired leaves are often united at the base and form a sheath about the stem. The leaf nodes are usually swollen.

PLANT CHARACTERISTICS: This low-tufted perennial is glabrous and glaucous and grows about 12 to 15 inches high. Its stems are simple or branched.

GARDEN VALUE: *Dianthus plumarius* is old fashioned in character and was formerly common in circle beds and as edgings. Plant it in small groups in the front of the border, the rock garden, and the wild flower garden or mass it in a naturalized area. The fragrant, colorful blossoms provide excellent cut flowers.

CULTURE: *Dianthus plumarius* grows best in full sun, in a warm, rich, well-drained, slightly alkaline soil.

Plant in spring. When preparing the bed for planting, incorporate lime into acid soils to enhance the growth of the plant. Add lime to acid or neutral soils again 1 or 2 times during the summer to keep the pH level high. Water regularly, and feed annually with a balanced fertilizer. After flowers have faded, prune the plant to promote new growth and to prevent the formation of seeds. When grown where winters are severe, the plants need protection; place evergreen boughs over the persistent foilage after the ground freezes. Individual plants in this species sometimes lose vigor after the second season of flowering and should be replaced.

The species is usually propagated by simply dividing the clumps in spring; it may also be propagated by layering or by cuttings.

ADDITIONAL NOTES: *Dianthus plumarius* has been used in breeding as a parent of Allwood's Pink and of the hardy or border carnations. Single and double forms of the species are available in the trade.

NATIVE HABITAT: Europe, but introduced to the United States in the colonial period.

SELECTED CULTIVARS: ◇ 'Cyclops': Red flowers. ◇ 'Dinah': Semi-double rose flowers with maroon centers. ◇ 'Evangeline': Softer-colored than 'Dinah.' ◇ 'Highland Queen': Vivid scarlet flowers borne over a longer period of time than the straight species. ◇ 'Nanus': A dwarf form. ◇ 'Pink Princess': Coral-rose flowers, 1½ inches across, fringed, and fragrant; borne for weeks, beginning in May, atop plants 15 inches tall. This plant, produced by the United States Department of Agriculture in Cheyenne, Wyoming, is a very hardy strain. ◇ 'Roseus': Rose flowers. ◇ 'Semperflorens': Double flowers.

HYBRID: *Dianthus X allwoodii:* Allwood's Pink. This cross between *Dianthus plumarius* and *Dianthus caryophyllus* was created by Montague Allwood of England. The colorful, very sweet-scented flowers are about 1½ inch across and mostly semi-double. They are borne lavishly in the spring and continue sporadically into the fall. The petals are fringed or entire and are colored red, pink, white, or a combination of these. The leaves are broad and glaucous. This hardy plant grows 12 to 18 inches high in a tufted mound and is an excellent garden plant. Remove faded flowers to stimulate further flowering. Propagation is usually by layering.
◇ 'Alpinus': Dwarf form. ◇ 'Blanche': Fragrant, double, white flowers. ◇ 'Doris': Double, light salmonpink flowers with a deeper, dark pink eye. ◇ 'Helen': Deep salmon. ◇ 'Jan': Deep, velvety red melting into black-red on the outer edge of the petals. ◇ 'Robin': Vermilion flowers. ◇

Dicentra

includes 19 species of perennial herbs, which are often stemless and usually have rhizomes or tubers. These plants, often included in the *Papaveraceae* family, are native to North America and Asia.

The name *Dicentra* is of Greek origin, derived from *dis*, meaning "two," and *kentron*, meaning "spur," because the corolla is spurred. The name was originally misprinted Diclytra, then spelled *Dielytra*.

Fumariaceae
(Fumitory family)

Dicentra eximia
Fringed Bleeding-heart
Also known as Plume Bleeding-heart, Wild Bleeding-heart, Turkey Corn, Staggerweed

FLOWERS: The delicate, heart-shaped, pink or purple flowers are borne in loose, nodding racemes 12 to 15 inches high and are produced almost continuously from May until August. The flowers are irregular and bisexual, and the scape is about as high as the leaves. There are 2 small, deciduous sepals. The 4-petaled, heart-shaped corolla is laterally flattened and closed at the top with 2 short, rounded spurs at the base. It is composed of an outer and an inner pair of petals, the inner pair protruding and the tips of the outer pair spread.

LEAVES: The attractive leaves are feathery and gray-blue in color. The basal leaves are ternately compound, and the stem leaves are dissected. The ultimate leaf segments are broadly oblong or ovate.

PLANT CHARACTERISTICS: This glabrous, stemless, somewhat glaucous perennial forms a large clump 12 to 15 inches high, depending upon the growing conditions. It has a short, fleshy, brittle rhizome.

GARDEN VALUE: This old-fashioned plant makes a fine display in the front of the perennial border, the wild flower garden, or the rock garden or as a ground cover. The flowers provide an unusual effect when used in cut flower arrangements.

CULTURE: The plant grows best in a rich well-drained soil in summer; it cannot tolerate a wet soil in winter or a dry soil in summer.

Placed in a partially shaded site, it will perform best and produce flowers all summer.

Dicentra eximia should be deeply planted in early spring, before new growth begins. Incorporate abundant amounts of peat moss into the soil, then plant, spacing the plants about 15 inches apart. Mulch with composted organic matter and keep plants moist during the growing season. Production of flowers may slow or stop during hot weather; however, if adequate moisture is provided, the plants usually flower during the summer heat. They will, in any case, resume flowering when temperatures become cooler. Do not disturb plants until they have increased to a large size, then divide them. They self-sow in the shade but do not become weedy.

Seeds may be sown in late summer or clumps divided in early spring.

NATIVE HABITAT: Mountainous areas from New York to Pennsylvania, and south to Georgia and Tennessee.

SELECTED CULTIVARS: ◊ 'Alba': White flowers, produced sparingly. ◊ 'Bountiful': Large fuchsia flowers, produced more abundantly in full sun, but tending to fade in hot weather, borne from May to July and in early autumn; heavier, bronzier leaves; grows 18 inches high. ◊ 'Clay's Variety': Vivid pink racemes borne constantly throughout the summer; produces no seed. ◊ 'Luxuriant': Fuchsia red flowers. ◊ 'Sweetheart': Pure white flowers. ◊ 'Zestful' ◊

Fumariaceae
(Fumitory family)

Dicentra spectabilis
Common Bleeding-heart

FLOWERS: The large, rosy-red flowers are borne, pendantly in simple, delicately nodding racemes up to 9 inches long, from April to June. The winsome, delicate flowers are irregular, bisexual, and up to 1¼ inches long. The heart-shaped corolla is laterally flattened; it has 2 short, rounded spurs at the base, is closed at the top, and consists of an outer and an inner pair of petals. The outer petals are rosy-red with reflexed tips; the inner petals are white and exserted.

LEAVES: The attractive bluish-green leaves are alternate or basal and predominantly ternately compound or dissected. The leaf segments are broad and range from obovate to cuneate. The foliage may disappear during the summer heat.

PLANT CHARACTERISTICS: The plant usually grows up to 2 feet high but can reach 3 feet if grown under optimum conditions.

GARDEN VALUE: This old-fashioned perennial is one of the best flowering perennials. Use it in a shady site in the perennial border or the wild flower garden. Because its foliage usually yellows and sometimes disappears in hot sunny sites, the plant should be placed next to plants that can cover the void during summer. The plant is effectively combined with spring bulbs, *Primula*, *Hosta*, *Lilium*, and ferns. It provides excellent cut flowers.

CULTURE: The plant grows in partial shade or full sun. If grown in full sun, it must have adequate moisture during the growing season. It prefers a rich, light, moist, well-drained, humus soil. The plants cannot tolerate wet winter soils or dry summer soils.

Plant in early spring before new growth has begun. Space 2 to 3 feet apart. If transplanted in early fall, provide a mulch during the first winter. Mulch with a composted organic material in the spring and keep plants moist during the growing season. Apply a balanced fertilizer annually in early spring. Once established, do not disturb them.

Seeds may be sown in August and September. Divide the plant in early spring. Take root and stem cuttings (3-inch pieces) in early June and place 2 inches deep in a rich soil.

ADDITIONAL NOTES: *Dicentra spectabilis* was brought to England from Japan by Robert Fortune in 1847. It was a favorite plant of Chinese mandarins, who named it *hong-pak-moutan-wha*. The

English called it Lyre Flower because the nodding flowers resemble lyres.

It is occasionally sold as *Dielytra spectabilis*.

NATIVE HABITAT: Japan.

SELECTED CULTIVARS: ◊ 'Alba': White flowers and weaker growth than the straight species.

RELATED SPECIES: *Dicentra cucullaria*: Dutchman's Breeches, White Eardrops. Nodding white flowers tipped with creamy yellow are borne, in simple racemes atop 10-inch stems, from mid-April to May. The two spurs are prolonged and widely divergent. The feathery leaves are basal, slender-petioled, ternately compound, and have linear segments. In hot climates the pale leaves die to the ground when flowering has ceased, usually about late June, but flowering may continue in cool, moist areas. The delicate, glabrous stems grow 5 to 10 inches high from a cluster of small tubers. This woodland species is attractive in the rock garden, the wild flower garden, or in a naturalized area. It needs a shady site with rich soil. If the plant does not flower after transplanting, incorporate a small amount of lime into the soil to encourage flowering. To propagate, divide the tiny tubers in spring or sow seeds in summer. Its native habitat is the area from Nova Scotia to Minnesota and south to Missouri and North Carolina. The plant receives its common name from the dainty white- or occasionally, pink-tinted flowers, which resemble a pair of inverted pantaloons. ◊

Dictamnus

contains a single, but extremely variable perennial herbaceous species. The origin of the name has not been definitely established; some botanists believe it to be derived from the Greek work *diktamnos*, meaning "ash-leaved," because its leaves resemble those of the ash tree, *Fraxinus*. Others suspect the name was derived from the Cretan habitat of the plant, Mt. Dikte.

Rutaceae
(Rue family)

Dictamnus albus (Dictamnus fraxinella)
Gas Plant
Also called Dittany, Fraxinella, Burning Bush

FLOWERS: The aromatic white flowers are about $1\frac{1}{2}$ to 2 inches long and are borne, on 2- to 3-foot-long, showy, terminal racemes, from late May to July. The flowers are borne on bracted pedicels and have 5 irregular sepals and petals. The ten curved stamens are prominent.

FRUIT: The aromatic fruit is an attractive, deeply 5-lobed capsule, ripening in late summer.

LEAVES: The handsome, aromatic, glossy, dark green leaves are leathery, alternate, and odd-pinnately compound. There are 9 to 11 3-inch-long leaflets, which are ovate, glandular-dotted, and serrulate. The dark, persistant foliage, which remains ornamental throughout the season, emits an ethereal, inflammable oil.

PLANT CHARACTERISTICS: This bold perennial is vigorous, long-lasting, and hardy, and is woody at the base. Sturdy and erect, the plant grows about 3 feet high and 3 feet across. A strong lemon fragrance emanates from the flowers and the foliage.

GARDEN VALUE: This beautiful permanent plant is excellent in the perennial border, grown alone as a specimen plant, or as a background plant in the small garden. *Dictamnus albus* provides desirable cut flowers. The attractive fruits can be dried and also used in dried flower arrangements.

CULTURE: The plant prefers well-drained soil ranging from average to rich and an open location in full sun, but it will tolerate light shade.

The plant is difficult to transplant and requires 2 or 3 years to become established. But once established in its permanent location, this long-lived plant is easy to grow and requires little maintenance.

Plant in spring, about 4 feet apart.

Young, flowering plants can be transplanted with a ball of soil. Initially they need a moderate amount of moisture, but, once established, they can tolerate drought conditions. Keep the ground cultivated, and apply a balanced fertilizer annually. Established clumps should not be divided and do not tolerate transplanting. The plants improve with age, producing more and longer flowering racemes.

The best method of propagation is by seed. Seeds sown in the fall will germinate the following spring and should not be disturbed for 2 years before they are transplanted into the permanent location. Seedlings will flower in 3 or 4 years. Division is usually difficult. Small plants can be purchased from specialists.

ADDITIONAL NOTES: The plants (especially their fruit) are poisonous.

Linnaeus discovered that by placing a small flame under the flower cluster and near the main stem on a still, sultry evening, the volatile oil can be made to ignite, causing a small burst of blue flame. Because of this phenomenon, the fire worshippers of India believed the plant to be sacred.

John Keats writes that the sacred dittany was once believed capable of frightening away serpents. The seed pods were used by early settlers as holders for small candles.

NATIVE HABITAT: From Southern Europe to Northern China.

SELECTED CULTIVARS AND VARIETIES:
◊ 'Purpureus': Large, dark purple flowers. ◊ 'Ruber': Rosy-purple flowers with deeper-colored veins borne in June. ◊ var. *caucasius*: The racemes are twice as long, and borne higher above the foliage, than those of the straight species. ◊

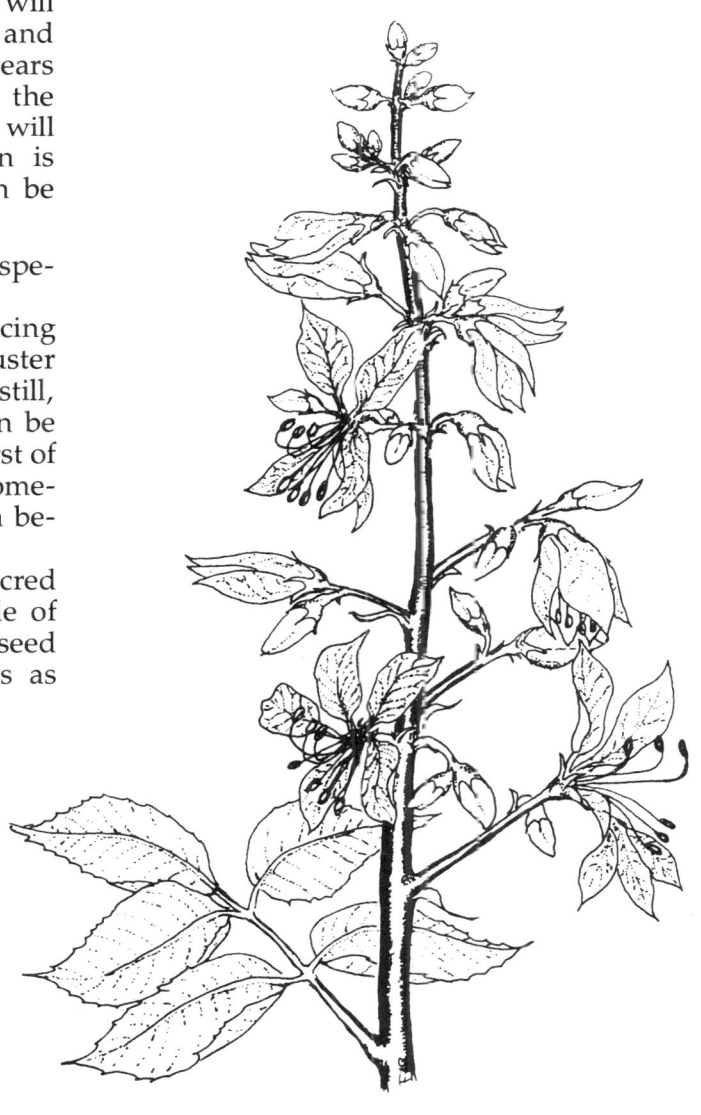

Digitalis

consists of about 19 species of perennial and biennial herbs, and rarely, subshrubs, that are native to Europe, Northwest Africa, and Central Asia.

The name *Digitalis* is derived from a Latin word meaning "finger-of-a-glove," referring to the flower shape. The origin of the common name Foxglove appears to have been lost in antiquity, although "fox" is thought to be a corruption of "folk," meaning the "little folk" or fairies.

Scrophulariaceae
(Figwort family)

Digitalis purpurea
Common Foxglove
Also known as Fairy Glove, Purple Foxglove, Finger Flower.

FLOWERS: The showy, drooping flowers are 2 inches long and are borne erect in terminal, often 1-sided racemes, up to 2 feet long, during June and July. The flowers are bisexual and irregularly symmetrical. The calyx is 5-parted and has ovate lobes. The corolla is purple (sometimes white or pink or, rarely, yellowish) and usually spotted on the inside; it is somewhat 2-lipped, up to 3 inches long, and has a campanulate corolla tube.

LEAVES: The leaves are alternate, simple, and rugose. The leaves in the basal rosette range from lanceolate to broadly ovate and are long-petioled. The stem leaves are sessile or short-petioled, and become smaller at the top of the stem.

PLANT CHARACTERISTICS: This stately plant grows 2 to 4 feet high. Usually biennial, it is sometimes perennial.

GARDEN VALUE: The popular, old-fashioned flower adds elegance and dignity to the garden. Use it in the perennial or mixed border, a natural-

108

ized area, or in the wild flower garden. The plant is more effective when massed; its vertical effect provides a relief to the horizontal forms of most garden plants. The plant combines well with *Lilium candidum*, *Dianthus barbatus*, and *Campanula medium*. The flower is reasonably good when cut.

CULTURE: *Digitalis purpurea* is easy to grow. It tolerates full sun, but prefers shady sites with a moist atmosphere. It grows best in a rich, acid, moist, well-drained soil; it will not grow in a wet soil, especially during the winter.

Plant in fall or early spring, and space plants 15 to 18 inches apart. Supply abundant water during dry periods in the growing season. Keep the foliage dry; the plants require good air circulation. Apply a balanced fertilizer annually. Mulch lightly during the summer to help retain moisture in the soil. Remove the racemes of the faded flowers just below the bottom flower, to encourage more flowers in midsummer. A light mulch applied during the winter as well provides them with protection. Apply a material such as straw or pine boughs around the bases of the plants; leaves, grass clippings, and compost applied to the base of the plant compact when wet, rotting the foliage.

The plants should be treated as biennials and renewed by seeds sown each August; this will produce flowering plants the following spring. Under ideal conditions, the plants self-sow and maintain themselves. The seeds are very tiny and should be covered lightly and kept moist.

NATIVE HABITAT: Europe and throughout North Africa.

ADDITIONAL NOTES: *Digitalis purpurea*, one of the most common English wildflowers, is the most popular *Digitalis* species.

The drug digitalis, a heart stimulant, is derived from the dried leaves.

SELECTED CULTIVARS: The Shirley Hybrids were developed by Rev. W. W. Wilkes of England from the plant native to that country. They have a full range of pastel colors, and the nodding flowers are borne on 1 side of the stem. Sutton's, an English seed firm, bred the Shirley Hybrids to an American variant, which had white flowers borne horizontally and encircling the stem. This superior strain, named the Excelsior Hybrids, retained the characteristic of flowers borne encircling the stem.

◊ 'Alba': White flowers. ◊ 'Campanulata': Large, campanulate flowers at the top of the raceme. ◊ 'Foxy': A strain that flowers in 5 months from seed and grows up to 3 feet in height. ◊ 'Gloxiniiflora' (*Digitalis gloxiniiflora*): A robust plant with a longer raceme and larger flowers that open simultaneously; one unusually large flower is at the top of the raceme. ◊ 'Isabellina': Yellow flowers. ◊ 'Maculata': Leopard Foxglove. Spotted flowers. ◊

FLOWERS: The pert white, magenta, or lavender flowers are borne, nodding in a 10- to 20-flowered umbel atop a reddish, slender, erect, smooth scape 8 to 24 inches high from April to June. The flowers are bisexual and regularly symmetrical. The calyx has long lanceolate lobes, and the corolla is 4- or 5-lobed, with linear-oblong lobes. The calyx and corolla lobes reflex to expose the yellow filaments and the purple, cone-shaped stamens and pistils. The corolla tube is usually maroon with a yellow band at the throat. The pedicels curve, so that the flowers nod, but as the fruits ripen, they straighten so that the mature fruits are borne erectly.

LEAVES: The leaves form a basal rosette. They are simple, glabrous, nearly entire or dentate-crenate, and range from ovate to oblong-linear; they often have a reddish base, taper into a more or less margined petiole, and grow up to 1 foot long and 1 to 2 inches across. The foliage completely disappears shortly after the plant has ceased flowering.

PLANT CHARACTERISTICS: Growing 1 to 2 feet high, this glabrous perennial has fibrous roots.

Dodecatheon

comprises about 14 species of scapose, perennial herbs, primarily native to North America.

The genus name comes from the Greek number *dodeka*, 12, and was used in Pliny's writing.

Primulaceae
(Primrose family)

Dodecatheon meadia
Common Shooting-star
Also known as American Cowslip, Prairie Pointers

GARDEN VALUE: *Dodecatheon meadia* should be placed against a background that will display its delicate flowers to their best advantage. Use the plant in the rock garden, the perennial border, or the wild flower garden, in the front row of a shrub border or in a naturalized area such as along a shady brook. The foliage tends to die back to the ground and leave a void in July, after the seeds have ripened. It is compatible with spring-flowering bulbs and with *Primula*.

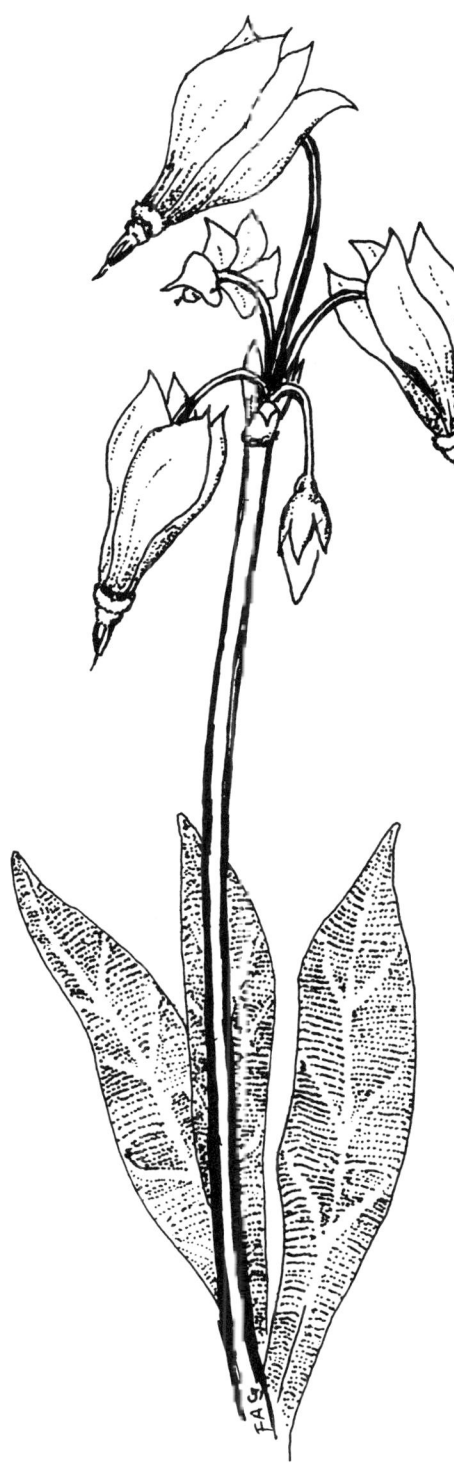

CULTURE: *Dodecatheon meadia* is not the easiest plant to grow in many areas. It prefers a cool shaded site but tolerates a sunny exposure. It will not grow well unless planted in a light, neutral, well-drained soil with a high humus content. It requires moisture during the growing season and dry conditions when dormant. The plant will succumb if water stands around the crown during winter.

Transplant in August, while the plant is dormant; transplant only container-grown plants in spring. Space 9 inches apart. Foliage will remain longer if the seed pods are removed before they develop. Hardy, vigorous specimens may need division after 3 or 4 years.

Sow seeds in late summer or early spring. Divide mature clumps in spring. Mulch well during the first winter.

ADDITIONAL NOTES: The specific epithet *meadia* commemorates Dr. Richard Mead (1673–1754), an English physician. The plant was first grown in England in 1774.

NATIVE HABITAT: From Pennsylvania to Southern Wisconsin and south to Georgia and Eastern Texas.

SELECTED CULTIVARS: ◊ 'Album': White flowers. ◊ 'Splendidum': Crimson flowers with a yellow circle. ◊

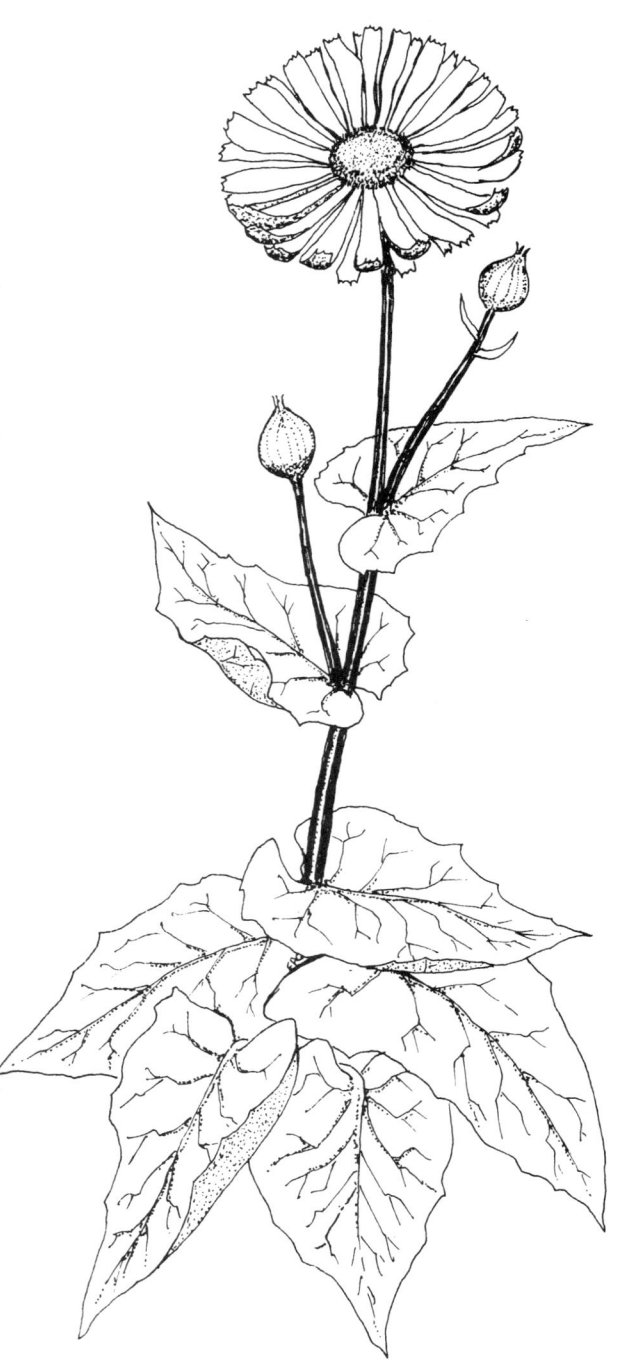

Doronicum

consists of at least 30 species of hardy perennial herbs native to Europe and temperate Asia.

The name *Doronicum* is a Latinized version of the Arabic name *doronig*. The common name Leopard's Bane evolved because arrows were once dipped in the juice of one species when hunting leopards. The roots are reputed to be poisonous.

Compositae—Senecio tribe
(Composite family)

Doronicum cordatum (Doronicum caucasicum)
Caucasian Leopard's Bane

FLOWERS: The bright yellow flower heads are radiate, 2 to 3 inches across, long-peduncled, and borne, singly on strong stems held high above the basal foliage, in April and May. The involucral bracts are in 2 or 3 rows and are nearly equal. The receptacle is usually naked. The disc flowers are yellow and bisexual; the ray flowers are yellow, female, and neutral.

LEAVES: The large, thick, green leaves, which range from cordate-ovate to ovate-lanceolate, are alternate, crenate-denate, and clasping. The basal leaves are long-petioled and ovate, with wavy, toothed edges. The stem leaves are alternate and often clasp the stem. The foliage disappears in the summer.

PLANT CHARACTERISTICS: This perennial forms large clumps. The stems grow 10 to 30 inches high and are simple or branched. The plant is shallow-rooted and has shallow fibrous rhizomes.

GARDEN VALUE: *Doronicum cordatum* is an excellent plant for the perennial border, the mixed border, or the rock garden. Use it in small clumps rather than in mass, because the foliage disappears in summer, leading to bare spots. It flowers at the same time as some of the spring bulbs and looks attractive when planted with *Dicentra eximia*, *Primula X polyanthus*, *Phlox divaricata*, and spring-flowering bulbs.

CULTURE: This sturdy plant is easy to grow. It prefers light shade, although it will grow in full sun in northern areas, and a deep, rich, moist, cool soil.

Plant in early spring before new growth begins, or in late summer. Set plants about 12 inches apart. Keep them reasonably moist and mulch to conserve moisture. Apply a balanced fertilizer annually in early spring. Keep plants cultivated. Divide them in August every second year.

Propagation is most easily done by dividing the clumps in late summer. Seeds germinate erratically, regardless of time of sowing, and 50% germination is average.

NATIVE HABITAT: Southeastern Europe and Western Asia.

ADDITIONAL NOTES: The straight species and the cultivar 'Madam Mason' are the most popular members of the genus.

SELECTED CULTIVARS: ◊ 'Finesse': Brilliant yellow flowers 3 inches across. ◊ 'Madam Mason': Often sold as 'Miss Mason,' this plant has slightly larger flowers and retains its foliage throughout the summer. ◊ 'Magnificum': Larger, clear yellow, single flowers that dry well. ◊ 'Spring Beauty': Many-petaled flowers. ◊

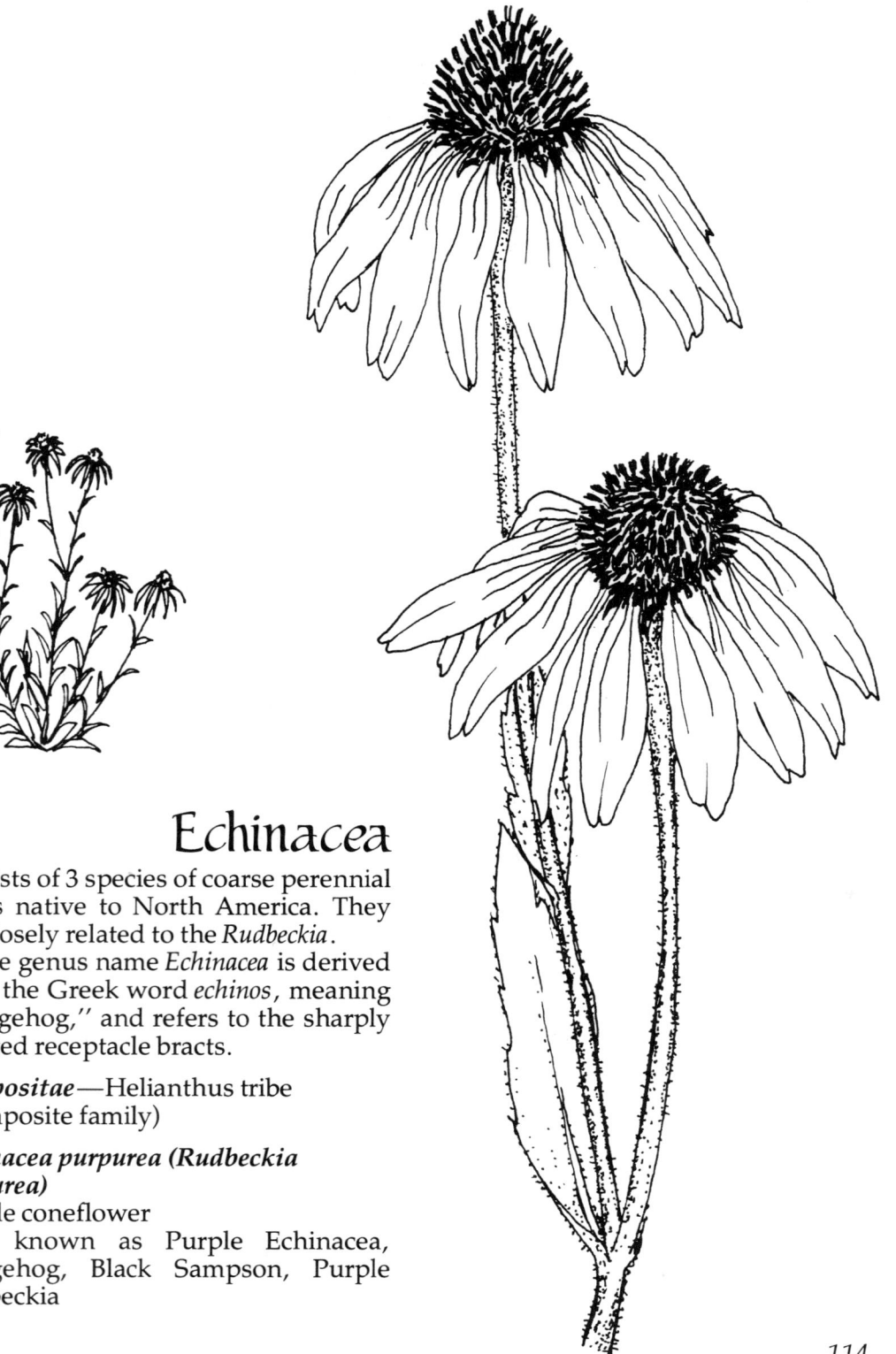

Echinacea

consists of 3 species of coarse perennial herbs native to North America. They are closely related to the *Rudbeckia*.

The genus name *Echinacea* is derived from the Greek word *echinos*, meaning "hedgehog," and refers to the sharply pointed receptacle bracts.

Compositae—Helianthus tribe (Composite family)

Echinacea purpurea (Rudbeckia purpurea)
Purple coneflower
Also known as Purple Echinacea, Hedgehog, Black Sampson, Purple Rudbeckia

FLOWERS: The coarse, attractive, unusual flower heads are radiate and up to 6 inches across; they are long-lasting and are borne, from July through August, on long peduncles, either singly or few in number. The receptacle is conical; the receptacle scales are stiff, spinescent, and longer than the disc flowers. The involucral bracts are imbricate in several rows, or nearly equal. The fertile, purple-brown disc flowers are borne in a distinct cone and are sparsely surrounded by the ray flowers. The broad, drooping ray flowers are rose-purple, female, sterile, and up to 2 inches or more in length. The resulting seed heads persist throughout the winter.

LEAVES: The large, bold leaves are alternate, simple, 2 to 8 inches long, and appear unkempt. The lower leaves range from ovate-lanceolate to broadly ovate, are denticulate or sharply serrate and usually 5-nerved, and have a long, margined petiole. The upper stem leaves are sessile, lanceolate, 3-nerved, and nearly entire.

PLANT CHARACTERISTICS: This plant reseeds itself easily and usually grows up to 3 feet high, occasionally reaching 6 feet. It has coarse, hairy stems and stiff, black, fibrous roots. The plant is drought resistant.

GARDEN VALUE: *Echinacea purpurea* should be used in the wild flower garden or in an open naturalized area, especially a dry, exposed site. The cultivars are attractive and are used, either as specimens or in groups of 3, for bold effects in the perennial border.

CULTURE: The plant thrives in sunny or windy sites and tolerates light shade, which protects the darker flower colors in hot weather. It prefers warm, rich, loamy soil that is well-drained during the winter

Plant in early fall or spring, spacing plants 18 to 24 inches apart. Keep the plants dry. Apply a balanced fertilizer annually in early spring. Remove faded flower heads to encourage a longer flowering season. Provide winter protection in northern areas. If the soil is not well-drained, the plants are not winter-hardy. Divide vigorously growing clumps every third spring to prevent deterioration of the clump.

The plants are usually easily propagated by division of the plants in spring, but they can also be easily started from seed. Cultivars may not grow true to type from seed.

NATIVE HABITAT: Fields and dry open woods from Ohio to Iowa and south to Louisiana and Georgia.

SELECTED CULTIVARS: The named cultivars are usually superior to the species. Most were developed by English and German breeders after World War I. ◇ 'Alba': White ray flowers and greenish disc flowers. ◇ 'Bright Star' ('Leuchstein'): Brighter rosy-red flowers than 'The King.' ◇ 'Robert Bloom': Purple ray flowers with orange disc flowers. ◇ 'The King': Beautiful coral-crimson flowers 5 to 6 inches across, with thick horizontal ray flowers and maroonish-brown disc flowers. ◇ 'White King' ('White Lustre'): Dull white ray flowers with bronze disc flowers. ◇

Echinops

comprises about 100 species of biennial and perennial herbs whose native range is from the Western Mediterranean region to Central Asia.

Echinops is derived from the Greek words *echinos*, meaning "hedgehog," and *op*, meaning "like"; it refers to the spiny involucral scales of the flower head.

Compositae—Carduus tribe
(Composite family)

Echinops ritro
Small Globe-thistle, Steel Globe-thistle

FLOWERS: The blue flowers are borne, in dense, globose heads, in July and September. Each flower is subtended by its own involucre, and the entire flower head is subtended by small, reflexed involucre. The outer involucral bracts are blue and bristly; the inner ones are linear or lanceolate. The disc flowers are perfect, usually fertile, and of varying shades of blue. There are no ray flowers.

LEAVES: The leaves are borne in rosettes or alternate on the stem and are pinnately lobed, with lanceolate or linear lobes. The leaves, up to 8 inches long, are a glossy green on the upper surface and densely white pubescent on the under surface.

PLANT CHARACTERISTICS: This tall, coarse, thistle-like perennial has silvery-white tomentose stems and grows 3 to 4 feet high.

GARDEN VALUE: *Echinops ritro* has strong character and interest. Use this plant in small groups for a bold, striking effect in the perennial or shrub border or the wild flower garden, or allow it to colonize in a naturalized setting. The plant contrasts nicely with *Alcea*, *Helianthus*, or *Macleaya*. The flower is a favorite to use for contrast in fresh flower arrangements. If cut just before the flower heads begin to age, the flowers dry splendidly for winter arrangements, although they fade in sunlight with age.

CULTURE: The plant needs full sun and a soil that is rich, light, sandy, and well drained.

Plant in spring at least 18 to 24 inches apart. Keep the soil dry, and apply a small amount of fertilizer annually. Divide the plant every 3 or 4 years.

The plant is usually propagated by dividing the clump in spring; cut the roots back to 6 to 8 inches long before replanting. Seed propagation is easy.

ADDITIONAL NOTES: *Echinops ritro* is the species most often grown in perennial gardens, and is the lowest-growing member of the genus. It attracts large numbers of bees.

NATIVE HABITAT: Europe

SELECTED CULTIVARS: ◊ 'Taplow Blue': Free flowering, intensely metallic blue flowers. ◊

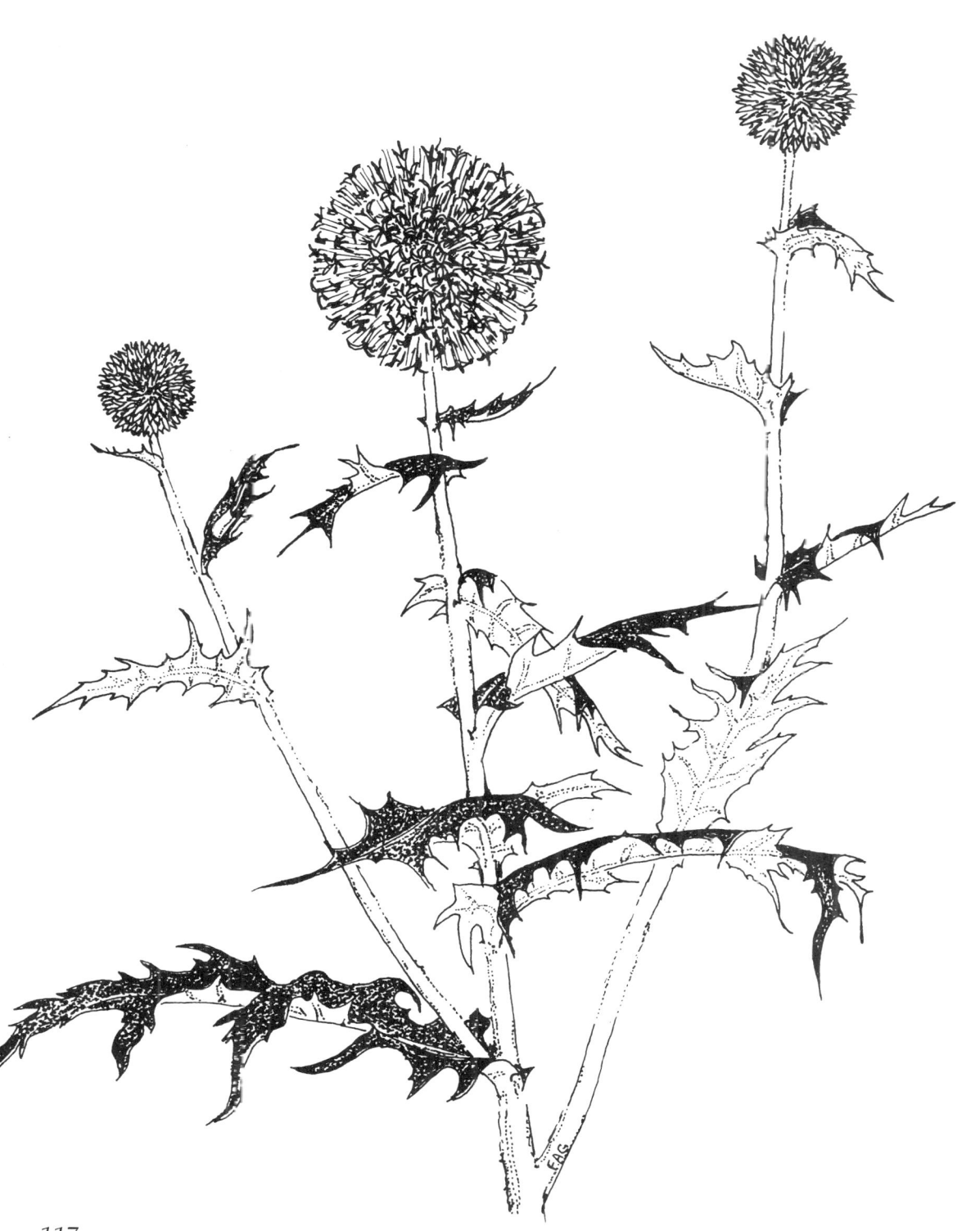

Epimedium

consists of about 21 species of low, rhizomatous perennials native to the temperate zones of Europe and Asia. The genus name, of Greek origin, means "like Medion"; it was named by the Greek medical writer Dioscorides, for a plant of ancient Media. The little-known genus includes some dainty ornamental plants suitable for the perennial border and the rock garden. The common name Bishop's-Hat refers to the square, flat flowers.

118

Berberidaceae
(Barberry family)

Epimedium X *rubrum* (*Epimedium alpinum* var. *rubrum*)
Red Alpine Epimedium

FLOWERS: The small, waxy flowers are 1 inch across and are borne, in loose, airy racemes, in May. The flower has 8 sepals, of which the outer 4 soon fall off; the inner 4 are petaloid and bright crimson. There are 4 flat, pale yellow or red-tinged petals that extend into slipper-like spurs.

LEAVES: The neat, interesting foliage appears delicate, but it has a stiff, leathery texture. The small leaves are basal, biternate, and arise on stiff wiry petioles; the small leaflets are irregularly cordate. The young foliage emerges reddish and becomes green with a red margin in summer, then chestnut in autumn, after the first frost. The foliage is not evergreen but is persistent when grown in a sheltered site. The leaves remain on the plant even when they are dead.

PLANT CHARACTERISTICS: The low rhizomatous perennial is long-lived, dependable, and extremely hardy. This neat plant grows 6 to 10 inches high.

GARDEN VALUE: *Epimedium* X *rubrum* is especially excellent for dense groundcover in full sun or shade; it even thrives under trees if fertilizer is applied occasionally. Use this plant in the rock garden or mass it in the shrub or perennial border or in a woodland area; it is most effective when combined with *Primula*, *Phlox*, and other spring-flowering dwarf perennials and bulbs. It is grown for its delicate flowers and superb foliage, and both are used for fresh flower arrangements. The cut flowers will last up to two months in water.

CULTURE: This plant prefers a sandy, well-drained, moist soil with abundant humus. Although it is partial to deep shade, the plant will grow in sun if the soil has sufficient organic matter to retain moisture.

Transplant potted plants in spring and clumps in early fall. Space plants 8 to 10 inches apart for a massed effect. Never allow the plants to dry out. If the persistent foliage is cut back in late March, a flush of new leaves is hastened. The plants may occasionally need to be divided, although they can remain undisturbed for many years.

They are easily propagated by division of rhizomes in spring or fall.

NATIVE HABITAT: Southern and Central Europe.

ADDITIONAL NOTES: *Epimedium* X *rubrum* is considered to be the showiest of the genus because it bears more flowers per cluster than other species. ◇

Eremurus

comprises nearly 40 species of perennial monocot herbs with thick, fibrous, or cord-like roots, native to Western and Central Asia.

Eremurus is derived from the Greek words *eremos*, meaning "solitary," and *oura*, meaning "tail," which probably allude to the tall, striking accent the plant provides in a solitary and desert site.

Liliaceae
(Lily family)

Eremurus X isabellinus (Eremurus X shelfordii)
Shelford Desert-Candle, Shelford Foxtail Lily

FLOWERS: The large, flashy flowers are borne, in June, in 1- to 4-foot-long racemes atop scapes up to 8 feet in height. The flowers may be shades of orange, buff, pale yellow, pink, bright pink, coppery-yellow, or white. The bisexual and regularly symmetrical flowers consist of 6 perianth segments, which are almost completely separated and are one- to several-nerved.

LEAVES: The succulent leaves are borne in a dense basal rosette. They are narrow and linear and usually disappear in late summer.

PLANT CHARACTERISTICS: The rosette usually grows up to 1 foot high; the erect flower stalk reaches up to 8 feet in

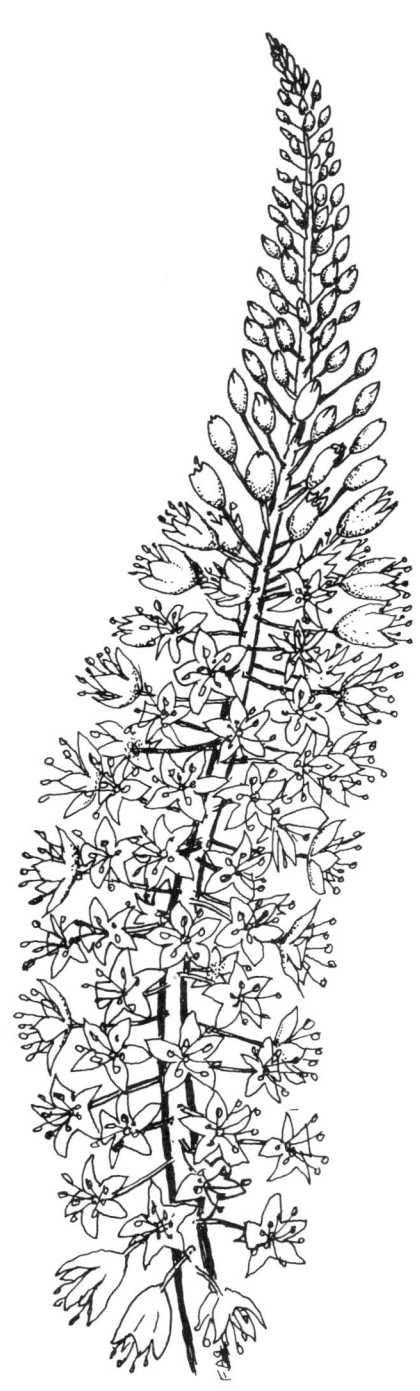

height. The roots are heavy, fibrous, and somewhat brittle. The plant is not too winter-hardy, especially in a soil that is poorly drained in the winter.

GARDEN VALUE: The beautiful *Eremurus* X *isabellinus* should be used as a vertical accent in the back of the large perennial border or against a green background such as a shrub border or hedge. This magnificent garden plant should be considered for many herbaceous borders. It combines well with *Iris* and *Delphinium* and provides splendid, long-lasting cut flowers for large arrangements.

CULTURE: Grow these plants in full sun, in a deep, rich, well-drained soil. They must have perfect drainage, particularly in winter. Select a site protected from summer winds.

Plant the roots in the fall, as soon as they arrive from the nursery. They are fleshy, brittle, and easily broken. Plant them 4 to 6 inches below the soil surface and surround them with coarse sand. They are heavy feeders and must be supplied regularly with abundant amounts of fertilizer. Plenty of water should also be provided during the flowering period, but not afterwards. In northern areas, plants not located in sheltered sites need winter protection; a mound of coarse sand over the crown is best. Any mulch that retains moisture is detrimental to the survival of the plants. Those left unprotected in the North often produce foliage but no flowers, and their early-formed buds are often killed by spring frosts. Failure in northern gardens is often caused by a lack of protection against freezing in early frosts and spring frosts. The plants increase rapidly and should be divided after every 3 years of flowering.

The plant is usually propagated by division. However, it can be grown from seeds, which need a cold treatment prior to being sown in spring. Seedlings take 3 to 5 years to produce flowers.

ADDITIONAL NOTES: *Eremurus* X *isabellinus* is a cross between *Eremurus olgae* and *Eremurus stenophyllus*. ◇

Erigeron

includes about 200 species of annual, biennial, and perennial herbs predominantly native to North America.

The genus name *Erigeron* is Greek in origin and dates back to the philosopher and naturalist Theophrastus. It is derived from the words *eri*, meaning "early," and *geron*, meaning "old man," possibly because of the early development of seed heads.

Compositae—Aster tribe
(Composite family)

Erigeron compositus
Fernleaf Fleabane

FLOWERS: The flower heads are usually radiate, up to 2 inches across, and are borne, on 12-inch flower stalks, in late June and July. The involucre ranges from campanulate to hemispherical; the involucral bracts are narrow and arranged in 2 or 3 rows. The receptacle is flat and naked. The disc flowers are bisexual and bright yellow. The ray flowers, borne in 2 rows, are female, fertile, and narrow and may be white, pink, or blue.

LEAVES: The dense clusters of leaves are alternate and rarely all basal; they are usually sessile, glandular, and covered with spreading, gray, coarse hairs. The basal leaves are up to 3 or 4 inches long and ternate. The few stem leaves are smaller and linear.

PLANT CHARACTERISTICS: This perennial grows up to 10 inches high and has a taproot.

GARDEN VALUE: *Erigeron compositus* is excellent for covering embankments, for use in the rock wall, or massed in the perennial border, the wild flower garden, or the rock garden. It combines well with foliages and provides fine cut flowers.

CULTURE: The plant grows well in a hot, dry, sunny site. However, protection from midday sun lengthens the flowering season. It requires a well-drained soil; a water-logged soil during the winter will cause it to succumb. A sandy soil of low fertility is most conducive to growth.

Plant in spring, and space plants 6 inches apart. They need a moderate amount of water and an annual application of a balanced fertilizer. Remove

faded flowers to prolong the flowering season.

Seeds sown in spring will flower the first season. Clumps should be divided in spring or fall.

NATIVE HABITAT: Western Idaho, Washington, and Oregon.

ADDITIONAL NOTES: *Erigeron compositus* is very popular in England. It is also reported to repel insects. ◇

Eryngium

includes about 200 species of perennial herbs that are native world-wide but primarily in the Mediterranean region. The genus name is derived from the Greek *eryngos,* meaning "thistle-like."

Umbelliferae
(Parsley family)

Eryngium amethystinum
Sea Holly
Also known as Amethyst Eryngium

FLOWERS: Small flowers are borne, from June to September, sessile in dense, oval heads ½ inch long and resemble those of thistles or teasels. The calyx is 5-lobed; the sepals range from ovate to lanceolate. The 5 petals are erect and range from ovate-oblong to nearly rectangular. The flower heads are subtended by 6 to 9 long, unequal, lanceolate, almost spiny involucral bracts. The peduncle is thick and sulcate. The flowers and the bracts range from steely gray to amethyst in color.

LEAVES: The handsome, blue-gray leaves are alternate, rigid, and leathery; they are obovate or oblong-ovate, bipinnate, and spinulose-dentate. The upper stem leaves are clasping, pinnately compound, and spinulose-dentate.

PLANT CHARACTERISTICS: This prickly, stiff, stout perennial grows 18 inches high and has many low branches, which are 4- or 5-forked at the tip. The upper stems are steely gray or amethyst in color. The long tap root is thick and cylindrical.

GARDEN VALUE: *Eryngium amethystinum* has a semi-formal, subtropical, and somewhat bizarre appearance that adds interest to the garden. The plants are best displayed in small groups, not massed; use in the perennial or the mixed border, the rockery, or the wild flower garden. The flowers can be used in fresh flower arrangements, or they can be dried and used in winter bouquets. Fully-opened flowers, which will keep their beautiful colors when dried, should be selected.

CULTURE: The plant grows best in full sun, in an infertile, dry, sandy soil; it requires excellent drainage. In rich soils, the plant grows energetically, losing its restrained character.

Plant in spring, and space plants 12 to 18 inches apart. Keep them moist, and occasionally apply a balanced fertilizer. Cultivate carefully around the plants. Clumps tend to spread slowly and can remain undisturbed indefinitely.

The best method of propagation is by seed sown as soon as it is ripe; germination will occur in the spring. Root cuttings can be taken in spring. Division, in spring or fall, is a severe shock to the plant and it requires time to recover.

ADDITIONAL NOTES: This plant is one of the best species of the genus. In the trade, however, *Eryngium planum* is often incorrectly labeled *Eryngium amethystinum*. *Eryngium planum* has less interesting flowers, lacks the attractive, colorful stems of the other species, is taller, and is difficult to transplant; it is attractive to bees and should be used only in the wild flower garden.

NATIVE HABITAT: Europe. ◇

Euphorbia

comprises over 1600 species of monoecious and dioecious herbs, shrubs, and trees that contain milky sap and are distributed world-wide.

According to Pliny, the genus name honors Euphorbus, the physician of a King Juba of Mauritania.

Euphorbiaceae
(Spurge family)

Euphorbia epithymoides (Euphorbia polychroma)
Cushion Euphorbia

FLOWERS: Several cyathias, containing small flowers, are produced in umbel-like cymes. They are borne, solitary, terminal, or axillary in axils of leaves or spines, from late April to early May. The unisexual flowers are inconspicuous and have no sepals or petals. They are subtended by 1-inch-wide, brilliant chartreuse-yellow, petaloid, involucral bracts; the 5 inner lobes alternate with from 2 to 4 glands.

LEAVES: The dark green leaves are simple, entire, petioled or sessile, and

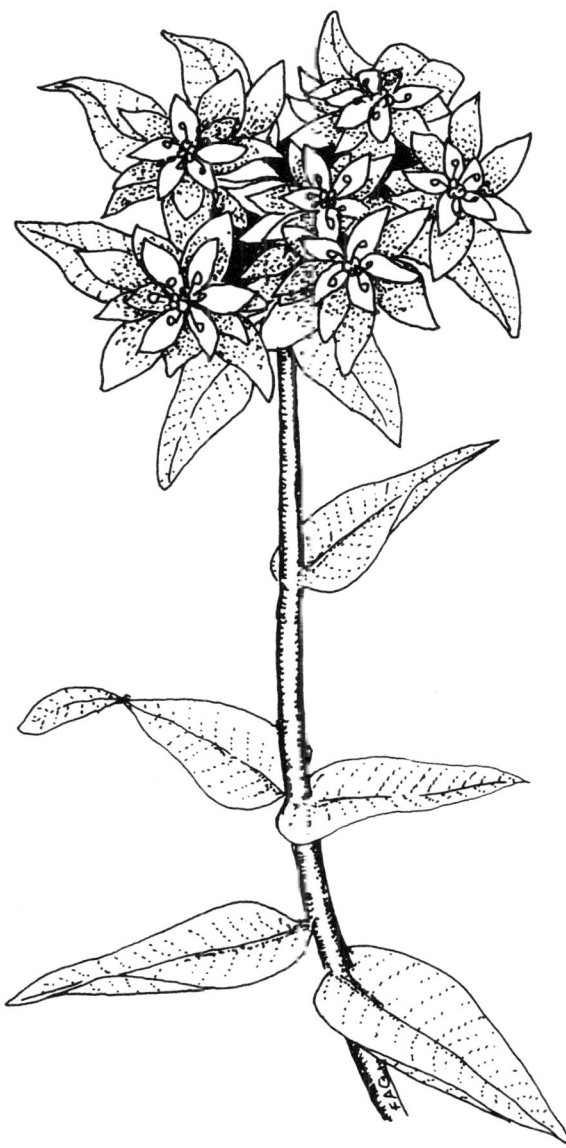

PLANT CHARACTERISTICS: The perennial grows up to 1 foot high and 2 feet across and has a creeping rootstock. The many-branched, 1-foot-long stems form a dense, hemispherical mound.

GARDEN VALUE: *Euphorbia epithymoides* is an excellent plant for the front of the perennial border, for use as a specimen plant, or for cut flowers.

CULTURE: This plant grows best in full sun, in a light, moderately fertile, well-drained soil.

Plant about 18 to 24 inches apart, in spring, before new growth is initiated. Keep plants somewhat dry, and feed annually with a balanced fertilizer. These long-lived plants dislike being transplanted.

Divide carefully to minimize damage of the heavy roots. Seeds may be sown in fall or early spring.

ADDITIONAL NOTES: The plant has a milky sap that can produce a dermatitis similar to poison ivy in susceptible persons.

To prepare flowers for cut flower arrangements, char the cut ends of the stems with a match and plunge them into deep water.

oblong-ovate. The foliage remains attractive all summer and becomes dark red in autumn.

NATIVE HABITAT: Eastern Europe. ◊

Euphorbiaceae
(Spurge family)

Euphorbia myrsinites
Myrtle Euphorbia

FLOWERS: Several cyathias, containing small flowers, are produced in 5- to 12-rayed umbels. They are borne solitary, terminal, or axillary in the axils of leaves or spines, in April or May. The unisexual flowers are inconspicuous and have no sepals or petals. The involucre of the cyathia has 5 inner lobes alternating with 4 glands. The flowers are subtended by attractive, pale yellow, petaloid involucral bracts.

LEAVES: The small, fleshy, glaucous blue-green leaves are borne in close spirals. The leaves range from obovate to obovate-oblong and are about $\frac{1}{2}$ inch long, abruptly short-mucrontae, and sessile. The leaves are evergreen in most areas, and they remain attractive throughout the year when placed in a site protected from winter wind or sun.

PLANT CHARACTERISTICS: This prostrate, herbaceous perennial is a very robust plant. The thick stems are 1 to 3 feet long, range from ascending to erect, and form a prostrate or decumbent wood base only a few inches high. The plant is very hardy when grown in well-drained sites.

GARDEN VALUE: Grown for its handsome foliage, *Euphorbia myrsinites* can be used in the perennial border, but it is especially suitable for rock outcroppings such as rock gardens, rock walls, or dry walls. The plant provides good cut flowers.

CULTURE: The plant grows best in a light, moderately fertile, well-drained soil in full sun.

Plant in early spring, spacing about 18 to 24 inches apart. Keep plants somewhat dry, and apply a balanced fertilizer annually in spring. When the plants begin to show signs of deterioration, they should be rejuvenated by pruning them, in early spring, to several inches above the ground. Although they are long-lived, any disturbance to the roots severely upsets them.

Propagation is usually by seed or division. Sow seeds in fall or early spring. Divide plants carefully to minimize damage to the heavy roots.

ADDITIONAL NOTES: The milky sap may produce dermatitis in susceptible persons.

To prepare the flowers for cut flower arrangements, char the cut end of the stems with a flame, then plunge into deep water.

According to folklore, the plants repel moles.

RELATED SPECIES: *Euphorbia cyparissias:* Cypress Spurge. Cyathias, containing small, inconspicuous flowers, are borne in many-rayed, umbel-like cymes in May and June. The petaloid bracts subtending the flowers range from ovate to triangular and are yellowish when young, later becoming purple or red. The yellow glands are crescent-shaped and have 2 short horns. The many dark green leaves are narrowly linear, 1 to 2 inches long, entire, and glabrous. This perennial plant grows up to about 1 foot high and has many short branches. Unless planted in a dry soil, it spreads voraciously from thick creeping rhizomes. This plant is sometimes used in naturalized plantings and to hold soil on dry banks. It may be used in smaller, formal areas as a ground cover or in the rock garden, but it should be located where its roots can be confined. The plant requires full sun. Once established, it can be very difficult to eradicate; each tiny piece of root remaining in the soil is capable of producing new plants. Its native habitat is Europe, but the plant grows in the Eastern United States, along roadsides, fence rows, on banks, and in cemeteries. ◊

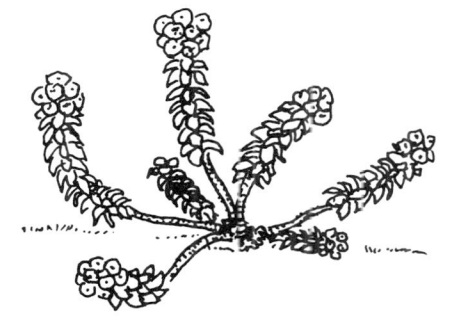

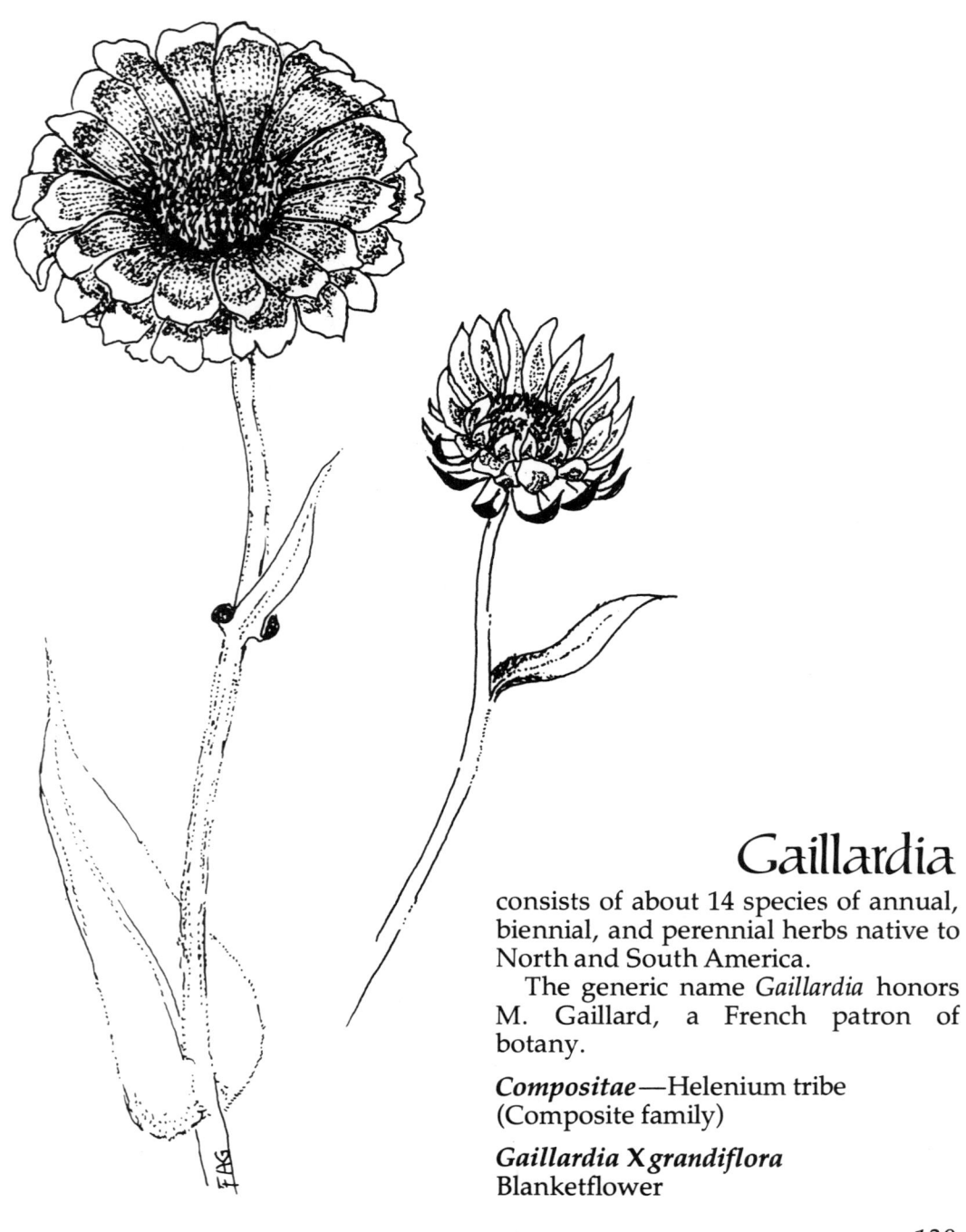

Gaillardia

consists of about 14 species of annual, biennial, and perennial herbs native to North and South America.

The generic name *Gaillardia* honors M. Gaillard, a French patron of botany.

Compositae — Helenium tribe (Composite family)

Gaillardia* X *grandiflora
Blanketflower

FLOWERS: The large, showy, flower heads are 2½ to 4 inches across and radiate, and are borne, solitary, from June until frost. The receptacle is hemispherical. The disc flowers are hairy, fertile, and yellow or reddish-purple. The ray flowers are sterile and yellow or red in color and have 3-tooth ligules.

LEAVES: The leaves are basal and alternate, toothed, spotted, and pubescent. The lower leaves are petioled; the upper leaves are sessile.

PLANT CHARACTERISTICS: This perennial grows 2 to 3 feet high and has erect or sprawling stems. It tolerates heat and droughty conditions.

GARDEN VALUE: *Gaillardia* is one of the most popular additions to the perennial border because of its bright, cheerful flowers and its long season of flowering. Use the plant singly or in groups in the perennial border, or mass it in the wild flower garden or in a naturalized area. The red-flowering cultivars are especially attractive when planted near *Chrysanthemum maximum*, *Delphinium*, white cultivars of *Phlox paniculata*, and dark blue cultivars of *Veronica*. The yellow-flowering cultivars are eye-catching when planted near purple cultivars of *Phlox paniculata*. It provides excellent cut flowers.

CULTURE: This plant is easily grown; it needs good air circulation and prefers full sun and a light, well-drained soil with a small amount of humus. A wet, rich soil causes a paucity of flowers, excessive foliage, and a hasty death.

Plant in spring, spacing 10 to 15 inches apart. Do not overwater. Occasionally apply a balanced fertilizer, and cultivate regularly. Stake the plants to

improve their habits of growth. Remove faded flowers to encourage flowering and to elimate seed production. The plants tend to die out unless the clumps are renewed every 2 or 3 years by division. *Gaillardia* is usually propagated by seed or by division. Seeds sown in spring will flower the same year but usually do not grow true to type. Cultivars are best propagated by division or by root cuttings in spring. Sink a spade in a circle 6 inches from the crown in the summer; the cut root will usually produce young plants ready for transplant in the spring. Softwood cuttings may be collected in August or September; while young, they will need winter protection.

ADDITIONAL NOTES: *Gaillardia* X *grandiflora* is a cross between *Gaillardia aristata* and *Gaillardia pulchella* and is tetraploid. Most of the plants in the trade under the name *Gaillardia aristata* are actually *Gaillardia* X *grandiflora*.

SELECTED CULTIVARS:

Yellow ray flowers—'Aurea' ◊ 'Aurea Pura' ◊ 'Golden Goblin' ◊ 'Golden Goddess' ◊ 'Goldkobold' ◊ 'Sun God' ◊ 'Yellow Queen'
Yellow-banded ray flowers—'Attraction' ◊ 'Baby Cole' ◊ 'Bremen' ◊ 'Dazzler' ◊ 'Goblin' ◊ 'Monarch' ◊ 'Sunset'
Others include—'Burgundy': Narrow wine-red ray flowers. ◊ 'Tangerine': Orange ray flowers. ◊

Galium

Rubiaceae
(Madder family)

includes about 300 species of slender herbs, usually square-stemmed, native to the temperate regions. *Galium* is the name of a plant used to curdle milk in ancient Greece.

Galium odoratum (Asperula odorata)
Woodruff
Also known as Sweet Woodruff, Woodroof

FLOWERS: The small, white flowers, which are up to ¼ inch long, are borne, in loose axillary or terminal cymes, from May to June. The corolla is 4-parted and campanulate.

LEAVES: The leaves are sessile in whorls of 6 to 8 and lanceolate; they grow up to 1½ inches in length, and are bristle-tipped and either finely toothed or roughish in the margins.

PLANT CHARACTERISTICS: This fragrant perennial grows 6 to 10 inches high. Its square stems are erect or ascending.

GARDEN VALUE: These small, creeping plants are an old-fashioned favorite and are useful in moist, shady sites. Plant in small groups in the rock garden, or use them as edging in the front of the border, as a ground cover, under ericaceous shrubs, or mass in a naturalized area.

CULTURE: The plant prefers a partly shaded to shaded site with moist, well-drained, fertile, acid soil. Under ideal conditions, it will grow luxuriantly until late fall. If grown in dry sunny areas, it becomes stunted and usually dies down completely before the end of the summer.

Plant in spring, spacing about 8 to 10 inches apart. Occasionally apply a balanced fertilizer, and keep the soil moist. They are usually propagated by division in spring.

ADDITIONAL NOTES: The dried leaves have a hay-like fragrance that lasts for years; it is often used to scent stored clothing. Cherished for flavoring wines and liquors, it is an important ingredient in the German May Wine, or *Maitrank*.

NATIVE HABITAT: Europe, North Africa, and Asia. ◇

Geranium

includes over 300 species of annual and perennial herbs primarily native to temperate regions and to mountainous areas.

The name *Geranium* comes from the Greek word *geranos*, meaning "crane"; it refers to the beaked fruit's resemblance to a crane's bill.

Geraniaceae
(Geranium family)

Geranium himalayense (Geranium grandiflorum)
Lilac Crane's Bill

FLOWERS: The showy flowers are borne, in a terminal cluster, from May to June. The flowers are regularly symmetrical. There are 5 imbricate sepals and 5 spreading, often ciliate petals that are pale lilac in color with dark purple veins. The flowers are 1 to $1\frac{1}{2}$ inches across and are borne above or with the leaves.

LEAVES: The attractive leaves are long-petioled and usually deeply, palmately 5- to 7-lobed; the incised lobes are broadly rhombic-obovate or obovate-spatulate.

PLANT CHARACTERISTICS: This perennial has thick ascending stems and grows 12 to 18 inches high.

GARDEN VALUE: *Geranium himalayense* is often used in the perennial and mixed borders, the rock garden, and the wild flower garden. It is quite outstanding when planted near yellow-flowering plants.

CULTURE: This plant is nearly indestructible. Although it flowers more profusely in sun, it will perform adequately in partial shade. Very hardy and adaptable to any well-drained garden soil, the plant spreads excessively when grown in a rich soil. In a dry, less fertile soil, it is smaller and more floriferous.

Plant in spring, and space plants about 12 inches apart. Cultivate them regularly, and apply a balanced fertilizer in early spring. Supply a moderate amount of water during the growing season, and mulch plants during the winter. Divide the plants after every fourth year of flowering.

ADDITIONAL NOTES: The popular garden geranium is not a member of this genus, but of *Pelargonium*.

NATIVE HABITAT: Turkestan, India, and Tibet.

RELATED SPECIES:
Geranium sanguineum: Blood-red Crane's Bill, Blood-red Geranium. The flowers are freely produced, usually singly on axillary peduncles, from late May to August. They are large, and vary in color from a bright purple-red to magenta. The attractive, white pubescent leaves are petioled and have from 5 to 7 lobes, divided nearly to the base, with lanceolate teeth. The foliage turns blood-red after the first hard frost. This perennial forms a broadly spreading mound that grows 12 to 18 inches high and 2 or more feet across and produces

a dense mat of foliage and trailing stems. Its native habitat is Europe and Asia.

◊ 'Album': White flowers. ◊ 'Prostratum': Bright pink flowers with red veins, freely borne all summer on a compact mound 6 inches high and 18 inches across.

Geranium ibericum: Iberian Crane's Bill. The dark purple flowers 2 inches across are borne, in erect terminal panicles, in July and August. The pedicels are glandular villous. The petals are obcordate, $1\frac{1}{4}$ inch long, and bearded. The large leaves are opposite and have from 5 to 7 toothed lobes, parted nearly to the base. The villous, erect stems form a clump 10 to 18 inches high. The plant is an attractive addition to the perennial border and deserves greater use. Its native habitat is China.

◊ 'Album': White flowers. ◊

Gypsophila

Carophyllaceae
(Pink family)

includes about 125 species of annual, biennial, and perennial herbs with glaucous, glabrous, or glandularly hairy foliage. The plants of this genus are primarily native to Eurasia. The genus name, derived from the Greek words *gypsos*, meaning "chalk," and *phileo*, meaning "love," refers to its preference for lime soils, which was also the origin of the common names, Chalk Plant and Gypsum Pink.

Gypsophila paniculata
Baby's Breath
Also known as Gypsum Pink, Mist, Chalk Plant

FLOWERS: Myriads of white (or occasionally, pink) flowers are borne, in diffuse panicles, in June and July. The flower bracts are usually scarious. The calyx has 5 ovate teeth and is less than

$\frac{1}{8}$ inch long; the 5 petals are linear-spatulate and about $\frac{1}{8}$ inch long. The flowers are borne on pedicels up to $\frac{1}{4}$ inch long.

LEAVES: The gray-green leaves are opposite, simple, entire, lanceolate, and acute; they grow up to 3 inches long, become smaller towards the inflorescence, and have parallel veins.

PLANT CHARACTERISTICS: This delicate, graceful perennial is "misty" and fine-textured in appearance, yet it is a very hardy plant. Growing $1\frac{1}{2}$ to 3 feet high and 4 feet across, it is glaucous and usually glabrous and has stout rhizomes. The stiff, wiry, diffusely branched stems are swollen at the nodes.

GARDEN VALUE: This old-fashioned favorite is valued as a perennial border plant because of its feathery texture and its small flowers. Use it to create a cloud-like effect, to soften coarsely textured plants such as *Gaillardia* and *Phlox*, and as a filler to hide the poor foliage of nearby plants—such as the early-fading foliage of *Papaver orientale* and spring-flowering bulbs.

The flowers are popularly mixed with other flowers in fresh bouquets and corsages; they also dry well for winter arrangements.

CULTURE: *Gypsophila paniculata* prefers full sun but tolerates partial shade. It prefers a moist, neutral-to-slightly-alkaline soil but will grow in almost any well-drained soil.

Because the plants are heavy feeders with deep roots, you should prepare the soil well before planting and spade in abundant amounts of organic matter. Plant in early spring, spacing about 2 feet apart. Because the double-flowered forms are usually grafted onto single-flowered forms, the graft union should be planted at least 1 inch below the soil surface so that it can develop its own root system. (Grafted plants are gnarled at the point where the stem and root join.) *Gypsophila* requires at least 2 years to become well established. Staking is usually necessary in windy sites, and occasional cultivation is beneficial. If the soil is acid, apply lime occasionally. Apply a balanced fertilizer regularly during the growing season. Prune off faded flowers after flowering has occurred to stimulate their continued production from August to October. The plant may have to be renewed occasionally after severe winters; however, it does not spread underground and can remain undisturbed indefinitely.

This plant should be propagated by cuttings collected in midsummer. Seeds are usually started in the greenhouse, in February, or outside, in April. The cultivars in the trade are best propagated professionally by grafting.

ADDITIONAL NOTES: *Gypsophila paniculata* is the most popular species.

The double-flowered forms are fairly common and generally flower more frequently than the single forms.

To prepare the flowers for dried arrangements, pick them when fully open, tie them in bundles, and hang them upside down in a shady airy spot until dry.

NATIVE HABITAT: Europe and Northern Asia.

SELECTED CULTIVARS: ◇ 'Bristol Fairy': Popular double, pure white flowers borne, repeatedly if cut, on 4-foot-high plants. ◇ 'Flore Pleno': Double flowers. ◇ 'Grandiflora': Large flowers. ◇ 'Pacifica': Pink flowers. ◇ 'Perfecta': Double flowers twice as large as those of 'Bristol Fairy.' ◇ 'Pink Fairy': Extra large, fully double, bright clear-pink flowers borne, until frost, on 18-inch-high plants.

RELATED SPECIES: *Gypsophila repens:* Creeping Gypsophila. The lilac, pale purple, or white flowers are profusely borne, in few-flowered panicles, from early June to mid-July. The pale blue-green leaves are linear, acute, and less than 1 inch long. This glabrous, prostrate perennial grows up to 10 inches high. Its stems grow up to 18 inches long and are trailing or prostrate and ascend at the ends. The root system consists of many corymbose rhizomes and long tap roots. Best when grown in full sun and a moist, well-drained limestone soil, *Gypsophila repens* is an excellent ground cover. It may be used as an edging, or in the rock garden, the mixed border, or a dry wall. As with other species in the genus, the delicate, rounded softness of the plant relieves harsh vertical lines and coarse textures elsewhere in the garden. The species is native to the area from Northwestern Spain to the Carpathian Mountains.

◊ 'Alba': A delicate cloud of tiny white flowers borne from June to frost, on a spreading plant up to 4 inches high. ◊ 'Bodgeri': Many, partially double, white-tinged pale pink flowers borne from late May until the first of July, on a plant 15 to 18 inches high; a cross between *Gypsophila repens* 'Rosea' and *Gypsophila paniculata*. ◊ 'Dorothy Teacher': Pink flowers on 4-inch stems. ◊ 'Dubia': Pink flowers on purple-green foliage. ◊ 'Frantensis': Very similar to 'Rosea.' ◊ 'Rosea': Pink flowers on a plant 6 inches high and $1\frac{1}{2}$ to 2 feet across; a useful ground cover, available in the trade. ◊ 'Rosy Veil' ('Rosenchlier'): Doubled pink-to-white flowers borne from June to August, and glabrous gray-blue foliage. ◊

Helenium

comprises about 40 species of hardy annual and perennial herbs native to North and South America. The genus name is either derived from that of Helenus, son of Priam, or named to honor Helen of Troy.

Compositae—Helenium tribe (Composite family)

Helenium autumnale
Sneezeweed

Also known as Common Sneezeweed, Yellow Star, False Sunflower, Helen's Flower, Swamp Sunflower

FLOWERS: The yellow flower heads are radiate, grow from 2 to 3 inches across, and are borne solitary or in corymbs on hairy, leafy peduncles. Myriads of flowers are produced from July to October. The involucre is flat; the involucral bracts are in 2 rows, are reflexed or spreading with age, and are covered with short whitish hairs. The receptacle is hemispherical and naked. The disc flowers are bisexual and yellow. The slightly drooping ray flowers are from bright to lemon yellow, wedge-shaped, and 3-cleft. Flowers may cover the entire top of the plant.

LEAVES: The bright green, moderately comes somewhat coarse, grows tall and from narrow to broadly lanceolate. They are glandular-dotted, frequently decurrent, usually serrate, 3 to 6 inches long, nearly glabrous, and sessile. The lower leaves are often deciduous.

PLANT CHARACTERISTICS: *Helenium autumnale* is a rank-growing perennial weed varying from 2 to 6 feet high. The rough, leafy stems are erect, stout, and branched and are winged by the alternate, decurrent leaf bases. The roots are fibrous.

GARDEN VALUE: Of limited horticultural value, *Helenium autumnale* becomes somewhat coarse, grows tall and lanky; it is best used in the wild flower garden or in a naturalized area. The medium-sized cultivars of this species are superior and may be used in the perennial border. They provide bright yellow flowers in late summer and early autumn—when most other perennials have finished flowering.

CULTURE: This plant prefers full sun and a moist, well-drained soil.

Plant in spring, spacing about 12 to 18 inches apart. Supply ample water during the growing season. Avoid over-fertilizing these plants, because it causes them to grow rankly and to produce excessive foliage. Pinch back the growing tips until mid-June to produce a bushier plant and more flowers. Staking is sometimes necessary when the plant becomes too straggly. The clumps should be divided every other year to stimulate new growth.

Seeds sown in early spring will probably flower sparsely the first fall, but more profusely the following year. Cultivars are usually propagated by division in spring.

ADDITIONAL NOTES: Most of the cultivars stem from *Helenium autumnale*. Their common name, Sneezeweed, should not prevent their use in the garden, for they do not actually provoke sneezing.

The leaves, stems, and particularly the flowers taste bitter and the flower heads have medicinal uses.

NATIVE HABITAT: A wide area from Canada south to Arizona and Florida.

SELECTED CULTIVARS AND VARIETIES:
◇ 'Bruno': Deep reddish-brown flowers atop a 3- to 3½-foot-high plant.
◇ 'Butterpat': Golden flowers atop a 3- to 3½-foot-high plant. ◇ 'Chippersfield Orange': Gold flowers streaked with crimson on a 3½- to 4-foot-high plant. ◇ 'Copper Spray': Copper-red flowers on a 3- to 3½-foot-high plant.
◇ 'Crimson Beauty': Bronze-crimson flowers on a 2- to 3-foot-high plant.

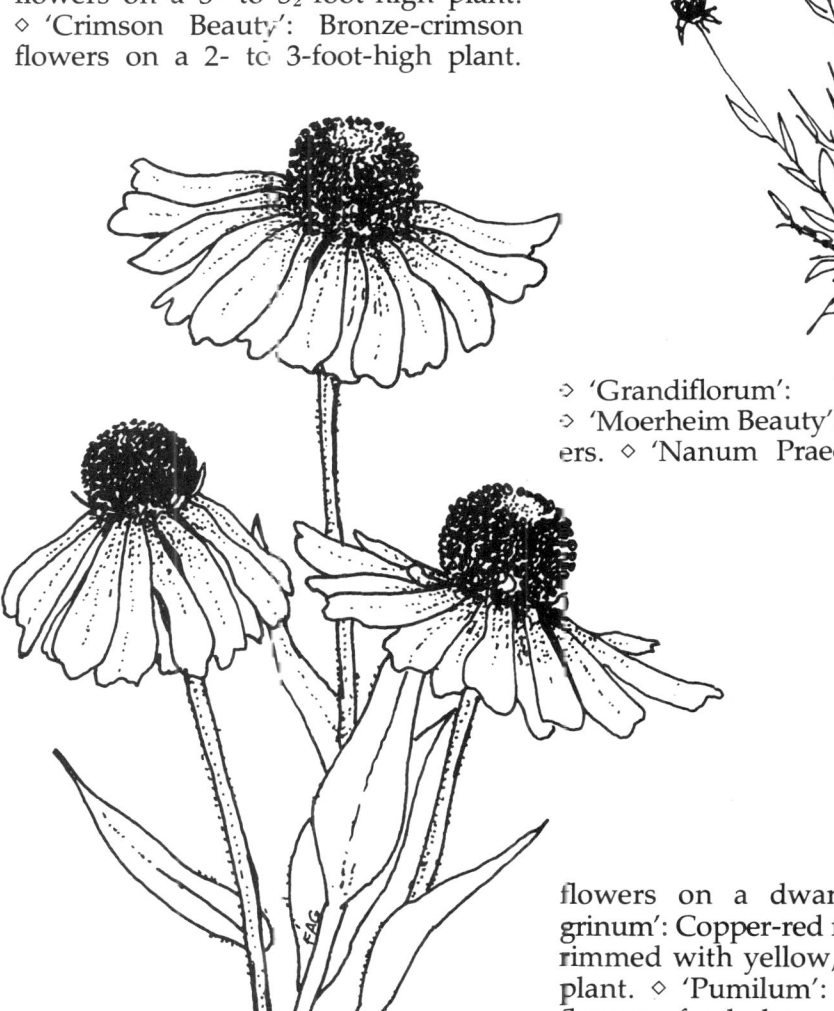

◇ 'Grandiflorum': Larger flowers.
◇ 'Moerheim Beauty': Bronze-red flowers. ◇ 'Nanum Praecox': Yellow disc flowers on a dwarf plant. ◇ 'Peregrinum': Copper-red ray flowers, faintly rimmed with yellow, on a 3-foot-high plant. ◇ 'Pumilum': Yellow and red flowers, freely borne on a 2-foot-high plant. ◇ 'Rubrum': Deep red flowers on a 4-foot-high plant. ◇ 'Superbum': Bright yellow ray flowers with wavy margins on a 4- to 5-foot-high plant. ◇

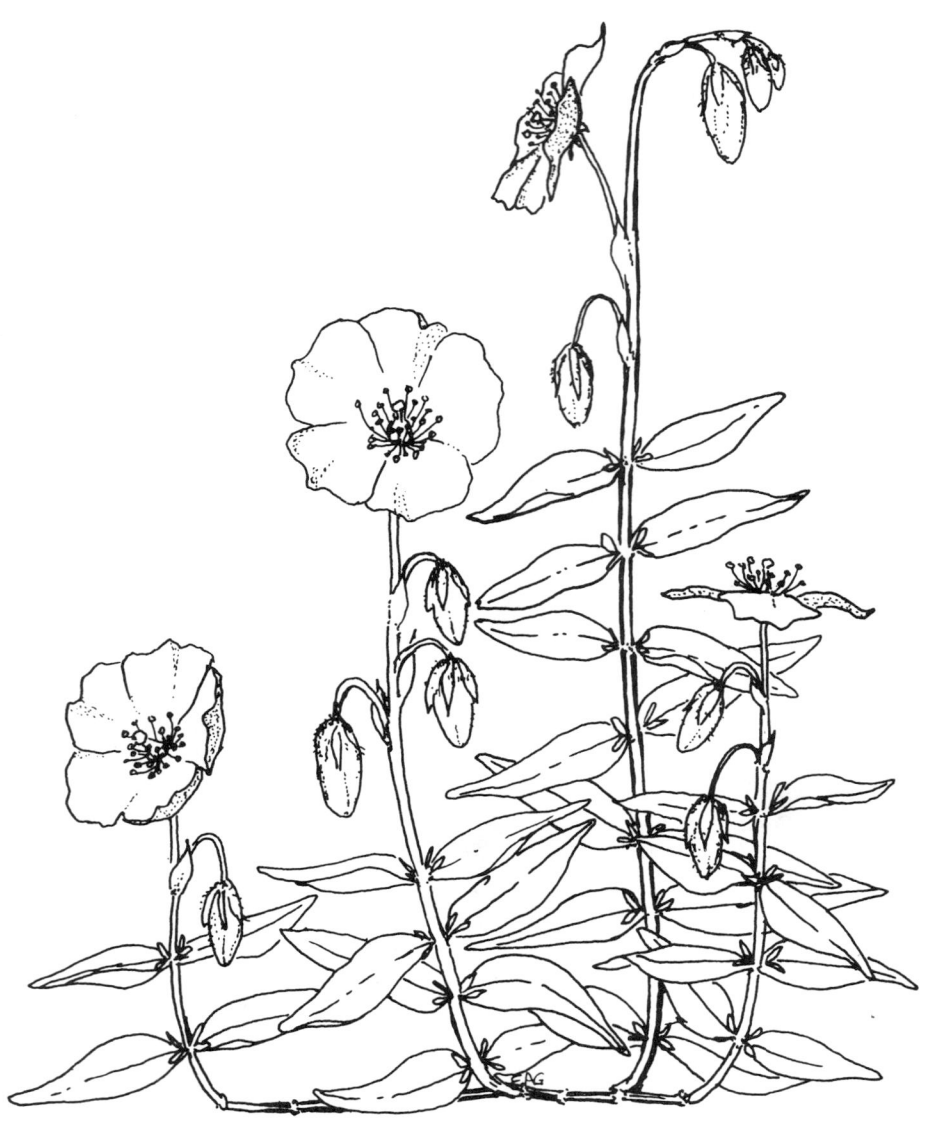

Helianthemum

Cistaceae
(Rock Rose family)

consists of about 110 species of semi-evergreen-to-evergreen herbs or subshrubs with showy flowers that are native to Europe and North and South America. The genus name, of Greek origin, means "sun flower."

Helianthemum nummularium
Common Sunrose

FLOWERS: The free-flowering, attractive, round flowers are usually yellow, but on rare occasions are cream, pale yellow, white, or pink. The regularly symmetrical flower consists of 5 petals, 5 sepals, and many conspicuous, showy, yellow stamens. The 1-inch-wide flower has a fine crêpe-papery texture and is borne, singly or in clusters of up to 12 on 1-sided racemes, from early June to July, then sparsely throughout the rest of the season.

LEAVES: The narrow green leaves are evergreen or semi-evergreen, usually opposite, and range from ovate to lanceolate. They are 1 to 2 inches long and gray tomentose on the underside, with flat or slightly revolute margins.

PLANT CHARACTERISTICS: This semi-woody perennial grows up to 18 inches high, forming a low-growing mound with procumbent branches. The *Helianthemum* tolerates dry soils.

GARDEN VALUE: Use this plant as a ground cover or in the perennial or mixed border or the rock garden. Its attractive foliage and masses of brilliant flowers contrast pleasingly with other plants. It grows well on steep banks where other plants fail because of the dry soil.

CULTURE: *Helianthemum nummularium* thrives in full sun. It prefers an alkaline soil that is poor, hot, dry, gravelly, and well-drained; it does not grow well in rich soils or respond to fertilization.

This species is difficult to transplant. Plant in spring. Keep the plants on the dry side. Provide periodic applications of lime if the soil is acid. Prune the plants in early spring to keep them dense and mat-like, especially when they are used as a ground cover. Prune again after flowering, about July 1, and they will flower again, quite heavily, in August and September. In the North, provide winter protection with an application of a medium-to-heavy mulch.

The plant is easy to propagate, from seed sown in spring or from cuttings taken in August.

ADDITIONAL NOTES: *Helianthemum nummularium* is the most commonly grown species of the genus. Its attractive foliage and flowers resemble those of small wild roses.

NATIVE HABITAT: Europe.

SELECTED CULTIVARS: ◊ 'Albo-plenum': Double flowers. ◊ 'Apricot Queen': Apricot-colored flowers, large shiny leaves, on a low-growing plant. ◊ 'Aureum': Deep yellow flowers. ◊ 'Buttercup': Masses of bright yellow flowers on 10-inch stems, borne in July to September; light green leaves, and a compact, dome-shaped growth habit. ◊ 'Citrinum': Golden-yellow flowers. ◊ 'Fire Nugget': Double yellow flowers. ◊ 'Macranthum': White petals with yellow blotches at the base. ◊ 'Mrs. Mould': An exquisite form with fringed salmon-pink petals and silvery foliage on stiff, erect stems. ◊ 'Mutabile' (*Helianthemum mutabile*): Flowers, opening light rose and changing to lilac, and fading to nearly white, borne in July and September; the dwarf plant likes full sun and requires winter protection. ◊ 'Rose Glory': Rose-pink flowers on 10-inch stems. ◊ 'Roseo-plenum': Double pale rose flowers. ◊ 'Rose Peach': Large peach-blossom-pink flowers and long, dark green, narrow leaves in a loose growing form. ◊ 'Rubro-plenum': Double red flowers. ◊ 'St. Mary's': White flowers. ◊ 'Stramineum': Petals with a bright straw-yellow blotch at the base and leaves with a white-tomentose underside. ◊

Helianthus

includes about 150 species of hardy annual and perennial herbs native to the Americas. The genus name, *Helianthus*, is derived from the Greek words *helios*, meaning "sun," and *anthos*, meaning "flower."

Compositae—Helianthus tribe (Composite family)

Helianthus decapetalus
Wild Sunflower
Also known as Thinleaf Sunflower, Rover Sunflower

FLOWERS: The flower heads are radiate, grow 2 to 3 inches across, and are borne, on long, slender peduncles, usually solitary or corymbose, from July until September. The involucre generally ranges from saucer-shaped to hemispherical; the involucral bracts are nearly equal and imbricate in 2 to 4 rows. The receptacle is flat-to-convex and scaly. The many disc flowers are bisexual, fertile, and light yellow. There are usually 10 or more female, sterile, yellow ray flowers in a single row.

LEAVES: The leaves have 2-inch-long petioles and are borne opposite in the lower part of the stem and alternate on the upper. The leaves are thin, simple, and range from ovate-lanceolate to ovate; they are acuminate, 3 to 8 inches long, sharply serrate, and scabrous-to-subglabrous.

PLANT CHARACTERISTICS: This dependable perennial grows 2 to 5 feet high. It has smooth stems and few branches and is a more upright-growing plant than *Heliopsis*.

GARDEN VALUE: *Helianthus decapetalus* makes a colorful addition to the middle of the perennial border, the evergreen border, or the wild flower garden or to a naturalized area. It is more effective massed than grown individually.

The plant provides long-lasting cut flowers.

CULTURE: *Helianthus* grows in almost any soil, but better flowers and plants result when located in a sunny site with a light, rich, moist, calcareous soil.

Plant in spring, spacing plants 1 to $1\frac{1}{2}$ feet apart. Keep the soil reasonably moist, especially during the dry periods in the growing season. Because they prefer a calcareous soil, apply lime occasionally to the soil around the base of the plants. Apply a balanced fertilizer, cultivate regularly, and stake if necessary. Remove faded flower heads to insure a longer flowering period. The roots are voracious feeders and quickly exhaust the soil; the plants should, therefore, be lifted, separated, and replanted in freshly prepared soil every 3rd year.

It is usually propagated by dividing the plants in spring, before new growth begins.

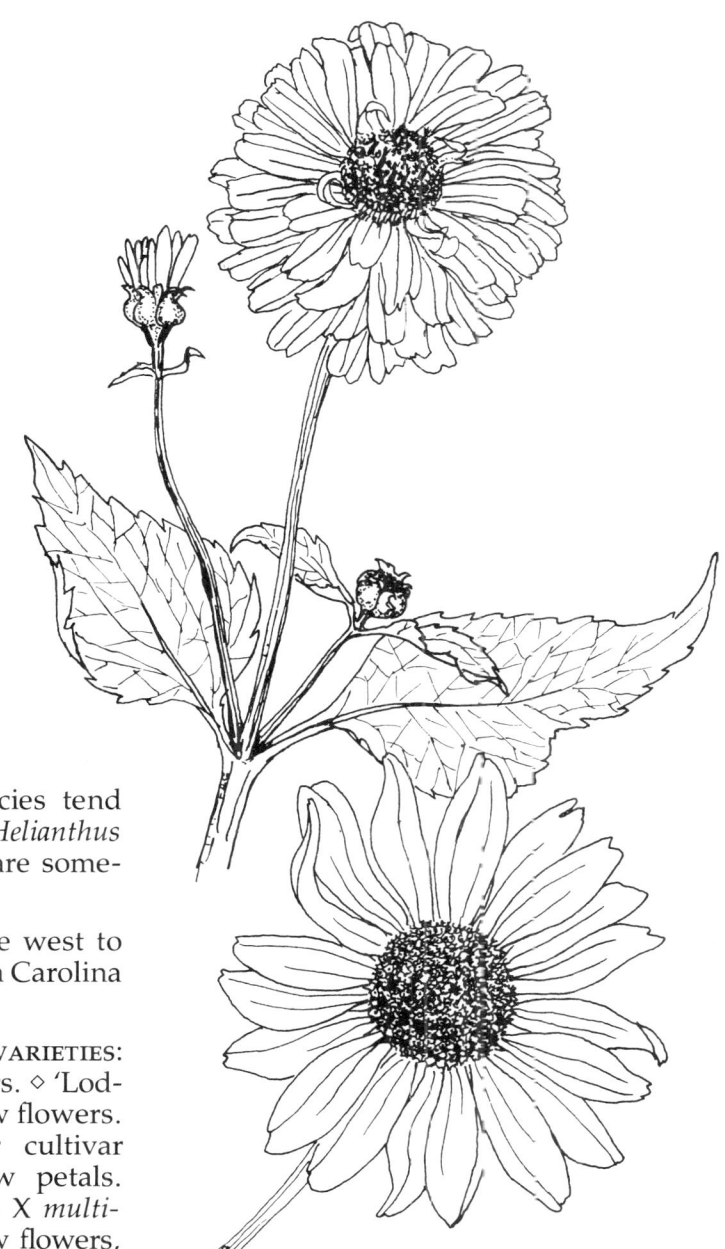

ADDITIONAL NOTES: The species tend to hybridize in cultivation. *Helianthus* and *Heliopsis* look alike and are sometimes confused.

NATIVE HABITAT: From Maine west to Wisconsin and south to South Carolina and Georgia.

SELECTED CULTIVARS AND VARIETIES: ◊ 'Flore-pleno': Double flowers. ◊ 'Loddon Gold': Double rich yellow flowers. ◊ 'Soleil d'Or': A popular cultivar with quilled, sulphur-yellow petals. ◊ var. *Multiflorus (Helianthus X multiflorus):* Single or double yellow flowers, 3 to 4 inches across, in late summer. ◊

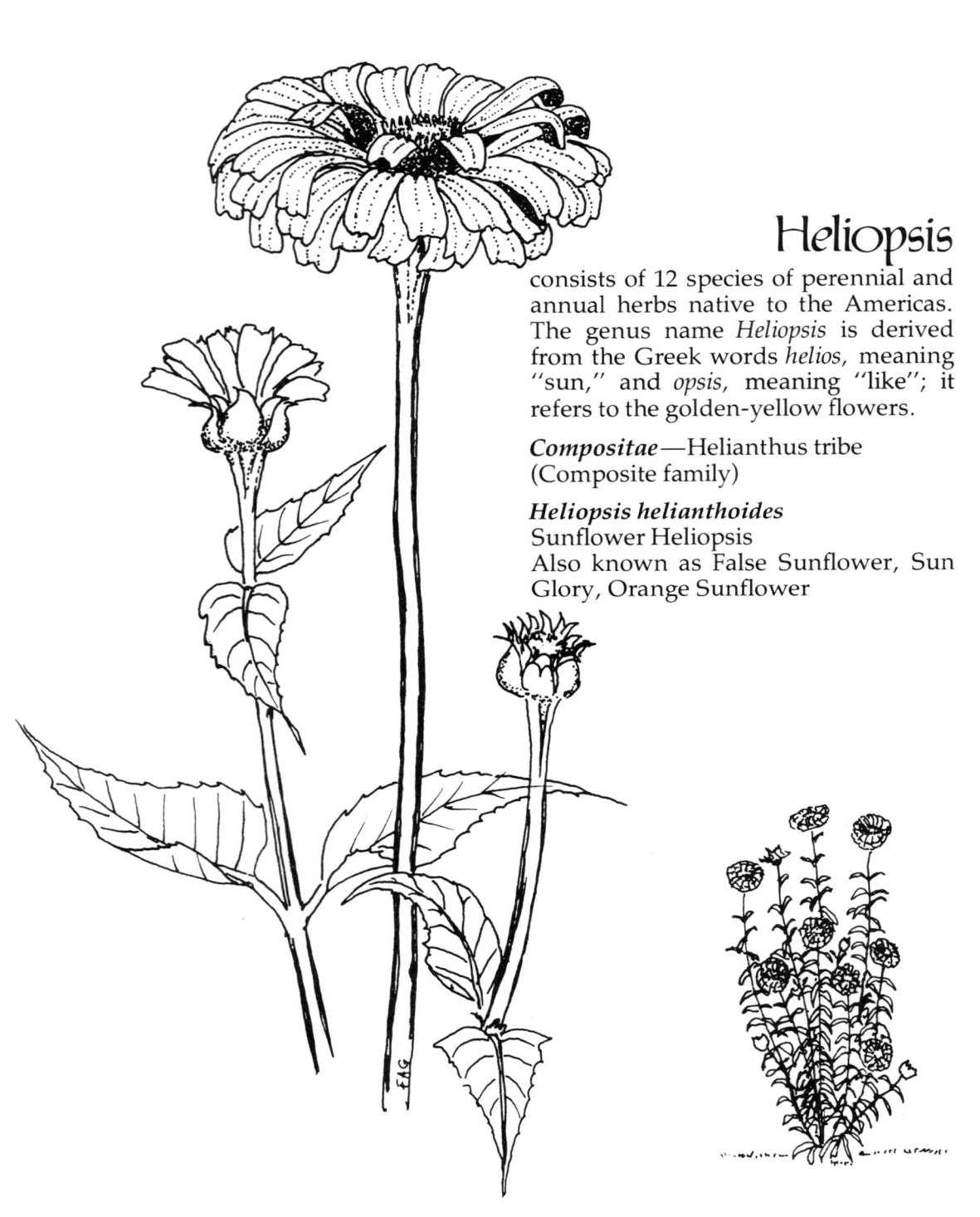

Heliopsis

consists of 12 species of perennial and annual herbs native to the Americas. The genus name *Heliopsis* is derived from the Greek words *helios*, meaning "sun," and *opsis*, meaning "like"; it refers to the golden-yellow flowers.

Compositae—Helianthus tribe (Composite family)

Heliopsis helianthoides
Sunflower Heliopsis
Also known as False Sunflower, Sun Glory, Orange Sunflower

FLOWERS: The long-stalked flower heads are radiate, grow up to 2½ inches across, and are borne, solitary and terminal on the branches, from July to October. The involucral bracts are nearly equal and arranged in 2 rows. The receptacle is convex-to-conical, scaly, and often hollow. The disc flowers are bisexual and brownish-yellow. The wide, pale yellow ray flowers are notched, female, and fertile and number from 10 to 20 in a flower head.

LEAVES: The thin leaves, which are opposite or in a whorl of 3, are simple, serrate, and range from lanceolate ovate to oblong-ovate. They are 3 to 5 inches long, 1½ to 2½ inches across, and on 1½-inch-long petioles.

PLANT CHARACTERISTICS: This perennial, growing 3 to 5 feet high, is nearly glabrous, coarse, and weedy; it grows vigorously, eventually forming a clump. The stem is erect and loosely branching.

GARDEN VALUE: Use *Heliopsis helianthoides* in the wild flower garden or a naturalized area; the plant is especially useful in dry sites. Use its cultivars in the perennial border, as small specimen plants or in small groups, to supply strong yellow flowers for months. The plant combines well with *Phlox*, *Delphinium*, and *Veronica* and provides excellent flowers for cutting.

CULTURE: The plant is easy to grow. It prefers full sun but tolerates partial shade. Any good, well-drained garden soil is satisfactory, but the best flowers and plants are grown in a soil containing abundant humus and moisture.

Plant in spring or fall, spacing plants 2 feet apart. Apply a balanced fertilizer occasionally, and cultivate as needed. Keep them on the dry side, but water during dry periods. Remove faded flowers to promote continued flowering until the first hard frost. Divide the plants every 3 or 4 years, when they become overcrowded.

To maintain the most desirable cultivars, propagation by division is usually best; root cuttings are easily started throughout the summer. Seedlings are also easy to grow, but they produce new seedlings of unknown types; 1-year-old seedlings do not bear flowers until August and September.

NATIVE HABITAT: Open places, from Ontario to Michigan and Northern Illinois, and south to Florida and Mississippi.

SELECTED CULTIVARS AND VARIETIES: ◊ 'Emiens': Chrome-yellow, 3-inch-wide flowers. ◊ 'Excelsa': Almost double, chrome-yellow flowers. ◊ 'Golden Plume': Double orange-yellow flowers. ◊ 'Goldgefieder': Double yellow ray flowers with green centers. ◊ 'Gold Greenhart': Double, buttercup-yellow flowers, opening with emerald-green centers that disappear as the flowers mature. ◊ 'Gratissima': Pale yellow ray flowers. ◊ 'Incomparabilis' (*Heliopsis incomparabilis*): Golden-yellow semi-double flowers. ◊ 'Light of Loddon': Bright yellow single flowers. ◊ 'Orange King': Bright orange flowers. ◊ 'Patula' (*Heliopsis patula*): Semi-double golden-yellow ray flowers, with 3 rows of incised petals. ◊ 'Pitcherana' (*Heliopsis pitcherana*): Large, more numerous, deeper-yellow flowers. ◊ 'Summer Sun': Clear orange-yellow flowers. ◊ 'Vitellina': Double golden-yellow flowers. ◊ 'Zinniiflora': Double golden-yellow flowers. ◊ var. *scabra* (*Heliopsis scabra*): Rough Heliopsis. Fewer flower heads, rough-pubescent foliage, and rough stems. ◊

Helleborus

includes nearly 20 species of perennial herbs native to the limestone regions of Europe and Asia. The genus name *Helleborus* is derived from the Greek words *helein,* meaning "to injure," and *bora,* meaning "food," because the bitter-tasting roots and leaves are poisonous when eaten. Crushed parts of the plant may cause severe dermatitis to susceptible persons. The name Christmas Rose was given to the plant because of its flowering season.

Ranunculaceae
(Crowfoot or buttercup family)

Helleborus niger
Christmas Rose
Also known as Winter Rose, Black Hellebore

FLOWERS: The white flowers, which are sometimes suffused with rose, are 2 to 4 inches wide and are usually borne solitary atop red-spotted peduncles. Environmental conditions control the flowering period, which may begin in November and continue until April. In the North, in a sheltered location (such as at the foundation of a building), the plant may flower in early spring and in late autumn. The flowers are cold-resistant, and individual flowers last a month or longer. They turn deep pink with age and in extremely cold weather. The flowers are bisexual and regularly symmetrical, with 5 petaloid sepals. The petals form small, inconspicuous, tubular nectaries behind the stamens, which are numerous, yellow, prominent, and pollen-bearing.

LEAVES: The attractive, dark green leaves are evergreen, mostly basal, erect, and palmately divided into 7, very thick, leathery leaflets. The leaf segments are ovate and slightly toothed toward the apex. The petioles are 5 to 7 inches long.

PLANT CHARACTERISTICS: This stemless perennial is evergreen, has short black roots, and forms ornamental clumps 12 to 15 inches high.

GARDEN VALUE: *Helleborus niger* is valued for its unusual flowering season. Place it in a sheltered location where it can be easily seen and enjoyed. Grow it in the front row of the perennial or mixed border, the rock garden, the wild flower garden or near a terrace, walk, or drive. The flowers are long-lasting in fresh arrangements. Sear the ends of the stems with a match before placing in water.

CULTURE: *Helleborus* prefers a site that is shaded fully in summer and partially in winter, beneath deciduous trees, for example. It suffers under full exposure to summer sun and heat. Avoid areas where it must compete with extensive tree roots. The plant grows best in a deep, fertile, light, moist but well-drained soil ranging from neutral to slightly alkaline.

Before planting, incorporate compost or leaf mold and superphosphate into the soil, as well as lime to raise the pH, if the soil is acid. Plant in spring, spacing 12 to 15 inches apart. Place the tops of the crowns 1 inch below the surface of the soil. Because the plants do not transplant well once established, plant them in their permanent location. Apply a 1-inch mulch of compost around the plant each spring to keep the roots cool and moist during the summer. Water well during drought periods in the summer. Apply a balanced fertilizer regularly, and cultivate to eliminate weeds. The clumps are slow to establish and improve with age; any disturbance to the roots severely upsets them.

In northern areas, more numerous flowers may be encouraged by placing a frame over the plants when the buds begin to develop. This also protects the flowers from snow, ice, and mud, and usually makes them last longer. The frame should consist of a small, ventilated plastic frame or box with a glass top; remove it in the spring.

The plants should not be divided. New plants are best propagated by seed; sow them immediately after they have ripened. Because they need a cold treatment, seeds will usually germinate the following spring. Seedlings take 3 or 4 years to produce flowers.

ADDITIONAL NOTES: The best garden species in the genus is *Helleborus niger; niger* refers to its black roots. Some plants cultivated in the trade under the name *Helleborus niger* are actually *Helleborus antiquorum*. In the 4th century B.C. the Greek naturalist and philosopher Theophrastus wrote in his *History of the Plants* that this species and those closely related to it had poisonous roots. Grown in Greece for centuries, the plant reached England in about 1596; it has long been used for medicinal purposes.

An ancient legend explains its unusual flowering season with the tale of Madelon, a country girl who accompanied the shepherds to see the Christ Child. Weeping because she had no gift for the Child, she was led outside by an angel, who touched the frozen ground. Immediately the plant sprang up, covered with flowers: it has flowered at Christmas every year since.

NATIVE HABITAT: Limestone regions of Europe.

SELECTED CULTIVARS: ◇ 'Altifolius': 3- to 5-inch-wide flowers, handsome foliage on petioles up to 1 foot long; superior to the species. ◇ 'Angustifolius': Smaller flowers. ◇ 'Praecox': Smaller flowers.

RELATED SPECIES: *Helleborus orientalis (Helleborus caucasicus):* Lenten Rose. The 2- to 3-inch-wide flowers, cream-colored on opening, turning a chocolate brown or purple, are borne, numbering 2 to 6, on a 15-inch high scape, from early March through April. The large, evergreen leaves are basal, light green, and up to 16 inches across; they are divided into 7 to 9 segments and are elliptic-oblong and sharply serrate. This evergreen plant grows up to $1\frac{1}{2}$ feet high; all its parts are poisonous. The plant is very popular in Europe but has not been grown much in the United States. Its native habitat is Asia Minor. The flowers do not last well when cut, but may be displayed floating in a bowl.

◇ 'Alba' ◇ 'Atropurpureus' ◇

Hemerocallis

consists of about 15 species of clump-forming, monocot perennial herbs native to the area from Central Europe to China and Japan. The genus name *Hemerocallis* is derived from the Greek words *hemera*, meaning "day," and *kallos*, meaning "beauty," because the single flowers remain open for only 1 day (however, new buds open daily so that the flower stalks are in flower for several weeks). The name was assigned in 1753 by the Swedish naturalist Linnaeus, in *Species Plantarum*.

Hemerocallis is usually included in the *Liliaceae* family, but it differs from the true lily in that it does not grow from bulbs and its flowers are borne on scapes.

Liliaceae
(Lily family)

Hemerocallis species
Daylily

FLOWERS: The fragrant flowers are yellow, orange, reddish, or purplish; they are ephemeral and are borne in clusters on long scapes. The slender scapes are erect, largely naked, and more or less branching at the top; they are borne from the low crown of the plant and extend above the foliage. Early cultivars flower with *Iris germanica*, immediately following *Tulipa;* most, however, flower after *Iris*. Some flower still later in the summer, and yet others re-flower well into the autumn. The flowers of a number of the cultivars open about sundown; others open during the day and remain open into evening.

The perianth is funnelform-to-campanulate and consists of 6 oblong or spatulate segments that join below into a tube. The inner 3 segments are petals; the outer 3 segments are sepals. The flowers range from under 2 inches to over 8 inches in width.

LEAVES: The graceful, arching, rich green leaves are basal, narrow, linear, and keeled. Some cultivars have foliage that is green all winter, and others are deciduous.

PLANT CHARACTERISTICS: This handy, dependable, long-lived, herbaceous perennial forms large clumps of foliage. Plants vary from under 1 foot to 8 feet in height; most cultivars in the trade are between 18 inches and about 5 feet high. The roots vary from fibrous to more-or-less tuberous; a few are rhizomatous.

GARDEN VALUE: Available in many colors and heights, *Hemerocallis* is quite versatile. It is effective when massed in a naturalized planting along a stream or pond, on a slope, in a woodland, or in an open area. It is also used on a sharp slope to control erosion. Use it also in the perennial border, the wild flower garden, along a lawn, wall, or terrace edge, or in a permanent landscape container.

The plant is displayed to its best advantage against a background such as a fence, a shrub, a hedge, or other herbaceous plants or evergreens. The background should be higher than the plants if the flowers are to be encouraged to face the viewer. They tend to lean toward the light, so each plant should be carefully placed for best effect. Some of the light-shaded varieties, especially yellow- or orange-flowered ones, are effective when seen from any direction and are particularly suitable in a location where the light comes from all sides. Most of the darker-flowered plants, however, are best viewed from the front.

Hemerocallis is often planted with spring-flowering bulbs such as *Tulipa* and *Narcissus* to hide their fading foliage and the subsequent void in the summer garden. Its various cultivars combine well with blue-and-white-bearded *Iris, Phlox, Aquilegia, Delphinium, Liatris, Chrysanthemum maximum, Papaver, Platycodon, Lilium*, and fall-flowering *Chrysanthemum*. *Hemerocallis* also provides good cut flowers.

CULTURE: Although *Hemerocallis* thrives on neglect and grows nearly anywhere, meeting its optimal cultural requirements will result in healthier plants and profuse flowering. The ideal exposure is full sun in the morning and light shade in the hot afternoon; the latter will somewhat reduce flowering, but the flowers will be of better quality. Some cultivars tend to fade, wilt, or "burn" in the hot afternoon sun. Severe wilting and fading occur when both the temperature and the humidity are high. Light yellow, pink, red, and dark-colored flowers are better when grown in partial shade. When grown in deep shade, the plants produce abundant foliage and few flowers.

The plants grow best in a well-drained, medium-heavy loam with abundant humus such as compost, leaf mold, or peatmoss incorporated into the soil. They are tolerant of either dry or wet soils but may suffer winter injury in wet soils in Northern areas.

Transplant from mid-August to early September to allow the roots to become established before the onset of winter. Space plants 2 feet apart.

The plants seldom need supplemental watering; they are very efficient in taking up water and storing it in their thick roots. Dry conditions usually do not kill the plant but cause injury; occasionally some cultivars may drop their flower buds. In a prolonged drought, supply water to a depth of 10 inches and let the soil dry out before adding more water. *Hemerocallis* is especially responsive to abundant moisture before flowering.

If the soil is a rich garden loam, little fertilizer is required. Too much nitrogen in the early spring may cause yellowish foliage that later becomes coarse and lushly green, a reduction in the number of flower scapes, the developement of a few coarse and inferior flowers with muted colors (especially those that are red or pink), and a lowered tolerance to midday sun. Incorporation of organic matter annually usually supplies the necessary nutrients and also improves the soil conditions. However, in an extremely poor soil or in light soil that leaches, several light applications of a complete fertilizer may be made in spring and early summer. Newly planted *Hemerocallis* plants should not be fertilized until they are completely established.

At the end of the flowering season, cut the scapes back to several inches above the ground. Established clumps can be kept from spreading by cutting around the crown with a sharp spade and removing crowns that extend out too far. Divide the old plants when the crowns become crowded and the flowers become less vigorous.

Dividing the plants in the early fall, from mid-August to early September, allows them to heal their wounds and become less susceptible to winter injury. Cut the tops back to 8 to 10 inches and trim off broken or diseased roots. The new growths that sometimes develop on the bracts of the flowering scapes can be rooted; sever the scape about 3 inches above and below the proliferation, place its crown 1 inch or more below the soil surface, and keep moist. Plants are easily grown from seed; however, the seedlings take 2 or 3 years to flower.

ADDITIONAL NOTES: This popular perennial has been known ever since the early Chinese advocated eating its petals to ease pain. It has been written about by such early authors as the Roman naturalist Pliny and the Greek herbalist Dioscorides.

Through the efforts of hybridizers in England and the United States, great improvements have been made in the last 100 years. The plant's color range has been expanded and new color patterns originated, the form and size of its flowers have been diversified, and its flowering period has been extended.

One new technique for breeding new cultivars is the use of colchicine to induce the growth of tetraploid plants. *Hemerocallis* is a diploid plant with 22 chromosomes in its cells; colchicine, applied to its growing points or its proliferations, doubles the number of chromosomes in the cells, making variations possible in all plant characteristics.

Hemerocallis is an integral part of the Chinese diet. The fresh flowers are collected, steamed, and dried and sold under the name *gun-jum*, golden vegetable, or *gum-tsoy*, golden needle. A gelatinous substance, it is used in soups and stews to add flavor. Before the flowering scapes appear, the tender center may be sliced for salads or cooked like asparagus. The fresh flower buds or flowers may be dipped in egg batter and fried. The tuber-like roots of *Hemerocallis fulva* 'Europa,' which are collected in late spring, are white and crisp, and, when eaten raw, have a sweet, nut-like flavor.

RELATED SPECIES:

Hemerocallis fulva: Tawny Daylily; also known as Orange Daylily, Corn Daylily, Fulvous Daylily. The rusty reddish or orangeish flowers are 5 inches long and $3\frac{1}{2}$ inches across; they are borne, in 6- to 12-flowered clusters on erect scapes, in July. The flowers are not fragrant. The long, linear leaves are 18 to 24 inches long and $1\frac{3}{8}$ inches across. The plant usually grows 4 to 5 feet high and forms clumps with its rapidly spreading rhizomes. Its main roots are fleshy. *Hemerocallis fulva's* rampant growth has led to a belief that all members of the genus are weedy. This pest can be eliminated only be removing all its roots and underground stems. It is native to Europe and Asia and has become naturalized in the eastern United States. This old, well-known, common plant is a self-sterile triploid and does not ordinarily set seed, although it produces pollen. The plant is used extensively in hybridizing to produce brilliant red cultivars.

◇ 'Cypriana': Coppery-red flowers with golden centers and a gold line in the middle of the segment; the leaves are glossy and the plant grows $4\frac{1}{2}$ feet across. ◇ 'Europa': Widely used along roadways to stem erosion and to crowd out weeds. ◇ 'Virginica': Double flowers, orange overlaid with rose. ◇ var. *kwanso* ('Flore Pleno'): A double-flowered plant known in Japan since about 1912. It, too, is sterile. The flowers occur later than those of the straight species and the leaves are occasionally striped white. ◇ var. *longituba*: Narrower leaves, up to $\frac{1}{2}$ inch wide, and the perianth tube is longer, $1\frac{1}{2}$ inches long. ◇ var. *rosea*: Discovered in Kiangsi Province, China, and sent to the New York Botanical Garden, where it was named in 1939. It is extensively used in breeding pink and red varieties.

Hemerocallis lilioasphodelus (Hemerocallis lilioasphodelus var. *flava; Hemerocallis flava)*: Medium-sized (about 4 inches long), lemon-yellow, faintly fragrant flowers are borne in May in 6- to 9-flowered corymbs on weak, arching scapes. The long, linear leaves are 18 to 24 inches long and $\frac{3}{4}$ inch wide. The plant grows up to 3 feet high and has spreading rhizomes. This is a favorite for the old-fashioned garden. Its native habitat is Eastern Asia. It has been superceded by superior cultivars.

◇ 'Major': Deeper yellow, larger flowers, on a taller plant. ◇ 'Rosea': Deep pink flowers, grows up to 40 inches high. ◇

154

Hesperis

includes about 24 species of biennial and perennial herbs with a branching and erect habit, native to the Mediterranean and Central Asia. The genus name is derived from the Greek word *hesperos*, meaning "evening"; it refers to the stronger fragrance that these plants have in the evening.

Cruciferae
(Mustard family)

Hesperis matronalis
Sweet Rocket
Also known as Dame's Rocket, Dame's Violet, Garden Rocket, Damask Violet

FLOWERS: The showy, fragrant flowers are $\frac{1}{2}$ to $\frac{3}{4}$ inch across and are borne, in loose, terminal, 3-foot, mostly paniculate racemes, from July to August. The profuse flowers are lilac or light purple, varying to white, in color. There are 4 sepals and 4 long-clawed petals that have spreading limbs, forming a cross. The flowers are regularly symmetrical and usually bisexual; there are single and double forms.

LEAVES: The leaves are alternate, narrow, and toothed, range from lanceolate to lanceolate-ovate, and grow up to 4 inches long.

PLANT CHARACTERISTICS: This usually hirsute (rarely glabrous) plant is hardy, erect, vigorous, and attains 2 to 3 feet in height. It sows seed freely and may become too weedy. This biennial or short-lived perennial is branched from the base and covered with showy, terminal pyramidal spikes of flowers.

GARDEN VALUE: *Hesperis matronalis* is a vigorously growing, old-fashioned hardy herb. Double-flowering forms, though rare, are more desirable; they grow less rampantly than the single-flowering forms. The double-flowering *Hesperis* is among the most floriferous plants in the perennial border; the single-flowering forms, however, are best used in the wild flower garden or in a naturalized area. The flowers are suitable for cutting.

CULTURE: Tolerant of a wide variety of soils, this plant prefers a moist, well-drained soil and a sunny or partially shaded site.

No special cultural practices are required. Plant in spring, spacing 15 to 18 inches apart. Apply compost in spring, keep the plants reasonably moist, and add regular applications of a balanced fertilizer; they are heavy feeders and exhaust the soil quickly. Cultivate them well. The heavy-headed flowers sometimes need staking. If the faded flowers are removed before seeds are formed, the plants may continue to flower until early fall.

The plants may be propagated from seed sown outside, in April, or inside, in March. Seedlings bear flowers the second year; because these vary considerably, and white, mauve, or purple flowers may appear, division is required to perpetuate a desired trait.

ADDITIONAL NOTES: This old-fashioned perennial somewhat resembles *Phlox* and is best considered a biennial. It is a variable species.

NATIVE HABITAT: Mediterranean and Central Asia, naturalized in North America as a wild flower.

SELECTED CULTIVARS: ◇ 'Alba': Pure white flowers. ◇ 'Alba Plena': Double, very fragrant, white flowers; a valuable form. ◇ 'Purpurea': Purple flowers. ◇

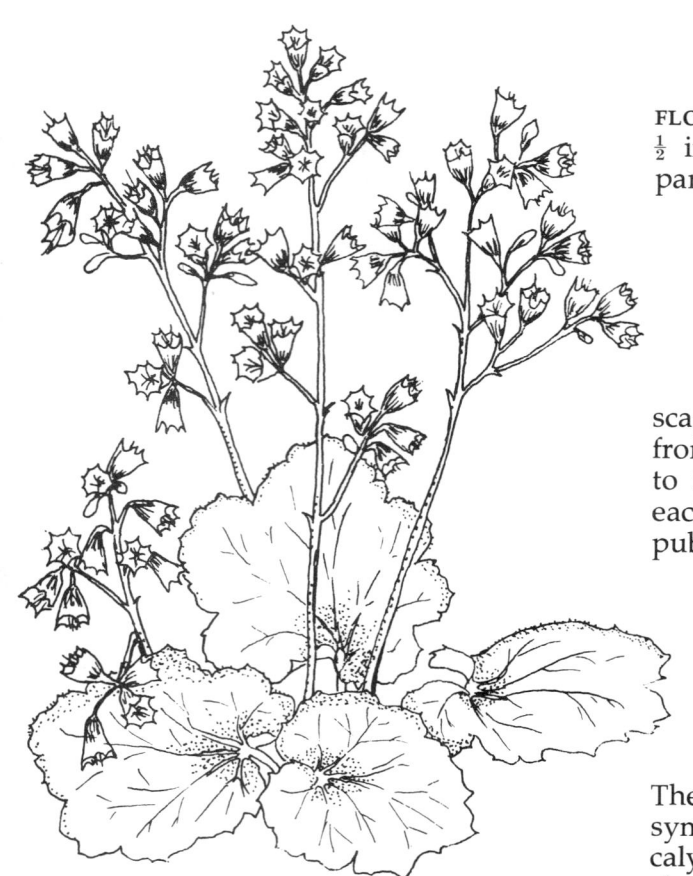

FLOWERS: Tiny bright red flowers, $\frac{1}{4}$ to $\frac{1}{2}$ inch across, are borne, in narrow panicles or racemes atop slender, wiry scapes held high above the foliage, from June through August. Several 18- to 24-inch-high scapes are borne on each plant; the scapes are glandular-pubescent above and pillose below.

Heuchera

contains between 35 and 50 species of perennial herbs native to North America, primarily inhabiting cliffs, hillsides, and mountains. The genus name honors Johann Heinrich von Heucher (1677–1747), a professor of botany from Wittenberg, Germany. The common name Coral Bells describes the color and shape of the flowers.

Saxifragaceae
(Saxifrage family)

Heuchera sanguinea
Coral bells
Also known as Crimson Bells, Alum Root

The flowers are bisexual and regularly symmetrical. The attractive, petalloid calyx tube is urn, cup, or saucer-shaped. There are 5 stamens, petals, and showy calyx lobes; the petals are shorter than the calyx lobes.

LEAVES: The rich, dark green, basal leaves are tufted, evergreen, and rounded-cordate or broadly 5- to 9-lobed. They are toothed, 1 to 2 inches across, and long-petioled. In appearance, the leaves are veined, mottled, or crinkled.

PLANT CHARACTERISTICS: The flower scapes reach 18 to 24 inches in height; the foliage, 8 to 10 inches. This hardy perennial is shallowly rooted and forms a decorative rosette.

GARDEN VALUE: A dainty plant, *Heuchera* is used in front of the perennial or mixed border, as an edging, in the rock garden, or to line a garden path. Cut, its flowers are long-lasting; they are often used as fillers in bouquets. They also press well for craftwork.

CULTURE: The plant tolerates filtered shade, especially in hot sites, but grows well in full sun. It needs a rich, loamy, well-drained soil with a high humus content. A poorly drained soil can be fatal in winter.

Plant in spring, spacing about 1 foot apart. Place the crown 1 inch below the soil's surface. Because the plants are shallow-rooted and do not tolerate drought, supply extra moisture during dry periods. Apply a balanced fertilizer and cultivate regularly. Remove faded flowers to prevent seed formation and to prolong the flowering season. In the North, apply a light mulch during winter months to reduce heaving during alternate periods of freezing and thawing. Do not smother the plants with heavy leaves. Because of this tendency to heave, crowns may have to be pushed back into the soil each spring. Divide the plants whenever they become overcrowded, usually after every 4 or 5 years of flowering.

The seeds germinate freely in spring, varying little from the parent plant. If sown in spring, the seeds provide flowering-sized plants in 1 year. Plants may be divided in spring or fall. Cuttings consisting of a leaf with a portion of the stem at the base of the petiole will root when collected in midsummer.

DISEASE PESTS: *Heuchera* suffers from crown rot—it can die out with winter injury.

ADDITIONAL NOTES: *Heuchera sanguinea* is the best and most popular species of the genus. It has been extensively bred in America and England with several other western species, resulting in hybrids which are superior garden

plants. The cultivars are more floriferous and are available in a range of colors from white to bright red.

NATIVE HABITAT: New Mexico, Arizona, and Northern Mexico.

SELECTED CULTIVARS: ◇ 'Alba': White flowers, comes true from seeds. ◇ 'Chartreuse': Light chartreuse-colored flowers. ◇ 'Chatterbox': Deep rose-pink flowers. ◇ 'Fire Sprite': Rose-red flowers. ◇ 'Garnet': Deep rose-pink flowers. ◇ 'June Bride' ◇ 'Matin Bells': Coral-red flowers. ◇ 'Oakington Jewels': Coral-red flowers and bronzy marbled leaves. ◇ 'Queen of Hearts': Large red bells; one of the best cultivars. ◇ 'Rhapsody': Excellent, clear rose-pink flowers. ◇ 'Rosamunda': Coral-pink flowers atop 24-inch stems; excellent cut flowers. ◇ 'Rosea': Rose-pink flowers. ◇ 'Sanguinea': Bright crimson flowers. ◇ 'Scarlet Sentinel': Vigorous scarlet flowers. ◇ 'Snowflakes': White flowers; perhaps one of the best white-flowered cultivars. ◇ 'Virginalis': White flowers. ◇ 'White Cloud': White bells, blending to cream, atop 18 inch spikes; flowers from June through September if the faded flowers are kept pruned. ◇

Hibiscus

is a polymorphous genus that comprises about 250 species of annual and perennial herbs, shrubs, and trees in the temperate and tropical regions. The name *Hibiscus* is Latin in origin and is believed to have been used, by Virgil, for a mallow.

Malvaceae
(Mallow family)

Hibiscus moscheutos
Common Rose Mallow
Also known as Swamp Rose Mallow, Mallow Rose, Wild Cotton

FLOWERS: The large, showy, funnelform flowers are 5 to 9 inches across. The flowers are borne solitary on long pedicels that arise from the leaf axils and are often fused basally to the leaf petioles. Flowers are borne from mid-July to frost but are heaviest in August and September. The flowers are regular and bisexual. There are 10 to 14 separate, lanceolate-linear, up-to-1-inch-long, involucral bracts, sometimes basally united or united to the calyx. The campanulate calyx is $\frac{3}{4}$ to $1\frac{1}{2}$ inches long, and sometimes prominently 10-veined, and has 5 triangular-ovate calyx lobes. The showy, campanulate corolla has 5 petals that are obovate, 3 to $4\frac{1}{4}$ inches long, and longer than the calyx. The white, pink, or rose-colored petals, usually with a crimson blotch at the base, are united at the base to the staminal column.

LEAVES: The large, hairy, gray-green leaves are alternate, simple, palmately veined, and either lack lobes or are shallowly 3- or 5-lobed; they are up to 8 inches long, crenate, and broadly ovate. The leaves are green on the upper surface and white pubescent on the under surface.

PLANT CHARACTERISTICS: This strong-growing perennial usually grows up to 5 feet high; in an extremely moist soil, it could reach 8 feet in height.

GARDEN VALUE: *Hibiscus moscheutos* is a good plant for the background of the perennial border, the wild flower garden, or the shrub border.

CULTURE: The plant grows best in full sun but tolerates partial shade. It prefers a rich, well-drained soil with abundant organic matter. Although tolerant of a wide range of moisture conditions, the plant grows best in a moist site.

Plant in spring. Set the crown about 3 to 4 inches below the surface of the soil, and space a minimum of 3 feet apart. Cultivate carefully around the plants in early spring as the new shoots appear late in the spring. Because the plants are heavy feeders, apply a balanced fertilizer annually. In northern areas, provide a light mulch during the winter months. Once the plant has become established, it can be left undisturbed for an indefinite period, because the plants do not spread underground.

Once established, the plant self-sows freely. Seeds sown in the spring will flower sparsely the first year but will come into full flower production in later years. Cultivars should be propagated by dividing the clump in spring.

ADDITIONAL NOTES: *Hibiscus moscheutos* is the hardiest, and one of the best, herbaceous species of the genus.

NATIVE HABITAT: A wetland plant, this species even grows in brackish salt marshes; it is found in the Eastern coastal states from Massachusetts to Florida, and is distributed as far west as Michigan and Alabama.

SELECTED CULTIVARS: Southern Belle and the Avalon Hybrids are strains that can be grown from seed. The named cultivars are more colorful than the species.
◇ 'Cotton Candy': Soft pink flowers.
◇ 'Satin': Velvety deep crimson flowers. ◇

Hosta

includes about 40 species of monocot perennial herbs with short rhizomes, primarily native to Japan.

Hosta was named after Nicolaus Thomas Host, a 19th-century Austrian physician. Its common name, Plantain-lily, compares its foliage pattern to that of the noxious lawn weed. The genus was once called *Funkia* and, erroneously, day lily; various species may still be listed under the obsolete name *Funkia*.

Liliaceae
(Lily family)

Hosta plantaginea (Hosta subcordata)
Fragrant Plantain-Lily

FLOWERS: The fragrant, waxy, pure white flowers are 5 to 6 inches long and are borne, tilted upward on terminal, bracted, 1-sided racemes atop $1\frac{1}{2}$- to $2\frac{1}{2}$-foot scapes held above the leaves, from mid-August through September. The flowers are bisexual, more or less irregularly symmetrical, and funnelform. The 6 perianth segments are united into a tube, the base of which is surrounded by a broad bract.

LEAVES: The handsome, large, bright greenish-yellow leaves are borne in basal clumps. The leaves are petioled, range from ovate to broadly ovate, are up to 6 inches long and 4 inches across, and have 7 to 9 nerves on either side of the midrib.

PLANT CHARACTERISTICS: This hardy, tufted plant grows 2½ feet high and 3 feet wide. The strong-growing plants have thick, durable rhizomes with large scars.

GARDEN VALUE: The plants in this genus have an ageless, noble appeal; favorites in the old-fashioned garden, they are still popular. The flowers and the foliage connote grandeur when used in appropriate plantings. Use them as a specimen plant, in the perennial border, as a ground cover, in the shrub border or as an edging for the patio, terrace, walk, or water garden. They blend well with fine-textured plants: ferns, *Dicentra*, *Astilbe*, and *Thalictrum* and also plants such as *Primula*, *Hemerocallis*, and *Pulmonaria* and ground covers such as *Ajuga*, *Asarum*, and *Galium*. The flowers and foliage both may be used in cut flower arrangements.

CULTURE: *Hosta* tolerates full sun or deep shade but grows best and with least care in partial shade, such as that under tall trees. Deep shade encourages lush foliage growth and few flowers; full sun promotes less luxuriant foliage, which may become pale or burn, except in cool, moist locations. In a deep, rich, moist, well-drained soil with abundant organic matter to retain moisture, the plants will continue to thrive for many years. They need a well-drained soil during the winter months.

The plants require little maintenance. Plant in spring, spacing about 3 to 4 feet apart to allow the plants to develop symmetrically. Keep plants moist during the growing season, cultivate regularly, and apply a balanced fertilizer annually, superphosphate in particular. Established plants usually do not need mulch; however, the plants may need winter protection in areas where winters are severe. Clumps improve with age and should remain in one permanent location if happily situated. Life spans of 20 years or more can be expected.

The plants may be easily propagated by seed or division of the clumps. Sow seeds as soon as they are ripe; seedlings do not flower for 2 or 3 years. Variegated forms and the hybrid 'Honeybells' will not produce true to type from seed. Divide plants that are 3 years old or younger; older plants have a very thick crown that is not easily separated, and the new sections may be difficult to transplant or establish.

ADDITIONAL NOTES: *Hosta plantaginea* is particularly known for its fragrant flowers.

NATIVE HABITAT: Japan and China.

SELECTED CULTIVARS: Many new hybrids are being introduced into the trade. ◊ 'Grandiflora' Longer, narrower, very fragrant, lily-shaped, pure white flowers, with more elongate leaves; the 2-foot spikes are borne in August and September.

RELATED SPECIES:

Hosta fortunei: Fortune's Plantain-lily, Tall Cluster Plantain-lily. The 1½-inch-long, pale-lilac-to-violet flowers are borne, on terminal, bracted, 1-sided racemes atop 3-foot scapes, in July. The flowers are funnelform; the 6 perianth segments, which are lanceolate, ascending, and half as long as the tube, are united into a tube. The glaucous, pale green leaves are cordate-ovate, 4 to 5 inches long and 3 inches wide, with 8 to 10 nerves on either side of the midrib. The flowers are held much higher than the leaves. The foliage provides interesting contrast to other plants. Its native habitat is Japan.
◊ 'Aurea' (*Hosta lancifolia* var. *aurea*): Thinner leaves, which are yellow when they open and become green in summer. ◊ 'Aureomaculata' (var. *albopicta*): Thinner, yellow leaves with a narrow green margin in spring. ◊ 'Glauca': Violet flowers and large blue-green leaves. ◊ 'Hyacinth': Pale lavender flowers and gray-green foliage. ◊ 'Marginata-albo': Large green leaves 12 inches long, borne in large picturesque clumps. ◊ 'Marginata-aurea': Green leaves with yellow margins. ◊ 'Picta': Lilac flowers and wavy, light green leaves with dark green edges.

Hosta sieboldiana (Hosta glauca): Siebold's Plaintain-lily, Blue-leaved Plantain-lily. The 1½-inch-long, pale lilac flowers are borne in short, dense, 6- to 10-flowered racemes on scapes that usually do not rise above the foliage. The flowers are funnelform, inclined, and have only one bract at the base. The leaves, which slowly mature to a powdery blue color, range from ovate to cordate, are 10 to 15 inches long and 10 inches across, and have about 12 nerves on either side of the midrib. They are usually very glaucous, thick, short-pointed, and rigid, with a welted texture. The plant grows up to 2½ feet high and 3 feet across. It is usually grown for its foliage and used in the shaded border. It produces seeds freely. Its native habitat is Japan.

◇ 'Aurea Marginata' ◇ 'Elegans'
◇ 'Variegata'

RELATED HYBRIDS:

Hosta decorata 'Thomas Hogg': Thomas Hogg Blunt-leaved Plantain-lily. The dark lilac flowers are small, narrowly campanulate, and 2 inches long; from few to many are borne on a racemose scape, in August. The leaves range from ovate to elliptic and are blunt-tipped, 6 inches long and 4 inches wide, with 4 or 5 nerves on either side of the midrib, a conspicuous silver-white margin, and winged petioles. This compact plant spreads by stolons and stays under 2 feet in height. It is excellent as an edging plant because of its small size and excellent foliage. Its native habitat is Japan. It may be listed as *Hosta* 'Thomas Hogg.'

Hosta 'Honeybells': Honeybells Plantain-lily. *(Hosta lancifolia X Hosta plantaginea)*. Fragrant, medium-sized, pale lilac-lavender flowers striped with blue pencilings are freely produced in July and August atop 3-foot stems. The grass-green leaves are nearly 1 foot long and 6 inches wide. ◇

Iberis

comprises about 30 species of small, evergreen, usually glabrous, annual and perennial herbs and subshrubs, that are sometimes woody and durable at the base and usually grow in limy soils in Southern and Central Europe and the Mediterranean region. The genus name *Iberis* is derived from *Iberia*, because many of its species are native to Spain. The common name, Candytuft (derived from Candia, the old English designation) refers to the flowers' appearance in tufts.

Cruciferae
(Mustard family)

Iberis sempervirens
Candytuft
Also known as Edging Candytuft, Evergreen Candytuft

FLOWERS: The white flowers are borne in lateral racemes 2 inches across, atop 8-inch stems that lengthen with age. The flowers are usually bisexual and consist of 4 deciduous sepals and 4 petals, the outer 2 being larger than the inner 2; the petals limbs spread to form a cross. These extremely floriferous plants usually flower from late April to early June, after the flowers of *Aurinia saxatilis* have faded, and thus remain effective for a long time.

LEAVES: The small, dark green leaves are alternate and almost evergreen; they are entire, narrow, linear or narrow-oblong, blunt, and 1 to 2 inches long.

PLANT CHARACTERISTICS: This compact, prostrate subshrub has a woody base and is glabrous or nearly so. Attaining 9 to 12 inches in height, the plant forms an irregular mat 2 or more feet in diameter.

GARDEN VALUE: One of the most popular dwarf garden plants, this excellent, refined plant may be used to hang over walls and ledges, as a ground cover or an edging, in rockeries, in the perennial border, in front of evergreen shrubs, in a separate bed in a garden nook, and in a porch box or hanging basket. Small masses are more attractive, especially when combined with spring-flowering bulbs. It combines well with *Aubrieta deltoides. Iberis sempervirens* provides good cut flowers.

CULTURE: This plant, which grows well in almost any well-drained garden soil, should have full sun but is tolerant of light shade.

Set out plants in early spring or fall, or when they are in full flower if they are potted. Space 12 to 15 inches apart. Trim the tops off after the flowers have faded and apply a light application of a balanced fertilizer to encourage new bushy growth. Without annual pruning, noticeable gaps in the center of the plant may develop. Water, and apply a balanced fertilizer regularly. In cold areas, protect plants against winter burn with a light mulch. These plants succeed best when left alone; they form a dense mat of foliage.

Cuttings taken in midsummer root easily. Although seeds germinate well in fall or spring, there is much seedling variation. Plants can be divided in spring; care must be taken because the roots are fragile.

ADDITIONAL NOTES: *Iberis sempervirens* is the most popular and the hardiest of the perennial species. It has been grown in England since the 16th century and was first known as Candie-mustard.

NATIVE HABITAT: Europe and Asia.

SELECTED CULTIVARS: ◇ 'Autumn Snow': Bears flowers in May and again in September until frost; use the compact, 7-inch-high plant in the perennial border, the rockery, or as an edging. ◇ 'Christmas Snow': Flowers almost constantly, even in winter, especially in milder climates. ◇ 'Compacta': A compact form. ◇ 'Little Gem': Densely covered with small clusters of pure white flowers; the compact plant grows about 5 inches high and 8 inches in diameter. ◇ 'Purity': Whiter flowers, more floriferous, and persistently longer-flowering; this hardy plant, an excellent selection, has luxuriant foliage that is always ornamental. ◇ 'Pygmea': White flowers atop a 4-inch-high plant. ◇ 'Snowflake': Large waxy flowers in large clusters; longer, broader dark green leaves on semitrailing stems, on a plant about 6 inches high and 3 feet across. ◇

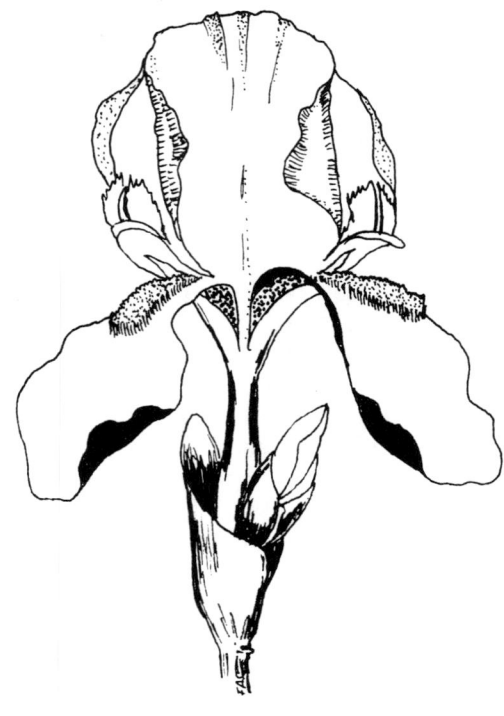

Iris

consists of at least 200 species of monocots, native to most of the Northern Temperate Zone, with rhizomatous or bulbous roots. Great variability and wide distribution are characteristic of the genus. Among the species are dwarfs for the rock garden, tender bulbs, and moisture-loving species for naturalizing in damp areas.

The genus name originates in Greek myth: Iris, Juno's messenger, is supposed to have traveled the rainbow between heaven and earth and was later transformed into a rainbow herself. The name is believed to signify the brilliant colors found in the genus. Pliny wrote of the plant as a source of perfume.

Botanically, *Iris* is divided into the bulbous species and the rhizomatous species. The general classes include: Tall Bearded; Dwarf Bearded; Intermediate; Japanese; Siberian; Bulbous; Beardless; Crested; Juno; Oncocyclus; Regelia; Reticulata; and Xiphium.

Iridaceae
(Iris family)

Bearded *Iris* cultivars
Iris

FLOWERS: The flowers are borne, in May and June, on stems with a 2-flowered terminal inflorescence and 2 lateral branches of different lengths, each of which has a single flower. The showy flowers, borne in 2 spathe valves, are of many colors and are usually called a "head." The perianth tube varies in length; the perianth has 6 segments. The "falls," the outer 3 segments, are obovate, cuneate, bearded, 2 to 4 inches long, and narrow basal. The petal-like portion of the fall is the "blade"; the "standards," the inner 3 segments, are obovate, connivent, usually erect and arching, narrowing into a claw, and sometimes spread or reflex. The "beard" is a pattern of hairs on the haft, which is the basal portion of the "fall." Inside the standards are 3 petal-like, very narrow "style branches."

LEAVES: The strong gray-green leaves are borne upright and sword-shaped and are 1 to $1\frac{1}{2}$ feet long.

PLANT CHARACTERISTICS: The thick rhizome grows near the surface of the ground. The flower stems are 2 to 3 feet high.

GARDEN VALUE: The bearded *Iris* provides flowers in the perennial garden for a short period of time after the spring-flowering bulbs have finished. This old-fashioned perennial is always effective when planted near other perennials that flower at the same time. The flowers last from 3 to 6 days. Although fragile, they may be used in cut flower arrangements if cut before the petals unroll.

CULTURE: Full sun promotes sturdy, erect, flowering stalks and maximizes flowering. An average, well-drained soil is required. If the soil is too acid, it can be corrected by incorporating lime; take care to keep lime and strong fertilizers from touching the rhizomes.

Transplant the rhizomes in July or August, and the plants will flower the following spring. If planted in early spring, flowers may be sacrificed that first year. Place the rhizomes 1 inch deep and 18 to 24 inches apart, and trim the foliage back to 6 inches high.

Divide clumps about every fourth season to prevent deterioration; replace old or weak rhizomes, and replant in freshly prepared soil. Each divided section should consist of 1 set of leaves in a fan, as well as the feeding roots below the rhizome.

The plant is usually propagated by dividing the rhizomes. Seeds should be sown immediately upon ripening; they usually germinate readily the following spring and will flower the year after germination.

ADDITIONAL NOTES: Cultivars are available in many blends of color and all the colors of the rainbow, as well as with ruffled or laciniated falls

The tall bearded *Iris* was formerly called *Iris germanica* (German Iris). However, the hybridization of *Iris germanica* (with many other species) and the development of tetraploids (plants with 4 sets of chromosomes instead of 2) have led to the use of the term "pogoniris" to signify the bearded types. Hundreds of new cultivars are registered every year, so no mention of selected cultivars will be made here. The bearded forms are classed, according to stature, as miniature dwarf, standard dwarf, intermediate, miniature tall, border, and standard tall.

Each year one outstanding selection is awarded the Dykes Medal (DM), the highest recognition an *Iris* can receive. The American Iris society makes several Awards of Merit (AM) to other outstanding cultivars. The awards are usually noted in catalogs from *Iris* specialists.

Iris kaempferi: Japanese Iris. Large beardless flowers up to 6 inches across are borne, in 2-flowered spathes atop 3- to 4-foot stalks, in late June and July. The colors range from white to blue, lavender pink, and reddish-purple. The perianth tube is $\frac{3}{4}$ inch long. The pedicles are $\frac{1}{2}$ to 2 inches in length. The falls are broadly ovate-oblong, obtuse, 2 to 3 inches long, and have a yellow spot on the short claw. The standards are narrowly oblanceolate, erect, connivent or spreading, and up to 2 inches long. The thin leaves are 1 to 2 feet long, ensiform, and have a prominent midrib. The slender, willowy leaves form graceful clumps. *Iris kaempferi* adds an aristocratic aura to the garden when it is well grown. Because the plant prefers moist soil, it can be handsomely sited around pools, fountains, and streams, especially when it is reflected in the water.

The plant grows equally well in full sun and partial shade. It grows best in

RELATED SPECIES:

Iris cristata: Crested Iris, Dwarf Crested Iris, Crested Dwarf Iris. Small, pale lilac flowers are borne, in 1- or 2-flowered spathes, in late April and May. The perianth tube is slender and $1\frac{1}{2}$ to 2 inches in length. A crest of petaloid tissue replaces the beard on the falls. The crested falls are obovate, yellow and white, and 1 to $1\frac{1}{2}$ inches long. The standards are shorter, oblanceolate, and naked. The green leaves are ensiform, grow 4 to 9 inches long and $\frac{3}{4}$ inch across, and are borne erect. The leaves die to the ground in midautumn. The slender rhizomes creep along the surface of the ground. This plant is ideal for the rock garden, and, although it tolerates sun, it grows better in partial shade. Do not cover the rhizomes with soil or they will rot. This is considered one of the best of the dwarf *Iris*. Its native habitat is from Maryland to the Carolinas and west to Missouri.

rich, mellow, acid soil that retains abundant moisture throughout the growing season but is dry in winter. Lime is fatal to it. Plant in spring or late summer, 1 inch deep and about 2 feet apart, and allow about 2 growing seasons for it to become established. Yellow foliage usually results from planting too deeply or from an insufficiently acid soil. The plant may be left undisturbed for a long period of time. Its native habitat is Japan. The specific epithet honors a Swedish consul who studied Japanese flora in the late 17th century.

Iris siberica: Siberian Iris. Medium-sized beardless flowers are borne, in 2- or 3-flowered spathes, in June; they are lavender, bluish purple, or grayish white in color. The spathe valves are brown and scarious. The perianth tube is about ½ inch long. The falls are reflexed, rounded-oblong, and 1½ to 2 inches long and ¾ inch wide. The standards are erect and shorter. The hollow stems grow up to 3½ feet high and branch toward the top. The leaves

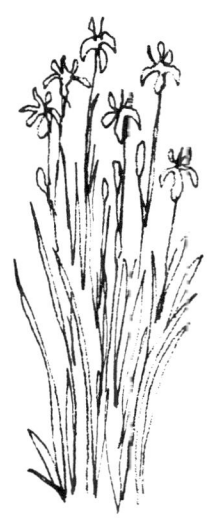

are green, linear, not rigid, and 1 to 2½ feet long. The plants form large compact clumps from which many flowering stems arise. The rhizomes are small, tough, and fibrous, making the Siberian Iris vigorous and relatively pest free. This popular *Iris* is used in the perennial or mixed border, or naturalized in colonies in wild areas. Although tolerant of poor soil, it performs best in a rich, moist, slightly acid soil in a sunny or slightly shaded site. Its native habitat is Central and Southern Europe and Russia. ◇

Kniphofia

includes about 70 species of stout, rhizomatous, perennial monocot herbs, usually stemless and thick-rooted, that are native to the high elevations of Madagascar and tropical and Southern Africa. The genus is named in honor of Johann Hieronymus Kniphof (1704–1765), a German professor of medicine at Erfurt.

Liliaceae
(Lily family)

Kniphofia X pfitzeri
Red-hot Poker
Also known as Poker Plant, Torch Lily, Tritoma

FLOWERS: The unusual, slender, orange-scarlet flowers are 1½ to 2 inches long and are borne, drooping on short, articulate pedicels in showy, lance-shaped spikes or dense racemes, along the top 12 inches of 3-foot-long stout scapes, from August to October. The flowers are bisexual and regularly symmetrical, with 6-segmented, cylindrical perianths; the perianth tube is longer than the 6 lobes. The 6 stamens are of 2 lengths, which equal or exceed the perianth.

LEAVES: The basal leaves are grass-like, up to 3 feet long, and narrowly lanceolate.

PLANT CHARACTERISTICS: This plant forms a tuft of foliage from which the flower spike arises in the center. The stout plants are stemless and have cord-like roots in a short vertical rootstock. The hybrids seem somewhat hardier than the species.

GARDEN VALUE: The sensational flowers provide a focal point in the garden; because they compete for attention with other floral accents, *Kniphofia* should be placed apart from them. The plant performs well in front of the shrub border or in the perennial garden, and the new dwarf forms do well in the rock garden. Place near shrubs, or near the white flowers of *Lilium*, *Phlox*, and *Delphinium*. The flowers are long-lasting in the garden and in the fresh flower bouquet.

CULTURE: The plant grows best in full sun and sandy, well-drained soils of low fertility. Wet soils, especially in the winter, are fatal. Avoid windy sites.

Plant in spring. Place roots about 2 to 3 inches deep and 2 to 3 feet apart. The plants are heavy feeders and require occasional applications of a balanced fertilizer. In northern areas, the plant is tender and needs to be well mulched during the winter. Rhizomes may be lifted and stored in sand or peat moss in a cool, dry place during the winter. The leaves should be left on the plant during winter and tied in a bunch over the crown to protect it from moisture, especially if hay or straw are mounded over the plants. Divide large clumps every third or fourth spring, after flowering.

The plants are usually started from divisions made in spring. They also come true from seed. Sow seeds in spring; 2 or 3 years are needed to produce a plant of flowering size.

ADDITIONAL NOTES: *Kniphofia X pfitzeri* is a cross between *Kniphofia uvaria* and another species. One of nature's unusual flowers, this plant is exotic and tropical in appearance. It attracts hummingbirds.

NATIVE HABITAT: Africa.

SELECTED CULTIVARS: The cultivars are superior to the species. Recent selections have increased the color range from pure white through shades of yellow to rosy red. The colors and flowering season have been expanded. Some cultivars flower from early summer to fall; most grow 2 to 2½ feet high or more.
◊ 'The Comte': Glowing scarlet at the tip, progressing to orange-gold and cream toward the bottom of the spike.
◊ 'White Giant': Large pale creamy-yellow flowers, becoming glistening white. ◊

Lathyrus

includes over 100 species of annual and perennial herbs of upright and climbing habit native to the Northern Temperate Zone and the mountains of Africa and South America.

Lathyrus, the genus name, Greek in origin, was applied to a leguminous plant.

Fabaceae (Leguminosae)
(Pea family)

Lathyrus latifolius
Perennial Sweet Pea
Also known as Perennial Pea Vine, Everlasting Pea

FLOWERS: The large, showy, rose or white flowers are 1 to 1½ inches across; from several to many are borne, on elongated peduncles in racemes, from late June to August. The calyx is 5-lobed and oblique-campanulate. The flower may not be as fragrant as the annual sweet pea. It is papilionaceous, and the standard is large, roundish, and notched, with a short claw. The wings are falcate-obovate or oblong, and the keel is shorter than the wings, incurved, and obtuse.

LEAVES: The somewhat glaucous leaves are alternate, mucronate, and even-pinnate, ending in a branched tendril. The 2 large leaf-like stipules are present at the base of the petiole.

PLANT CHARACTERISTICS: This glabrous, perennial climber is a rampantly sprawling plant that usually reaches 4 to 5 feet of height but can attain 9 feet. The plant climbs by tendrils or by falling over itself. Its stems are flattened and broadly winged and the inner nodes grow longer in the spring than under intense summer heat. The plant is dependable year after year, even when neglected.

GARDEN VALUE: Support must be provided or the plant tends to mound up on itself. Use it on a trellis, wall, fence, brush, or rock. It may be used to cover wild, rough sites. This species is showy but can become a nuisance with its propensity to climb and spread over other plants and objects. It provides suitable cut flowers.

CULTURE: *Lathyrus latifolius* is difficult to kill. Tolerant of all types of soil and exposure, it grows best in full sun and in almost any well-drained soil. Space plants 18 to 24 inches apart. Remove faded flowers to extend the flowering season. The roots are long and fleshy and, when once established, do not require further attention.

Propagate from seed sown, very early, in the open to secure a cool root run. Divide or take cuttings in the fall.

ADDITIONAL NOTES: *Lathyrus latifolius* is the common Perennial Sweet Pea, one of the hardiest and most easily cultivated species of the genus. Pink, reddish, purple, and pure white flower forms are available.

NATIVE HABITAT: Southern Europe; widely naturalized in the United States.

SELECTED CULTIVARS: ◇ 'Albus': White flowers. ◇ 'Splendens': Dark purple-red flowers; does not come true from seed. ◇

Lavandula

consists of about 20 species of aromatic, perennial herbs, subshrubs, and shrubs native to dry and hilly waste areas from the Canary Islands to India. *Lavandula* is derived from the Latin word *lavo*, meaning "to wash," dating back to when the Romans used the fragrance from the flowers and the foliage in baths.

Labiatae
(Mint family)

Lavandula angustifolia
Lavender

FLOWERS: The fragrant, $\frac{3}{8}$-inch-long purple flowers are borne, in 6- to 10-flowered verticillasters in upright spikes, from June to August. The calyx is erect, nearly equal, and ovoid-tubular; it is $\frac{1}{4}$ inch long, 13-nerved, slightly 5-toothed, and densely pubescent. The corolla, usually purple, is a corolla tube twice as long as the calyx and is 2-lipped; the upper lip is 2- to 10-lobed, and the lower lip is 3-lobed. The lobes are ovate and equal.

LEAVES: The fragrant silvery-green leaves are opposite, entire, and oblong-linear or lanceolate; they have backward-rolled margins, grow 1 to $1\frac{1}{2}$ inches long, and are white tomentose when young, later becoming green. Younger leaves often cluster in the axils. The semi-evergreen foliage is often more fragrant than the flowers.

PLANT CHARACTERISTICS: This dense tomentose subshrub grows 1 to 3 feet high, with a compact, rounded growth habit. The stems are square in cross

section. This species lives many years undisturbed. All parts of the plant are aromatic.

GARDEN VALUE: Its low growth habit, ornamental flowers, and foliage provide an attractive plant for ornamental use; the silvery-green foliage makes a nice contrast with the foliage of nearby plants. Use it in the rock garden, on rock walls, in front of the perennial border, as an untrimmed dwarf hedge, as an edging along walks, or on a dry sunny bank. Allow space for the plant to spill outward when in full flower. The lovely, fragrant flowers are often cut for fresh arrangements or dried for winter arrangements.

CULTURE: *Lavandula angustifolia* grows well in full sun and light, sandy, well-drained, moderately fertile soils. In heavier, fertile soils the growth becomes lax and the plant is less hardy. It is a fine plant for dry, calcareous, rocky soils.

Plant at 15- to 18-inch intervals in early spring, before any new growth begins. Keep moderately moist, but if nutrition and moisture are too abundant, the plants become soft and more prone to winter injury. Prune them lightly in April to remove dead wood and to keep plants from becoming straggly; do not cut the plant back too far, however, or new buds will not break. Remove faded flowers to encourage new flowers in August and to produce a compact growth habit. Provide a heavy mulch during winter. Allow the plant to grow undisturbed indefinitely.

Sow seeds, not too deeply, in spring. The plant is best propagated by taking cuttings from 1-year-old wood in spring or autumn. Propagate cultivars by cuttings. Shade young plants and, to encourage a bushier plant, do not allow first-year seedlings to flower.

ADDITIONAL NOTES: The pungent fragrance of the flowers and foliage lingers for years. Lavender is famous for its use in sachets or potpourris; the flowers and leaves also produce a fine, very expensive oil, "oil of lavender." The plant, which belongs in every herb garden, has been dubbed "queen of all herbs."

Lavandula officinalis, *Lavandula spica*, or *Lavandula vera* may be found in the trade under the name *Lavandula angustifolia*.

SELECTED CULTIVARS: ◇ 'Alba': White, not very attractive flowers. ◇ 'Atropurpurea': Dark purple flowers. ◇ 'Fragrance': Very heavily scented flowers. ◇ 'Gray Lady': Deep lavender flowers, grows 2 feet high. ◇ 'Hidcote': Rich, purple flowers on vigorous stems atop a compact plant. ◇ 'Munstead': Mauve flowers borne, in fan-like clusters in long spikes, in early June; the compact, rounded plant grows 15 inches high. ◇ 'Munstead Dwarf': Dark heliotrope flowers, a dwarf plant. ◇ 'Twickel Purple': Short dark blue spikes, silvery leaves, reaches 18 inches in height. ◇ 'Waltham': Deep purple flowers. ◇

Liatris

consists of about 40 species of hardy perennial herbs native to North America. The origins of the genus name are not known.

Compositae —Eupatorium tribe (Composite family)

Liatris spicata
Blazing Star, Spike Gayfeather

FLOWERS: The discoid flower is about ½ inch wide and is borne in groups of 8 to 13 in a long, closely sessile, neat, dense terminal spike 6 to 12 inches long, in July and August. Flowering is always initiated with the uppermost flower head first, progressing down the stem. Secondary racemes usually develop after the main stem has been cut, which prolongs the flowering period. The involucre ranges from cylindrical to turbinate-campanulate. The involucral bracts are orbicular and imbricate in several rows and have scarious, usually purple, margins. The receptacle is naked. There are no ray flowers; the disc flowers are bisexual, tubular, and purple or rose-purple in color.

LEAVES: The leaves are alternate, simple, entire, usually resin-dotted, and glabrous or slightly hairy. The lower leaves range from linear to linear lanceolate and are from 1 to 6 inches long; the upper leaves are linear and smaller.

PLANT CHARACTERISTICS: The perennial varies from 2 to 5 feet in height and usually has 1 stout, erect, leafy stem arising from underground tuberous roots.

GARDEN VALUE: *Liatris spicata* makes a striking color accent. Place a small group in the rear of the perennial border, or mass plants in the wild flower garden or in a naturalized area, such as a low spot or along a waterway. Plant near *Gysophila paniculata* and *Limonium latifolium* to provide relief to its stiff, erect growth habit.

The long-stemmed flowers last well in fresh arrangements and dry well for winter bouquets.

CULTURE: The plant requires no special care. It grows best in full sun or partial shade and will grow in poorer soils than most garden plants; however, a sandy, fertile soil is best. The plant will tolerate a quite moist soil during the growing season but, because wet conditions reduce its hardiness, it must have a well-drained soil in winter.

Plant in early spring, spacing 12 to 15 inches apart. Abundant amounts of water are required once flowering begins. The plant may require staking. When cutting the flower stems, leave at least a third of each stem on the plant for continued plant growth, otherwise the plant may die. Divide when the clumps become overgrown, usually after every third or fourth year of flowering.

Seeds are sown in spring and produce plants of flowering size the second year. Although white forms reproduce relatively true to type from seed, division in early spring is the best method of propagation for the cultivars.

ADDITIONAL NOTES: The genus *Liatris* is widely grown in the garden because it attracts large numbers of bees and butterflies.

NATIVE HABITAT: Eastern and Southern North America.

SELECTED CULTIVARS: ◊ 'Kobold': Compact, rosy-purple flowers borne in August. ◊ 'Silver Tips': Lavender flowers. ◊

Limonium

includes about 150 species of primarily perennial herbs that are occasionally woody at the base and are widely distributed throughout the world. *Limonium* is derived from the Greek word *leimon*, meaning "meadow," and refers to the native habitat of many of the species. The botanical name *Statice* is often incorrectly applied to the plants in the genus.

Plumbaginaceae
(Leadwort family)

Limonium latifolium (Statice latifolia)
Sea-lavender
Also known as Hardy Statice, Wide-leaf Sea-lavender

FLOWERS: Masses of tiny, bright mauve-lavender flowers are borne, sessile or nearly so in great misty panicles atop tall branched scapes, from July to August. The inflorescence is almost spherical and contains 1- or 2-flowered spikelets. The flowers are bisexual, regular, and 5-merous. The calyx is tubular, short, and slightly hairy, and the 5 lobes are clawed and united at the base. The corolla is bluish lavender.

LEAVES: The green leaves, borne in a basal rosette, are entire, oblong-elliptic, obtuse, up to 10 inches long, and narrow to a long petiole. The leaves are leathery and partially evergreen.

PLANT CHARACTERISTICS: This many-branched perennial has short stellate hairs, deep roots, and a woody base and grows 1 to 2 feet high. It is salt tolerant.

GARDEN VALUE: *Limonium latifolium* is airy in appearance, much like *Gypsophilia*. It is an excellent plant for the late-summer garden; use it to soften coarser textures, stiff forms, and gaudy colors in the perennial border, particularly in the seacoast garden.

The large panicles provide excellent cut flowers to use either fresh or dried. To dry, cut the flowers just before they are fully open, hang upside down in a shady, airy room until dry, and store until ready to use.

CULTURE: The plant tolerates partial shade but grows best in full sun. It will thrive indefinitely in a light, well-drained soil; rich, heavy soils encourage weak stems that require staking. It can be grown in a salty marsh.

Plant in early spring or fall. Prepare deep holes to accomodate the long roots, and space 18 to 24 inches from other plants. Apply a small amount of a balanced fertilizer annually. Because the plants do not acquire their majestic

beauty until they have become well established, their roots should not be disturbed. The plants require little care.

Plants may be divided in very early spring. Root cuttings are not very successful. Seeds may be sown in early spring or late fall and require 3 or 4 years to provide a plant of flowering size.

ADDITIONAL NOTES: *Limonium latifolium* is not only the finest species of the genus, it is one of the finest and hardiest of all perennials.

NATIVE HABITAT: Europe and Asia.

SELECTED CULTIVARS: ◊ 'Blue Cloud': Large mauve florets. ◊ 'Chilwell Beauty': Very large, deep violet-blue flowers. ◊ 'Collier's Pink': Pink flowers. ◊

Linum

consists of about 200 species of annual and perennial herbs and subshrubs native to temperate and subtropical regions, primarily of the Northern Hemisphere.

The genus name *Linum* is derived from the Celtic word *lin*, meaning "thread," because of *Linum usitatissimum*, Common Flax, the fiber and seeds of which are used as, respectively, clothing fiber and a source of linseed oil.

Linaceae
(Flax family)

Linum perenne
Perennial Flax, Common Blue Flax

FLOWERS: The chicory-blue flowers are about 1 inch across and are borne, in terminal or axillary, many-branched panicles, from June to August. The flowers are bisexual and regularly symmetrical, having 5 sepals and 5 petals. The attractive, graceful, arching stems are about 2 feet high and produce flowers, in great profusion, that last only one day.

LEAVES: The delicate, blue-green leaves are alternate, simple, entire, and acute; they range from linear to lanceolate and are 1 inch long. The upper leaves are 1-nerved.

PLANT CHARACTERISTICS: This glabrous perennial grows 1 to 2½ feet high, and is finely textured. The thin, erect, branching, gracefully arching stems resemble small, feathery bushes and are leafless or almost leafless on the lower part.

GARDEN VALUE: This low-growing species, with its delicately colored flowers and fine texture, is an excellent plant for the rock garden or the foreground of the perennial border. It is especially handsome when used in combination with perennial and annual forms of *Delphinium, Lupinus*, and other coarse-textured plants. Because the individual flowers last for only one day, they do not make good cut flowers.

CULTURE: Full sun and a light, well-drained, fertile soil are ideal. The plant is easy to grow. Plant, spacing 12 to 18 inches apart, in spring. Keep plants fairly moist during the growing season, and remove faded flowers to prolong the flowering season. Provide a light winter mulch in areas where plants tend to die out over the winter; it self-seeds readily, however, and can usually perpetuate itself.

The plant does not divide well. Cuttings can be collected from non-flowering stems in summer and will flower the following season. Sow seeds in spring, and the plants will flower the second summer.

ADDITIONAL NOTES: *Linum perenne* is probably the most common species of the genus.

NATIVE HABITAT: Europe. ◇

Liriope

includes about 5 species of stemless, evergreen, perennial, monocot herbs, tufted or rhizomatous, and native to Japan, China, and Vietnam. The name of the genus orignated with the mythical Greek nymph Liriope.

Liliaceae
(Lily family)

Liriope spicata
Creeping Lily-turf

FLOWERS: The flowers are ¼ inch across, range from pale-violet to nearly white in color, and are on a violet rachis; they are borne, in axillary fascicles arranged in slender, terminal racemes atop erect, light violet-brown scapes, in July and August. The bisexual, regularly symmetrical flowers are produced in scapes higher than the leaves. The 6 perianth segments are separate.

LEAVES: The arching, evergreen leaves are green, thin, prostrate, 18 inches long and ¼ inch wide, and serrulate with translucent teeth. They remain green in the North until about Christmas, then stay a pale green until spring.

PLANT CHARACTERISTICS: This stemless, evergreen plant grows up to 10 inches high. The rhizomes are short, thick, and often stoloniferous. The plant forms a heavy, almost impenetrable mass; it tolerates heat, drought, ocean exposure, and salt spray.

GARDEN VALUE: The plant is often used as a ground cover, a substitute for grass, or in the rock garden.

CULTURE: Tolerant of either sun or shade, the plant grows best in light shade and a moist, rich garden loam. In sun or deep shade, the plant will grow very slowly unless the soil is sufficiently moist.

Space plants 12 inches apart; they become so thick that they crowd out everything, including grass and weeds. Winter protection should be provided in northern areas. Cut off old leaves in spring to encourage growth of new foliage.

The plant can be easily divided in the spring.

NATIVE HABITAT: China, Japan, and Vietnam.

RELATED HYBRID: *Liriope muscari* 'Majestic' *(Liriope majestica)*: Violet flowers in fasciated inflorescences, with narrow leaves. ◇

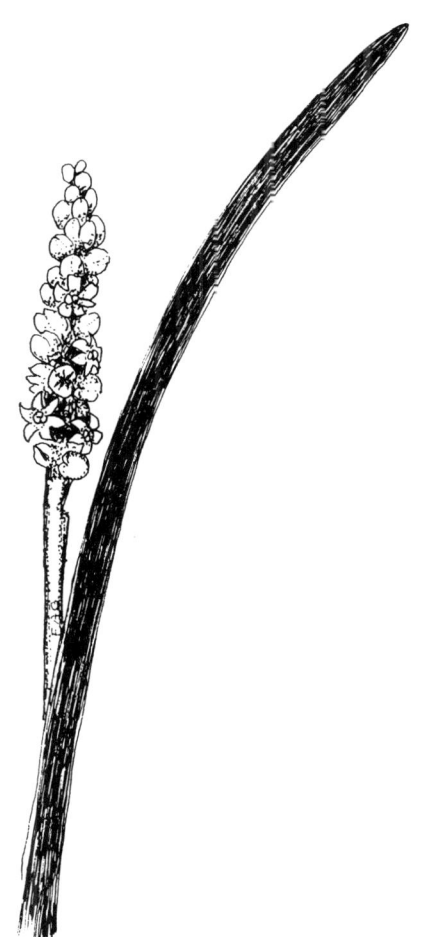

Lobelia

comprises about 370 herbaceous and woody plants, primarily native to the tropical and warm-temperate regions. Linnaeus named the genus in honor of the Flemish botanist, author, and physician to King James I, Matthia Lobel or L'Obel (1538–1616).

Lobeliaceae
(Lobelia family)

Lobelia cardinalis
Cardinal-flower
Also known as Indian Pink, Scarlet Lobelia, Red Lobelia, Red-birds

FLOWERS: The handsome, bright scarlet flowers are borne, on erect, long, narrow, terminal racemose spikes, from late July to early September. The irregularly symmetrical flowers have narrow bracts, are inverted by a twisted pedicel, and are borne in nearly 1-sided clusters. The calyx is 5-parted and hemispherical, and the calyx tube is much shorter than the long, linear lobes. The corolla is irregular, 5-lobed, $1\frac{1}{2}$ inch long, and mostly 2-lipped; the upper lip has 2 distinct lobes, and the lower lip has larger, 3-cleft lobes. The 1-inch-long corolla tube is split along the upper edge almost to the base. The 5 stamens are united into a protruding tube surrounding the single style.

LEAVES: The leaves are in a basal rosette and alternate, simple, and irregularly serrate. They range from lanceolate to oblong-ovate, taper at both ends, and grow to 4 inches. The petiole is very short or absent. Where winters are not too harsh, the basal foliage is usually evergreen.

PLANT CHARACTERISTICS: This short-lived perennial usually grows 2 to 4 feet high. The tall, straight, unbranched stem is glabrous, or nearly so, and usually purple-red in color.

GARDEN VALUE: With their tall spikes and bright crimson color, the flowers create a vivid sparkle of color in the late-summer, shaded garden. Use the plant as a vertical accent in the wetter areas of the perennial border, the mixed garden, or the wild flower garden or in a naturalized area.

The flowers are good when cut if the stems are first seared with a lit match.

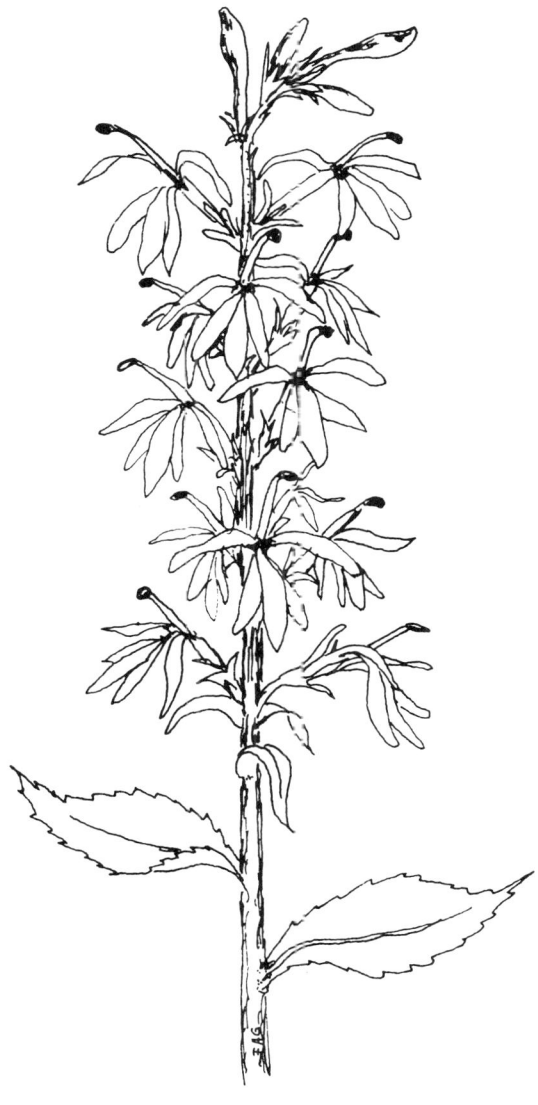

CULTURE: The plant prefers a shady site, but it is not necessary if adequate moisture is available, and the soil is rich. Flowers exposed to full sun in areas with hot, sunny summers will fade.

When preparing the site prior to planting, incorporate abundant amounts of peatmoss into the soil. Plant, spacing 12 inches apart, in early spring. Pinch the plants back to about 6 inches to produce a compact specimen. Water well during drought periods, and, for best results, occasionally apply a balanced fertilizer. Mulch well to keep the soil cool and moist in the summer and to provide sufficient moisture in the winter; the plants often winter-kill in a dry soil. Because the plants do not persist in the average border when self-sowing does not occur naturally, you should, to perpetuate the plants, either sow seed around them to keep vigorous new plants coming or divide and replant the clusters of new basal growth in the fall.

Seeds germinate easily when sown in fall or spring. The plant may be easily divided. Stem cuttings may be collected in midsummer.

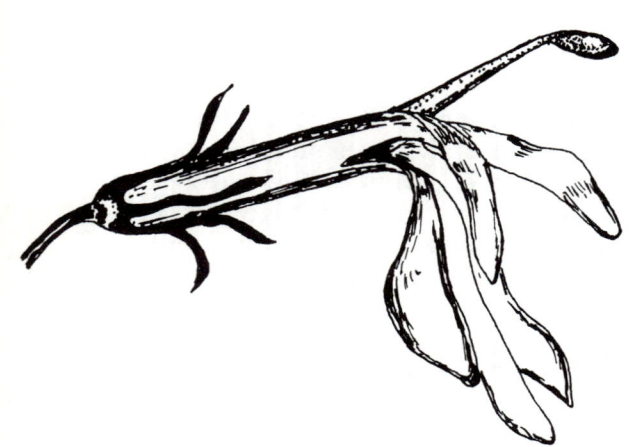

ADDITIONAL NOTES: *Lobelia cardinalis* is one of the few native plants that bees are not able to pollinate; only the hummingbirds can reach the nectaries at the base of the corolla tube.

NATIVE HABITAT: *Lobelia cardinalis* is found in large colonies in damp meadows or along streams in the eastern half of Canada and the United States, as far south as the Gulf of Mexico.

SELECTED CULTIVARS: ◇ 'Alba': White flowers. ◇ 'Rosea': Pink flowers.

RELATED SPECIES: *Lobelia siphilitica*. Great Lobelia, Blue Cardinal Flower; also known as Great Blue Lobelia, Big Blue Lobelia. The deep blue or purplish-blue flowers are about 1 inch long and are borne, in dense, terminal, racemose spikes atop stout stems, from July to October. The flower pedicels have a bract in the middle. The calyx is hairy and has 5 lance-acuminate lobes auricled at the base. The blue corolla is about 1 inch long. The leaves are thin, rather coarse, alternate, and slightly pubescent; they range from oblong-ovate to broadly lanceolate, are usually 2 to 6 inches long, and are acute and irregularly dentate or crenate-denticulate. The lower leaves are petioled; the upper, sessile. The basal foliage is evergreen in areas with mild winters. This usually simple-stemmed perennial grows 2 to 3 feet high and has stout, leafy, hairy stems. Stiffly erect, the plant is a strong, weedy perennial that is weedier but easier to grow than *Lobelia cardinalis*. Seedlings vary in the color of their flowers and in the time of flowering. This plant is interesting in the bog-garden, in a moist perennial border, and in the wild flower garden, as well as naturalized. It grows easily in wet soils, less vigorously in dry soils. Self-sowing freely, it may become weedy, but the seedlings are shallow-rooted and easily removed. It may be propagated by means of offsets. Its native habitat is moist woods from Maine west to South Dakota and south to Mississippi and Kansas. ◊

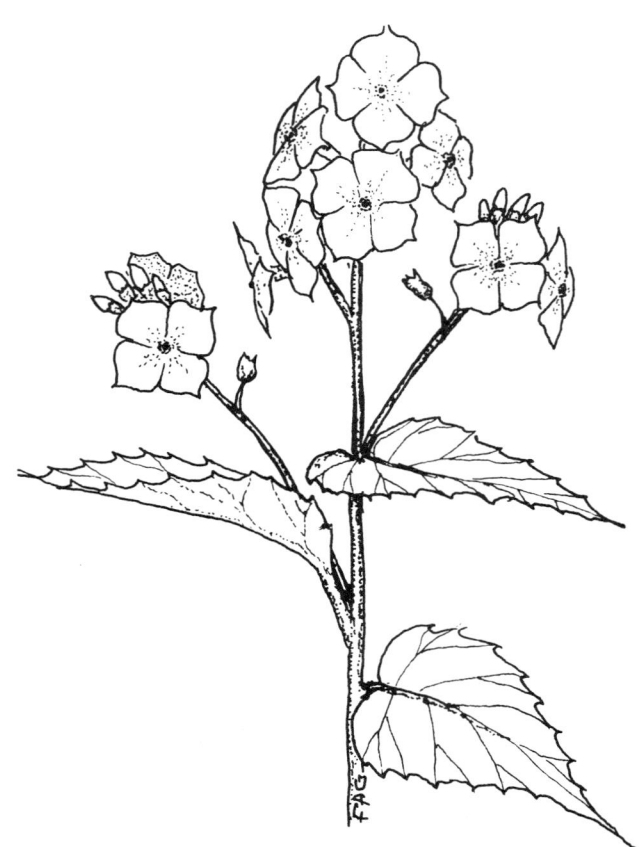

Lunaria

comprises 2 or 3 species of erect, branching annual, biennial, and perennial herbs of Europe.

The genus name *Lunaria* is derived from the Latin word *luna*, meaning "moon," and describes the silvery, satiny part of the seed pods. Its common name Honesty refers to the fact that the seeds can be seen through the pods.

Cruciferae
(Mustard family)

Lunaria annua (Lunaria biennis)
Honesty, Dollar Plant
Also known as Bolbonac, Silver Dollar, Penny Flower, Money Plant, Moneywort, Moonwort

FLOWERS: The numerous, large, showy, fragrant, pink-purple flowers are borne, on terminal racemes, in May and June. The flowers are regularly symmetrical and usually bisexual. The 4 sepals are decidous; the 4 petals are long-clawed, spreading to form a cross.

FRUIT: The fruit is a very flat silicle, ranging from oblong-elliptic to nearly orbicular, with deciduous values and a thin, persistent, satiny, paper-white septum.

LEAVES: The large leaves are alternate, succulent, coarsely and irregularly toothed, and more or less cordate. The upper leaves are sessile or subsessile.

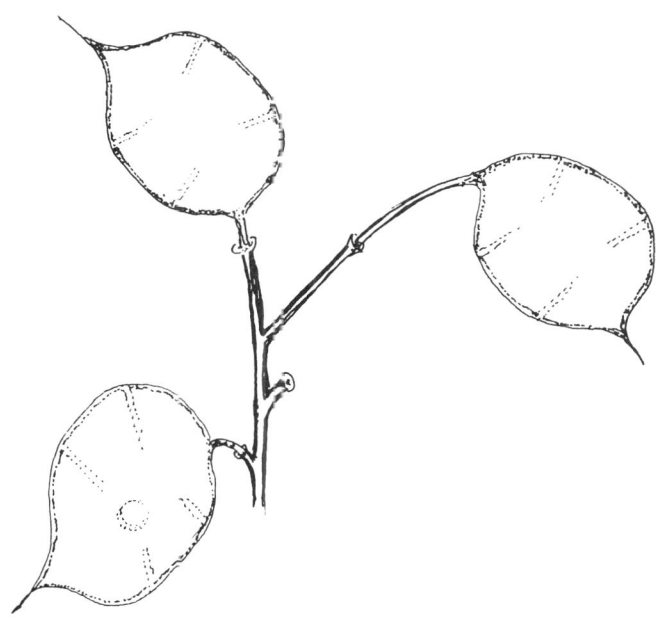

PLANT CHARACTERISTICS: This plant grows 1½ to 2½ feet high, branching as it matures. Although it is a biennial, it is sometimes grown as an annual.

GARDEN VALUE: The gay flowers and unusual fruits help to create a most unusual plant that adds considerable interest to the perennial or mixed border. *Lunaria annua* is an old-fashioned plant, popular for centuries. The flowers are attractive in fresh arrangements and also dry well; and the dried fruits are much sought after for winter bouquets.

CULTURE: *Lunaria annua* prefers partial shade but will grow in full sun. It grows well in almost any well-drained garden soil.

The plants are easily grown. Space 12 to 15 inches apart. Keep plants moist, cultivate regularly, and annually apply a well-balanced fertilizer. It readily self-sows and usually perpetuates itself, but it sometimes escapes from gardens.

The plants can be propagated by division but are usually started from seed. Sow seeds outdoors, where they are to grow, in the fall or spring. If sown in very early spring, the plant may flower in the summer.

ADDITIONAL NOTES: The perennial species of *Lunaria* is not as attractive as the biennial.

To preserve the pods, cut the branches as the fruits begin to dry; if allowed to ripen on the plant, they may rot during wet weather. Rub off the 2 outer coverings from the fruits to expose the central septum. Tie in loose bundles and hang the branches upside down to dry in a cool, airy dark spot.

NATIVE HABITAT: Southern Europe, naturalized in Europe and North America. ◊

Lupinus

consists of about 200 species of annual and perennial herbs and subshrubs that are widely distributed but especially prevalent in Western North America. A variable genus in the garden, the plants are grown primarily for ornamental use.

The genus name *Lupinus* is derived from *lupus*, "wolf," in Latin; it refers to an ancient myth that the plants destroyed fertility. Actually, some of the species are used to build up exhausted soil, as well as for fodder. As a legume, the *Lupinus* utilizes nitrogen from the air and stores it in the nodules on the roots.

Fabaceae (Leguminosae)
(Pea family)

Lupinus polyphyllus
Lupine

FLOWERS: The showy, free-flowering, deep blue flowers are pedicelled and alternately borne, on dense terminal racemes up to 2 feet long, from June to September. The 5-toothed calyx is deeply divided into unequal upper and lower parts. The flower is papilionaceous; its standard is erect, simple, and broadly ovate with reflexed margins, and its wings are united at the apex and enclose the keel.

LEAVES: The beautiful, very distinctive leaves are alternate, palmately compound, long-petioled, lanceolate, and glabrous on the upper surface, silky-haired on the underside. The lower leaves have 5 to 15 leaflets that are entire, acute, and 2 to 6 inches long; the upper leaves are smaller. The stipules are united to the petioles.

PLANT CHARACTERISTICS: This stout, erect perennial forms tufts 2 to 5 feet high.

GARDEN VALUE: Stately columns of dazzling colors, *Lupinus* commands attention in the perennial border; its attractive foliage contrasts pleasingly with the other plants in the garden. For the best effect in the perennial border, grow in small groups of 3 or 4 plants, all of a single color; mixed colors grown together are not as striking. Avoid overplanting them in one border, or great gaps will be left in it after the flowering season is over.

The highly prized flowers are magnificent when used in fresh arrangements.

CULTURE: *Lupinus* grows in full sun or light shade and performs best in a light, well-drained soil ranging in pH from slightly acid to neutral and containing little organic matter. It prefers a soil low in nitrogen but high in phosphorous; it will not grow in a soil containing lime. *Lupinus polyphyllus* thrives in cool areas with high humidity, such as the Pacific Northwest. The high temperatures and unfavorable soil types of the Midwest can result in poor development of the plant and flowers so that only a few flowers develop along the raceme.

Plant in early spring or fall, spacing at 18-inch intervals. Sprinkle bonemeal around the bases of the plants in spring and fall to encourage flower development. Mulch to retain soil moisture, water the plants liberally during dry periods, and cultivate carefully. Remove all faded flowers before seed pods develop. When cutting stems, leave all possible foliage on the plant. Provide a light winter mulch in northern areas. Do not transplant the plants once they are well established; leave clumps undisturbed until they begin to lose vigor, then replace.

Divide large clumps in early spring. Probably the best method of propagation is by seed; sow in late summer and transplant seedlings to their permanent location in early spring. Before sowing, dust the seeds with a nitrifying powder available from seed companies.

INSECT PESTS: Cyclamen mites may attack *Lupinus polyphyllus*.

ADDITIONAL NOTES: *Lupinus polyphyllus* is the best and most popular species of the genus. Yet the hybrids, of which *Lupinus polyphyllus* is a parent, surpass that species in beauty and bear flowers with an increased color range. The Russell Hybrids, developed by George Russell of England, are known for their vigorous plants, beautiful flowers, and long flower stalks and are tolerant of heat. ◇

Lychnis

includes about 35 species of erect annual and perennial herbs native to the Northern Temperate and Arctic regions. The name of the genus is derived from the Greek word *lynchos*, meaning "lamp," and refers to the flaming red flowers of some of the species.

Caryophyllaceae
(Pink family)

Lychnis chalcedonica
Maltese Cross
Also known as Scarlet Lychnis, Jerusalem Cross, Scarlet-lightning, London Pride.

FLOWERS: The vivid scarlet flowers are borne, 10 to 50 to a dense head or capitate inflorescence on 3-foot stems, in June and July. The flowers are bisexual or sometimes unisexual, 1 inch across, and have 10 stamens. The calyx is 5-toothed, 10-veined, sometimes inflated, and $\frac{3}{4}$ inch long. The 5 petals are 2-lobed, with coronal scales at the juncture of blade and claw. The flowers resemble small Maltese Crosses.

LEAVES: The leaves are simple, opposite, entire, ovate or acute, sparsely hispid, and parallel-veined. The stem leaves clasp the stem. The lower leaves are 2 to 4 inches long.

PLANT CHARACTERISTICS: This hispid perennial grows 1½ to 3 feet high and forms a rosette. The stems are erect, usually simple, and stout.

GARDEN VALUE: *Lychnis chalcedonica* is one of the best of all old-fashioned flowers. Although it has harsh coloring and a brief flowering period, small groups add brilliance to the perennial border in summer. Grow it also in the wild flower garden and in a naturalized area. It is a good source of cut flowers.

CULTURE: The species prefers full sun and a light, well-fertilized, well-drained soil. A wet soil during winter can be fatal.

It transplants well if potted; field-grown plants can be moved in early spring. Space 12 to 15 inches apart. Remove faded flower heads to induce continued flowering. The crown may need to be thinned after 3 or 4 years of flowering.

Divide in spring or fall. Propagate all except the double-flowering types by seed; sow seeds outdoors in April and transplant in May, or sow seeds where plants are to grow.

ADDITIONAL NOTES: *Lychnis chalcedonica* was brought from Russia to England in 1593 and was later introduced along the westward trail by homesick American pioneers.

NATIVE HABITAT: Northern USSR, naturalized in the Eastern United States.

SELECTED CULTIVARS: The white forms are not especially interesting. ◇ 'Alba': White flowers. ◇ 'Carnea': Flesh-pink flowers. ◇ 'Grandiflora': Large, flaming scarlet flowers. ◇ 'Rubra Plena': Double red flowers. ◇ 'Salmonea': Unusual, pastel, salmon-colored flowers. ◇

Caryophyllaceae
(Pink family)

Lychnis coronaria (Agrostemma coronaria)
Rose Campion
Also known as Mullein Pink, Dusty Miller

FLOWERS: The rounded, purplish (or, rarely, white) flowers are borne, singly on long pedicels sporadically from June to the end of August. The bisexual or sometimes unisexual flowers have 10 stamens. The calyx is 5-toothed, 10-veined, sometimes inflated, and up to ¾ inch long. The 5 petals have coronal scales at the juncture of the blade and claw and are 1½ inches across.

LEAVES: The sparse leaves are simple, opposite, entire, and oblong-ovate or oblong-spatulate. They are 1 to 4 inches long, parallel-veined, and white-woolly. The lower leaves are obtuse and petioled, the upper leaves are sessile.

PLANT CHARACTERISTICS: The densely white-woolly plant is usually biennial. The angular stems are erect, often branching at the top, and 1½ to 2½ feet high.

GARDEN VALUE: This is another old-fashioned flower for the rock garden, perennial border, wild flower garden, or a naturalized area. Use it in small groups. The flowers contrast with the silver-gray foliage to add a bright spot to the summer garden. It has a short life span but provides good cut flowers.

CULTURE: The plant requires full sun and a very light, fertile, well-drained soil. The plant may not survive the winter in wet soil.

Plant in early spring, and space about 12 to 15 inches apart. The plant transplants easily only if moved as a potted plant or a young field-grown plant. It self-sows freely but may be kept under control by eliminating those seedlings that overcrowd themselves or extend beyond their range.

Divide in spring or fall. Sow seeds outdoors in April and transplant in May, or sow seeds where plants are to grow.

NATIVE HABITAT: From Northwest Africa to Southeastern Europe and Central Asia; naturalized in several places in the United States.

SELECTED CULTIVARS: ◊ 'Alba': White flowers. ◊ 'Atrosanguinea' (*Agrostemma atrosanguinea*): Dark red flowers. ◊

Caryophyllaceae
(Pink family)

Lychnis viscaria (Viscaria viscosa, Viscaria vulgaris)
German Catchfly

FLOWERS: The small, dark purple or pink-purple (or rarely, white) flowers are borne, in 3- to 6-flowered, opposite, short-stalked clusters forming a panicle atop 18-inch stems, in late May and June. The flowers are bisexual or, sometimes, unisexual, with coronal scales at the juncture of the blade and claw, and are often emarginate.

LEAVES: The dark green leaves are evergreen, opposite, simple, entire, mostly basal, and petioled. They range from long-linear to lanceolate and are basally ciliate, parallel-veined, and about 6 inches in length.

PLANT CHARACTERISTICS: This hardy perennial usually grows in attractive clumps from 6 to 20 inches high. The stems range from glabrous to hairy above the nodes, but are viscid just below.

GARDEN VALUE: Although the plant has a limited life span and is harshly colored, it is often used in the perennial border and the rock garden. It may be grown also in the wild flower garden and in a naturalized area. It provides good cut flowers.

CULTURE: This plant flowers profusely in full sun and a light, well-drained soil. In a wet soil, it probably will not survive the winter.

Plant in spring. It transplants best if potted plants or young field-grown plants are used. Space 12 to 15 inches apart. Keep well-fertilized. Sow a few seeds in fall to provide for possible winter loss. The plant self-sows freely, which becomes a nuisance; this must be kept under control by eliminating those seedlings that are crowded or that extend beyond their range.

Divide in spring or fall. Sow seeds outdoors in April and transplant in May, or sow seeds where plants are to grow.

ADDITIONAL NOTES: *Lychnis viscaria* does not resemble the others in the genus. The common name refers to its viscid stems, from which insects cannot free themselves.

Single and double flowers are available in the trade.

SELECTED CULTIVARS: ◊ 'Alba': White flowers. ◊ 'Rosea': Pink flowers. ◊ 'Splendens': Rose-pink flowers. ◊ 'Splendens Flore-Pleno': Magenta flowers; a popular double-flowering form. ◊ 'Zulu': Red flowers. ◊

Lysimachia

consists of about 165 species of annual and perennial herbs or, rarely, shrubs, widely distributed throughout the temperate and subtropical regions of the world. The genus may have been named for King Lysimachus of Thrace, who first discovered its medicinal properties; or the name may have been derived from Greek words meaning "a release from" and "strife," implying peacemaking. Considered to have great medicinal properties, the plant's branches, when laid on the shoulders of quarreling oxen, have also been reported to cause instantaneous reconciliation. Supposedly, it could also dye the hair yellow, stop bleeding, and, when burnt, drive away serpents with its smoke.

The common name Loosestrife is used for the 2 genera *Lysimachia* and *Steironema*, both of the *Primulaceae* family.

Primulaceae
(Primrose family)

Lysimachia nummularia
Moneywort
Also known as Creeping Jenny, Creeping Charlie, Wandering Jenny, Wandering Sally

FLOWERS: Many small, bright yellow flowers about $\frac{3}{4}$ inch across are borne, solitary, axillary, or stalked, in June, and sporadically throughout the summer if the soil is kept moist. The flowers are bisexual and regularly symmetrical. The calyx is 5- or 6-lobed. The sepals are cordate or lanceolate, acute, and half as long as the corolla lobes. The corolla is rotate or campanulate, 5-lobed, oval, and sparsely dark-dotted.

LEAVES: The leaves are simple, opposite, and entire; they are dotted with black glands, are nearly orbicular, and grow up to 1 inch long on petioles $\frac{1}{2}$ to 1 inch long.

PLANT CHARACTERISTICS: This glabrous, prostrate perennial grows 3 to 4 inches high and forms large patches. The creeping or trailing, leafy stems may be as much as 2 feet long, rooting at the nodes throughout the entire length.

GARDEN VALUE: If it were not for its weedy tendency, *Lysimachia nummularia* would be a good ground cover for shady sites. The plant covers banks, rustic walls, and stumps and has been grown under apple trees to cushion fallen fruit. It can be effective on a wall, where it would be restrained naturally. The creeping stems can become a nuisance in the lawn; however, it brings a bright spot to dark corners where its invasive habit would not be a problem. *Lysimachia nummularia* is best suited to the wild flower garden or to naturalization along the edges of lakes, streams, and pools. It may also be grown in a hanging basket.

CULTURE: *Lysimachia nummularia* is easily cultivated and, generally, adapts to almost any situation. It will grow in sun or shade and prefers a moist, fairly rich soil; it will not thrive in a dry soil.

Plant in spring, and space about 15 inches apart. Add supplemental water during drought periods. Periodically divide or reduce the size of the clumps. It is usually propagated by cuttings, by division, or by seeds sown in the spring.

NATIVE HABITAT: Europe, but naturalized in the area from Newfoundland south to Virginia and west to Illinois.

SELECTED CULTIVARS: ◊ 'Aurea': Yellow foliage.

RELATED SPECIES:

Lysimachia clethroides: Gooseneck Loosestrife, Japanese Loosestrife. The white, ½-inch-wide flowers are borne, in very long, slender, curving racemes, in July and August. The unique racemes are bent into a gooseneck shape. The calyx is blackish, lanceolate, acute, and shorter than the corolla. The corolla lobes are ovate-lanceolate and obtuse. The flowers are borne on short pedicels and have subulate bracts. The leaves are opposite, ovate-lanceolate, and sessile; they taper at both ends and grow 3 to 6 inches long. In autumn, they are occasionally bronze-yellow in color. The plant is a pubescent perennial, reaching 2 to 3 feet in height. An old-fashioned garden plant, it tends to spread rapidly; it is usually planted in the wild flower garden or in a naturalized area where space is not a problem. The plant provides interesting cut flowers. It grows best in a semi-shaded site with moist soil. Its native habitat is China and Japan.

Lysimachia punctata: Garden Loosestrife, Yellow Loosestrife. The yellow flowers are borne, in axillary whorls, in June and early July. The corolla lobes are oval, denticulate, and glandular-ciliate. The leaves are whorled in 4's (sometimes 3's); they range from lanceolate, ovate to cordate-ovate and are subsessile. This erect perennial reaches up to 4 feet in height; it prefers partial shade and a soil rich in humus. Its native habitat is Europe, but the plant has become naturalized, to a limited extent, in the Eastern United States. ◊

Lythrum

consists of about 30 species of annual and perennial herbs, with 4-angled or winged stems, native to Europe and North America. The genus name *Lythrum* is derived from the Greek word *lythron*, meaning "black blood"; it refers either to the color of some of its flowers or to the styptic properties of some species.

Lythraceae
(Loosestrife family)

Lythrum salicaria
Purple Loosestrife
Also known as Purple Willow Herb, Red Sally, Spiked Loosestrife, Black Blood

FLOWERS: The rosy-purple flowers are about ¾ to 1 inch across and are borne, from July to August, in whorled clusters or solitary, in the axils of leafy, interrupted, slender spikes 1 to 3 feet long. The flowers are regularly symmetrical and bisexual. The calyx tube is cylindrical with 4 to 6 calyx lobes alternating with appendages 2 or more times the length of the calyx lobes. There are 4 to 8 obovate petals.

LEAVES: The leaves are usually opposite or in whorls of 3; they are entire, lanceolate, cordate at the base, and 2 to 3 inches long.

PLANT CHARACTERISTICS: This slender, rapidly spreading perennial grows 2 to 4 feet high. The erect stems are 4-angled, branched, tough, and woody and die back to the ground each year.

GARDEN VALUE: *Lythrum salicaria* is limited to extremely moist locations; it is best grown in a naturalized planting along a pond or stream, in a difficult, soggy terrain, or in a moist, sunny, semi-wild site. When it dominates a marshy meadow, it provides a dazzling display of summer flowers.

Today's hybrids are excellent plants about 3 feet high that can be grown in the perennial border or mixed border if the soil is sufficiently moist. Single specimens are attractive, but groups of 3 make an especially pleasing summer display. The plant provides good cut flowers.

CULTURE: The plant prefers full sun but tolerates light shade. It requires moist soil that may be either low or high in fertility.

Lythrum salicaria needs little attention. Space plants 15 to 18 inches apart. Keep them moist at all times and feed occasionally with a balanced fertilizer.

Because seedlings display some variation, the cultivars are usually propagated by division in spring or fall. Softwood cuttings root easily in summer.

ADDITIONAL NOTES: An old-fashioned plant, Shakespeare called it "Long Purples" and wrote that Hamlet's mother Gertrude made garlands from it.

Lythrum salicaria is the best species of the genus. Recent cultivars, being superior to the straight species, have increased its prestige.

NATIVE HABITAT: Found in marshes and wet meadows, where its vigorous growth chokes out other vegetation, *Lythrum salicaria* is native to Europe and has been naturalized in Australia and in North America.

SELECTED CULTIVARS: ◊ 'The Beacon': Fading red flowers on a weedy plant, not as good as 'Morden Gleam.' ◊ 'Brightness': Brilliant rose-pink flowers and dark foliage which turns scarlet-colored in the autumn. ◊ 'Dropmore Purple': Flowers vary in color from a clear purple in cool areas to a muddy dark purple in hot ones. The flowers are profusely borne from late June through September. ◊ 'Happy': Dark pink flowers atop an 18-inch-high plant. ◊ 'Morden Gleam': Deep carmine flowers and ruddy, juvenile foliage. ◊ 'Morden Pink': Rose-pink flowers borne on trim spikes nearly all summer; a bud sport of *Lythrum virgatum*, which originated at the Dominion Experiment Station in Morden, Manitoba, Canada. This excellent plant grows 3 feet high and has a nice, compact growth habit. Tolerant of both wet and drought conditions, it is excellent for the perennial or mixed border, the wild flower garden, and a naturalized area. The clumps increase rapidly in size. The plant is sterile and

produces no seeds. ◊ 'Robert': Rose-red flowering dwarf whose foliage turns scarlet in autumn. ◊ 'Roseum Superbum': Larger, brighter rose-colored flowers; a more robust plant about 4 to 6 feet high, which flowers from July to September. ◊

Macleaya

consists of 2 species of large perennial herbs with yellow sap, native to Eastern Asia. The genus name honors Alexander Macleay, the secretary of the Linnean Society in the early 19th century. Its former genus name *Bocconia* honors Dr. Paolo Bocconi, a Sicilian author and botanist.

Papaveraceae
(Poppy family)

Macleaya cordata (*Bocconia cordata*)
Pink Plume Poppy, Tree Celandine

FLOWERS: The numerous small, delicate, creamy-pink flowers are borne, in showy, terminal, erect panicles up to 1 foot long and raised high above the foliage, in July and August. The flower buds are bronze. The flowers are apetalous, bisexual, and regularly symmetrical. The 2-colored sepals fall early. There are 24 to 30 pollen-bearing stamens.

FRUIT: The fruit is a stalked capsule that resembles the flowers, continuing the plant's plume-like effect into the autumn.

LEAVES: The bold, elegant leaves are alternate, simple, and cordate; they are palmately lobed and veined, glaucous, and up to 8 inches across. The leaves are gray-green on the upper surface and have short, white, dense pubescence on the underside.

PLANT CHARACTERISTICS: This vigorously growing perennial grows 5 to 8 feet high and can spread enough to become a nuisance. A hardy plant, it has yellow sap and a spreading root system.

GARDEN VALUE: This tall, robust plant belongs in the large garden. Place it in the rear of the perennial border, among shrubbery, in a naturalized area, or in the wild flower garden. It is also used as an accent plant in an isolated bed to display its attractive, bold growth habit. It is a good background plant and looks attractive with trees and shrubs.

The flowers are good for cutting or for drying for winter use. To dry the flowers, cut the panicles when the flowers are $\frac{3}{4}$ open, hang in a dry, well-ventilated room until dried, then store until ready for use. The handsome seed pods are also used in dried floral arrangements.

CULTURE: Select a site in full sun that has soil of only average fertility, because the plant tends to spread quite rapidly in shade or in a rich soil. It will tolerate wet soils. Some protection from the wind helps in an open site.

Plant in spring, spacing about 2 to 3 feet apart. Keep the soil moderately moist. Because the plants are heavy feeders, apply a balanced fertilizer in early spring, and again during the growing season. Divide the large clumps after every 3 to 4 years of flowering.

The plant is propagated in the spring by seed or by dividing the clumps. Seeds germinate readily and will produce flowering plants the next season.

ADDITIONAL NOTES: The whole plant secretes a yellow sap which stains.

NATIVE HABITAT: Japan and China.

SELECTED CULTIVARS: ◊ 'Kelway's Coral Plume': Rich coral-pink flowers. ◊

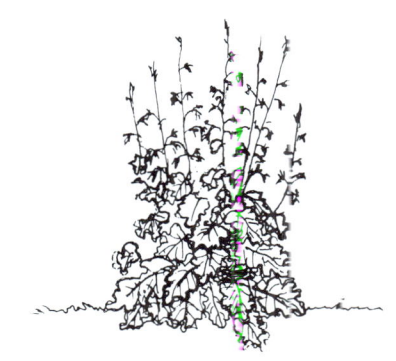

Mertensia

includes about 45 species of glabrous and hairy perennial herbs with thickened roots, native to the cooler regions of Asia, Europe, and North America, especially their woods and thickets. The genus was named for Franz Carl Mertens, a 19th-century professor of botany. It is one of the relatively few plants that bear flowers truly blue in color.

Boraginaceae
(Borage family)

Mertensia virginica
Blue Bells
Also known as Virginia Bluebells, Cowslip, Virginia Cowslip, Roanoke Bells

FLOWERS: The brightly colored flowers are borne in a congested, bractless, scorpioid cyme that is either racemose or panicled. The gracefully nodding, somewhat 1-sided clusters of 20 or more flowers are carried, axillary or terminal along the stems, in very early spring. The tubular or funnelform corolla is about 1 inch long; the calyx and the corolla are both 5-lobed. The flower buds and newly opened flowers are bright pink; the older flowers have a purple tube and a blue bell.

LEAVES: The handsome, light bluish-green leaves are alternate, simple, entire, and glabrous, often with pellucid dots. The basal leaves are petioled; the stem leaves are often sessile. The 2- to 5-inch-long leaves are oblong, oval or obovate in shape, obtuse at the apex, and conspicuously pinnately veined. Growth begins in very early spring, before shade beneath the trees becomes dense. The foliage dies back to the ground by June.

PLANT CHARACTERISTICS: This strong, erect, glabrous perennial usually grows in clumps 18 to 30 inches high. Several stout, succulent, many-branched stems with longitudinal ridges arise from the thickened rhizome.

GARDEN VALUE: When in flower, large masses of these plants are very effective; however, the void left in the garden after the foliage dies to the ground challenges the landscaper to place these plants carefully. They are quite handsome in various nooks and crannies of the rock garden, in the perennial border, and in the all-blue border. They are most often used in the wild flower garden and in a naturalized area such as a woodland setting, a moist bottomland, and along a ravine. In the perennial garden, place them among *Primula, Hosta, Vinca,* and ferns with spreading summer foliage to hide their summer barrenness.

CULTURE: *Mertensia virginica* prefers partial shade but grows well in full sun. In northern areas, the plant flowers better if it has full sun during early spring, such as that found under late-leafing deciduous trees or trees with filtered shade, and adequate moisture during spring. The plant needs a cool, moist, rich soil containing plenty of organic matter such as leaf mold, compost, or peatmoss.

Incorporate organic matter into the soil before planting. Plant in fall, place crowns 1 to 2 inches deep, and mulch well. The plants will not survive transplanting from the wild when in flower. Apply well-rotted compost in the spring and apply a balanced fertilizer regularly. For best performance, the plants need adequate moisture in spring. Because they are difficult to transplant, they should be left undisturbed once established.

Sow seeds in spring or fall. Divide or transplant from the wild only in early autumn. Root cuttings about 2 inches long can be collected in early fall, set shallowly into the ground, and protected during winter. Very early in spring, when the plant breaks dormancy, plant the seedlings and rooted cuttings in their permanent location. The random pink forms do not propagate true to type, suggesting that the coloration may be due to soil conditions.

NATIVE HABITAT: *Mertensia virginica* dwells along rivers, in bogs, and in rich woods and thickets. It is distributed over a large area from New York south to Tennessee and Alabama and west to Kansas.

SELECTED CULTIVARS: ◊ 'Alba': Rare, beautiful, fragile, white flowers. ◊ 'Rubra': Pink flowers. ◊

Monarda

consists of about 12 species of annual and perennial aromatic herbs native to North America and Mexico.

The genus was named for Nicolas Monardes, a Spanish physician and botanist of the 16th century. Its common name Oswego Tea was attached to the plant by John Bartram, who discovered that early settlers near Oswego, New York steeped its leaves to brew a tea. The common name Bee Balm was attached to the plant because bees are attracted to its fragrance. The Indians had their name, *O-gee-chee*, which meant "fiery flower."

Labiatae
(Mint family)

Monarda didyma (Monarda coccinea)
Bee Balm
Also known as Oswego Tea, Red Balm, Monarda, Bergamot, Horsemint, Fragrant Balm

FLOWERS: The fragrant, vivid scarlet-red flowers are usually borne in a solitary, terminal, or axillary, dense, head-like verticillaster 3 to 4 inches across. The verticillaster is subtended by many leafy, reddish bracts. The calyx is tubular, ½ inch long, narrow, 15-nerved, and 5-toothed; it has bristly teeth and is usually villous in the throat. The corolla tube is notched at the apex, is longer than the calyx, being up to 1¼ inch long, and is glabrous within. The

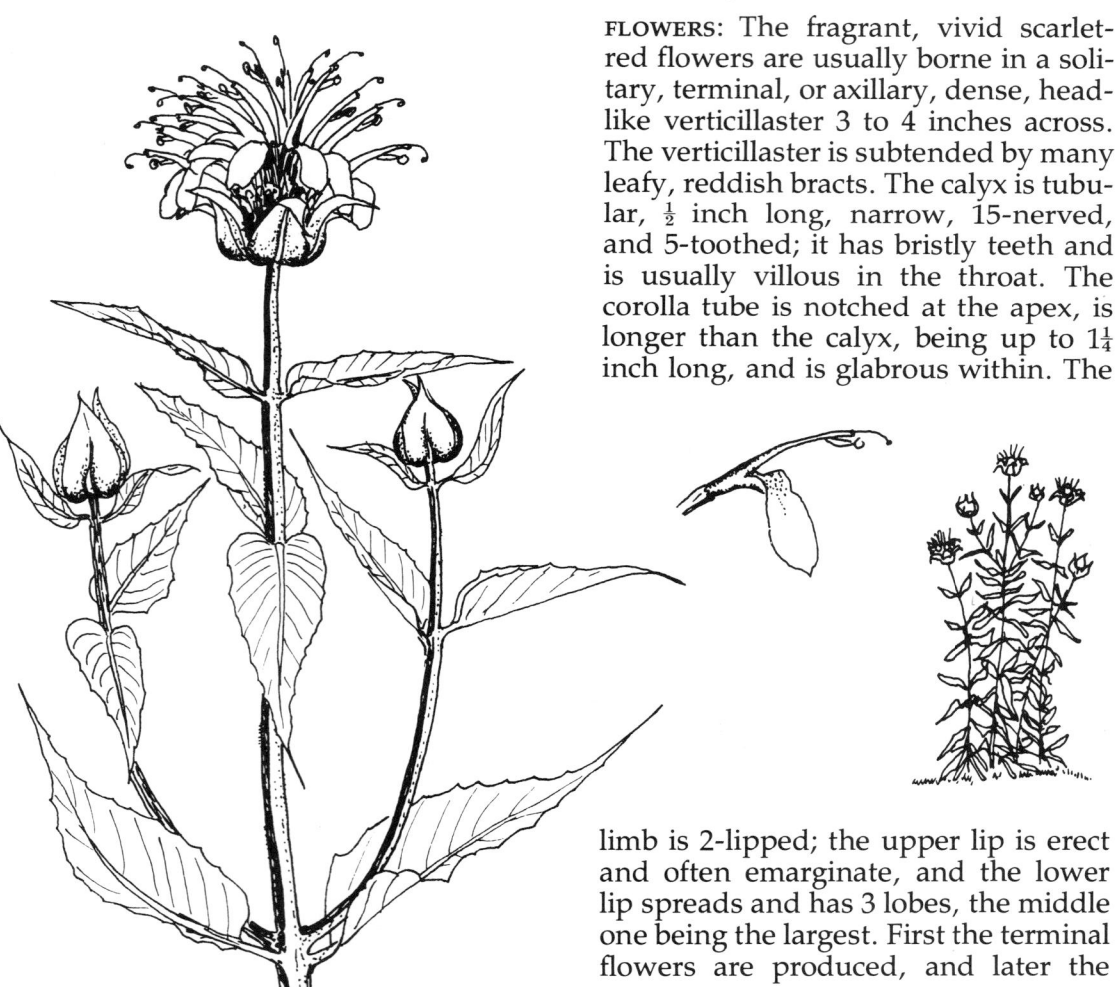

limb is 2-lipped; the upper lip is erect and often emarginate, and the lower lip spreads and has 3 lobes, the middle one being the largest. First the terminal flowers are produced, and later the secondary side shoots emerge to extend the flowering season from June to August.

LEAVES: The thin, dark green leaves are opposite, simple, ovate-lanceolate, and acuminate. They are serrate-dentate, sparsely pubescent, and up to 4 inches long, and they have short petioles.

PLANT CHARACTERISTICS: This rather coarse, erect, robust perennial, reaching to 3 to 4 feet in height, emits a delightful minty fragrance from both flowers and leaves. The stems are hollow, stout, and square in cross section. The plant may spread rapidly and become invasive by forming mats of shallow rhizomes.

GARDEN VALUE: *Monarda didyma* is a useful plant for areas too moist for other plants. Especially striking when massed, the plant should be used in bold groups in the wild flower garden or in a naturalized area, especially along a stream or beside a pond. Use as an accent in the perennial border, among evergreens, or in front of a shrub border. The plant combines well with *Anthemis*, *Heliopsis*, *Phlox*, *Delphinium*, *Iris siberica*, and *Hemerocallis*. It provides splendid cut flowers.

CULTURE: The plant grows best in a shaded, moist, well-drained site with abundant organic matter. In full shade the plant tends to get floppy and requires staking; if placed in adequate sun, this is not necessary. Cultivars will grow in full sun if provided with adequate moisture.

The plant is easily cultivated. Space 12 to 15 inches apart. Apply a balanced fertilizer regularly, cultivate, and supply water in dry periods. Remove faded flowers to prolong the flowering season. If neglected, the plants usually grow into irregular thickets of lean plants. Divide when the plants become crowded (under drier conditions they usually do not spread as rapidly), and place in newly prepared soil.

Seeds sown in the spring germinate well, but the flowers vary in color. Divide plants only in the spring. Propagate cultivars by division to maintain a particular color.

DISEASE PESTS: *Monarda didyma* is subject to mildew, especially on the leaves, on hot humid nights.

ADDITIONAL NOTES: One of our most brilliant native wild flowers, *Monarda didyma* was introduced to England in 1752 and was popular for over 100 years. The plant attracts bees, butterflies, and hummingbirds. It is added to some oils and perfumes to mask the odor of the chemicals. The cultivars are far superior to the straight species.

NATIVE HABITAT: Moist woodlands and stream banks from Quebec and Michigan south to Tennessee and Georgia.

SELECTED CULTIVARS: ◊ 'Adam': Rose-red flowers. ◊ 'Blue Stocking': Violet-purple flowers. ◊ 'Cambridge Scarlet': Bright crimson flowers. ◊ 'Croftway Pink': Rich rose-pink flowers.◊ 'Granite Pink': Pink flowers atop a 10-inch-high plant. ◊ 'Mahogany': Deep red-brown flowers. ◊ 'Salmonea': Delicately shaded salmon-pink flowers in large heads. ◊ 'Salmon Queen': Salmon-pink flowers. ◊ 'Snow Maiden': White flowers. ◊ 'Snow Queen': White flowers in large heads. ◊ 'Sunset': Dark red flowers. ◊ 'Violet Queen': Violet flowers. ◊

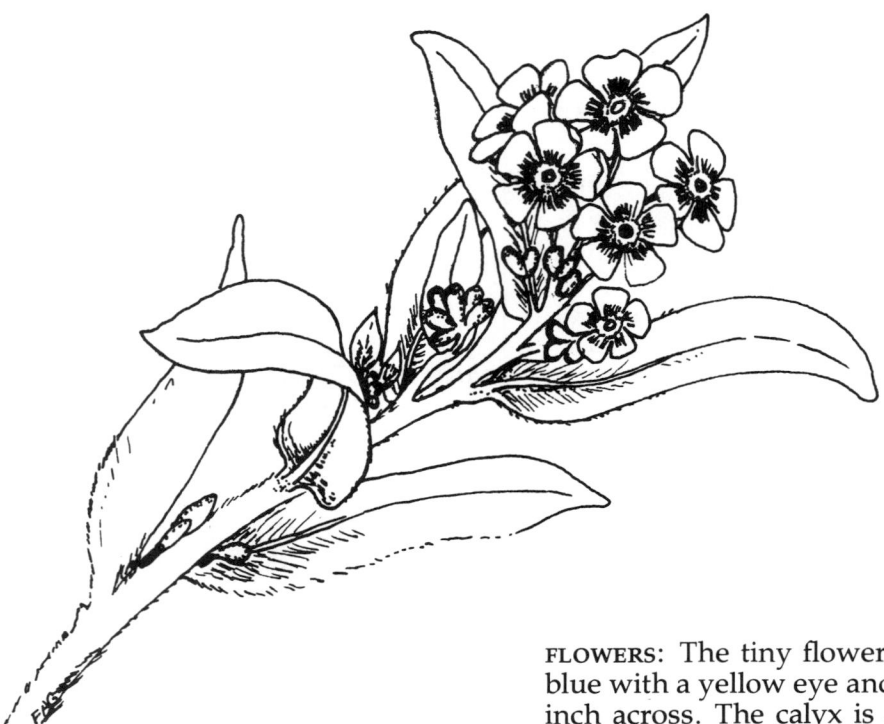

Myosotis

consists of about 50 species of hairy annual, biennial, and perennial branching, diffuse, or erect herbs native to the Temperate Zone. The genus name *Myosotis* is from a Greek word meaning "mouse-ear" and refers to the shape of the leaf.

Boraginaceae
(Borage family)

Myosotis sylvatica (Myosotis oblongata)
Garden Forget-me-not, Woodland Forget-me-not

FLOWERS: The tiny flowers are usually blue with a yellow eye and are about $\frac{5}{16}$ inch across. The calyx is 5-lobed with hooked hairs; the corolla is salverform and 5-lobed on a pedicel nearly twice as long as the calyx. The flowers are borne in May on bractless, 1-sided, long, loose, terminal inflorescences or branched scorpioid cymes.

LEAVES: The gray-green leaves are evergreen, alternate, simple, and entire; they range from oblong-linear to oblong-lanceolate. The basal leaves are petioled; the stem leaves are sessile.

PLANT CHARACTERISTICS: This 1-foot-tall, erect, hairy plant is branched, hirsute, and green or light gray in color. It is an annual or biennial and is often not too hardy.

GARDEN VALUE: *Myosotis sylvatica* is an old-fashioned garden favorite, which is used in the perennial border, the rockery, the wild flower garden or in a naturalized area. It is effective with *Hyacinthus*, *Tulipa*, and *Viola*, providing an undermat of blue. Frequently found in porch boxes and hanging baskets, it provides excellent flowers for cutting.

CULTURE: This plant will grow practically anywhere but prefers light shade and a cool, rich, moist soil.

Planting is safest in early spring; space plants about 9 to 12 inches apart. Cultivate regularly. Apply a balanced fertilizer regularly and mulch with compost around the plants in the spring. Mulch plants to provide winter protection. Divide after 3 or 4 years of flowering.

Propagate plants from seeds sown in March to flower the following year. It is best to divide the plant in late summer; the cuttings root easily in summer. However, the plant self-sows so readily that, once it is planted, it spreads.

ADDITIONAL NOTES: The perennial species of *Myosotis* are doubtlessly secondary to the biennial *Myosotis sylvatica*. It varies when cultivated and is often confused in the trade; the plant known as *Myosotis dissitiflora* is actually *Myosotis sylvatica*.

NATIVE HABITAT: Europe and Asia, sparsely naturalized in North America.

SELECTED CULTIVARS: ◊ 'Alba': White flowers. ◊ 'Compacta': Dense, compact form. ◊ 'Fischeri': Bluish-purple flowers on a dwarf plant. ◊ 'Oblongata Perfecta': Large blue flowers, borne earlier than those of the straight species. ◊ 'Robusta Grandiflora': Large flowers on a vigorous plant. ◊ 'Rosea': Rose flowers. ◊ 'Stricta': Erect branches. ◊

Oenothera

includes about 80 species of stemless, decumbent, or erect annual and perennial herbs widely distributed throughout the Western Hemisphere. Generally speaking, the genus includes Evening Primroses (which usually flower in the evenings) and Sundrops or Suncups (which usually flower in the day); however, the plants do not always behave in this manner.

The genus name *Oenothera* is derived from the Greek words *oinos* meaning "wine," and *thera*, meaning "taste," because according to legend the roots of certain species induce a thirst for wine.

Onagraceae
(Evening Primrose family)

Oenothera missouriensis
Sundrops
Also known as Missouri Primrose, Ozark Sundrops

FLOWERS: The few, very showy, clear yellow flowers often redden with age. They can swell 3 to 5 inches across and are borne, solitary and axillary in panicles, from June to August. Lightly fragrant and cup-shaped, the flowers have 4 sepals and 4 petals which are 1 to $2\frac{1}{2}$ inches long and very broad; they open in the evening. The calyx has a tube with 4 lobes.

LEAVES: The thick, dull, gray-green leaves are alternate and simple. They are entire or remotely denticulate, acuminate, narrowly lanceolate or oval, and 5 inches or less in length, narrowing to a petiole.

PLANT CHARACTERISTICS: This 9- to 12-inch-high perennial forms an attractive, low, broad mound. The stout, erect, reddish, strigose stems trail and ascend at the tips.

GARDEN VALUE: *Oenothera missouriensis* is best used in the wild flower garden or a naturalized area. An occasional specimen may be placed in the perennial border or the large rock garden or

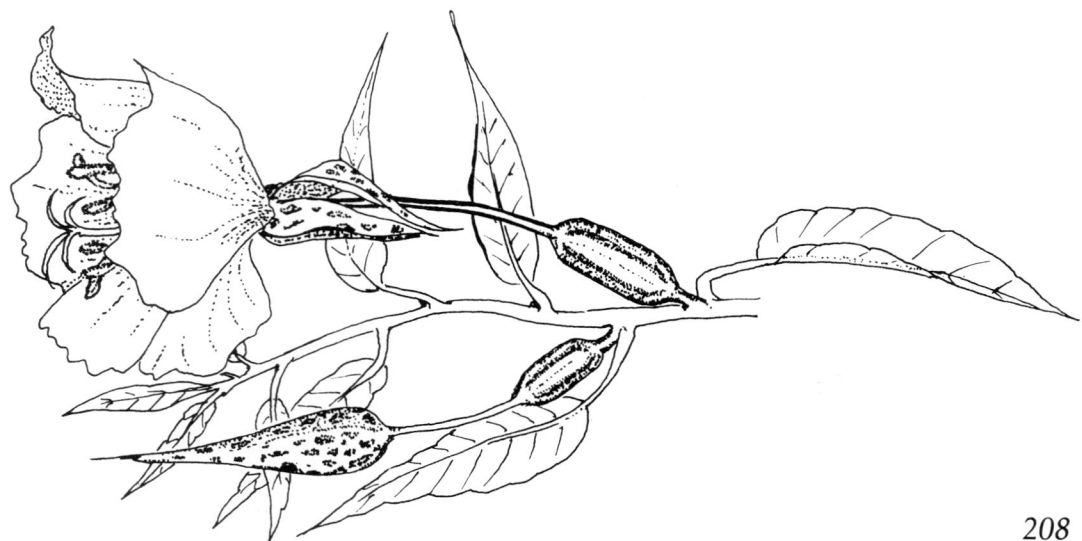

208

it may be used in mass in front of the shrub border or in the dry wall. It provides excellent cut flowers.

CULTURE: The plant prefers full sun but tolerates light shade. It grows best in a light, moderately rich, deep, well-drained soil. Without good drainage in winter, it will winter-kill.

Plant in either fall or spring, spacing plants 12 to 15 inches apart. Water during prolonged dry periods. Apply a balanced fertilizer in the spring, and cultivate regularly. Remove faded flowers to prolong the flowering period. In northern areas, apply a light mulch in the winter. When plants become overcrowded they should be divided.

Seeds may be sown in spring or fall. The cultivars should be propagated by cuttings in late summer.

ADDITIONAL NOTES: Moths are attracted to this night-flowering species, and the flowers attract bees.

NATIVE HABITAT: From Missouri west to Kansas and south to Texas.

RELATED SPECIES: *Oenothera tetragona* (*Oenothera fruticosa* var *youngii*): Young's Sundrops. The bright lemon-yellow, cup-shaped, diurnal flowers are borne from June to August. A few 1 to 1½-inch-long flowers are borne along the upright spike. The shiny, green leaves are firm, lanceolate, 4 inches long, and slightly glaucous. The erect plant grows 2 to 3 feet high. It is usually a perennial but may be biennial. *Oenothera tetragona*, often confused in the trade with *Oenothera fruticosa*, is weedy and unassuming, but it is colorful when in flower. Often used as a filler, it should not be used in the perennial border. Grow this plant in the wild flower garden or in a naturalized area. Its native habitat is the Eastern United States.

◁ 'Fyrverkerii': Numerous 2-inch golden-yellow flowers, borne on a 1-foot-high plant; the flower buds and young stems are a glossy reddish-brown.
◁ 'Illumination': Fine yellow flowers on a 12-inch-high plant; excellent for the rock garden or the perennial border. ◊

Paeonia

consists of about 33 species of stout-to-coarse perennial herbs and diffuse shrubs, native to the northern temperate region of Eurasia and to Western North America.

The genus name honors Paeon, a Greek physician of myth; Pluto is said to have changed Paeon into a flower to repay him for his successful cure after Hercules defeated Pluto.

Paeoniaceae
(Peony family)

Paeonia lactiflora (Paeonia albiflora)
Peony
Also known as Chinese Peony, Common Garden Peony

FLOWERS: The large, showy, fragrant flowers, usually white but often in shades of red and pink, are 4 to 8 inches across and are borne, singly or in groups at the ends of stems, in May and June. The flowers are bisexual and regularly symmetrical. There are 5 persistent, large, leaf-like sepals, and 5 to 10 very showy petals. The numerous stamens are golden yellow and spirally arranged.

LEAVES: The large, handsome leaves are alternate and compound. The lower leaves are bi-ternate; the leaflets range from elliptic to lanceolate and are entire or occasionally lobed and red-veined, with rough-scabrous margins. The foliage changes from reddish shoots in April to lustrous green leaves in summer, becoming occasionally crimson-tinted in autumn, until a hard frost kills the foliage to the ground.

PLANT CHARACTERISTICS: This coarse perennial is rhizomatous with thick, tuberous roots often 12 to 15 inches deep. The glabrous stem grows 2 to 3 feet high and usually branches to bear 2 to 5 flowers. Very hardy and tolerant of sub-zero temperatures, *Paeonia lactiflora* flowers each year on shoots that rise from the crown; it dies completely to the ground with the onset of winter.

GARDEN VALUE: Hardy, easily cultivated, fragrant, and beautiful, this plant is a prized perennial. It is an all-time favorite of the perennial garden; it also is used in the shrub border or as a hedge consisting of a single cultivar. Plant in clumps of 3 or in mass among other plants. Plant behind spring-flowering bulbs or intersperse with annuals and medium-height *Dahlia* for summer flowers and *Chrysanthemum* transplanted when in flower for autumn coloration. Or group with *Phlox* or *Hosta* for contrasts of foliage and time of flowering. The plant also combines well with *Iris, Papaver, Heuchera,* and climbing roses. *Paeonia lactiflora* supplies excellent cut flowers. All forms are cultivated commercially for cut flowers.

CULTURE: The plant grows best in a deep, rich, well-drained soil with abundant organic matter. The fleshy roots require excellent drainage. Full sun is recommended, although a lightly shaded site prevents the delicately tinted cultivars from fading. Select the site carefully; the heavy flowers should be protected from winds. Also avoid sites where radiating heat from adjacent buildings could result in premature spring foliage that would be susceptible to injury by late frosts.

Plant divisions that have 3 to 5 eyes during August or early September. The "eye," the reddish bud at the top of the tuberous roots, should be set about 1 inch below the soil surface; if planted too deeply, the plant will not flower. Space plants at least 2 to 3 feet apart. Usually, 3 years is required for the plant to become fully established.

The plant is a heavy feeder. Apply a balanced fertilizer around the plant and work it into the soil in spring. Supplemental watering is required in the first year to establish the root system. Mulch in summer to eliminate weed competition and to retain moisture; mulch also in winter to protect against freezing and thawing when establishing new plantings.

Disbudding is recommended; it is a technique whereby large, single flowers are produced. All the buds on the stem except the top or crown bud are removed. Thus the energy of the plant goes into producing a few superior flowers. As soon as the axillary buds are visible, roll each one off with your finger to eliminate a visible stump of scar.

The plants should be staked to prevent the heavy flowers from being bruised by rain and wind and from touching the ground. Before the buds begin to open, place stakes carefully into the ground away from the fleshy roots. Use a soft twine that does not cut the stems or foliage, or use a circular ring on stakes that allows the plant to maintain its natural form.

Remove the faded flowers to prevent seed development, which utilizes the carbohydrates that would otherwise go into manufacture of food for storage, in the roots, to produce the following year's flowers. Leave all the foliage on the plant. When the foliage dies in the autumn, cut plants back to the ground; burn the cut stems and leaves to destroy disease organisms that overwinter on the dead foliage. Once established, do not disturb plants until obvious deterioration is visible. The planting may last 20 years or more.

It may take 5 to 7 years to produce a flowering plant from seed; commercial growers may use tissue culture in coming years to reduce the time required to produce a saleable-sized plant. Division is the usual method of propagation: dig the plants in August or early September; using a sharp knife, cut the heavy root mass into sections with 3 to 5 eyes and prune the old roots back to at least 6 inches. The grafting of cultivars is usually accomplished in late summer or early fall by grafting the eyes of 1 cultivar onto a piece of tuber of another that has had all the eyes removed. Store the tuber over winter, and plant outside in the spring.

COMMON PAEONIA PROBLEMS: If the plant fails to flower, it could be because the plant has too much shade or because the location is poorly drained. Other reasons for a non-flowering plant include: fewer than 3 buds on a root; cutting back the foliage before it turned brown the previous fall; eyes planted deeper than the 1 inch recommended; and a late spring frost, which may kill the flower buds.

Anthracnose produces lesions on stems, leaves, bud scales, and flower petals. The infection usually occurs when the leaf and stem tissue are quite succulent.

Botrytis attacks stems, buds, and leaves and is most prevalent in cool, humid weather during midsummer. Early in the spring, young stems attacked at ground level wilt and fall over. Young buds turn black and fail to mature. Older buds turn brown and become covered with a brown mass of fungal spores. Usually the stalks become rotted for a short distance below the diseased buds. Irregular dark brown spots occur in the leaves.

Phytophthora blight is less common than *Botrytis* but has similar symptoms. The stems, leaves, and buds develop dark brown or black leathery lesions. Infection spreads from buds down the stem. The stem rots at ground level and falls over.

To prevent the dissemination of disease during the growing season, cut off all wilting or rotting stems at the soil surface and immediately burn the diseased material. To prevent the overwintering of disease organisms, cut off and burn all the foliage after it turns brown in late fall.

ADDITIONAL NOTES: For fresh flower arrangements, cut the flowers when the buds swell half-way open and quickly plunge the stems into deep water. Leave at least 3 full sets of leaves on the stem to produce food reserves. Cut flowers can be kept in the refrigerator for 1 to 3 weeks.

Ants are prevalent on the plants during the flowering period. They are not harmful to the flowers but feed on the sweet sap or the buds.

Paeonia was cultivated in China over 2,500 years ago. Much breeding has been done in the genus; today hundreds of *Paeonia* cultivars, which stem primarily from *Paeonia lactiflora,* range in color from deep red, through red, pink, white, and cream, to yellow and may be up to 6 inches across. The American Peony Society recognizes 5 basic types of flowers: the single or Chinese, Japanese, anemone, semi-double, and double.

The single or Chinese peonies have a single row of 5 or more broad petals surrounding a prominent cluster of yellow stamens. Japanese peonies have long-curved petals; anemone peonies have broad central petals. Semi-double peonies have broad central petals; doubles have central petals as wide as the outer petals.

NATIVE HABITAT: Tibet, China, Siberia.

SELECTED CULTIVARS: ◊ 'Bowl of Cream': Huge creamy-white flowers. ◊ 'First Lady': Deep-pink flowers, borne early. ◊ 'Krinkled White': Ruffled, white, single flowers with a yellow center. ◊ 'Moonstone': Double creamy-pink flowers. ◊ 'Raspberry Sundae': Raspberry-colored flowers. ◊ 'Scarlet O'Hara': Fiery-red flowers. ◊ 'Sweet 16': Soft pink flowers.

For other fine cultivars, consult your specialty catalogues and growers. ◊

Paeoniaceae
(Peony family)

Paeonia suffruticosa (Paeonia moutan, Paeonia arborea)
Tree Peony

FLOWERS: The huge, showy, fragrant flowers range in color from rose-pink to white, with a magenta blotch at the base of the petals; they often reach 6 to 8 inches across. The flowers are borne, singly or in small groups at the ends of stems, in May and June. The flowers are bisexual and regularly symmetrical. There are 5 persistent, large, leaflike sepals and 5 to 10 very showy petals. A mature plant may bear from 25 to 50 flowers each season.

LEAVES: The handsome, large, deciduous leaves are alternate and bipinnate. The leaflets are deeply divided, acute, and glabrous.

PLANT CHARACTERISTICS: This hardy, coarsely branched, deciduous shrub grows 3 to 6 feet high and 3 to 6 feet across. It grows slowly and is as permanent as the herbaceous *Paeonia lactiflora*.

GARDEN VALUE: Although less common than the herbaceous perennial, *Paeonia suffruticosa* is an aristocrat of the garden. It is best used as an accent near an entrance or in a large perennial border or shrub border. It is often used in formal plantings.

CULTURE: Even though its requirements are similar to those of *Paeonia lactiflora*, *Paeonia suffruticosa* is somewhat more difficult to grow. Select a site protected from wind and exposed to sun for several hours during the day, preferably in early morning and late afternoon. The hot midday sun tends to fade the flowers.

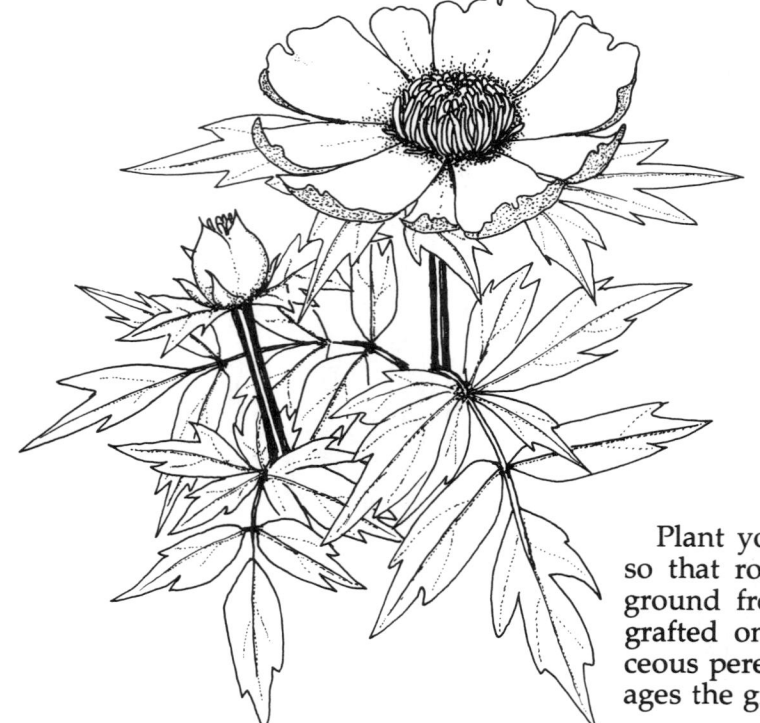

Plant young plants in mid-October so that roots can develop before the ground freezes. Because the plant is grafted onto the roots of the herbaceous perennial, deep rooting encourages the grafted portion to develop its own roots. The graft is the union of the stem and root and is usually visible by a ridge in the stem and a different bark texture.

Water occasionally to keep the soil moist. Mulch in summer. Apply lime annually to an acid soil. Provide a protective mulch of hay or leaves during the first winter. Prune only to remove old or weak wood.

Seed propagation demands great patience because the seedlings do not flower for 5 or 6 years. Old plants can be divided in August but must be protected during winter. The usual method, however, is to graft the plants; a scion of a *Paeonia suffruticosa* cultivar is grafted onto a 4- to 6-inch root of *Paeonia lactiflora*. Grafted plants should flower well in 3 years.

DISEASE PESTS: *Paeonia suffruticosa* is subject to *Botrytis*, *Anthracnose*, and *Phytophthora* blight. (See the discussion under *Paeonia lactiflora*.)

ADDITIONAL NOTES: *Paeonia suffruticosa* was greatly honored and cherished in its native habitat. In China around 500 A.D. it was regarded as a sacred plant and considered a great treasure in the Imperial Gardens. It was also prominent in the art and literature of the time. Strictly protected from export, the plants reached Japan and, finally, England about 1787.

Many named cultivars are available: single- or double-flowered in colors of white, pink, red, purple, and light yellow. Some hybrids were developed by crossing *Paeonia suffruticosa* with *Paeonia lutea* and other species; the three types are known as European, Japanese, and *Lutea* Hybrids.

NATIVE HABITAT: Northwestern China.

SELECTED CULTIVARS: ◊ 'Age of Gold': Double or semi-double, soft creamy-gold flowers. ◊ 'Argosy': Single, clear yellow flowers with red blotches at the base. ◊ 'Banksii': Double pink flowers. ◊ 'Bijou de Chusan': Pure white creamy-centered flowers. ◊ 'Canary': Single, bright yellow flowers. ◊ 'Fragrance Maxima Plena': Fragrant, double, salmon-pink flowers. ◊ 'Gesseka': Large, double white flowers with crinkly petals. ◊ 'Higurashi': Bright crimson flowers. ◊ 'Hinode-no-seki': Large, double rosy-pink flowers. ◊ 'Howgan': Double, delicate, flesh-pink flowers. ◊ 'Kamada-fugi': Double wisteria-blue flowers. ◊ 'Reine Elizabeth': Fully double rose flowers. ◊ 'Rimpo': Purple-black flowers. ◊ 'Souvenir de Ducker': Double deep violet flowers with a red tinge. ◊ 'Suisho Haku': Semi-double white flowers. ◊ 'Tamafuyo': Semi-double, light rosy-pink flowers. ◊ 'Uka-tama': Large, nearly double satiny-maroon flowers. ◊ 'Yachiyo Tsubaki': Salmon-pink-centered flowers, fading to light pink at the edge. ◊ 'Yo Yo-no-homare': Semi-double flesh-pink flowers.

RELATED SPECIES: *Paeonia tenuifolia*: Fernleaf Peony, Fringed Peony. The deep crimson flowers are 2 to 4 inches across and appear to rest on the leaves. The flowers are borne, singly and erectly, in May and June. The fern-like leaves are ternate and glabrous; the leaflets are dissected into narrowly linear segments. This densely leafy plant grows 1 to 1½ feet high, forming rounded clumps. Its native habitat ranges from Southeastern Europe to the Caucasus.

◊ 'Laciniata' (*Paeonia laciniata*): Taller plant with broader leaflet segments. ◊ 'Plena': Double flowers. ◊ 'Rosea': Rose-red flowers. ◊

Papaver

includes over 50 species of annual and perennial herbs and, rarely, subshrubs, with milky sap. These plants are primarily native to Europe.

The genus name *Papaver* is of Latin origin and means "poppy." The common name Poppy is believed to be derived from the Anglo-Saxon word *popig,* meaning "sleep," because a drink made from the seeds of certain species induces sleep; early poets also associated poppies with sleep.

Papaveraceae
(Poppy family)

Papaver orientale
Oriental Poppy

FLOWERS: The flaming scarlet flowers have a blackened base at the center and are borne, solitary on a long, single-flowered scape, in late May and June. The flowers are 6 to 10 inches across, bisexual, and regularly symmetrical. The plump, hairy buds arise nodding before opening into the spectacular flowers. The flowers have 2 deciduous sepals. There are 4 to 6 elegant petals, or sometimes double that number; they are crumpled in bud, obovate or ovate, up to 3 inches long, and have a tissue-paper texture. The many prominent stamens are black and bear pollen.

FRUIT: The fruit is an obovate capsule with a flat disc.

LEAVES: The light green, basal leaves are pinnately dissected, hispid, coarsely-toothed, and lobed. The lobes are lanceolate or oblong. The upper lobes are coarsely serrate; the lower ones are incise-dentate. The foliage dies to the ground and disappears in early July, leaving large vacant spots in the garden. The new foliage begins growth in September and persists during the winter.

PLANT CHARACTERISTICS: This robust perennial has fleshy roots and grows 3 to 4 feet high.

GARDEN VALUE: *Papaver orientale* is a popular, flamboyant perennial for the garden. Place the spectacular plants so that they are not combined with others that flower at the same time, or place them near other plants whose flower colors do not clash. Use this plant in the perennial or mixed border, in the wild flower garden, or in a naturalized area. Select neighboring plants carefully, choosing those that will spread and fill the void left after the foliage dies. *Gypsophila, Anemone* hybrids, *Phlox,* dwarf forms of *Aster,* and most *Hemerocallis,* as well as many annuals, are suggested plants.

The flowers are attractive in fresh arrangements. Cut the flowers just as the buds begin to open and immediately char the stems thoroughly with a match, before placing them in warm water. The dried fruit is attractive in dried flower arrangements.

CULTURE: The plants prefer full sun or partial shade and a rich, very well-drained soil. A soggy soil in the winter encourages root rot.

Plant in late summer. Transplanting garden plants in the spring usually severs the long tap root, causing the plants to wilt; however, container-grown plants may be transplanted in the spring. Space the plants about 15 to 18 inches apart, and set the root crown 3 inches deep. Allow plenty of room for the plants to develop. Keep them fairly moist, but not wet, when in flower; after flowering has ceased, keep the plants dry. Because they are heavy feeders, apply a balanced fertilizer annually in early spring. Tall plants usually need staking in windy sites. Do not move established plants. Cultivate in late summer, taking care to avoid damage to the roots.

Divide the clumps in late July or August when the plants are dormant. Propagate the cultivars by division or by root cuttings taken in late summer, and cut into lengths of about 4 to 6 inches. Sow seeds soon after ripening. Cultivars do not grow true from seed and usually revert to less desirable types.

218

ADDITIONAL NOTES: Although the genus contains several popular annuals, *Papaver orientale* is the most popular perennial for the garden. All species have a milky sap. The culture of the annual *Papaver somniferum*, the opium poppy of Greece and the Middle East, is strictly controlled in the United States. The drug is derived from the milky sap that oozes from the young capsules. The seeds have no narcotic properties and produce a valuable oil.

NATIVE HABITAT: The Mediterranean region and Persia; the plant is widely grown and sometimes naturalizes.

SELECTED CULTIVARS: The many modern cultivars are superior to the straight species; they range in color from white through various shades of pink to dark red. Many have a black blotch at the base of each petal. The flowers vary from 6 to 12 inches across. The hairy-leaved plants grow from 1½ to 4 feet high. Most white forms are not as long-lived and often become gray from their own pollen. ◊ 'Barr's White': Large, pure white flowers with a purplish-black blotch at the base of the petals. ◊ 'Beauty of Livermore': Oxblood-red flowers. ◊ 'Big Jim': Popular oxblood-red flowers. ◊ 'Carmine': Red flowers with black splotches. ◊ 'Carnival': Base of petal is ivory; upper half, nasturium red. ◊ 'Carousel': Snow-white flowers with border of red. ◊ 'Crimson Pompom': Medium-sized, orange-scarlet flowers. ◊ 'Curlilocks': Deep rose-pink flowers. ◊ 'Harvest Moon': Clear orange flowers. ◊ 'Lavender Glory': Deep lavender flowers with large black basal spots. ◊ 'Mahogany': Mahogany flowers, not easy to grow well. ◊ 'Maiden's Blush': A 2-inch-wide pink band around the edge of white flowers. ◊ 'Marshall Vonder Glotz': Large pure white flowers. ◊ 'May Curtis': Watermelon-red flowers. ◊ 'Mrs. Perry': Salmon-pink flowers with an apricot tinge. ◊ 'Olympia': Bright red flowers. ◊ 'Pandra': Clear salmon-pink flowers with a blood red spot at the base. ◊ 'Pinnacle': Petals fading from light pink on the edge to white in center. ◊ 'Salmon Glow': 8-inch-wide flowers that vary from orange to salmon. ◊ 'Show Girl': Large pink crinkled petals with a white center. ◊ 'Snowflame': Petals a brilliant orange-red in the upper portion, white in the lower portion; the width of the white ring varies in the individual flowers. ◊ 'Spring Morn': Flesh-pink flowers blending to a deeper pink in the center. ◊ 'Watermelon': Pink flowers. ◊

Phlox

comprises 60 species of annual and perennial herbs and subshrubs primarily native to North America.

The genus name is derived from the Greek word *phlego*, meaning "flame," which refers to the brilliance of the flowers. This name was once applied to the plants in the *Lychnis* genus.

Polemoniaceae
(Phlox family)

Phlox divaricata (Phlox canadensis)
Wild Sweet William
Also known as Spring Phlox, Blue Phlox, Canadian Phlox, Woodland Phlox, May Phlox.

FLOWERS: The showy, mildly fragrant, pale violet-blue flowers are 1 inch across and are borne, erect and solitary or in terminal cymes subtended by leafy bracts on 12- to 15-inch stems, from April to June. The flowers are bisexual, regularly symmetrical, and convolute in bud. The 5-lobed calyx has narrow, subulate lobes. The salverform corolla has 5 flat, spreading lobes, usually notched or erose.

LEAVES: The leaves are opposite (with the upper leaves sometimes alternate), simple, entire, up to 2 inches long, ranging from ovate to oblong, and mostly acute. The leaves of the sterile shoots are usually more rounded than those of the flowering stems.

PLANT CHARACTERISTICS: This attractive perennial grows 8 to 18 inches high and has a shallow root system. The stems are slender and pubescent. The basal stems are prostrate and stoloniferous and slowly spread into colonies.

GARDEN VALUE: Use the plant in front of the border, in a naturalized area, in the wild flower garden, or as a woodland ground cover. It is very effective when planted in mass and featured with *Narcissus, Tulipa,* and *Pulmonaria*.

CULTURE: The plant will grow in full sun if there is sufficient moisture during the growing season. It prefers a semi-shaded site with a moist, humus soil. When grown in full sun and dry soil, the plant becomes partially dormant, loses many of its leaves, and looks unsightly.

Plant in fall or spring. Space plants 8 to 12 inches apart. Mulch them to protect the shallow roots. Shear, after flowers have faded, to stimulate branching and to initiate new foliage that is attractive all season. To prevent deterioration, divide these plants every 2 or 3 years. This is best done in late summer.

This plant is most easily propagated by division of the plant in spring; divide clumps that have flowered for 2 years. Stem cuttings gathered in summer will produce flowers the following season.

DISEASE PESTS: *Phlox divaricata* is occasionally affected by rust or mildew.

NATIVE HABITAT: From Quebec to Michigan and south to Florida.

SELECTED CULTIVARS AND VARIETIES: ◇ 'Alba': A good form with pure white flowers. ◇ var. *laphamii:* Deeper blue flowers with rounded, obtuse, entire corolla lobes and ovate leaves; a stronger-growing plant, with a longer flowering season than the species. ◇

Polemoniaceae
(Phlox family)

Phlox paniculata (Phlox decussata)
Garden Phlox

Also known as Perennial Phlox, Summer Phlox, Tall Phlox, Phlox

FLOWERS: The bright pink-purple flowers are 1 inch across and are borne, in large, terminal cymes, from late June to September. The flowers are bisexual, regularly symmetrical, and convolute in bud. The calyx is 5-lobed; the corolla is salverform, with 5 flat, spreading lobes.

LEAVES: The thin leaves are opposite (with the upper leaves usually alternate), simple, oblong-lanceolate, acute or acuminate, and up to 6 inches in length.

PLANT CHARACTERISTICS: This clump-forming perennial has stiff, erect, nearly woody, glabrous stems that grow 2 to 5 feet or more in height.

GARDEN VALUE: *Phlox paniculata* is an immensely popular garden flower. Plant it in groups of 3 in the large perennial garden or mixed garden for indispensable summer color. The attractive plants are compatible with most garden flowers, and they contrast well with *Heuchera, Gypsophila,* and *Limonium.* The flowers are excellent in fresh flower arrangements, but they drop individual florets each day.

CULTURE: *Phlox paniculata* is easily grown. The plant grows best in full sun, but light shade is not detrimental. The bluish-flowered forms tend to deteriorate into a lilac color under direct hot sun. The plant needs a deep, well-drained, fertile soil with ample organic matter and applications of superphosphate to help deep rooting.

Plant in spring or fall, and space about 18 to 24 inches apart. When the new growth in the spring is about 4 to 6 inches high, thin each clump to 4 or 5 shoots spaced 4 to 6 inches apart, to encourage large flower clusters. Because the plants are heavy feeders, apply a balanced fertilizer annually in spring. Provide a mulch during the summer to keep the soil moist and water well during drought periods. Cut off faded flower clusters immediately below the lowest flowers to promote lateral branching and the development of additional flower buds. Removal of the faded flowers before seed formation prevents seedlings (the

seedlings usually revert to the undesirable magenta color of the species), which crowd out the superior cultivars. Mulch to provide winter protection against low temperatures in northern areas. Clumps need to be divided every 4 or 5 years and replanted after the ground is cultivated and composted organic matter is added. Division is necessary because the plants become overcrowded.

Seeds may be sown in winter or spring; however, if sown in spring, they must be stratified first. Seedling plants usually need 3 years to produce flowering plants. Garden Phlox are usually not propagated by seed. Plants may be divided in spring or fall; replant only the new outer shoots. Sections of root cuttings about 2 inches long are taken in fall and placed, upright or horizontal, under ¾ inch of a light soil medium in the cold frame or the cool greenhouse; they flower in 2 years.

INSECT AND DISEASE PESTS: During hot, dry weather red spiders may seriously infect plants growing in poor, dry soil. Gradually yellowing leaves with brown spots on the lower surfaces usually indicate the presence of these pests.

Aster yellows, leaf spot, rust, and powdery mildew are diseases that may severely affect *Phlox*.

NATIVE HABITAT: *Phlox* is one of our finest native plants. Its native habitat is the area from New York to Georgia, and west to Illinois and Arkansas. The plant was introduced to Europe in the 19th century.

SELECTED CULTIVARS: The late Capt. B. Symons-Jeune of England was responsible for many great advances in hybridization of the species. The cultivars

have a wide range of superior colors of white, salmon, scarlet, purple, and lilac and usually bear a distinct "eye" at the base of the petals. The flowers are larger and are borne in fuller, larger panicles, up to 12 to 14 inches high and 6 to 10 inches across. The flowering period is extended from late June to September. ◊ 'Ann': Mauve flowers. ◊ 'Brigadier': Brick-red flowers. ◊ 'B. Symons-Jeune': Rose-pink flowers with red eyes. ◊ 'Charles Curtis': Variable—from some sources it may be identical with 'Red Glory,' from others it may be identical with 'Spitfire.' ◊ 'Dodo Hanbury Forbes': Clear pink flower heads, up to 16 inches across. ◊ 'Dresden China': Soft shell-pink flowers on a 2-foot-high plant. ◊ 'Elizabeth Arden': Elegant soft pink flowers. ◊ 'Fairy's Petticoat': Pale pink flowers with darker pink eyes. ◊ 'Leo Schlageter': Flowers vary from crimson to scarlet. ◊ 'Lilac Time': Large, clear lilac-blue flowers. ◊ 'Mary Louise': Snow white flowers. ◊ 'Orange perfection': Salmon-orange flowers. ◊ 'Progress' ◊ 'Royalty': Rich dark purple flowers. ◊ 'San Antonio': Plum flowers; the color does not fade. ◊ 'Sir John Falstaff': Huge salmon florets about 1¾ inches across. ◊ 'Spitfire': Flamboyant orange-scarlet flowers. ◊ 'Star Fire': Brilliant red flowers. ◊ 'Vintage Wine': Rich claret-red flowers. ◊ 'White Admiral': Enormous, white, fragrant flower heads and side branches. ◊ 'Windsor': Salmon-tinted-rose flowers. ◊

Polemoniaceae
(Phlox family)

Phlox subulata
Moss Pink or Moss Phlox
Also known as Mountain Pink, Flowering Moss, Ground Pink

FLOWERS: The flowers range from red-purple to violet-purple, pink, or white, occasionally have a contrasting "eye" at the base of the petals, and are ¾ inch across. They are borne in small terminal cymes or panicles atop short, flowering branches. The flowers are bisexual, regularly symmetrical, and convolute in the bud; they are profusely borne from March to May. The calyx is 5-cleft; the corolla is salverform, with 5 shallowly notched, spreading, cordate lobes.

LEAVES: The prickly leaves are evergreen, opposite (with the upper leaves sometimes alternate), and simple and range from linear to subulate. They are ciliate, stiff, crowded or fascicled (except on the flowering stems), and up to 1 inch in length.

PLANT CHARACTERISTICS: This prostrate, semi-evergreen perennial grows 6 inches high and forms a dense hummock, often 2 feet across. It has a sparse, shallow root system.

GARDEN VALUE: A prized old garden plant, used for colonizing and to provide a mass of early spring flowers, *Phlox subulata* creates a carpet-like mat. Use it for edging, on walls, in the rock garden, as a ground cover, and on a slope. Its foliage complements *Colchicum*, which flowers without leaves in autumn.

CULTURE: The plant is easy to grow in a sunny site on almost any well-drained soil. It prefers a coarse, dry, porous soil with abundant gritty material.

Plant in the spring or fall, about 8 to 12 inches apart. Cultivate frequently to reduce competing weeds. Shear off the tops of the plants about halfway after the flowers have faded, to encourage new foliage and a second sparse flowering. Divide occasionally.

The plants may be propagated by layering or division, after flowering in the spring, or by late fall cuttings allowed to root in a sandy medium in a cold frame. Because the root system is shallow and sparse, the foliage should be cut back halfway before the divided plants are replanted.

INSECT AND DISEASE PESTS: In hot weather, red spiders may become a problem on plants that are not kept watered. Gray spotting on the undersides of the leaves, which gradually turn yellow, usually indicates the presence of this pest.

Rust, usually indicated by brownish-black spots on the foliage, can also damage the plant.

NATIVE HABITAT: Its native habitat is in sandy, open woods from New York to Michigan, and south to North Carolina. *Phlox* is another of our fine native plants and has been widely cultivated.

SELECTED CULTIVARS: Many named selections have been developed. These superior plants often bear flowers 1 inch across in clear colors of white, lavender, blue, pink, and red. ◊ 'Alexander's Beauty': Pink flowers. ◊ 'Alexander's Surprise': Pink flowers. ◊ 'Atropurpurea': Rose-purple flowers with a crimson ring. ◊ 'Blue Hills': Blue flowers. ◊ 'Brilliant': Magenta-colored flowers. ◊ 'Chuckles': Pink flowers. ◊ 'Emerald Cushion': Pink flowers; a smaller plant. ◊ 'Intensity': Cerise-colored flowers. ◊ 'Lilacina': Lilac flowers; a compact plant. ◊ 'Rosea' ◊ 'Scarlet Flame': The first true red-flowered cultivar. ◊ 'Schneewitchen': Abundant tiny white flowers; a very compact mat with silky gray-green foliage. ◊

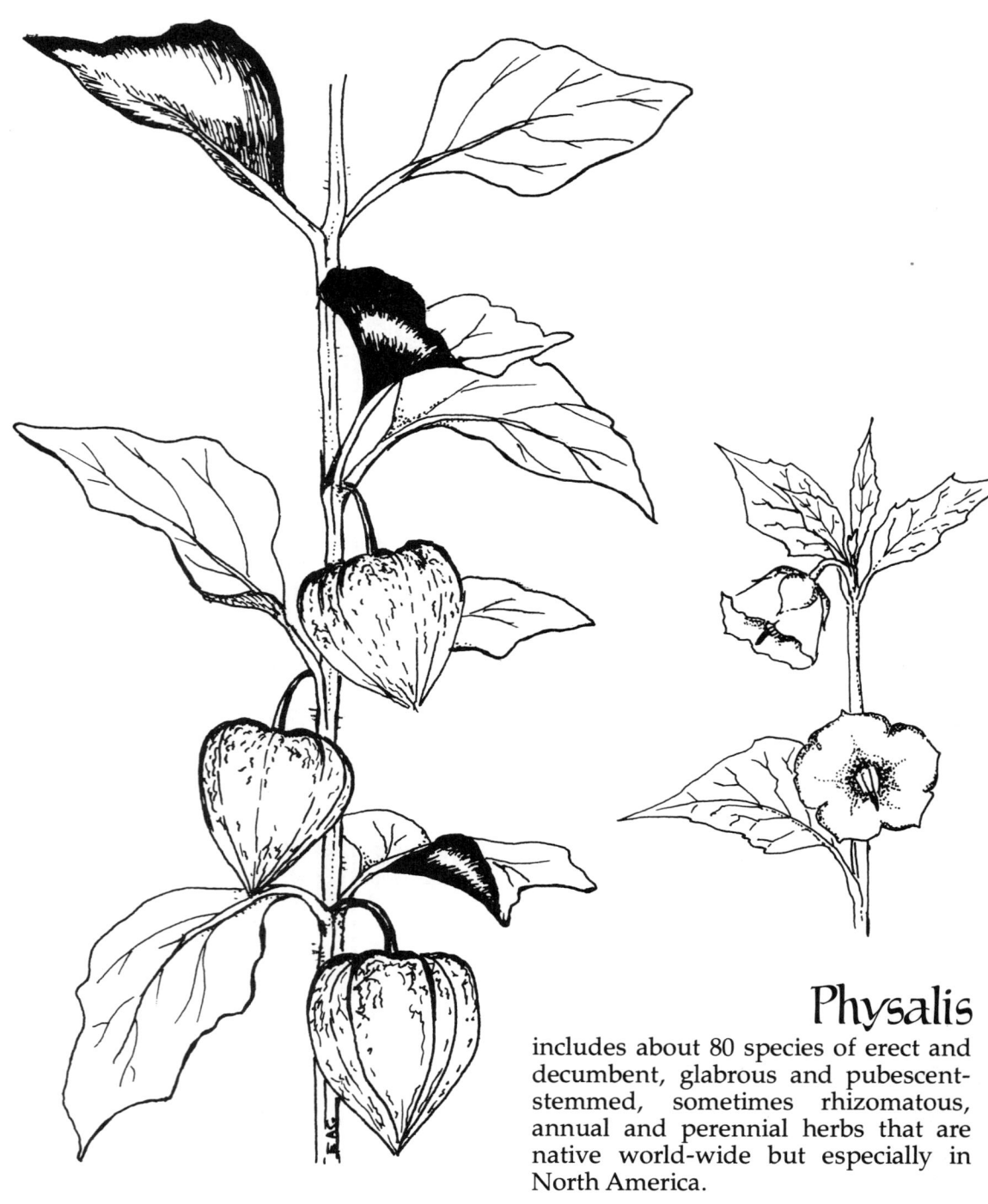

Physalis

includes about 80 species of erect and decumbent, glabrous and pubescent-stemmed, sometimes rhizomatous, annual and perennial herbs that are native world-wide but especially in North America.

The genus name comes from the Greek name *physa*, meaning "bladder," and refers to the enlarged calyx.

Solanaceae
(Nightshade family)

Physalis alkekengi
Chinese Lantern Plant

Also known as Alkekengi, Winter Cherry, Japanese Lantern, Strawberry Tomato, Strawberry Ground Cherry, Bladder Cherry

FLOWERS: The small, inconspicuous white flowers are $\frac{1}{2}$ inch across, pedicelled, and usually borne, solitary in leaf axils, and obscured by the foliage, in August. The bisexual flowers have a 5-toothed, persistent calyx that becomes a 2-inch, bladder-like lantern covering the ripened fruit. The corolla is white, hairy, and deep yellow in the center; it is rotate and usually 5-lobed.

FRUITS: The showy fruits are globose, red berries enclosed in an inflated, vermillion-red, 2-inch-long calyx. They are edible and have many seeds.

LEAVES: The leaves are alternate and simple, range from ovate to ovate-rhombic, are entire or undulate, and grow up to 3 inches long. The petiole widens at the top.

PLANT CHARACTERISTICS: An ornamental perennial sometimes grown as an annual, *Physalis alkekengi* has long rhizomes and can become weedy in the garden. It usually grows 12 to 18 inches high but can attain 2 feet in height. The straight, glabrous or glabrescent stems usually zigzag, and are mostly simple, angled, and setose.

GARDEN VALUE: *Physalis alkekengi* may be grown in the vegetable garden, the cut-flower garden, or in the perennial border. Set the plants apart, or in a confined space, because they spread and tend to overwhelm other ornamental plants.

This plant is often grown for its fruit; it is edible and is used fresh or in preserves, pickles, pies, salads, or jams. The fruit also may be gathered when ripe and dried for winter bouquets. To prepare the lanterns for winter bouquets, cut the stems just as the lanterns begin to turn red, remove the leaves, hang the stems upside down in a shaded, airy location until dry, and then store until ready to use.

CULTURE: The plant prefers full sun and a warm site and will grow in almost any rich garden soil.

Space plants 2 feet apart. Keep them from spreading into other planting beds; the long creeping rhizomes are difficult to eliminate. The plants can remain undisturbed indefinitely.

Divide clumps in spring or fall. Plants may be propagated from root division in fall or spring. Seeds may be sown in spring. All these methods will produce fruit the first growing season.

ADDITIONAL NOTES: *Physalis alkekengi* is the only species used as an ornamental in the perennial garden.

NATIVE HABITAT: From Southeastern Europe to Japan.

SELECTED CULTIVARS: ◇ 'Gigantea': Larger fruits. ◇ 'Montrosa': ◇

Physostegia

includes about 15 species of perennial herbs native to North America.

The genus name *Physostegia* is of Greek derivation, from *physa*, meaning "bladder," and *stege*, meaning "covering," and refers to the inflated fruiting calyx. The plants were often confused with the plants in the *Dracocephalum* genus commonly called Dragonhead and came to be known as False Dragonhead. Because each flower, if twisted on the stem, remains in that position, the plant has also been called Obedient Plant.

Labiatae
(Mint family)

Physostegia virginiana
False Dragonhead
Also known as Virginia Lion's-head, Obedient Plant

FLOWERS: The flowers, ranging from purplish-red to rosy-pink and lilac, are 1 inch long and are borne, in dense, terminal, solitary or leafless panicled spikes, from late July through August. The flowers are arranged on the 8- to 10-inch spikes in 4 widely-spaced horizontal rows and are subtended by small lanceolate bracts. The calyx is tubular-campanulate, 10-nerved, viscid-glandular, and short-toothed, with the tube much longer than the calyx. The corolla is up to $1\frac{1}{4}$ inches long and is inflated at the mouth, with a 2-lipped limb. The upper lip is erect and nearly entire; the lower lip is 3-lobed.

LEAVES: The dark green leaves are opposite, simple, lanceolate, acute, serrate, and 3 to 5 inches long. The upper leaves are reduced and sessile; the lower leaves are petioled. The leaves are prominent on the stem up to the inflorescence.

PLANT CHARACTERISTICS: The glabrous perennial forms large clumps, usually 3 to 4 feet high. The stems are simple, erect, slender, and square in cross section. The plant is stoloniferous and tends to be weedy.

GARDEN VALUE: *Physostegia virginiana* flowers at a time when most other plants have finished flowering. Place an occasional plant toward the rear of the perennial border or in the shrub border. Mass the plant in the wild flower garden or in a naturalized area. It grows well beside a stream bank. The plant provides plenty of long-stemmed flowers for cutting.

CULTURE: *Physostegia virginiana* is a carefree plant that performs equally well in moist and dry soils, in sun and partial shade. When grown in full sun and light soil it has stiffer stems and spreads less. It is an excellent plant for a problem wet spot.

This plant needs very little attention. Plant in spring or fall and space 2 feet apart. Keep soil moist at all times; occasionally apply a balanced fertilizer.

Taller plants with brittle stems are top heavy and may need staking in windy areas. Divide plants after 2 years of flowering to keep them neat.

Divide in October or in spring. Sow seeds in spring; seedlings show wide variability.

INSECT PESTS: Red spider can seriously affect the plant.

ADDITIONAL NOTES: *Physostegia virginiana* is the only species of the genus that is a common garden plant. Externally, the genus more resembles the *Scrophulariaceae* (Figwort) family than the *Labiatae*.

NATIVE HABITAT: Moist, slightly acid soil from New England to Minnesota and south to the Carolinas and Texas.

SELECTED CULTIVARS: ◊ 'Alba': Pure white flowers borne on erect 12-inch stems in July and August; the plant grows 1 to 3 feet high and does not creep. ◊ 'Bouquet Rose': Rose flowers borne from August to October. ◊ 'Rosy Spire': Rose-pink flowers atop $3\frac{1}{2}$-foot spikes in early September; a cross between 'Grandiflora' and 'Vivid.' ◊ 'Summer Glow': Pale pink flowers borne earlier, atop 3- to 4-foot spikes. ◊ 'Summer Snow': Translucent white flowers, grows up to 2 feet high. ◊ 'Vivid': Claret-colored flowers, grows to 2 feet high, and flowers in September; discovered in a St. Louis nursery around 1935. ◊

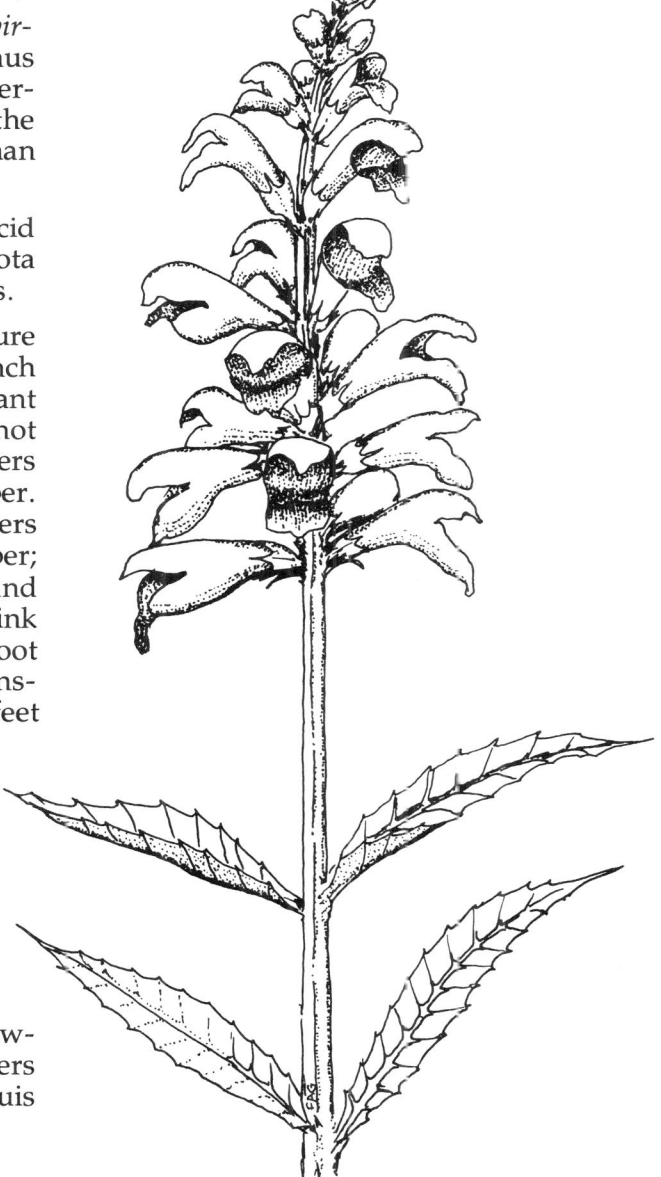

which swell before the starry petals unfold. The buds pop resoundingly when squeezed.

Campanulaceae
(Bellflower family)

Platycodon grandiflorus
Balloonflower
Also known as Chinese Bellflower, Japanese Bellflower

FLOWERS: The unique flower buds inflate to resemble a balloon before they open. The 5-lobed corolla, ranging from broadly campanulate to nearly rotate, may be 2 to 3 inches across and in colors from deep blue to pale blue, lilac, white, and blue-tinged white; the calyx tube is adnate and 5-lobed. The flowers are borne erect, solitary, and terminal, from late June to early September, on 2- to 3-foot stems.

LEAVES: The glossy, dark green, leathery leaves are sparse, often opposite or whorled, subsessile, and glabrous. They range from ovate to ovate-lanceolate and are 2 to 3 inches long and sharply dentate.

PLANT CHARACTERISTICS: This hardy, long-lived perennial forms clumps 2 feet across and 2 to 3 feet high. Glaucous, glabrous, erect, and densely branched, the plant does not spread.

GARDEN VALUE: *Platycodon grandiflorus* is at home in the perennial border, the mixed garden, the all-blue garden, the wild flower garden, and the shrub border and in a naturalized area. Used singly or in small groups, this plant is a

Platycodon

consists of 1 species. The genus name is derived from the Greek words *platys*, meaning "broad," and *kodon*, "bell," and it refers to the shape of the flower. The popular name Balloonflower describes the inflated balloon-like buds, good companion for *Phlox, Hemerocallis* (yellow cultivars), and *Anthemis*. The *Platycodon* also extends the season of its relative *Campanula* into late summer. *Platycodon grandiflorus* is considered to have the purest blue of the ornamental perennial plants, and its flowers are excellent in floral arrangements.

CULTURE: Either full sun or partial shade is satisfactory. Partial shade is better for the pink cultivars. The plant prefers light, moist, well-drained soil with abundant organic matter. Unable to tolerate poorly-drained soils, or stagnant, damp ground, especially in winter, the plant suffers from winter rot and suddenly dies.

Plant in spring; barely cover the crown with soil, and space plants 12 to 18 inches apart. Take care in spring cultivation to avoid damaging the dormant crown; the plants come up late in the season and could inadvertently be damaged. Occasionally apply a balanced fertilizer. Cultivate regularly around the plants. Stake plants early in the season to avoid breaking the stems. Removal of the faded flowers before seed development lengthens the flowering season. In autumn the old stems should not be cut away; the plant should be allowed to die back naturally to avoid injury to the crown. Old clumps do not spread.

New plants are easily started from spring-sown seeds, but they require 2 years of growth before flowering. Because of the fleshy rootstock, division should be done only in the spring. Cut off sections of the thick crown, including buds and roots; some will survive. Dust the cut surfaces with a fungicide. New plants are rather slow to develop, but after 2 or 3 years they will perform rewardingly.

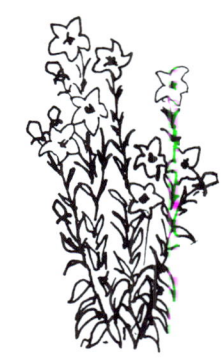

ADDITIONAL NOTES: *Platycodon grandiflorus* was first placed in the *Campanula* genus and later in the *Wahlenbergia*. These genera are closely related.

To use the flowers for fresh arrangements, either char the stems well with a match or allow them to wilt freely before placing in deep, warm water.

NATIVE HABITAT: Eastern Asia and Japan.

SELECTED CULTIVARS AND VARIETIES: All modern cultivars stem from variations found within this species. Double-flowering forms with petaloids in the throat have been developed. ◊ 'Albus': White flowers. ◊ 'Autumnalis': Late-flowering form. ◊ 'New Alpine': Blue flowers; breeds true from seeds. ◊ 'Shell Pink': Soft shell-pink flowers which are best when grown in semi-shade.

Double forms (created by Alex Cummings from crosses of a chance double blue with single flowers in all colors) are tolerant of drought conditions. ◊ 'Bristol Bells': Lavender flowers. ◊ 'Bristol Bride': White flowers. ◊ 'Bristol Blush': Flesh-pink flowers. ◊ 'Bristol Bluebird': Deep blue flowers.

◊ var. *mariesii*: Marie's Balloonflower. Large, bright blue flowers on a compact dwarf from Japan, which is not over 18 inches tall. It has cultivars 'Albus' and 'Roseus.' ◊

Polemonium

comprises nearly 25 species of annual and perennial herbs that are often viscid and rhizomatous. The plants are native to Europe, Asia, South America, and the Western regions of North America.

The origin of the botanical name of the genus is uncertain. Some botanists suggest that it is named after the philosopher Poleman; others suggest it is derived from the Greek word *polemus*, meaning "war." According to Pliny, 2 kings claimed that they had discovered the merits of the plant and engaged in war to resolve the issue.

Polemoniaceae
(Phlox family)

Polemonium caeruleum
Jacob's-ladder
Also known as Greek Valerian, Charity

FLOWERS: Many dainty sky-blue flowers, $\frac{3}{4}$ to 1 inch across, are borne, nodding and solitary-to-capitate in terminal or axillary cymes atop 1-foot stems, from May to July. The flowers are bisexual and regularly symmetrical. The calyx is campanulate, with 5 acute, oblong lobes; the corolla is campanulate to funnel-form, with 5 obovate lobes. The 5 stamens alternate with the corolla lobes.

LEAVES: The handsome, feathery, apple-green leaves are alternate, odd-pinnate, and leathery and are borne on petioles 6 or more inches in length. The leaflets number 19 to 27 and are lanceolate-to-elliptic and entire; the terminal leaflet is distinct. The stem leaves are smaller and short-petioled or sessile near the top of the stem.

PLANT CHARACTERISTICS: This plant grows 15 to 36 inches high and 12 to 15 inches across and forms a dense, tufted hummock that is attractive all season. It is among the first perennials to initiate new growth in the spring. The erect stems are slightly pubescent, somewhat glandular, and angled.

GARDEN VALUE: *Polemonium caeruleum* is a plant associated with cottage gardens. Its interest lies in its blue flowers and attractive compound foliage. Use the plant in the rock garden, in front of the perennial or shrub border, in the wild flower garden or in a naturalized area. It contrasts well with *Primula*, *Doronicum*, and *Narcissus*. The flowers are long lasting when used in fresh arrangements.

CULTURE: The plant is tolerant of a

wide variety of garden conditions. It grows well in full sun but prefers partial shade. Moist, rich, well-drained soils that contain abundant humus produce the most attractive plants.

Plant in spring, spacing about 18 inches apart. Supply additional water in dry periods; where the moisture is sufficient, the neat foliage remains attractive and decorative throughout the summer. The plant self-sows freely. Divide to prevent overcrowding after 3 or 4 years of flowering.

It is relatively easy to propagate. Sow seeds in spring, take cuttings of cultivars in midsummer, or divide the clumps in late summer. The color of the blue flowers will vary considerably in seedlings.

ADDITIONAL NOTES: The common name of the species, Jacob's Ladder, refers to the pinnate leaves on long leafy stalks, which resemble a ladder.

NATIVE HABITAT: Europe.

SELECTED CULTIVARS: Most yellow-flowering forms are disappointing. ◊ 'Blue Pearl': Shiny, clear cobalt-blue flowers with yellow eyes; a floriferous cultivar, flowering in May. ◊

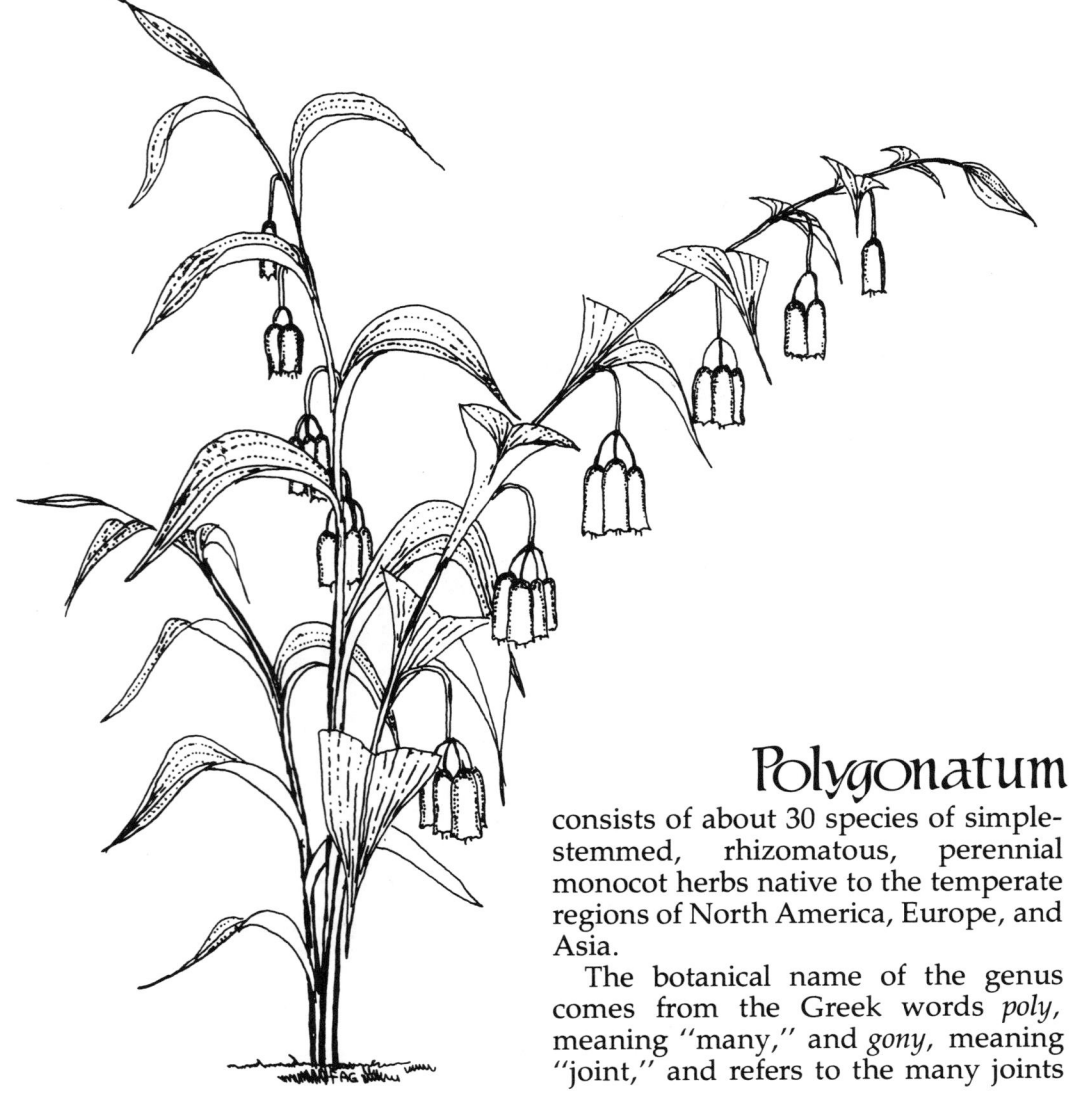

Polygonatum

consists of about 30 species of simple-stemmed, rhizomatous, perennial monocot herbs native to the temperate regions of North America, Europe, and Asia.

The botanical name of the genus comes from the Greek words *poly*, meaning "many," and *gony*, meaning "joint," and refers to the many joints of the rhizomes. The common name, Solomon's Seal, refers to the seal or scar on the rhizome, which occurs when the annual stem arising from the rhizome at that point dies.

The genus often resembles *Smilacina*, False Solomon's Seal, which has similar foliage but bears its flowers and fruits on a terminal panicle.

Liliaceae
(Lily family)

Polygonatum biflorum
Small Solomon's Seal

FLOWERS: Small greenish-white flowers are borne, on 1 to 3 usually 2-flowered peduncles, in late May and June. The flowers are borne pendulously from the leaf axils along unbranching, arching stems. They are bisexual and regularly symmetrical. The perianth is cylindrical, ½ to 1 inch long, and has 6 short, greenish lobes.

FRUIT: The shiny, glaucous, blue-black berries have several seeds and mature in autumn.

LEAVES: The leaves are alternate, sessile, and range from ovate to elliptic-lanceolate; they are strongly veined, and 2 to 4 inches long and 1½ to 2 inches across. The underside is pale and pubescent; the upper side is glabrous. The foliage is attractive throughout the growing season.

PLANT CHARACTERISTICS: This simple, graceful perennial grows from 8 inches to 3 feet high, with arching stems. It spreads by fleshy, knotted, horizontal rhizomes but does not become weedy.

GARDEN VALUE: *Polygonatum biflorum* makes a good perennial border plant, but it looks most appropriate in a naturalized area. Grow it in the wild flower garden, under large trees, or among shrubs. It is a good ground cover in a shady, wooded area. The plant combines well with *Trillium, Digitalis, Convalaria*, medium-sized ferns, and other spring wildflowers. The plant provides interesting cut flowers that last well.

CULTURE: The plant grows best in a deep, cool, moist, rich soil in a shaded site. It prefers partial shade but will tolerate full sun if it has adequate moisture.

Plant in the spring. Place the rhizomes horizontally, 1 to 2 inches below soil level and about 1 foot apart. Keep the plants watered at all times. Apply a balanced fertilizer in early spring and during the summer. Cultivate around the base of the plant, taking care to prevent damaging the rhizomes.

Propagate by division in early spring or fall. Seeds may be sown in autumn.

ADDITIONAL NOTES: *Polygonatum biflorum* is the most common species of the genus. *Polygonatum canaliculatum* is similar and native to the same area.

NATIVE HABITAT: From New Brunswick to Michigan, and south to Florida and Texas. ◇

Primula

consists of about 400 species of usually scapose perennial herbs, sometimes short-lived, usually spring-flowering, and primarily native to the Temperate Zone of the Northern Hemispere (although a few species are native to the Southern Hemisphere).

The botanical name *Primula* is derived from the Latin word *primus,* for "first," which refers to the very early flowering of the genus.

Primulaceae
(Primrose family)

Primula X polyantha
Polyantha Primrose

FLOWERS: The fragrant many-colored flowers, about 1 inch across, are borne, in many-flowered, erect umbels or solitary on scapose stems 8 to 15 inches high, in April and May. The flowers may be single or double, striped or blended, in combinations of white, gray, ivory, yellow, pink, lavender, blue, purple, salmon, burnt orange, copper, bronze, chestnut, and brown. The flowers are bisexual and regularly symmetrical. The calyx is 5-toothed. The corolla has 5 spreading lobes ranging from entire to 2-lobed, and is funnelform or salverform; the corolla tube is longer than the calyx. The bracts of the involucre are sometimes leaf-like.

LEAVES: The long, light green leaves are basal, evergreen, simple, entire, and obovate, tapering to winged petioles. The foliage remains handsome all season. The leaves pucker between the veins, giving them wavy margins.

PLANT CHARACTERISTICS: This 6- to 12-inch perennial forms large clumps. Sometimes short-lived, the plant prefers a cool moist climate.

GARDEN VALUE: *Primula* has much to offer in shaded areas. Use it in the rock garden, in the forepart of the perennial border, as an edging, and in the porch box and permanent landscape container. Single plants are seldom effective; they should be grown in mass. Place the plants under flowering dogwoods (*Cornus florida*), redbuds (*Cercis canadensis*), crabapple or apple trees (*Malus* species). Mass or naturalize them in the wild flower garden, in an open woodland, along a shaded brook, or as carpeting in a shrub border. The fragrant, brightly colored flowers last well when cut.

CULTURE: *Primula X polyantha* grows best in partial shade and a rich, well-drained, acid soil, with plenty of humus to retain the moisture during

236

summer. If the shade is too dense, abundant foliage and few flowers are produced.

Set plants out in spring or early fall, or, very carefully, when in full flower. Space plants about 6 to 12 inches minimum apart for a massed effect. Mulch in spring with composted organic matter. During the growing season, apply a balanced fertilizer; water well during drought periods, because the plants will not survive high summer temperatures if allowed to become dry; and cultivate frequently, taking care to avoid damage to the shallow roots. Provide a winter mulch. The plants should be divided after 4 years of flowering and immediately after flowering has ceased.

Divide plants in September or in spring; the cultivars must be reproduced asexually to maintain a specific color. Seeds may be sown as soon as ripe for the best germination. Pre-treat spring-sown seeds in the refrigerator for 2 months, with several periods of alternate freezing and thawing.

INSECT PESTS: When grown in the sun, this plant is subject to red spider attacks. They occur most frequently in hot dry summers, as well as when grown in a nutrient-deficient soil. The underside of the leaf becomes rusty-colored, and the upper side chlorotic.

ADDITIONAL NOTES: *Primula* X *polyantha* is probably the most easily cultivated and most popular hybrid group of the hardy *Primula* in the United States. It is available in nearly every color, tint, and shade.

Primula X *polyantha* includes all the polyanthus types. *Primula elatior* (Oxslip), *Primula veris* (Cowslip), and *Primula vulgaris* (Common Primrose) have been interbred for many years.

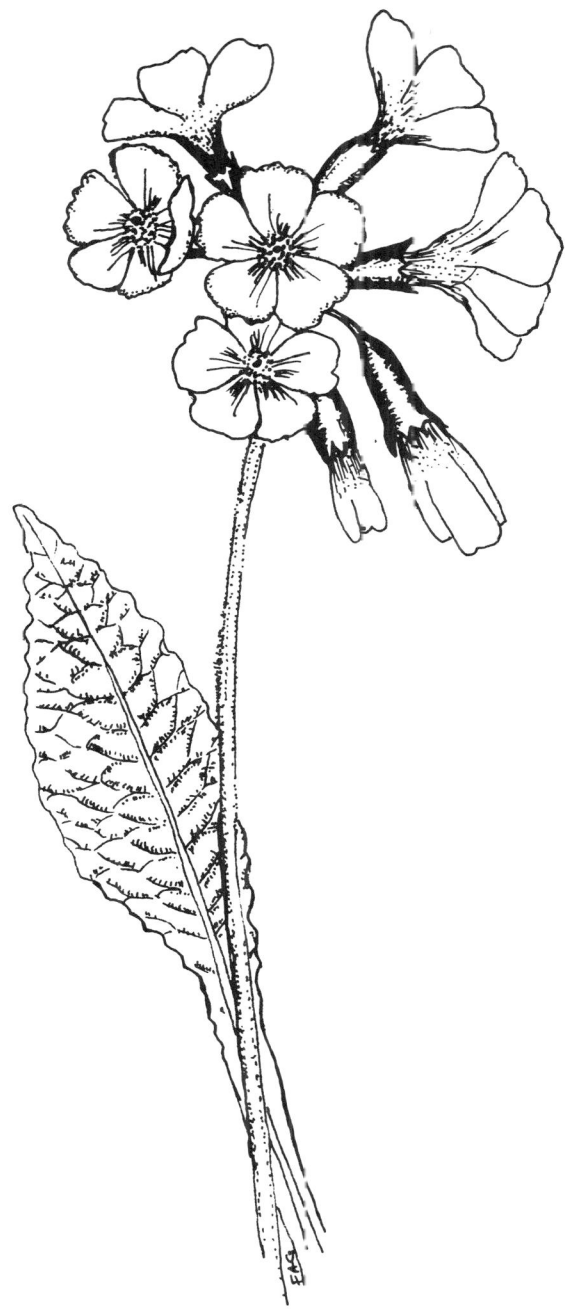

Breeding of the genus began in England; many hybrids have been developed specifically for the Pacific Coast region and for the New England region. ◊

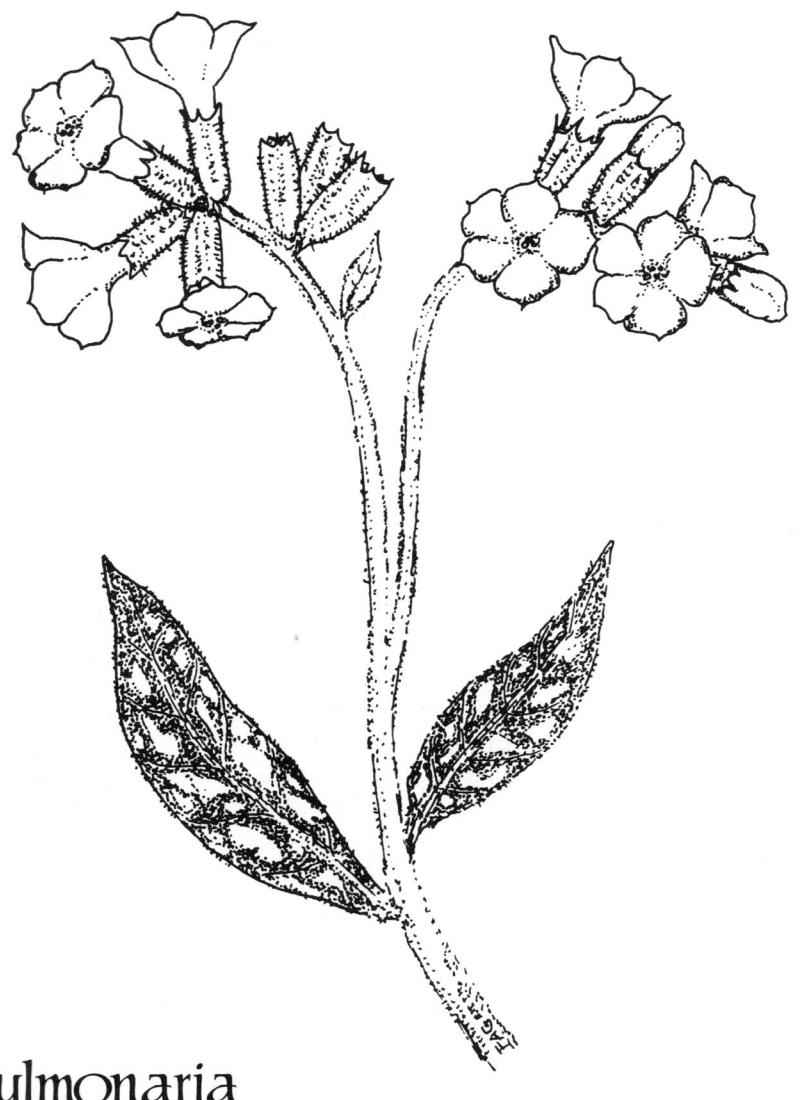

Pulmonaria

consists of about 12 species of hairy, spring-flowering perennial herbs with creeping rhizomes, native to Europe and Asia. The Latin word *pulmo*, meaning "lung," gives the genus its scientific name, probably because 1 species *(Pulmonaria officinalis)* was once believed to resemble the lung and to have medicinal properties to cure lung disorders.

Boraginaceae
(Borage family)

Pulmonaria angustifolia (Pulmonaria azurea)
Cowslip Lungwort, Blue Lungwort

FLOWERS: The blue flowers are borne in primarily bracted, terminal, forked cymes on 12-inch-tall stems. The calyx is tubular-campanulate and 5-lobed, and the corolla is also 5-lobed. The small, attractive flowers are produced in April and May and frequently contrast in color with the flower buds.

LEAVES: The plain, green, decorative foliage is uniquely attractive in all seasons. The basal leaves are simple and long-petioled, and range from linear-lanceolate to oblong-lanceolate. The stem leaves are few, simple, and alternate, and range from linear-lanceolate to linear-elliptic.

PLANT CHARACTERISTICS: This compact, setose perennial grows 8 to 12 inches high and has creeping rhizomes.

GARDEN VALUE: *Pulmonaria angustifolia* is a delightful plant for a shaded area. Use it in the rock garden, in the perennial border, as an edging, or as an undercarpet for shrubs. It flowers at the same time as *Forsythia* and combines well with *Narcissus* and *Primula*.

CULTURE: This plant prefers full shade but tolerates partial shade. Grown in full sun, it struggles, appearing listless by late summer. A cool, moist, peaty soil is best, but the soil does not have to have a high fertility content.

The genus thrives on neglect. Plant in early fall, very early spring, or when plants are in full flower. Space 10 inches apart. Water during prolonged dry periods. To prevent overcrowding, divide after every fourth season of flowering.

Divide in late summer, and water heavily afterwards; plants propagated by seed may show widespread variation. Seeds sown early in spring are able to develop good root systems before winter. Plants will flower the next season either from seed or division.

ADDITIONAL NOTES: *Pulmonaria angustifolia* was sometimes referred to as Soldiers-and-Sailors or Mary-and-Joseph in England. Certain intensely blue-flowered forms were occasionally designated *Pulmonaria azurea*, but they are listed in the trade as April Opals.

NATIVE HABITAT: Europe.

SELECTED CULTIVARS: ◇ 'Alba': White flowers. ◇ 'Azurea': Sky-blue flowers. ◇ 'Johnston's Blue': Beautiful gentian-blue flowers. ◇ 'Munstead Blue': Deep blue flowers. ◇ 'Rubra': A name that covers deviations of reddish shades. ◇ 'Salmon Glory': Clear coral-to-salmon flowers. ◇

Compositae—Helianthus tribe (Composite family)

Rudbeckia hirta
Black-eyed Susan
Also known as Brown-eyed Susan, English Bull's Eye, Yellow Oxeye Daisy

FLOWERS: The flower heads are radiate, 2 to 3 inches wide, and borne, terminally or on axillary stalks, from June to September. The receptacle is conical and scaly. The involucral bracts are hairy and imbricate in several rows, or nearly equal in 2 rows. The brownish-purple disc flowers are fertile. The 10 to 20 orange-yellow ray flowers are sterile, spreading, and notched at the end.

LEAVES: The thick, rough, hairy leaves are alternate, simple, pinnatifid or compound, toothed or entire, and 2 to 5 inches long. The lower leaves are petioled, ovate, and twice as long as they are broad. The upper leaves are sessile and narrow.

PLANT CHARACTERISTICS: This coarse, annual or biennial plant is nonrhizomatous, grows up to 3 feet high, and drops seed freely. The stems are hispid and simple or somewhat branched.

GARDEN VALUE: *Rudbeckia hirta* can be used in small groups in the perennial border for a summer display of flowers. Excessive use of the plants in the garden imparts a coarse impression, but they can be massed in an open naturalized area and have a less offensive effect. The plants sometimes abound in neglected borders; however, they should not be allowed to self-sow or a future weed problem is

Rudbeckia

consists of about 25 species of annual, biennial, and perennial herbs native to North America. The species are coarse, and have attractive, unusual yellow flowers in summer, similar to those of *Echinacea*.

The genus name *Rudbeckia* honors Olaf Rudbeck and Son, Swedish botanists at Uppsala during the 18th century. The nomenclature of this group of plants has been somewhat confused.

inevitable. They combine well with certain summer-flowering perennials, especially those in the blue colors: *Aster* X *frikartii*; *Aster amellus*; and *Lythrum*. The flowers are good when cut.

CULTURE: The plants prefer full sun but tolerate light shade; they will grow in a well-drained soil of average fertility. The plants thrive in a moist site but tolerate dry conditions.

Plant in the spring. Space plants 12 to 15 inches apart. Apply a balanced fertilizer each spring to produce finer plants. Cultivate regularly. Divide the plants after every third season of flowering to prevent overcrowding.

The plants may be divided in March or April; or seeds may be sown in early spring, in a cold frame, and the seedlings transplanted when the soil warms.

DISEASE PESTS: This plant is susceptible to mildew and rust.

ADDITIONAL NOTES: *Rudbeckia* and several other genera are referred to as "Coneflowers" because of the conical shape of the disc flowers.

NATIVE HABITAT: From Western Massachusetts west to Illinois, and south to Georgia and Alabama.

SELECTED CULTIVARS: The new, improved cultivars are far superior to the straight species, many of which are considered weeds. ◇ 'Gloriosa Daisy' and 'Double Gloriosa Daisy': Coarser plants, with flower heads over 6 inches across; these cultivars are tetraploid strains that flower the first year from seed. ◇

Saponaria

consists of about 30 species of hardy, usually coarse, annual, biennial, and perennial, erect and decumbent herbs, native to Eurasia but chiefly to the Mediterranean region.

The genus name is of Latin extraction, from *sapo*, meaning "soap"; several species have mucilaginous juices in the root that create a lather when mixed with water; the juices are easily extracted by pounding the root on a hard surface. In earlier days in England, the plants were supposed to be effective against grease spots; the leaves and stems of some species have been used to make soap.

Caryophyllaceae
(Pink family)

Saponaria ocymoides
Rock Soapwort

FLOWERS: Masses of bright purple flowers are borne, in a broad, loose, cyme, in June and sporadically until September. The calyx is cylindrical, 5-toothed, glandular-hairy, and up to $\frac{1}{2}$ inch long. The 5 petals are clawed, with coronal scales at the juncture of claw and blade, and are entire or emarginate. 10 stamens emerge from the middle of the flower.

LEAVES: The neat leaves are opposite, simple, entire, flat, and acute. They have parallel veins, range from nearly spatulate or elliptic to ovate-lanceolate, and are usually less than 1 inch long. The lower leaves are short-petioled; the upper leaves are sessile.

PLANT CHARACTERISTICS: This hardy perennial, growing up to 10 inches high and 2 feet across, forms a broad mound that tends to encroach upon other plants just by sprawling over them. The stems are reddish, much-branched, and range from procumbent to ascending.

GARDEN VALUE: A popular garden plant, *Saponaria ocymoides* adds interest to an edging, a dry wall, or a sandy perennial border. It is of prime interest in the rock garden, where it can be kept from spreading. The plant supplies good cut flowers.

CULTURE: Full sun and sandy soil with perfect drainage are best; however, the plant tolerates poor soils. It is unable to survive in a wet soil during winter.

Plant in spring. Keep the plants reasonably moist, and occasionally apply a balanced fertilizer. Cut back severely after flowering, to keep the plant neat and compact. Provide winter protection in areas of variable winters.

Division is the easiest method of propagation and is safest in very early spring. Sow seeds in spring or early fall. Cuttings will root easily in midsummer.

ADDITIONAL NOTES: *Saponaria ocymoides* is the most widely cultivated species in the genus.

NATIVE HABITAT: Southern and Central Europe; it is seen in great masses along railways in the Alps in Switzerland.

SELECTED CULTIVARS: ◇ 'Alba': Pure white flowers, considered less interesting than those of the straight species. ◇ 'Rosea': Bright rose flowers. ◇ 'Rubra': Deep red flowers. ◇ 'Splendens': Larger, more intense rose flowers. ◇

Scabiosa

includes 80 or more species of annual and perennial herbs or, rarely, subshrubs, with more or less woody bases. They are native to Europe, Asia, and Africa, but primarily to the Mediterranean region.

The genus name is derived from the Latin word *scabies*, meaning "itch"; it refers to the medicinal value of the genus.

Dipsacaceae
(Teasel family)

Scabiosa caucasica
Pincushion Flower
Also known as Caucasian Scabious

FLOWERS: The light blue flowers are freely borne, in long-petioled, flattened, dense involucrate heads up to 3 inches across, from June to September. The attractive flowers are irregular, symmetrical, bisexual, and subtended by non-spiny receptacle bracts. The calyx is cup-shaped, has 5 bristly teeth, and is enveloped by a cup-shaped, gray-tomentose involucre. The corolla, which is sometimes 2-lipped, has 4 or 5 nearly equal lobes; the marginal corolla is usually larger. It has a tufted central cushion from which the prominent dark gray stamens protrude, usually adding a neat contrast to the flower.

LEAVES: The leaves are opposite and glaucous or whitish. The basal leaves are lanceolate-linear and acute; the stem leaves are divided.

PLANT CHARACTERISTICS: This hardy perennial reaches 18 to 30 inches in height and forms a mounded rosette.

GARDEN VALUE: *Scabiosa caucasica* is an excellent garden plant and lends itself well to massing in the perennial or mixed border. It also may be used in the rock garden. The plant provides long-lasting cut flowers.

CULTURE: Because the plant flourishes so well in cool, humid climates, such as those of the Pacific Northwest or the British Isles, special attention is necessary for it to survive in sultry regions. The plant requires full sun and a well-drained, richly fertile soil. Added humus and perfect drainage should meet its needs for summer moisture and winter dryness. If the soil is acid, add lime to maintain the soil near neutral pH.

Plant in spring, spacing 12 to 15 inches apart. Cultivate regularly, and occasionally apply a balanced fertilizer. Mulch each spring, and water during dry periods. Remove faded flowers before seeds develop, to encourage additional flowering. The plants may need winter protection in northern areas. Clumps should be divided after every 2 to 4 years of flowering to prevent overcrowding.

Seeds may be sown as soon as ripe, in early fall or in spring. Cultivars are usually propagated by division in the spring, but this is a slow method.

ADDITIONAL NOTES: The common name Pincushion Flower is derived from the flower's globular shape, with its protruding stamens resembling pins.

NATIVE HABITAT: Southern Europe, Asia, and North Africa.

SELECTED CULTIVARS: Many fine English strains, especially from Isaac House of Bristol, are superior to those available in America. The seed strains have increased the flower color range to include mauve, lavender, violet, and blue to white. ◇ 'Alba': White flowers. ◇ 'Blue Lady': Gentian-blue flowers. ◇ 'Constancy': Amethyst-colored flowers. ◇ 'Magnifica': Large deep lavender-blue flowers. ◇ 'Miss Wilmott': Snowy-white flowers. ◇ 'Perfecta': Large, fringed flowers. ◇

Sedum

contains as many as 600 species of succulent, mostly hardy, perennial herbs and subshrubs of the Northern Temperate Zone and the tropical mountains.

Sedum is derived from the Latin word *sedo,* meaning "to it." The common name Stonecrop refers to the plant's propensity for flourishing on or around rocks and stony ledges.

Crassulaceae
(Orpine family)

Sedum spectabile
Showy Sedum
Also known as Showy Stonecrop, Live-forever

FLOWERS: Numerous pink flowers $\frac{1}{2}$ inch wide are borne, in large, flat, terminal umbellate cymes 3 to 4 inches across, from August to frost. The 5 sepals are whitish and linear-lanceolate; the 5 petals are slightly concave. The stamens are larger than the petals.

LEAVES: The bold, succulent, gray-green leaves are opposite and decussate or in whorls of 3 or 4. They are scarcely petioled, obovate or spatulate, glaucous, and entire and grow 3 inches long and 2 inches wide. The leaves are attractive throughout the growing season and stems die to the ground each winter.

PLANT CHARACTERISTICS: This hardy, compact perennial grows 18 to 24 inches high. Robust, glaucous, and glabrous, it has simple, erect, thick stems and tuberous roots but does not spread. The plant is drought-tolerant.

GARDEN VALUE: *Sedum spectabile* is grown for its unusual foliage and its flowers. It is useful in the perennial border, the wall garden, the rock garden, and the porch box or in a permanent landscape container. It is a good cut flower.

CULTURE: The plant grows equally well in full sun or light shade. It will grow in almost any garden soil that is well-drained.

Plant in the spring and space 18 to 24 inches apart. Do not disturb the clumps except to propagate. The plants may be propagated by spring-sown seeds. The cultivars should be propagated by stem cuttings taken in spring and summer.

ADDITIONAL NOTES: *Sedum spectabile* is the showiest and most popular species in the genus.

NATIVE HABITAT: China and Korea.

SELECTED CULTIVARS: ◇ 'Album': Creamy white flowers. ◇ 'Atropurpureum': Rosy-crimson flowers. ◇ 'Brilliant': Raspberry-colored flowers; attracts butterflies. ◇ 'Carmine': Rose-red flowers. ◇ 'Meteor': Very large, wine-red flower clusters. ◇ 'Rubrum': Crimson flowers. ◇ 'Star Dust': Ivory-colored flowers. ◇ 'Variegatum': Ice Plant. Poor, muddy-white flowers; white and yellow foliage markings that occasionally revert to the normal green foliage color. ◇

Crassulaceae
(Orpine family)

Sedum spurium
Two-row Stonecrop

FLOWERS: Numerous pink/purple or white flowers ½ to ¾ inch across are borne in dense, terminal, 2-inch-wide, umbellate cymes with about 4 forked branches. The flowering stems are ascending, reddish, and up to 6 inches high and are borne from mid-July to early August. The 5 sepals are linear-oblong; the 5 petals are lanceolate, acute, entire, and twice as long as the calyx. The anthers are reddish and speckled.

LEAVES: The dark green, succulent leaves are opposite, obovate-cuneate or spatulate, and ¾ to 1¼ inches long. They are crenate-serrate toward the apex, papillose-ciliate, and short petioled. The leaves are usually attractive throughout the growing season but occasionally begin to deteriorate. Many are deciduous, but those near the end of the stem remain on the plant, turning red during the winter.

PLANT CHARACTERISTICS: This hardy, glabrous but somewhat papillose perennial grows up to 6 inches high. It forms a dense carpet with its reddish, decumbent stems that root at the nodes.

GARDEN VALUE: *Sedum spurium* is a good ground cover for an arid bank or sunny open site or for the wall garden. It becomes weedy in the formal garden.

CULTURE: The plants need full sun and well-drained sandy soil. They can be transplanted at almost any time during the growing season. Keep them weed free.

Propagate cultivars by cuttings or divisions taken anytime during the growing season. The species may be propagated by seeds sown in the spring; however, some cultivars will not reproduce true-to-type from seed.

NATIVE HABITAT: Asia Minor.

SELECTED CULTIVARS: ◊ 'Album': White flowers. ◊ 'Bronze Carpet': Reddish-bronze leaves throughout the season. ◊ 'Coccineum': Flowers vary from deep pink to red. ◊ 'Schorbusser Blut': Dragon's Blood. Ruby-red flowers and scarlet leaves.

RELATED SPECIES: *Sedum acre:* Wall Pepper, Mossy Stonecrop, Gold Dust, Love Entangle, Golden-carpet, Gold Moss, Goldmoss Stonecrop. Bright yellow, star-like flowers up to $\frac{1}{2}$ inch wide are borne in 1-sided cymes atop 2- to-3-inch stems, from May to July. The sepals are leaflike, and the petals are lanceolate, acute, and longer than the stamens. The glabrous, light greenish-yellow leaves are alternate, overlapping, ovate, slightly succulent, sessile, and $\frac{3}{16}$ inch long; they taste acrid. This glabrous perennial forms an evergreen mat up to 5 inches high; it is quite weedy, except when used as a ground cover under full sun. Small pieces broken off and left lying on the soil will quickly form roots. This is an excellent plant for use between stepping stones, to trail over rocks and walls, or to use in a naturalized area. It is drought-tolerant and grows best in a poor soil. It is easy to propagate by division and cuttings. *Sedum acre* is one of the most commonly cultivated species. Its native habitat is from Northern Africa to Europe and Western Asia. The plant has become naturalized in the Northern part of the United States.

There are many other excellent species available, so check your garden center and catalogues. ◊

Sempervivum

comprises about 40 species of succulent, usually stemless, perennial herbs native to Europe, Morocco, and Western Asia.

Sempervivum is of Latin origin and means "live forever," which describes the long lives of many of the species.

Crassulaceae
(Orpine family)

Sempervivum tectorum
Common Houseleek
Also known as Roof Houseleek, Hen and Chickens, Old Man and Woman

FLOWERS: Purplish-red flowers about ¾ to 1 inch across are borne in midsummer, in compact cymes atop stout, terminal, leafy, densely pilose peduncles. The calyx is densely pilose, and the calyx segments are lanceolate. The petals are separate, linear, erect, keeled, and spreading.

LEAVES: The green, often purple-tipped leaves are evergreen; 50 to 60 are borne in dense, basal rosettes. The leaves are alternate, succulent, glabrous, and range from oblong to obovate-cuneate; they are broad-based, cuspidate, and 1 to 3 inches long and ¾ inch across.

PLANT CHARACTERISTICS: This hardy perennial has open, flattened rosettes 3 to 4 inches across and is stoloniferous. The new rosettes are crowded and sessile.

GARDEN VALUE: Valued for the color, form, and hardiness of the rosettes, *Sempervivum tectorum* is excellent when used in the rock garden, in front of the perennial or mixed border, as an edging, in a carpet bed, and in a porch box or planter box. It is a companion plant for *Sedum*, which has similar requirements. It is also ideal for a dry wall or a sunny naturalized area with poor soil, such as a thin rock outcropping. A few offsets wedged between layers of rock grow and spread despite a nearly complete lack of soil.

CULTURE: The plant is very easy to culture. It grows best in full sun in a hot, dry site. It requires good drainage. Remove weeds and keep the plant on the dry side.

The plant is usually propagated by separation of the small outer rosettes from the parent plant; it may also be started easily from cuttings or seeds.

ADDITIONAL NOTES: According to an old Central European superstition, neither fire or lightning would harm a home if this plant were grown on the roof.

Sempervivum tectorum is an old-fashioned plant that is very popular in the United States. A variable species, it appears in many forms and under many names. It may be brought into the house in autumn to be kept during winter as a houseplant.

NATIVE HABITAT: Europe.

SELECTED CULTIVARS AND VARIETIES: ◊ 'Atroviolaceum' ◊ 'Robustum': Purple-tipped leaves in rosettes that are 7 inches across. ◊ 'Violaceum' ◊ var. *calcareum*: Pale red flowers ¾ inch across are borne in 3 or 4 panicles; it has glaucous leaves with conspicuous brownish-purple tips. ◊

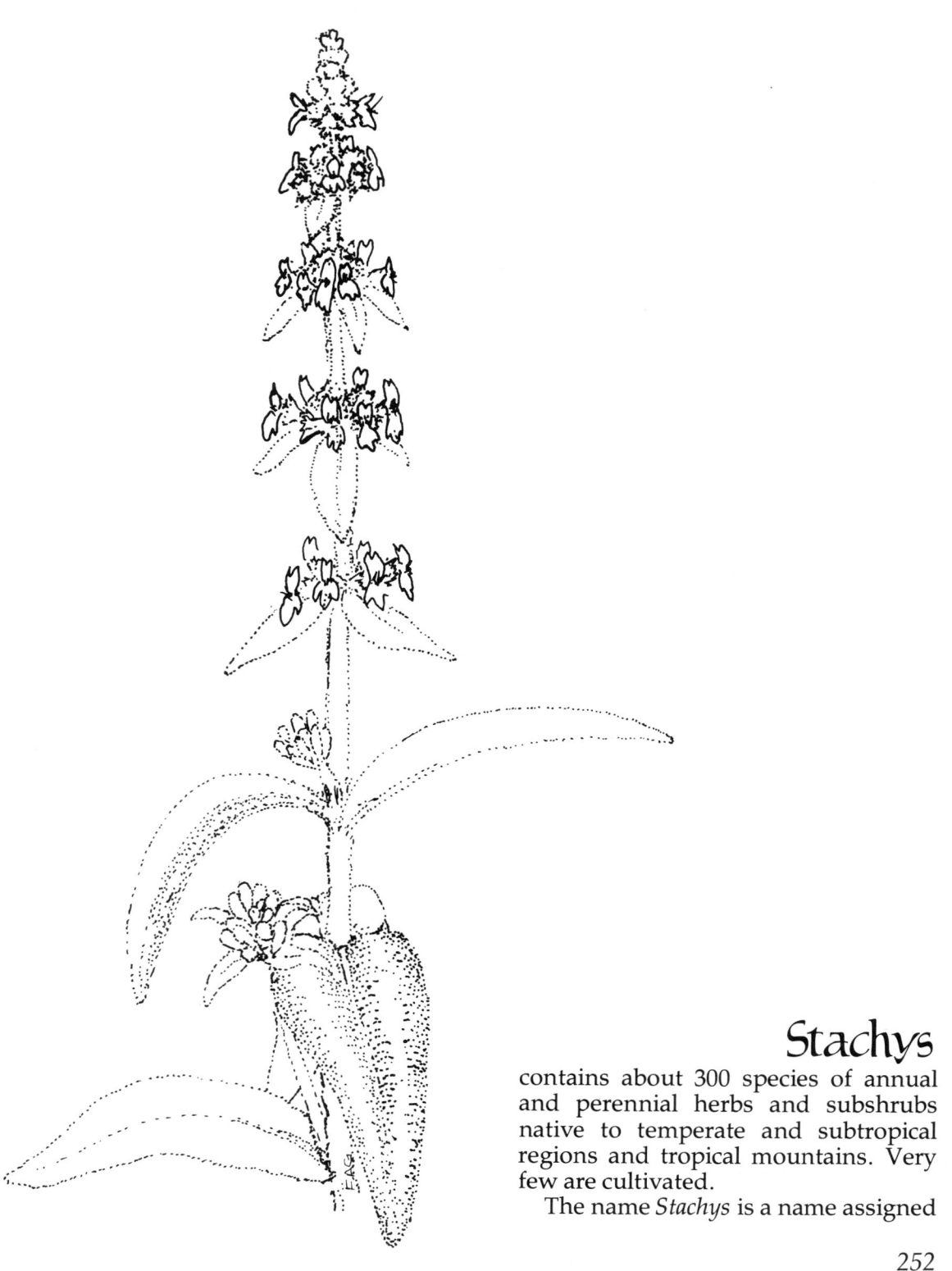

Stachys

contains about 300 species of annual and perennial herbs and subshrubs native to temperate and subtropical regions and tropical mountains. Very few are cultivated.

The name *Stachys* is a name assigned

by Dioscorides to a different group of plants; it is probably derived from a Greek word, *stachys,* meaning "spike," because the flowers of the genus are arranged in whorls or spikes. The common name Lamb's Ears describes the silky, woolly leaves that resemble lamb's ears.

Labiatae
(Mint family)

Stachys byzantina (Stachys lanata, Stachys olympica)
Lamb's Ears
Also known as Woolly Betony, Woolly Woundwort

FLOWERS: Small pink or purple flowers are borne sessile or short-pedicelled in dense, 30- or more-flowered, terminal verticillasters. The flowers are borne from June and July until frost on stout, woolly stems 1 foot or more high. The tubular-campanulate calyx is 5- to 20-nerved, bristly toothed, and up to $\frac{1}{2}$ inch long. The pink or purple, densely white-woolly corolla is a cylindrical tube, up to 1 inch long and often hairy inside, and has a 2-lipped limb. The upper lip is often concave and 2-lobed; the lower lip is 3-lobed.

LEAVES: The soft, silky, woolly leaves are opposite, entire or toothed, 4 to 6 inches long, and densely tomentose. The lower leaves are oblong-elliptical; the upper leaves, smaller and elliptic.

PLANT CHARACTERISTICS: This white-woolly hardy perennial grows up to 1 or $1\frac{1}{2}$ feet high.

GARDEN VALUE: *Stachys byzantina* provides an unusual accent wherever it is grown. Place the plant in the front of the perennial border or in the large rock garden or use it as an accent in the perennial garden. It has often been used as a bedding plant. The flowering stems and leaves are suitable for flower arrangements; the stems are weak until swelled with water.

CULTURE: The plant needs a sunny location and a light, loamy, well-drained soil. *Stachys byzantina* is easy to grow; plant 12 to 18 inches apart in spring or fall. Remove faded flowers to keep plants producing attractive leaves. Thin annually to rejuvenate the plant.

It is propagated by division in early spring or early fall. Sow seeds in early spring.

ADDITIONAL NOTES: Several species are sometimes listed under *Betonica,* an invalid name.

NATIVE HABITAT: Turkey and Southwest Asia.

RELATED SPECIES: *Stachys grandiflora (Betonica grandiflora):* Betony, Big Betony. Rich purple-violet flowers 1 inch across are borne, in 10- to 20-flowered verticillasters atop 18-inch flowering stalks, in late June and early July. The leaves are ovate, coarsely crenate-serrate, and up to $2\frac{3}{4}$ inches long. This villous, rosette-forming perennial grows up to 18 inches high. It tends to spread but does not become weedy. Grow it in partial shade to prolong flowering. Its native habitat is Asia Minor.

◊ 'Alba' ◊ 'Superba' ◊

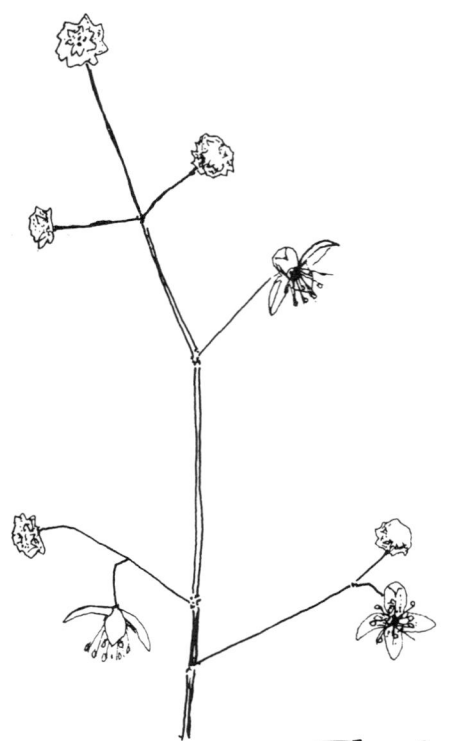

Thalictrum

includes about 100 species of perennial herbs primarily located in the Northern Temperate Zone.

Thalictrum, which is derived from the Greek word *thaliktron*, was used by Dioscorides for a plant with compound leaves.

Ranunculaceae
(Buttercup or Crowfoot family)

Thalictrum rochebrunianum
Lavender Mist

FLOWERS: The small flowers are borne in panicles from mid-July to early September. The flowers are bisexual and apetalous. There are 4 or 5 white, petaloid, sepals, which are deciduous, oblong, and $\frac{1}{4}$ inch long. The many primrose-yellow stamens are club-shaped and $\frac{1}{4}$ inch long. The color of the light, airy flowers is provided by the petaloid sepals, which quickly drop off, and by the numerous stamens.

LEAVES: The delicate leaves are ternately compound or decompound. The upper leaves are alternate and bipinnate. The leaflets are obtuse, entire, and leathery, and the terminal leaflet is 3-lobed.

PLANT CHARACTERISTICS: This glabrous plant forms 4- to 6-foot clumps and tends to be a short-lived perennial in the Midwestern section of the United States.

GARDEN VALUE: *Thalictrum rochebrunianum* deserves greater popularity; the plant is valued for its light, airy flowers and delicately compound foliage. Place it in the rear of the perennial border, in the wild garden, or in a naturalized area. Plant it beside *Papaver orientale* to disguise the vacant spot left by the latter's lack of foliage in the summer.

CULTURE: A woodland plant, it is accustomed to light shade and a well-drained soil. The plant tolerates full sun if the soil is rich and fairly moist.

Plant in spring or fall. Space at least 2 feet from other plants. Keep moderately moist and cultivate regularly. The plant may need staking in windy sites. Divide the clumps after a few years of flowering; spring is the best time to divide them. If divided in early fall, provide protection during the first winter. Sow seeds in fall.

ADDITIONAL NOTES: *Thalictrum rochebrunianum* is probably the finest species in the genus.

NATIVE HABITAT: Northern Japan. ◊

Ranunculaceae
(Crowfoot or Buttercup family)

Thalictum speciosissimum (Thalictrum glaucum)
Dusty Meadow Rue

FLOWERS: The numerous small, slightly fragrant flowers are borne, on erect, crowded panicles, in June and July. The flowers are perfect and apetalous. There are 4 or 5 pale yellow, petaloid sepals, which are deciduous and less than $\frac{1}{8}$ inch in length. The many showy stamens are bright yellow and $\frac{1}{2}$ inch long. The color of the cloud-like clusters is provided by the petaloid sepals and the numerous stamens.

LEAVES: The blue-gray leaves are 2- to 3-pinnately compound. The leaflets are ovate-orbicular, with 3 deeply toothed lobes.

PLANT CHARACTERISTICS: This stout perennial forms 2- to 5-foot-high clumps. The stems are erect, round, and glaucous.

GARDEN VALUE: Place the plant near the rear of the perennial border, in the wild flower garden, or in a naturalized area. *Thalictrum speciosissimum* is excellent when grouped with *Delphinium* or *Campanula persicifolia*. Placed behind *Heliopsis*, *Phlox*, *Echinacea*, or *Iris*, the plant adds softness and daintiness to the planting. Place it near *Papaver orientale* to hide the void left by the latter's foliage, which dies back in the summer. The flowers and foliage are valued for fresh bouquets.

CULTURE: The plant prefers a light, shaded site with a moist, rich, well-drained soil. Plant 15 to 18 inches apart in spring or fall. Provide plenty of water in dry periods during the growing season. Unless planted deeply, winter protection may be needed. Leave the clumps undisturbed except to propagate.

Sow seeds in late summer or autumn to produce flowering-sized plants 2 years later. Division is best performed in spring; however, it may be done in fall if winter protection is provided.

NATIVE HABITAT: Western Mediterranean region.

SELECTED CULTIVARS: ◊ 'Illuminator': Lemon-yellow flowers; a superior form. ◊

Thermopsis

comprises about 20 species of herbs native to North America and Northeastern Asia.

The genus name *Thermopsis* is derived from the Greek words *thermos*, meaning "lupin," and *opsis*, meaning "like." The plant was so named because of the resemblance of its flowers to those of *Lupinus*.

Fabaceae (Leguminosae)
(Pea family)

Thermopsis caroliniana
Carolina Lupine
Also known as Carolina Thermopsis, Aaron's Rod, Bush-pea, Golden-pea

FLOWERS: The sparkling yellow, rather large flowers are borne, in dense, erect, rigid, terminal, many-flowered racemes up to 10 inches long, in June and July. The calyx is narrowly campanulate and 5-lobed, with sub-equal lobes. The flower is papilionaceous. It has an orbicular standard, oblong wings, and a keel equaling or slightly longer than the wings.

LEAVES: The light green leaves are alternate, palmately compound, ternate, and long-petioled. The leaflets range from ovate to obovate and are up to 3 inches long, pubescent, and glaucous on the underside. The leaf-like, large stipules are free and clasping. The foliage remains fresh until frost.

PLANT CHARACTERISTICS: This hardy perennial forms clumps 3 to 4 feet high and 1 foot across. It has deep roots and is drought tolerant. The stems are stout, simple, smooth, and erect.

GARDEN VALUE: *Thermopsis caroliniana* is grown for its beautiful flowers and handsome foliage. Use it in the back of the perennial or mixed border. This plant combines well with blue or purple cultivars of *Delphinium* and can be used in place of yellow cultivars of *Lupinus*, because it is easier to grow and has a greater color range. The plant supplies useful racemes for cut flower arrangements.

CULTURE: Although full sun is ideal, *Thermopsis caroliniana* will tolerate partial shade. It grows best in deep, light, well-drained soil. It will tolerate quite dry sites if there is adequate moisture prior to flowering.

Because the plant makes rapid growth in early spring, plant 3 to 4 feet apart in fall. Use nitrogen fertilizer sparingly around the plant. When grown in a rich, fertile soil, it may grow tall enough to require staking.

Because seeds do not remain viable long, sow the seeds in late summer; they will germinate readily. Before planting, dust the seeds with a nitrogen-fixing bacteria available from a seed company. Seeds sown in the summer will flower 2 years later. Divisions can be made in very early spring, but the old clumps are hard to dig and divide.

NATIVE HABITAT: Mountainous areas of North Carolina and Georgia. ◇

Thymus

comprises about 300 to 400 species of aromatic perennial herbs, subshrubs, and small shrubs native to Europe and Asia.

Thymus is an ancient Greek name used by Theophrastus.

Labiatae
(Mint family)

Thymus serpyllum
Mother-of-thyme
Also known as Creeping Thyme, Wild Thyme, Lemon Thyme

FLOWERS: The tiny rose or lilac flowers are borne, in several-flowered verticillasters that are sessile and congested into terminal spikes, from late May through July. The erect flower stems are hairy on 4 sides and grow up to 4 inches high. The calyx ranges from cylindrical to campanulate and is 10- to 13-nerved, hairy in the throat, and 2-lipped to the middle. The teeth of the upper lip are triangular and glabrous or ciliate; the teeth of the lower lip are lanceolate and ciliate. The corolla tube is straight, $\frac{1}{4}$ inch long, 2-lipped, and displays the stamens inside.

LEAVES: The aromatic leaves are opposite, small and entire, range from linear to elliptic or oblong, are nearly sessile, and grow ¼ to ½ inch long. The leaves are predominantly evergreen and remain attractive throughout the season.

PLANT CHARACTERISTICS: This mat-forming perennial or subshrub grows up to 4 inches high. Its wiry stems are mostly square in cross section and are woody at the base, prostrate below and ascending above, and root wherever nodes touch the ground.

GARDEN VALUE: Common in old gardens, *Thymus serpyllum* is an invaluable plant today, prized as a ground cover, an evergreen edging, and a cover for a rockwall. It is planted in a border, along a walk or path, between flagstones, in a naturalized area, along a dry stream. It may be walked on as well as mowed.

CULTURE: *Thymus serpyllum* will grow in a sunny location in any kind of soil. It performs better in poor, rocky or sandy soil than in fertile soil.

Plant about 12 inches apart in spring or early fall. Give winter wind protection where possible.

The plant is easily divided in spring. Cuttings root easily in early summer. Seeds germinate well but may not produce seedlings true to type.

ADDITIONAL NOTES: *Thymus serpyllum* has been a popular garden plant in America since Colonial days. A variable species, many *Thymus* grown in American gardens appear to be of confused identity and are often mislabeled.

NATIVE HABITAT: Northwestern Europe.

SELECTED CULTIVARS AND VARIETIES: ◇ 'Albus': White flowers abundantly borne in late spring and minute green leaves on a plant 2 to 4 inches high. ◇ 'Argenteus': Silver-margined leaves. ◇ 'Aureus': Variegated golden leaves. ◇ 'Coccineus': Bright red flowers, handsome dark green evergreen leaves which turn reddish-green in autumn; grows 1½ to 3 inches high. ◇ 'Lanuginosus': Woolly Mother-of-thyme. Small, roundish, gray-pubescent leaves; grows 3 inches high. ◇ 'Roseus': Pink flowers. ◇ 'Variegatus': Leaves variegated with white. ◇ 'Vulgaris': Lemon Thyme. Leaves that are smaller, strongly veined, and strongly lemon-scented. ◇

Tradescantia

comprises over 20 species of hardy perennial herbs with erect and trailing stems native to North and South America.

The genus was named in honor of John Tradescant, a plant collector and gardener to King Charles I of England.

Commelinaceae
(Spiderwort family)

Tradescantia virginiana
Spiderwort
Also known as Common Spiderwort, Widow's-tears

FLOWERS: The violet-purple flowers (rarely, white or rose) are 1 to 2 inches across and are borne, from June to July, in terminal and axillary inflorescence or in paired sessile cincinni. Each flower lasts only 1 day, usually opening during the morning; however, there is a long flowering season. Each pair of flowers is subtended by leaf-like or spath-like bracts, usually paired when terminal and single when axillary. Generally, the flowers are bisexual and regularly symmetrical. The sepals and petals are separate and equal. The 3 small sepals are bright green, somewhat turgid, and villous; the 3 petals are equal and obovate. The 6 conspicuous, bright yellow stamens and the purple filaments with long purple hairs attract close-up interest to the flower. After the petals have closed, the pedicels (which bear the flowers upright) curve downward, so that the fruits develop in a recurved position.

LEAVES: The delicate leaves are alternate, simple, entire, and parallel-veined. They are linear-lanceolate, 6 to 15 inches long and $\frac{1}{2}$ to 1 inch across, and clasping; they are often channeled down the center.

PLANT CHARACTERISTICS: This hardy, long-lived perennial grows from 1 to 3 feet high and may become slightly weedy. The erect or ascending stems are rather weak and succulent and contain mucilaginous sap.

GARDEN VALUE: *Tradescantia virginiana* is not a tidy plant for the formal garden. The foliage may dry and become straggly after it has flowered. This plant is best displayed in a shaded area where a good ground cover is desired, in the wild flower garden, or in a naturalized area. Place the plants in groups of at least 3 or 5 to create a good impression. The cut foliage of this plant often combines well with other cut flowers.

CULTURE: The plant tolerates full sun or light shade and grows in almost any soil, although it performs best in a rich, well-drained soil.

Tradescantia virginiana is easy to grow and tolerates neglect. Plant in spring or fall, and space plants 12 to 15 inches apart. By midsummer, the stems have become long and floppy. If cut off at ground level, new shoots will come up and bear flowers during the autumn. Keep plants well watered during drought periods.

Seedlings may vary in flower color. Plants should be divided in the spring, after a few years of flowering. Seeds may be sown in spring or summer and will produce flowers the following summer.

ADDITIONAL NOTES: In the 17th century, when the Commonwealth of Virginia extended to the Mississippi River, John Tradescant collected this plant and sent it back to England. *Tradescantia virginiana* is the only species of real garden value in the genus and closely resembles its relative, the Dayflower *(Commelina communis)*, which is smaller and has less showy flowers. Most plants in the trade named *Tradescantia virginiana* are *Tradescantia x andersoniana*. The cultivars are a great improvement over the native species. Breeders in Europe and the United States Department of Agriculture have developed 18-inch-high plants that have violet-blue, pink, red, or white flowers 1½ to 3 inches across.

SELECTED CULTIVARS: ◊ 'Blue Stone': Deep blue flowers. ◊ 'Innocence': Pure white flowers. ◊ 'Iris Frichard': White flowers with a blue hue. ◊ 'James C. Weguelin': Large porcelain-blue flowers. ◊ 'Osprey': Huge, feathery white flowers tinted blue in the center. ◊ 'Pauline': Large, pale pink flowers. ◊ 'Purple Dome': Brilliant rosy-purple flowers that are freely borne all summer. ◊ 'Red Cloud': Rosy-red flowers; grows 15 to 18 inches high. ◊ 'Snow Cap': Large pure white flowers. ◊

Trollius

includes some 20 species of perennial herbs that are primarily native to moist or marshy areas of the Northern Temperate Zone.

The name of the genus is derived from the old German word *trol*, meaning "something round"; it came to be called "trollblume," or globeflower.

Ranunculaceae
(Buttercup or Crowfoot family)

Trollius europaeus
Globeflower
Also known as Common Globeflower, European Globeflower

FLOWERS: The globular, lemon-yellow flowers are 1 to 2 inches across and are borne, solitary or in 2's on terminal stems, from May to late August. The bisexual flowers have large, showy sepals. The 5 or more, petaloid, pale or greenish-yellow sepals are ovate and incurved. The 5 or more yellow petals are usually small and spatulate. There are many stamens.

LEAVES: The basal leaves are petioled and palmately 3- to 5-lobed; the stem leaves are sessile and 3-lobed. The leaves are dark green on the upper surface and paler on the undersurface.

PLANT CHARACTERISTICS: This simple perennial grows 15 to 24 inches high and has thick fibrous roots.

GARDEN VALUE: *Trollius europaeus* is a neat attractive plant for a damp area. Place this plant in a small group in the rock garden and the perennial border; naturalize it in a wet, sunken, or bog garden, a moist meadow, the wild flower garden, or along a stream and around a pond.

CULTURE: The plant grows in sun or partial shade. It is best suited to a rich, moist, heavy soil with a high moisture content; however, it cannot tolerate a stagnant bog-like condition.

Plant in clumps in spring or fall and set 10 to 12 inches apart. Provide sufficient amounts of water during drought periods. Remove faded flowers to prolong the flowering season.

Divide in late summer when the plants become oversized, usually after 5 years of flowering.

Plants may be divided or propagated by seed. Sow seed directly after flowering. The seeds will germinate and flower the following season.

ADDITIONAL NOTES: When raised from seed *Trollius europaeus* is highly variable in leaf shape and flower color. The Scots called these plants Butterballs.

NATIVE HABITAT: *Trollius europaeus* is native to damp places in Northern Europe, especially the English and Welsh river valleys.

SELECTED CULTIVARS: ◊ 'Superbus': 2-inch-wide bright lemon-yellow flowers. ◊ 'Loddigesii': Deep yellow flowers. ◊

Verbena

includes about 200 species of annual and perennial herbs and subshrubs native to the tropics and subtropics of North and South America.

The name *Verbena* is an ancient Latin name for the common European species.

Verbenaceae
(Verbena family)

Verbena canadensis
Rose Verbena
Also known as Clump Verbena, Creeping Vervain, Rose Vervain

FLOWERS: The reddish-purple or magenta flowers, about $\frac{5}{8}$ inch across, are borne, in elongated spikes, from May to June. The bracts and calyx are glandular-pubescent. The calyx is tubular and 5-ribbed, and has 5 unequal teeth. The corolla is salverform or funnelform, and slightly 2-lipped. The petal lobe is $\frac{1}{2}$ to $\frac{3}{4}$ inch across, spreading, and oblong or obovate.

LEAVES: The shiny dark green leaves are opposite, ovate or ovate-oblong, 3-cleft, incisely toothed and lobed, and 2 to 4 inches long.

PLANT CHARACTERISTICS: This branching perennial ranges from pubescent with stiff hairs to nearly glabrous and grows 6 to 18 inches high. The stems are usually 4-angled and ascending or decumbent.

CULTURE: The plants prefer an open, sunny site with a rich, well-drained soil. They are easy to grow. Plant in spring, spacing about 12 inches apart. Remove faded flowers to prolong the flowering season. The plants are usually propagated by seeds or cuttings.

NATIVE HABITAT: From Virginia to Colorado, and south to Florida and Mexico.

SELECTED CULTIVARS: ◊ 'Candidissima': White flowers. ◊ 'Compacta': Denser and shorter plant. ◊ 'Rosea': Fragrant rosy-purple flowers, borne continuously over a long period. ◊

Veronica

comprises about 250 species of annual and perennial herbs of the North Temperate Zone. The genus name *Veronica* honors St. Veronica.

Scrophulariaceae
(Figwort family)

Veronica longifolia (Veronica maritima)
Veronica
Also known as Clump Speedwell, Beach Speedwell

FLOWERS: The numerous, small, lilac flowers are borne, in dense, erect, axillary or terminal racemes, from late July until September. The flowers are bisexual and irregularly symmetrical. The calyx is 4- or 5-parted; the corolla is rotate and 4- or 5-lobed.

LEAVES: The leaves are opposite, or, sometimes, in a whorl of 3, in the lower part of the plant; the upper leaves are more or less whorled; the flower stem leaves are alternate. The leaves are simple, lanceolate or oblong, 2 to 4 inches long, very acute, sharply serrate, and short-petioled.

PLANT CHARACTERISTICS: This strong, leafy perennial grows 2 to 4 feet high. Its erect stem is usually smooth.

GARDEN VALUE: *Veronica longifolia* is excellent for the perennial border, especially after the plant has become well established. It blends well with other plants and is especially striking when planted near *Anthemis tinctoria* or near red cultivars of *Phlox*. It provides tall spikes of blue flowers, a color frequently lacking in midsummer. With a careful selection of species and their cultivars, a display of *Veronica* can be seen almost throughout the growing season. This popular, old-fashioned perennial furnishes good cut flowers.

CULTURE: *Veronica longifolia* is easy to grow. The plant prefers full sun but will tolerate partial shade. It grows in most garden soils but will succumb to a poorly drained soil in the winter. Plant in spring or early fall. Space the plants 18 to 24 inches apart. Remove faded flowers to lengthen the flowering season. Divide plants occasionally to preserve a neat appearance. Seeds sown in late spring will produce plants with some variation. Stem cuttings collected in late spring are easily rooted and will produce flowers the following year. Division can be done in spring or fall.

ADDITIONAL NOTES: *Veronica longifolia*, probably one of the best species of the genus, has been used as a parent for modern cultivars, to which it is inferior. Many garden varieties are probably hybrids of *Veronica longifolia* X *Veronica spicata*.

NATIVE HABITAT: Wet areas of Central and Eastern Europe and Northern Asia; the plants have become naturalized in Eastern North America.

SELECTED CULTIVARS AND VARIETIES: ◊ 'Alba': White flowers atop a 1- to 1½-foot-high plant. ◊ 'Blue Champion': Medium-blue flowers from July 1 until the end of August. ◊ 'Blue Spires': Deep blue flowers. ◊ 'Icicle': Pure white flowers produced from June to September, providing long-lasting cut flowers. ◊ 'Rosea': Pink flowers on a much-branched 2-foot-high plant. ◊ 'Sunny Border': Navy-blue flowers from July to September. ◊ var. *subsessilis:* Clump Veronica. The larger, royal-blue flowers are borne, in longer spikes on slender 2-foot stalks, from August to October. The leaves are very short petioled and are 2 to 4 inches long. The plant is more erect and compact than the straight species. A very popular plant found in Japan about 1878.

RELATED SPECIES:

Veronica incana: Woolly Speedwell. Many porcelain-blue flowers on short pedicels are borne, in several terminal racemes up to 6 inches long, in June and July. The soft white-tomentose leaves are opposite, oblong on the lower part and lanceolate on the upper, acute, 1 to 3 inches long, obtusely crenate, and petioled. This white-pubescent perennial forms gorgeous clumps, up to 2 feet high, of strong upright or ascending stems. Valued for its grayish leaves and slender racemes, the plant has a good appearance with or without flowers. The flowers and foliage provide contrast when used in the rock garden, in the front row of the perennial border, or as an edging plant. It requires perfect drainage and full sun. Its native habitat is Northern Asia. ◊ 'Rosea': Rose-pink flowers on a more desirable plant, which does not reproduce reliably from seed. ◊ 'Rubra': Red flowers. ◊ 'Saraband': Deep violet flowers borne all summer. ◊ 'Wendy': Striking violet-blue flowers, gray foliage, 18-inch-high plant; a cross between *Veronica incana* and *Veronica spicata.*

Veronica spicata: Spike Speedwell. Showy, clear blue or pale pink flowers are borne, on pedicels in 6-inch-long, dense, erect racemes, from late June to early August. Thick soft-green leaves are opposite or verticillate, oblong to lanceolate, crenate, downy, and 1½ to 2 inches long. The plant is a clump perennial, growing 2 to 4 feet high. The slender stems are erect or ascending and well branched, and grow from a creeping root stock. The plant thrives in a sunny, open site. Popular because of its handsome foliage, it is used in the rock garden or in front of the perennial border. Its native habitat is Northern Europe and Asia.

◇ 'Alba': White flowers. ◇ 'Blue Peter': Blue flowers; when grown in poorer soils, the plant has poor foliage. ◇ 'Nana': Blue flowers on a dwarf plant. ◇ 'Rosea': Showy purplish-pink flowers from July to early autumn.

A group of superior hybrids developed by Alan Bloom of England flower all summer: ◇ 'Barcarolle': Deep rose flowers. ◇ 'Minuet': Soft pink flowers. ◇ 'Pavanne': Medium rose flowers. ◇

Viola

consists of about 500 species of annual and perennial herbs, and, rarely, subshrubs, which are widely distributed throughout the temperate regions. The large, well-known family includes Violas, Pansies, and Violets. Closely related species freely hybridize in nature. Many produce 2 kinds of flowers: those borne in early spring which are showy and sterile; and those borne in summer, which are apetalous and produce many seeds (cleistogamous).

These self-pollinated flowers remain on short peduncles under the soil until the seeds ripen, at which time the peduncle elongates and lifts the capsule into the air, dispersing the seeds.

The genus name *Viola* was used by Virgil and Pliny.

Violaceae
(Violet family)

Viola cornuta
Tufted Pansy
Also known as Horned Violet, Viola, Bedding Pansy

FLOWERS: The showy, nodding flowers are $\frac{1}{2}$ to 2 inches across and are borne from April to September if the seeds are not allowed to develop. The flowers are bisexual and irregularly symmetrical. The 5 violet-colored petals are obovate-obtuse; the lower petal is a slender spur, acute and shorter than the petals. The other 4 petals are in 2 unlike pairs; the petals in each pair are symmetrically alike. The 5 sepals persist on the fruit.

LEAVES: The simple leaves are subcordate-ovate and crenately serrate and have long peduncles. The large, triangular stipules are dentate and persistent.

PLANT CHARACTERISTICS: The plant is more or less tufted and grows 4 to 8 inches high. A dependable perennial, it spreads by stolons and seed, which may become weedy in the garden and lawn.

GARDEN VALUE: *Viola cornuta*, an old-fashioned plant, is excellent in the perennial border, as a bedding plant, specimen, or edging, in a limited mass planting in the rock garden, or in the wild flower garden or a naturalized area. The flowers are good cut, but they may have short stems.

CULTURE: The plant grows best in sun or slight shade. It does best in a fairly rich, well-drained soil with some humus content.

Plant in the spring. Because the plant requires lots of moisture, water frequently during the growing season. Remove faded flowers to promote continued flowering. It transplants easily.

The plant self-sows. It may be propagated by cuttings, division, or seed. Divide in early spring or late summer, and prune the long shoots back to reduce wilting. Sow seeds in late summer, protect the seedlings from low temperatures during the winter, and transplant in April. Seeds may also be sown indoors in January and should produce flowers after the plants are set out in April.

INSECT AND DISEASE PESTS: *Viola cornuta* is often damaged by 2-spotted mite and mildew.

NATIVE HABITAT: Spain and the Pyrenees.

SELECTED CULTIVARS: ◊ 'Admiration': Deep purple flowers. ◊ 'Alba': White petals. ◊ 'Apricot': Rich apricot-bronze flowers. ◊ 'Arkwright Ruby': Terra cotta flowers. ◊ 'Atropurpurea': Dark purple petals with small yellow centers. ◊ 'Beauty of Laronne': Large blue flowers. ◊ 'Chantryland': Apricot flowers. ◊ 'Jersey Gem': Very popular purple flowers. ◊ 'Papilio': Very large flowers with violet petals and purple centers. ◊ 'Perfection': Soft blue flowers. ◊ 'Purpurea': Purple petals. ◊ 'White Perfection': Milky white flowers. ◊ 'Scottish Yellow': Bright yellow flowers. ◊

Violaceae
(Violet family)

Viola odorata
Violet
Also known as Sweet Violet, Garden Violet, Florist's Violet, English Violet

FLOWERS: The showy, fragrant, nodding flowers are about ¾ inch across and are borne in April and May. The 5 petals are deep violet (rarely, rose or white) and the lower petal is a short, nearly straight, obtuse spur. The other 4 petals are in 2 unlike pairs; each pair is symmetrically alike. The 5 sepals persist on the fruit. The flowers are bisexual and irregularly symmetrical. Cleistogamous flowers are produced in the summer unless the plant is growing in wet ground.

LEAVES: The leaves are simple, range from cordate-ovate to reniform, and are obtusely serrate. The often leafy, persistent stipules are ovate-lanceolate.

PLANT CHARACTERISTICS: This somewhat pubescent, stemless plant forms broad, tufted clumps about 8 inches high. Having long prostrate stolons it becomes weedy and is difficult to eradicate.

GARDEN VALUE: This old-fashioned favorite is useful for limited massing, as an edging, or as a specimen plant in the rock garden or perennial border as well as in the wild flower garden or a naturalized area. The flowers are good cut, but the stems are usually extremely short.

CULTURE: The plants prefer a cool, semi-shaded site with a fertile, well-drained soil. Plant in spring. Water frequently throughout the growing season. Remove faded flowers to encourage additional flowering.

They may be propagated in early spring or late summer; prune the long stolons to reduce wilting. Sow seeds in late summer. Remove offsets in late winter or early spring, and root in sand.

ADDITIONAL NOTES: *Viola odorata*, the best known species, is the fragrant violet in the florist's bouquet and in poetry. It has long been important as a source of perfume and in the florist's trade. A number of garden forms are available, varying in growth habit, size, and flower color and with single or double flowers.

NATIVE HABITAT: Europe, Asia, and Africa.

SELECTED CULTIVARS AND VARIETIES: ◇ 'Parma': Double-flowered cultivar, flowering from mid-April through May. ◇ 'Rosina': Rosy-pink flowers. ◇ 'Royal Robe': Dark purple, very fragrant flowers are borne atop 8-inch stems; plant 1 foot apart in the rockery, or use as an edging or ground cover. ◇ 'Semperflorens': Flowers borne later, into early summer. ◇ 'White Czar': Faint yellow and blue streaks through chalky white petals. ◇ var. *rosina*: Many very fragrant, deep rose flowers are borne on 6-inch plants in early spirng. ◇

Waldsteinia

comprises a few species of hardy strawberry-like perennial herbs, with creeping rhizomes near the surface of the ground, native to the Northern Temperate Zone.

The genus was named after Franz Adam (1759-1823), the Count of Waldstein-Wartenburg.

Rosaceae
(Rose family)

Waldsteinia ternata
Barren Strawberry
Also known as Yellow Strawberry

FLOWERS: The small yellow flowers about ½ inch across are borne, in 3- to 8-flowered corymbs on bracted scapes up to 8 inches high, in May and June. The 5-petaled flowers are bisexual, regularly symmetrical, and sterile. The 5 sepals alternate with the 5 bracteoles. The calyx tube is inversely conical. There are many stamens.

LEAVES: The bright, glossy-green leaves are alternate, evergreen, mostly basal, and ternately palmately compound. The 3 leaflets are 1 to 2 inches long, dentate or crenate except at the base, and broadly cuneate.

PLANT CHARACTERISTICS: This 6- to 12-inch-high tufted perennial spreads slowly by short rhizomes and short stolons.

GARDEN VALUE: *Waldsteinia ternata* is grown as a low ground cover, in a rock garden, or as an edging plant for the perennial or shrub border.

CULTURE: The plant grows well in sun or shade but requires a well-drained garden soil.

The plant is easy to grow. Plant 10 to 12 inches apart in the spring. In dry, hot summers, water well to keep it lush; in dry soil, the plant loses the rhizomes and part of the stolons. Propagation is by division of terminal tip cuttings.

ADDITIONAL NOTES: Its sterile flower does not produce fruits. *Waldsteinia ternata* is not related to the strawberry genus and should not be mistaken for any of the strawberry plants, many of which are weeds.

This plant is sometimes sold as *Waldsteinia fragarioides*.

NATIVE HABITAT: Woody areas from Southern Canada to the Northeastern United States. ◇

Yucca

contains about 40 species of long-lived, stemless or erect, woody-trunked monocots in the warmer regions of North America.

Yucca, the native name for Manihot or Cassava, was erroneously applied to the members of this genus.

Agavaceae
(Yucca family)

Yucca smalliana
Spanish Bayonet
Also known as Adam's Needle, Needle Palm, Spanish Dagger, Bear Grass, Yucca, Soapweed, Heavenly Candles

FLOWERS: The nearly white, bell-shaped flowers are 2 inches across and are borne, pendulously on scapose panicles, usually glabrous, 4 to 6 feet high, from late June to July. The flowers are especially fragrant at night and last for a long time. The 6-segmented perianth is cup-shaped and partly united.

LEAVES: The long basal leaves are rigid, evergreen, scarcely glaucous, and spatulate; they narrow abruptly to a stout, terminal spine and grow $2\frac{1}{2}$ feet long and 1 inch across. Long curly threads dangle from the tips and margins of the leaves.

PLANT CHARACTERISTICS: These bold, stiff plants grow stemless in a rosette 2 feet high and 3 feet across; it grows wider as it produces offshoots at the base. A long-lived perennial, it has deep roots and is drought resistant.

GARDEN VALUE: *Yucca smalliana* is primarily grown for its exotic foliage effects and is even more effective when the plant is in flower. Use the plant as a bold accent plant and for formal effects in the large border, the perennial border, as a specimen among the shrubbery or elsewhere, or in a permanent landscape container. The large fruits are attractive in dried flower arrangements.

CULTURE: The plant performs best when grown in full sun and in a dry, arid soil. The plant is easy to grow. It is difficult to transplant when it is an old plant because its roots are deep. Water sparingly. The plant needs little fertilizer.

Instead of digging and transplanting the heavy root mass, sever the rooted offshoots from around the edge of the parent plant. Seeds usually germinate easily, but they take 2 or 3 years to produce a flowering-sized plant.

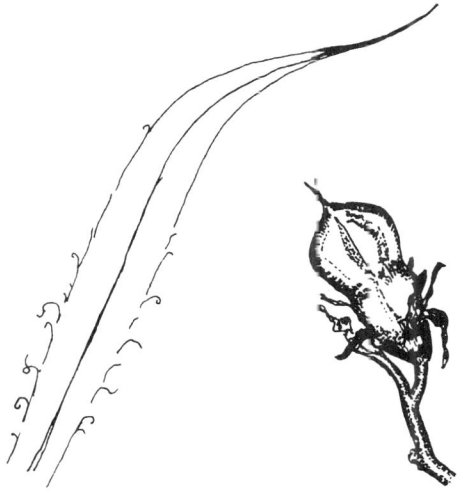

ADDITIONAL NOTES: *Yucca smalliana* is the only species of the genus that is dependably winter hardy and grown throughout the country. Much material distributed under this name is actually *Yucca flaccida*. This plant is also often mistakenly sold as *Yucca filamentosa*.

Early settlers discovered *Yucca smalliana* growing in sandy soils, many miles from the beaches along the Mid- and Southern Atlantic Coast. They made spoons from its stiff concave leaves and cords from the strong leaf fibers.

NATIVE HABITAT: North Carolina, south to Florida and Mississippi.

SELECTED CULTIVARS ◊ 'Bright Edge': Variegated foliage. ◊

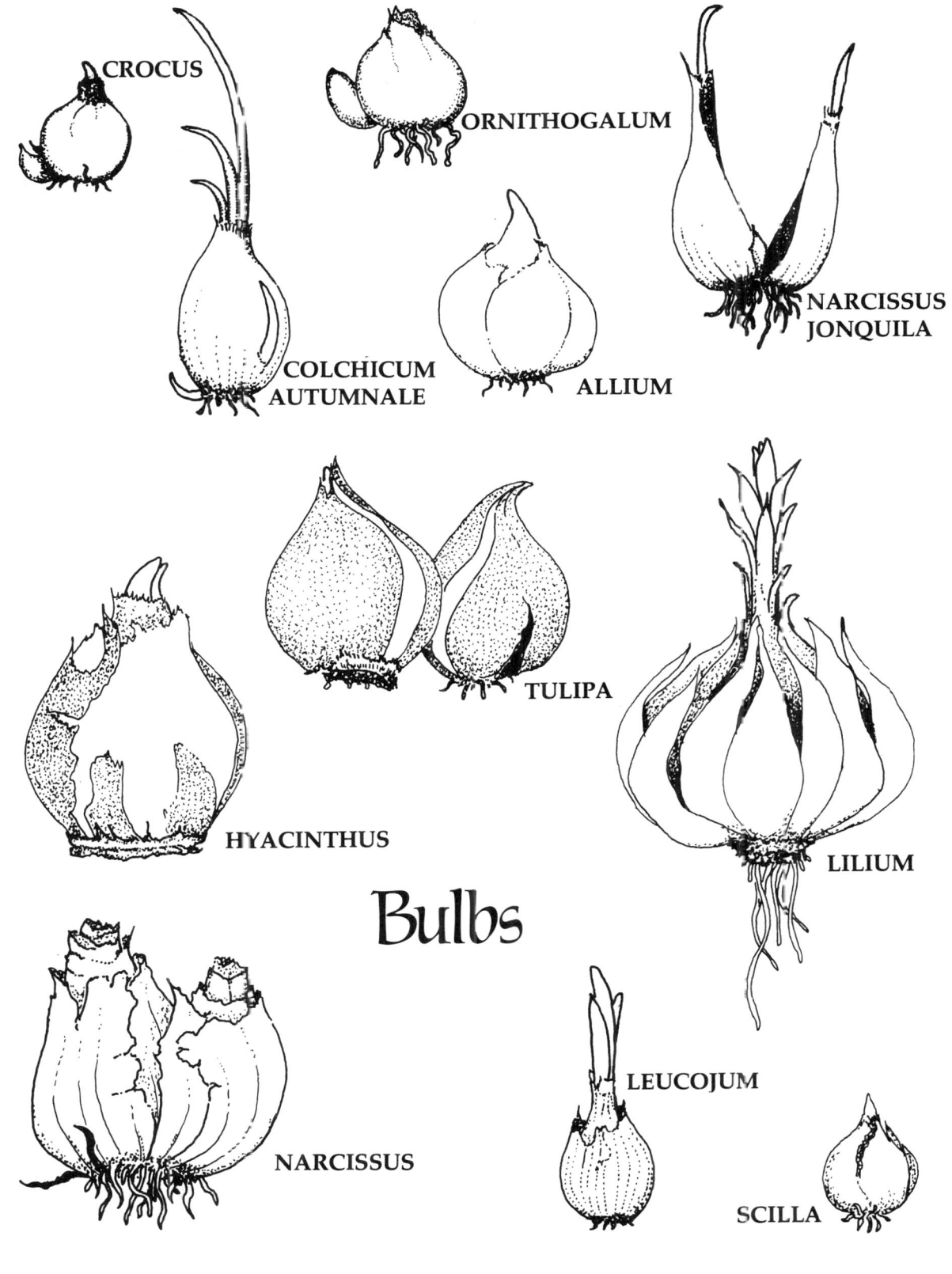

Allium

comprises over 400 species of rhizomatous and bulbous herbs that are primarily native to the Northern Hemisphere. The species, which are strongly odorous when bruised, vary in time of flowering (spring, summer, or autumn) and in height, from 6 inches to 5 feet. The genus contains edible species—onions, leeks, shallots, chives, and garlic—as well as unusual ornamental species. The genus name *Allium* is an ancient Latin name for garlic.

Amaryllidaceae
(Amaryllis family)

Allium christophii (Allium albopilosum)
Star-of-Persia

FLOWERS: The numerous small, metallic, lilac flowers are borne, in a rounded umbel 8 to 12 inches across atop a strong scape 2 feet high, in early June. The umbel is subtended by a short spathe or 1 or 2, or more, valves. The pedicels are nearly the same length. The stellate perianth has 6 segments, which are narrow and $\frac{1}{4}$ to $\frac{3}{4}$ inch long, becoming rigid and persistent.

LEAVES: There are 3 to 7 strap-shaped, basal leaves, 1 to 2 inches across and 18 inches long, somewhat glaucous, and white pubescent on the underside.

PLANT CHARACTERISTICS: The solitary bulbs are spherical and strongly scented. The bulb coat is membranous and gray. The stout scape grows to 2 or 3 feet high.

GARDEN VALUE: Because of its unusual, globelike flower head, this species is a striking accent when grown in mass or in the perennial or mixed border.

This plant provides excellent, long-lasting cut flowers. The odor of the cut stem disappears when placed in water. The flowers can be easily dried for winter arrangements; hang in a dry, warm, dark place until the flower head is completely dried, in order to retain the flower color.

CULTURE: *Allium christophii* is easy to grow. It does best in full sun and tolerates most soils.

Plant the bulbs in spring or fall. Place 6 inches deep and 8 inches apart. Apply a balanced fertilizer in spring, after new growth has been initiated. In northern areas, apply a winter mulch to protect the bulbs from heaving during periods of alternate freezing and thawing. Clumps may be left undisturbed for years. Replant when they have become too crowded to flower freely.

The plants may be propagated from seed. Sow seed as soon as it has ripened; seedlings require 2 or 3 years to reach flowering size. They are also propagated by offsets and by bulblets in the umbel.

ADDITIONAL NOTES: *Allium christophii* is probably the largest-flowering species of the genus, and one of the most beautiful.

NATIVE HABITAT: Iran and Asia Minor. ◇

Amaryllidaceae
(Amaryllis family)

Allium giganteum
Giant Onion

FLOWERS: The small bright lilac flowers are densely borne, in many-flowered globose umbels 4 or 5 inches across, in June. The umbels are subtended by a spathe of 1 or more valves and terminate in a 4- or 5-foot-high scape. The pedicels are nearly the same length. There are 6 perianth segments. The flowers open green and slowly turn to lilac, reversing to green upon maturity. The color changes begin at the top of the umbel and progress downward.

LEAVES: The glaucous straplike leaves are 2 inches wide and 18 inches long.

PLANT CHARACTERISTICS: This strongly scented plant grows 3 or 4 feet high. The bulb is ovoid with a membranous bulb coat.

GARDEN VALUE: *Allium giganteum* is planted in the perennial or mixed border. This plant provides fine cut flowers. The odor of the cut stem disappears when the stem is placed in water. The flowers can be easily dried for winter arrangements; hang in a dry, warm, dark place until the flower head is completely dried in order to retain the flower color.

CULTURE: *Allium giganteum* is easy to cultivate; it will grow in most garden soils in a sunny location.

Plant the bulbs in spring or fall. Place bulbs 6 inches deep and 8 to 10 inches apart. Apply a balanced fertilizer in spring, after new growth has been initiated. The scape may need staking. In northern areas, apply a winter mulch to protect the bulb from heaving during periods of alternate freezing and thawing.

The plant is usually propagated by offsets and bulblets. Seed sown as soon as it has ripened produces flowering-sized plants in 2 or 3 years.

NATIVE HABITAT: Central Asia. ◊

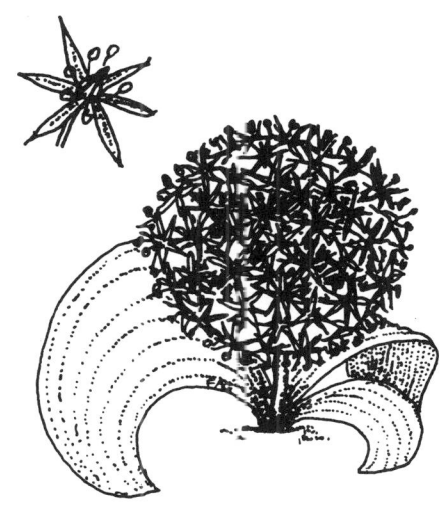

Amaryllidaceae
(Amaryllis family)

Allium karataviense
Turkestan Onion

FLOWERS: Small reddish flowers are borne, in a many-flowered globose umbel 3 to 4 inches across, terminating in a scape 10 inches high, in May and June. The flower head is subtended by a spathe of 1 or 2, sometimes more, valves. There are 6 narrow perianth segments, up to ½ inch long. The pedicels are 2 to 5 times as long as the flowers.

LEAVES: The glaucous leaves range from broadly ovate to elliptic and are 2 to 5 inches across and 6 to 12 inches long.

PLANT CHARACTERISTICS: This strongly scented plant grows up to 10 inches high. The bulb is ovoid and has a membranous outer bulb coat.

GARDEN VALUE: *Allium karataviense* is grown in the perennial or mixed border or planted in mass. The plant provides excellent cut flowers. The odor of the cut stem disappears when placed in water. The flowers can be easily dried for winter arrangements; hang them in a dry, warm, dark place until the flower head is completely dried in order to retain the flower color.

CULTURE: *Allium karataviense* is easy to cultivate; it grows in most soils and in full sun.

Plant the bulbs in spring or fall. Place 4 inches deep and 6 inches apart. Apply a balanced fertilizer in spring, after new growth has been initiated. In northern areas, apply a winter mulch to protect the bulbs from heaving during periods of alternate freezing and thawing. The clumps may be left undisturbed for years. Replant when they become too crowded to flower freely.

The plants are usually propagated by offsets and by bulblets. Seed may be sown as soon as it has ripened; however, seedlings require 2 or 3 years to reach flowering size.

NATIVE HABITAT: Turkestan. ◊

Amaryllidaceae
(Amaryllis family)

Allium moly
Lily Leek
Also known as Leek Lily, Golden Garlic

FLOWERS: The small, bright yellow flowers are borne, in many-flowered umbels 2 or 3 inches across, terminating in a scape 6 to 18 inches high, in late May and June. The flower head is subtended by a spathe of 1 or 2, or more, united valves. There are 6 stellate, $\frac{1}{4}$"- to $\frac{1}{2}$-inch-long, papery, and persistent perianth segments. The pedicels are 1 to 3 times as long as the flowers.

LEAVES: The 2 glaucous basal leaves are flat, lanceolate, and narrow toward the apex and the base, and grow 1 to 2 inches across and 8 to 12 inches long.

PLANT CHARACTERISTICS: This strongly scented plant is hardy in the North and grows 6 to 18 inches high. The ovoid bulb has a pale membrane covering the outer, leathery, bulb coat.

GARDEN VALUE: *Allium moly* is a popular bulb for massing and for rock garden use. It combines well with *Delphinium* in the perennial border.

This plant provides excellent cut flowers. The odor of the cut stem disappears when placed in water. The flowers can be easily dried for winter arrangements; hang in a dry, warm, dark place until the flower head is completely dried, in order to retain the flower color.

CULTURE: *Allium moly* is easy to grow and does best in full sun, in most garden soils.

Plant the bulbs in spring or fall. Place 4 inches deep and 6 inches apart. Apply a balanced fertilizer in spring, after new growth has been initiated. In northern areas, apply a winter mulch to protect the bulbs from heaving during periods of alternate freezing and thawing. The clumps may be left undisturbed for years. Replant when they become too crowded to flower freely.

The plants may be propagated from seed. Sow seeds as soon as they have ripened; seedlings require 2 or 3 years to reach flowering size. However, it is usually propagated by offsets and by bulblets.

ADDITIONAL NOTES: Homer wrote of *Allium moly* as having medical qualities because the plant was said to have prevented Ulysses from being changed into a pig. Today its presence in the garden is supposed to bring good fortune and prosperity.

NATIVE HABITAT: Southern Europe. ◇

Amaryllidaceae
(Amaryllis family)

Allium schoenoprasum
Chives

FLOWERS: The small, bright purple flowers are borne in many-flowered umbels terminating a scape 18 to 24 inches high. The umbel is subtended by a spathe of 1 or more valves. There are 6 ¼-inch-long perianth segments. The pedicels are unequal and shorter than the flowers.

LEAVES: The numerous leaves are hollow, slender, cylindrical or semicylindrical, and 4 to 6 inches long.

PLANT CHARACTERISTICS: These strongly scented plants have an outer membranous bulb coat. The scape is hollow and grows to 1 to 1½ feet high.

GARDEN VALUE: The plant may be placed in the perennial or mixed border, in the herb or vegetable garden, or in mass plantings. The foliage is used for seasoning, growing readily as it is cut.

This plant provides excellent cut flowers. The odor of the cut stem disappears when placed in water. The flowers can be easily dried for winter arrangements; hang in a dry, warm, dark place until the flowerhead is completely dried, in order to retain the flower color.

CULTURE: *Allium schoenoprasum* is easy to grow and does best in full sun and in most soils.

Plant the bulbs in spring or fall. Place 2 inches deep and 2 inches apart. Apply a balanced fertilizer in spring, after new growth has been initiated. Remove the flower scapes when they begin to become straggly, to encourage the plant to produce foliage until late fall. In the northern areas, apply a winter mulch to protect the bulbs from heaving during periods of alternate freezing and thawing. The clumps may be left undisturbed for years. Replant when they become too crowded to flower freely.

The plants may be propagated by offsets, bulblets, or by seed. Sow seed as soon as it has ripened; however, seedlings require 2 or 3 years to reach flowering size. Chives readily multiply by seedling around the clump.

NATIVE HABITAT: Europe and Asia. ◇

Anemone

includes about 120 species of hardy perennials native to the Northern Temperate Zone and to mountainous regions. *Anemone* is derived from the Greek word for "wind."

Ranunculaceae
(Crowfoot or buttercup family)

Anemone blanda
Greek Anemone

FLOWERS: Sky-blue flowers about 2 inches across are borne, solitary atop erect stems, in early spring. There are no petals; there are 10 to 14 petaloid, elongated, and obtuse sepals. The many stamens are shorter than the sepals. The flower is glabrous.

LEAVES: The basal leaves are divided; the principal divisions are sessile. The stem leaves form an involucre below the flower.

PLANT CHARACTERISTICS: This tuberous-rooted plant grows 3 to 8 inches high and is villous.

GARDEN VALUE: *Anemone blanda* is suitable for the perennial or mixed border, the rock garden, and the wild flower garden. The plants are effective when planted in mass with spring-flowering shrubs.

CULTURE: The plants prefer a fertile, humusy, well-drained, sandy soil, but they will grow in any good garden soil. They grow best in full sun or partial shade. In southern areas, they need protection from the sun during the heat of the day.

Plant in fall or very early spring. Soak tubers in tepid water up to 48 hours before planting. Set tubers 2 inches deep and 4 to 6 inches apart. They require moisture during the flowering period. In northern areas, protect the plants with a deep winter mulch such as wood chips.

Plants may be propagated by root division or seed. Sow seeds shallowly, in early fall or early spring. Seedlings require 18 months to reach flowering size. Divide roots in early spring before new growth begins.

NATIVE HABITAT: Southeastern Europe and Asia Minor.

SELECTED CULTIVARS: ◊ 'Atrocoerulea': Deep blue flowers, freely borne in March. ◊ 'Blue Star': Large, intensely blue single flowers. ◊ 'Pink Star': Pink flowers with yellow centers. ◊ 'Radar': Sepals are bright red on the outer part and whitish in the center. ◊ 'White Splendour': Snow-white flowers with golden centers. ◊

Ranunculaceae
(Crowfoot or buttercup family)

Anemone coronaria
Poppy-flowered Anemone

FLOWERS: Red, blue, or white flowers 2 to 3 inches across are borne solitary in early spring. The petals are absent; there are 6 to 8 petaloid, elliptic sepals. The numerous stamens are blue and are shorter than the sepals.

LEAVES: The basal leaves are biternate and petioled. The stem leaves form an involucre below the flower and are divided and sessile.

PLANT CHARACTERISTICS: This perennial plant grows 12 to 18 inches high from tuberous rhizomes.

GARDEN VALUE: The plant is usually grown in the perennial border, among ground covers, in the wild flower garden, in the rock garden, or on a bank.

The flowers are long-lived when cut. When collecting them, use a sharp knife or shears to cut the stems close to the ground. If you pull the stems, you could tear the crown of the tuber.

CULTURE: *Anemone coronaria* thrives in a fertile, humusy, well-drained, sandy loam in a sunny or lightly shaded site. In southern areas, these plants need protection from the sun during the heat of the day. They grow best in a temperate, moist climate, such as that of the Pacific Northwest.

Plant in spring or fall. Soak the tubers in tepid water up to 48 hours before planting. Set tubers 6 inches apart and 3 inches deep. In northern areas where the plants are not able to survive winter, the tubers may be lifted each fall, stored in dry peatmoss, perlite, or vermiculite at 55° to 60°F, and replanted in the spring. They must remain completely dry in storage.

Propagate by seed or root division. Sow seeds shallowly in early fall or early spring, to produce flowering-sized plants in 18 months. Divide roots in early spring before new growth begins.

ADDITIONAL NOTES: *Anemone coronaria* is the most common species in the florist's trade.

NATIVE HABITAT: Mediterranean region.

SELECTED CULTIVARS: ◊ 'Chrysanthemiflora': Many petals, giving a full, rounded shape. ◊ 'DeCaen': Single flowers ranging through white, pink, red, purple, and blue with black centers, providing good cut flowers. ◊ 'Flore Pleno': Double flowers in many colors, scarlet is most common. ◊ 'His Excellency' ◊ 'Mr. Fokker' ◊ 'St. Bridget': Semi-double flowers in mixed colors; named after St. Brigid, 452 to 523 A.D., the patronness of Ireland. ◊ 'Sulphide' ◊ 'The Bride' ◊

Ranunculaceae
(Crowfoot or Buttercup family)

Anemone X hybrida (Anemone hupehensis Japonica)
Japanese Anemone

FLOWERS: The pink and white flowers are usually borne solitary. The petals are absent and the sepals are petaloid and broad. The numerous stamens are shorter than the sepals.

LEAVES: The basal leaves are 5-lobed and usually cordate, with twice-serrated lobes. The stem leaves form an involucre below the flower.

PLANT CHARACTERISTICS: This delicate, soft plant may grow to 4 feet and is covered with many flowers.

GARDEN VALUE: *Anemone X hybrida* is usually grown in the perennial or mixed border.

CULTURE: *Anemone X hybrida* thrives in a fertile, humusy, well-drained sandy loam in a sunny or lightly shaded site. In southern areas, these plants need protection from the sun during the heat of the day. They grow best in a temperate, moist climate such as that of the Pacific Northwest.

Plant in spring or fall. Set tubers 3 inches deep and 12 inches apart. In northern areas where the plants are not able survive winter, the tubers may be lifted each fall, stored in dry peatmoss, perlite, or vermiculite and replanted in the spring. They must remain completely dry in storage.

Propagate by seed or root division. Sow seeds shallowly in either early fall or early spring, to produce flowering-sized plants in 18 months. Divide roots in early spring, before new growth begins.

ADDITIONAL NOTES: *Anemone X hybrida* was produced in the Royal Gardens, England, in 1848. It is a cross between *Anemone hupehensis* var. *japonica* and *Anemone vitifolia*. It is sometimes offered as *Anemone japonica*.

SELECTED CULTIVARS: ◊ 'Alba': White flowers. ◊ 'Crispa': Leaves crisped. ◊ 'Lesseri': Crimson flowers. ◊ 'Rosea Superba': Rose flowers. ◊ 'Rubra': Waxy-red flowers. ◊

Ranunculaceae
(Buttercup or Crowfoot family)

Anemone pulsatilla (Pulsatilla amoena, Pulsatilla vulgaris)
Pasque-flower, European Pasque-flower

FLOWERS: The reddish-purple to bluish flowers 1½ to 2½ inches across are borne, on an erect 12-inch stem, in April. There are no petals; the 5 sepals are petaloid. The numerous stamens are shorter than the sepals.

LEAVES: The basal leaves develop after the flowers. The leaves are 4 to 6 inches long on slender petioles and 3-pinnate, and have linear segments. Stem leaves form an involucre below the flower. The involucral leaves are 1 inch long and sessile, and have linear lobes.

PLANT CHARACTERISTICS: This villous plant has erect stems which grow up 10 or 12 inches high when in flower, becoming 15 inches high when in fruit.

GARDEN VALUE: *Anemone pulsatilla* is a valued rock garden plant that prefers dry soil. It is also popularly planted in the perennial and the mixed border.

CULTURE: *Anemone pulsatilla* thrives in a site that has sun for half the day and a well-drained or rocky soil. Plant in spring or fall. Soak the tubers in tepid water overnight before planting. Set tubers 2 inches deep and 12 inches apart. In northern areas where the plants are not able to survive winter, the crowns may be lifted each fall, stored in dry peatmoss, perlite, or vermiculite and replanted in the spring. They must remain completely dry in storage.

Propagate by seed or root division. Sow seeds shallowly in either early fall or early spring, to produce flowering-sized plants in 18 months. Divide roots in early spring before new growth begins.

ADDITIONAL NOTES: *Anemone pulsatilla* has been used medicinally. A nonpermanent green dye is extracted from the purple petals and is used to color Easter eggs.

NATIVE HABITAT: Europe and Asia.

SELECTED CULTIVARS: ◊ 'Alba': White flowers. ◊ 'Albicyanea': Bluish-white flowers. ◊ 'Rubra': Burgundy-red flowers. ◊ 'Vulgaris': Woolly buds, opening purple and turning to violet. ◊

Ranunculaceae
(Buttercup or crowfoot family)

Anemone vitifolia

FLOWERS: The silvery-pink flowers 2 or 3 inches across are borne, solitary in open cymes. There are no petals, and the 5 sepals are petaloid and hairy on the outside. The numerous stamens are shorter than the sepals.

LEAVES: The large basal leaves are 3- to 7-lobed. Stem leaves form an involucre below the flower.

PLANT CHARACTERISTICS: The tuberous plant grows 1 to 3 feet high.

GARDEN VALUE: *Anemone vitifolia* is usually grown in the perennial or mixed border.

CULTURE: *Anemone vitifolia* grows best in a fertile, humusy, well-drained, sandy loam in a sunny or lightly shaded site. In southern areas, these plants need protection from the sun during the heat of the day. They prefer a temperate, moist climate such as that of the Pacific Northwest.

Plant in spring or fall. Soak the tubers in tepid water overnight before planting. Set tubers 3 inches deep and 10 inches apart. In northern areas where the plants are not able to survive winter, the tubers may be lifted in fall, stored in dry peatmoss, perlite, or vermiculite and planted in the spring. They must remain completely dry in storage.

Propagate by seed or root division. Sow seeds shallowly in either early fall or early spring, to produce flowering-sized plants in 18 months. Divide roots in early spring before new growth begins.

NATIVE HABITAT: Nepal.

SELECTED CULTIVARS: ◇ 'Robustissima': Pale pink flowers on a plant that grows to $2\frac{1}{2}$ feet high. ◇

Colchicum

includes nearly 70 species of perennial herbs native to Europe, North Africa, and Western and Central Asia. The species grow from corms, produce their stems and scapes underground, and usually flower in the autumn.

The genus name *Colchicum* is derived from Colchis, a country in Asia Minor, one of the native habitats of the genus.

Liliaceae
(Lily family)

Colchicum autumnale
Autumn Crocus
Also known as Fall Crocus, Wonder Bulb, Meadow Saffron, Mysteria

FLOWERS: The purple-to-white crocus-like flowers are single or sometimes double, up to 4 inches across, and are borne, 1 to 4 in each spathe, during August and September. The 6 perianth segments are joined basally into a long tube extending underground.

LEAVES: There are 3 to 8 linear, lanceolate leaves 9 to 12 inches long and 1½ to 2 inches across, borne in the spring and usually dying back to the ground by June.

PLANT CHARACTERISTICS: The plant grows 3 or 4 inches high from a corm. The stem and the scape are borne underground.

GARDEN VALUE: *Colchicum autumnale* is most effective when planted in mass. It is usually grown in the rock garden, perennial border, or mixed border. The flowers are borne in August and September, when the herbaceous borders begin to lose their freshness. Although individual flowers are short-lived, others follow in quick succession to prolong the flowering period. Because the leaves die down before the flowers are borne, these plants should be planted against other plants with low-growing foliage, such as *Phlox subulata*, *Sedum* species, and dwarf species of *Artemisia* and *Aster*.

CULTURE: The plant is easy to cultivate. It grows best in an open, sunny or partially shaded site, and prefers a deep, fertile, light, sandy loam.

Plant in August or early September, or as soon as the tubers are available. A delay in planting usually results in having the plants flowering in the package. Place the tips of the corms 2 or 3 inches below the surface of the soil and 6 to 9 inches apart. Provide a winter mulch to protect the plants during winter. Do not disturb until plants show signs of deterioration—fewer flowers and poor foliage.

Propagate by division of corms and by seed. Divide corms in June or early July. Seeds should be sown as soon as they ripen. Seedlings require 3 to 5 years to attain flowering size.

ADDITIONAL NOTES: Colchicum, a medicine, and Colchicine, a mutagenic agent used in plant breeding, are derived from the dried corms and seeds of this plant.

NATIVE HABITAT: Europe and Northern Asia.

SELECTED CULTIVARS: ◇ 'Album': White flowers. ◇ 'Minus': Dwarf form. ◇ 'Roseum': Rose-pink flowers. ◇

Crocus

comprises about 80 species of bulbs primarily native to the Mediterranean region. The showy plants grow from a tunicate corm and bear flowers in spring or autumn.

The genus name *Crocus* is of Greek origin, meaning "saffron."

Iridaceae
(Iris family)

Crocus species
Spring-flowering Crocus

FLOWERS: The showy white, yellow, or lilac-to-deep purple, funnel form flowers are borne erect and appear in early spring. The perianth tube is long and slender; there are 6 equal or nearly equal perianth segments. The 3 prominent yellow stamens are attached to the throat of the perianth tube and are shorter than the segments. The peduncle and ovary are subterranean.

LEAVES: The linear leaves are grasslike. The flowers are produced before the leaves are fully developed. The foliage continues to grow after the flowers fade, becoming arched and 8 to 10 inches long when mature.

PLANT CHARACTERISTICS: These stemless plants arise from tunicate corms.

GARDEN VALUE: Many forms of *Crocus* are popularly grown. They are planted in the rock garden, perennial border, mixed border, and wild flower garden and are naturalized in the lawn, as well as in the foundation planting. Plant, in masses of 6 or more corms, closely together in 1 spot for a more effective display of flowers. The flowering season can be lengthened by proper selection of species or by planting in a protected, warm site where they may flower 2 weeks earlier than in an open exposed site.

CULTURE: *Crocus* thrive in a sunny site with a perfectly-drained soil, free from clay and decaying humus or manure. They perform best in regions that have cool or cold winters.

Plant corms in September or October. Inspect all corms and plant only the healthy ones. Bruised corms are susceptible to fungal disease. Place bulbs 3 or 4 inches deep and 2 or 3 inches apart.

Scatter a light application of bonemeal or balanced fertilizer on the soil each fall. Occasionally mice, chipmunks, and squirrels eat the corms.

When naturalized in the lawn, the foliage of the plants must be allowed to mature and die back to the ground before the lawn is mowed. If the leaves are removed prematurely, the plants will not last more than 1 or 2 years.

Because new corms form on top of old ones, the plants tend to grow out of the ground. Replant the strongest corms every 2 or 3 years. When the plants begin to form tight clumps and produce few flowers, they should be lifted and separated. This is usually done in late June, after the leaves have died down, or in early September.

Seeds are produced freely but are often overlooked because they form at the surface of the soil. These germinate easily in the spring and produce flowers in the third season.

ADDITIONAL NOTES: Saffron, a yellow food coloring and flavoring, is derived from the stigmas of *Crocus sativus*.

Crocus sativus is probably the most satisfactory of the fall-flowering types. The flowers appear in the fall without foliage.

HYBRID: *Crocus* 'Dutch Hybrids': The Dutch hybrids are primarily bred from *Crocus maesiacus* and have larger flowers than the species. The stigmas are brilliant orange or yellow. ◊ 'Snowstorm': White flowers. ◊ 'Striped Beauty': White flowers with lilac stripes. ◊ 'Yellow Mammoth': Large yellow flowers. ◊ 'Remembrance': Soft purplish-blue flowers.

SPECIES:

Crocus angustifolius: Cloth-of-gold Crocus. The bright orangish-yellow starlike flowers are borne in February and March. The perianth segments are 1 to 1½ inch long, acute, and reflexed. Outer segments are usually brown or striped on the outside. There are 6 to 8 leaves, in a tuft, linear, with revolute edges and a band of white down the middle of the leaf. The plant grows 3 to 6 inches high; the corm is ¾ inch in diameter. Its native habitat is in the Crimean Mountains in Southwestern Russia.

Crocus korolkowii: Celandine Crocus. The shiny orangish-yellow starlike flowers are borne in early March. The perianth tube is shortly exserted; the perianth segments are ¾ to 1 inch long. The outer segments have dense brown speckles and are often veined on the outside. There are 8 to 12 very narrow leaves, with reflexed edges and a central white band down the middle. The plant grows 3 to 6 inches high. The corm is large and flattened. *Crocus korolkowii* is a popular rock garden plant. Its native habitat is Southeastern Europe.

◊ 'Vinosus': Perianth segments are purple-veined on the outside.

Crocus sieberi: Sieber Crocus. The dark purple-to-white starlike flowers with orangish-yellow throats are borne in winter. The perianth tube is shortly exserted. The perianth segments spread, are oblong and 1 to 1½ inches long, and have darker streaks or darker feathering on the outside. The 4 to 6 leaves grow as high as the flowers. The leaves are glaucous on the underside and ¼- to ½-inch wide. The globular corm is ¾ inch in diameter. Its native habitat is Greece and Crete.
◇ 'Firefly': Bright lilac-pink flowers with orange stamens. ◇ 'Hubert Edelsten': Violet-purple flowers with richly colored outer petals that have broad white bands, and paler inner petals. ◇ 'Purpureus': Dark-colored flowers.

Crocus vernus: Dutch Crocus, Common Crocus. The white-to-lilac or purple starlike flowers with white bearded throats are borne in early spring. The flowers are often feathered or striped darker purple on the outside. The perianth segments are 1 to 1½ inches long. There are 2 to 4 leaves, ¼ inch across and 3 to 6 inches high. They are green on the upper surface and glaucous beneath, with reflexed edges and a central white band. The globose corm is 1 inch or less in diameter. It is one of the most commonly cultivated species. Its native habitat is Central and Southern Europe.
◇ 'Vanguard'

Crocus versicolor: Cloth-of-silver Crocus. The white flowers are suffused with lilac and starlike, with a white-to-pale-yellow glabrous throat. The perianth segments are up to 1½ inch long. The inner segments are feathered purple on the outside. There are 4 or 5 leaves, 3 to 6 inches long. The corm is ½ to ¾ inch in diameter. Its native habitat is Southern France.
◇ 'Picturatus': Pure white flowers with feathery outer perianth segments. ◇

Eranthis

consists of about 7 species of low perennial herbs native to Europe and Asia.

Eranthis is derived from the Greek words *er*, meaning "spring," and *anthos*, meaning "flowers," because the flowers open very early in the spring.

Ranunculaceae
(Buttercup or Crowfoot family)

Eranthis hyemalis
Winter Aconite

FLOWERS: The bright yellow, honey-scented flowers about 1 inch across are borne solitary from February to March, or as soon as the ground is free from frost. The flowers are borne sessile above a horizontally spreading involucre. The petals are modified into small, 2-lipped nectaries. There are usually 6 petaloid, oblong sepals. There are many stamens.

LEAVES: The basal leaves are usually solitary, orbicular, palmately dissected, and long-petioled. The involucral leaves are sessile. The foliage usually dies back to the ground by mid-May.

PLANT CHARACTERISTICS: This hardy, erect, glabrous plant grows 5 to 8 inches high and has a tuberous rootstock. It tolerates snow and sleet well; unseasonable heat usually shortens the flowering season.

GARDEN VALUE: *Eranthis hyemalis* is especially lovely in the rock garden and massed in large numbers in naturalized areas. Plant it in the perennial or mixed border. Do not place *Eranthis hyemalis* in the lawn because it does not compete well with grass.

CULTURE: *Eranthis hyemalis* thrives in a rich, humusy soil in full sun or light shade, in a site protected from the wind.

Plant in late summer or early autumn placing about 2 inches deep and 3 to 4 inches apart.

If the tubers are dried when they arrive, soak them overnight in water and plant immediately. The plants can be moved when in flower if they are transplanted without removing the soil clinging to them. Mark the location of the tubers so that they can be protected against disturbances, such as from cultivation, after the foliage has died down. Do not allow the soil to dry out in summer.

Propagate by division of tubers in late summer. The plants are self-sowing; however, the seedlings require 2 or 3 years to produce flowers.

ADDITIONAL NOTES: *Eranthis* should not be confused with the true aconites (*Aconitum*), which are summer-flowering perennials.

NATIVE HABITAT: Europe and Asia. ◊

Fritillaria

includes about 100 species of perennial herbs native to Western North America, Europe, Asia, and North Africa. They are hardy, spring-flowering, mostly low-growing, bulbous plants with drooping or nodding flowers.

The genus name *Fritillaria* is derived from the Latin word *fritillus*, meaning "checker-board" or "dice box."

Liliaceae
(Lily family)

Fritillaria imperalis
Crown Imperial, Imperial Fritillary

FLOWERS: Clusters of nodding reddish-orange flowers up to 2 inches long are borne pendant on curved pedicels below a crest of leaves, at the end of a naked terminal peduncle. The musky-scented flowers are borne, atop $2\frac{1}{2}$- to 4-foot stems, in late April and May. There are 6 perianth segments, of which at least the inner segments are separate; they are nearly equal, ovate or oblong, and bear a nectar gland.

LEAVES: The numerous leaves are alternate, lanceolate, and crowded, and up to 6 inches long and $\frac{1}{2}$ to 1 inch across. The stem leaves are alternate or whorled, sessile, and narrow. The leaves die to the ground by early summer.

PLANT CHARACTERISTICS: The tunicate bulb has several fleshy scales and is 3 or 4 inches in diameter. Several scapes 2 or 3 feet high emerge from each bulb. The vigorous plant has a skunklike odor.

GARDEN VALUE: Because this old-fashioned plant has a musky odor and its leaves die down in early summer,

Fritillaria imperalis is usually planted in the perennial or shrub border.

CULTURE: *Fritillaria imperalis* requires a well-drained, warm, deep, rich, sandy soil with a pH of 6.0 to 7.5, which has been deeply cultivated. The plants are longer-lived and produce larger flowers if provided shade from the midday sun.

Plant in early fall. Place bulbs about 8 inches apart and 6 inches below the surface of the ground. Apply a balanced fertilizer when new growth emerges in spring and a pinch of lime at flowering time. Water well during dry periods in spring. Divide plants in early summer after the leaves have died down, about every 2 or 3 years.

They are usually propagated by division of the bulbs. The plant is rarely propagated by seeds; the seedlings take 4 to 6 years to reach flowering size.

NATIVE HABITAT: Iran, Afghanistan, and Northern India.

SELECTED CULTIVARS: ◇ 'Aurea': Red-orange flowers. ◇ 'Lutea': Yellow flowers. ◇ 'Maxima': Strong-growing plant with orange-red flowers. ◇ 'Rubra': Large red flowers. ◇ 'Sulphurea': Yellow flowers.

RELATED SPECIES: *Fritillaria meleagris*: Checkered Lily, Snake's Head, Guinea Hen Tulip. Drooping, dull purplish flowers 1½ inches long are borne, usually solitary, sometimes in 2's or 3's, in April. The flowers are campanulate, checkered, and veined with shades of reddish-purple. The segments are oblong, narrow at both ends, and 1½ inches long. The leaves are alternate, ranging from linear to oblanceolate, and 3 to 6 inches long. The bulb is tunicate and has 2 fleshy scales. The stem grows 12 to 15 inches high. The plant is usually short-lived. The species needs a light background to be displayed effectively. The bulbs prefer a light, moist, well-drained soil and partial shade. Select a sheltered site that does not face east, to reduce frost damage. Set bulbs 3 to 4 inches deep and 3 or 4 inches apart. Its native habitat is from England and Norway, through central Europe to the Caucasus.

◇ 'Alba': White flowers. ◇ 'Purpurea': Purplish flowers. ◇

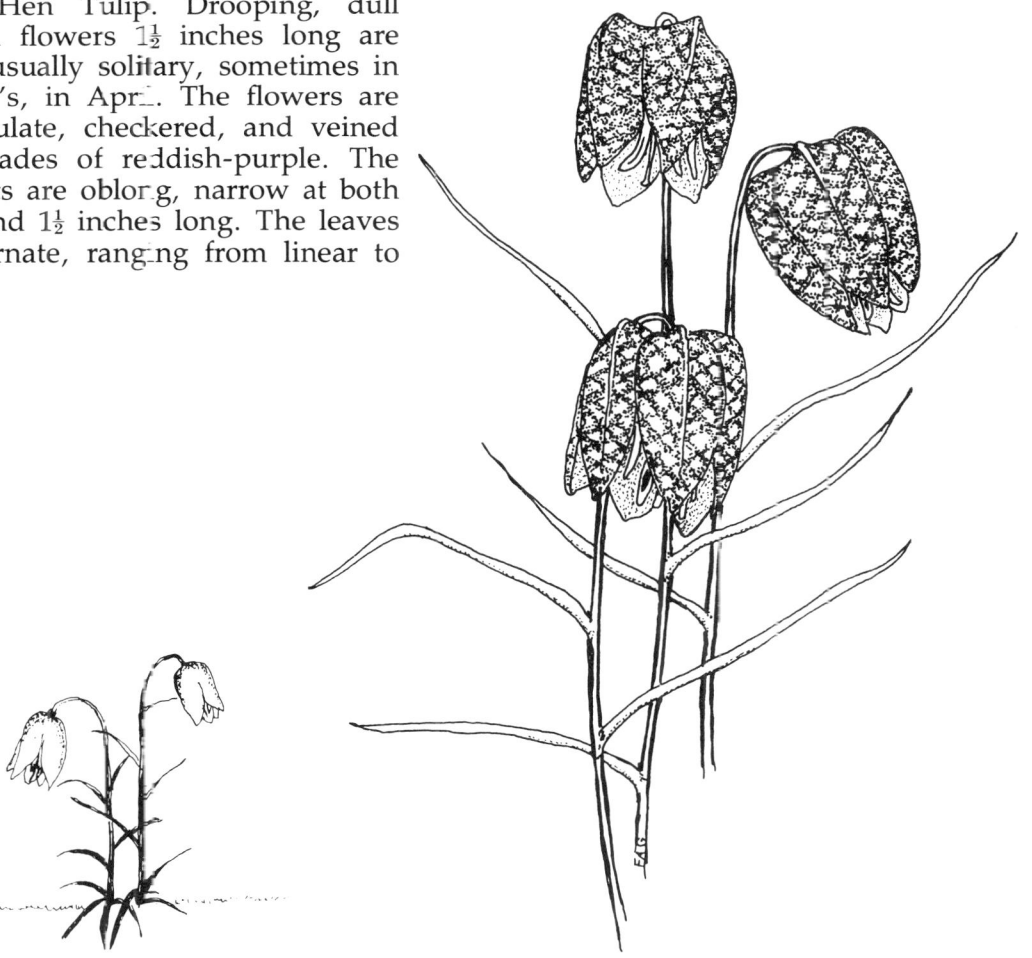

Galanthus

consists of about 12 species of herbs native to Europe and Asia. The species are bulbous and mostly spring-flowering, with solitary, nodding white flowers.

The genus name *Galanthus* is a Greek word, meaning "milkflower."

Amaryllidaceae
(Amaryllis family)

Galanthus nivalis
Common Snowdrop

FLOWERS: The small, nodding translucent flowers about 1 inch across are borne solitary in March. The flowers are subtended by a papery spathe, split on one side. The perianth segments are separate; the 3 inner ones are shorter, with the overlap appearing tubular, and are white with green markings around the sinus. The outer segments are white and oblong. There are 5 stamens.

LEAVES: The 2 dark, shining leaves are basal, glaucous, linear, 4 to 9 inches tall and $\frac{1}{4}$ inch wide, and channeled. The leaves appear with the flowers, reach their full growth after the flowers have faded, and usually die down in midsummer.

PLANT CHARACTERISTICS: The small, globose, tunicated bulb is membranous-coated. The plant grows 6 to 9 inches high and usually bears a single flower.

GARDEN VALUE: The flowers of *Galanthus nivalis* are among the smallest and daintiest of the hardy, commonly cultivated, spring-flowering bulbs. They often flower in early March, before all the snow has gone. The plants grow well under deciduous trees or with an evergreen ground cover; they are well suited to naturalizing in a lawn or in the wild flower garden.

CULTURE: *Galanthus nivalis* is easy to grow. It performs well in most garden soils and does best in partial shade, and in cooler climates rather than in warm ones. Under proper conditions—shady, moist, and cool—the plants increase without attention.

Plant in autumn. Place bulbs 3 or 4 inches deep and 2 to 4 inches apart in large masses. Do not fertilize. The bulbs can be divided soon after flowering. They should be replanted immediately so that the roots do not dry out.

They are easily propagated by offsets and by seed. Seedlings need 3 or 4 years to reach flowering size.

ADDITIONAL NOTES: This European species is the most commonly cultivated species in America.

NATIVE HABITAT: Europe.

SELECTED CULTIVARS: ◊ 'Flore Pleno': Doubled flowers. ◊ 'Lutescens': Yellow markings on the inner segments and the ovary. ◊ 'Simplex': Single flowers. ◊

Hyacinthus

is a popular spring-flowering, fragrant, bulbous, perennial herb native to the Mediterranean region and Asia Minor.

Hyacinthus was created by Apollo, according to Greek mythology, to express his grief at having accidentally killed the youth Hyacinthus.

Liliaceae
(Lily family)

Hyacinthus orientalis
Common Hyacinth, Dutch Hyacinth, Garden Hyacinth

FLOWERS: The intensely fragrant flowers are white, yellow, red, pink, or blue, 1 inch long, occasionally doubled, and are borne, in a dense cylindrical raceme 6 to 10 inches long terminating a stout, hollow scape 8 to 12 inches high, in early spring. The perianth is funnelform and has 6 oblong-spatulate lobes.

LEAVES: The 4 to 6 thick green leaves are basal, strap-shaped, 8 to 12 inches long and $\frac{1}{2}$ to $1\frac{1}{2}$ inches wide, and many-nerved.

PLANT CHARACTERISTICS: This stemless plant grows 8 to 12 inches high and has a tunicate bulb.

GARDEN VALUE: The brightly colored flowers have a delightful fragrance and are popular in the spring garden, the rock garden, the perennial or mixed border, or the foundation planting. A few hyacinth plants carefully placed provide colorful spring interest. It flowers at the same time as the midseason Tulips.

CULTURE: The plant grows best in full sun and a well-drained soil.

Plant in September and October. Place the bottoms of the bulbs about 5 or 6 inches below the surface of a properly prepared soil, spacing them 6 to 9 inches apart. Mulch thoroughly with wood chips or salt hay for winter protection. In colder areas, the bulbs should be lifted in fall, stored in a dry, cool spot, and replanted in early spring. The flowers become smaller during the second season because the large bulb splits into 2 or more smaller bulbs. In order to have a bed of large flowers each spring, new bulbs should be planted every other year.

Propagate by separation of offsets from old bulbs or from bulblets, which will produce flowering-sized bulbs in 2 or 3 years.

ADDITIONAL NOTES: *Hyacinthus orientalis* is grown in Southern France as a source of perfume. It has been cultivated for centuries.

NATIVE HABITAT: Syria, North Africa, and from Greece to Asia Minor.

SELECTED CULTIVARS: ◇ 'Amsterdam': Salmon-pink flowers. ◇ 'Anne Marie': Clear pink flowers. ◇ 'Blue Jacket': Bright navy-blue flowers with black stems. ◇ 'City of Haarlem': Primrose-yellow flowers. ◇ 'Delft Blue': Blue flowers. ◇ 'Jan Bos': Carmine-red flowers. ◇ 'King of the Blues': Rich indigo-blue flowers. ◇ 'L'Innocence': Pure white flowers. ◇ 'Lady Derby': Light shell-pink flowers. ◇ 'Orange Boven': Soft salmon-orange flowers. ◇ 'Perle Brilliant': Light blue flowers. ◇ 'Pink Pearl': Deep pink flowers. ◇ 'Princess Irene': Rose-pink flowers. ◇ 'Princess Margaret': Rose-pink flowers. ◇

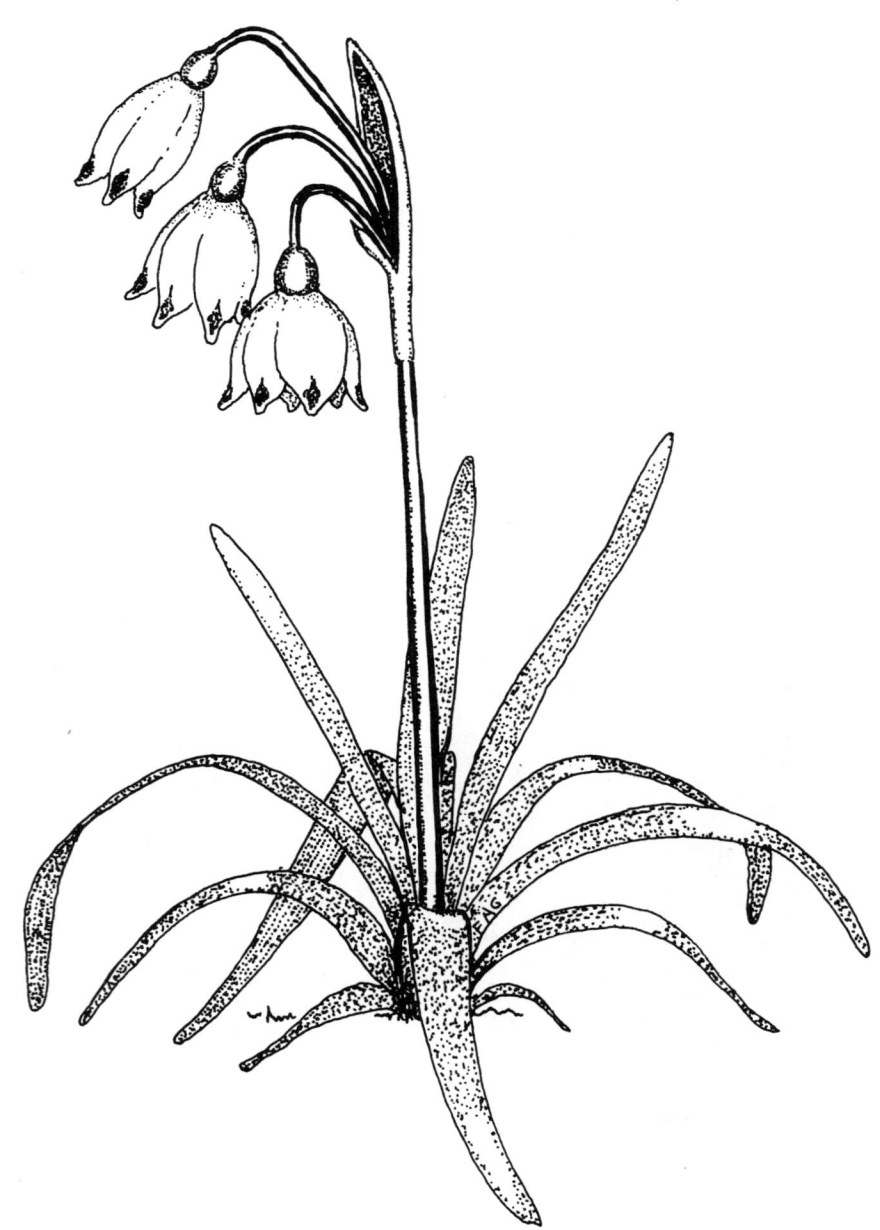

Leucojum

comprises about 9 species of small, hardy, bulbous herbs native to Europe and the Western Mediterranean region.

The genus name *Leucojum* was assigned to these plants by Linnaeus. "Leucoion" is derived from the Greek *leukos*, meaning "shining, white," and *ion*, meaning "violet." Plants of the *Leucojum* genus flower with the early white violets and sometimes have a delicate violet-like fragrance.

Amaryllidaceae
(Amaryllis family)

Leucojum aestivum
Giant Snowflake, Summer Snowflake

FLOWERS: The nodding, white, campanulate flowers are tipped with green and borne in a 2- to 8-flowered umbel on a hollow scape 10 to 15 inches high. The flowers are $\frac{3}{4}$ inch long and are borne, on long nodding pedicels, in April and May, after most spring-flowering bulbs are finished. The flowers are subtended by a spathe. The perianth segments are separate, uniform, ovate or oblong, and spreading.

LEAVES: The green leaves are slender, strap-shaped, 1 to $1\frac{1}{2}$ feet long and $\frac{1}{2}$ inch across. The foliage usually dies back to the ground by the end of June.

PLANT CHARACTERISTICS: This hardy plant grows up to 1 foot high. The rootstock is an ovoid bulb that is 1 to $1\frac{1}{2}$ inches in diameter.

GARDEN VALUE: *Leucojum aestivum* are best planted in large clumps under deciduous trees. They may also be planted in the perennial border and the rock garden, or naturalized in the lawn or the wild flower garden. The plant provides unusual cut flowers.

CULTURE: *Leucojum* grows best in full sun or light shade and in a well-drained soil.

Plant the bulbs in autumn, as soon as they are available. Place them 3 inches deep and 4 inches apart. Late planting may result in the delay of flowering until the second season. Provide a good mulch for winter protection. Leave the bulbs undisturbed.

They are usually propagated from the offsets. Seedlings take about 3 years to flower.

ADDITIONAL NOTES: *Leucojum* is related to *Galanthus* but is less popular.

NATIVE HABITAT: Central and Southern Europe.

SELECTED CULTIVARS: ◇ 'Gravetye': Up to 9 flowers are borne on each stem of a plant 18 inches high. ◇

Lilium

comprises nearly 90 species of perennial bulbs native to the North Temperate Zone.

Lilium is said to be derived from the Celtic word *li*, meaning "whiteness," a reference to the white flower of *Lilium candidum*.

The Royal Horticulture Society and the North American Lily Society have divided the genus into nine groups based on origin and flower form: Asiatic Hybrids; Martagon Hybrids; Candidum Hybrids; American Hybrids; Longiflorum Hybrids; Aurelian Hybrids; Oriental Hybrids; Unclassified Hybrids; and True Species.

Liliaceae
(Lily family)

Lilium species
Lily

FLOWERS: The flowers are borne solitary and terminal or in terminal racemes, panicles, or umbels. They are white, red, purple, maroon, orange, and yellow, but never blue, and may have spots on the inside of the perianth. The flowers are perfect. They are borne from June until September, depending upon the species or hybrid. The perianth is funnelform, campanulate, or cup-shaped, and has 6 spreading or reflexed segments, each with a basal gland containing nectar. Each flower has 6 conspicuous stamens and 1 long pistil.

LEAVES: The bright green leaves are linear or lanceolate, usually sessile but with short petioles in a few species, and are borne alternate or whorled the length of the stem.

PLANT CHARACTERISTICS: *Lilium* is a herbaceous perennial with a scaly bulb. The stems are single, smooth or pubescent, and usually bright green, but sometimes tinged with brown or purple. Many species produce fibrous roots above the bulb from the underground portion of the stem.

GARDEN VALUE: The *Lilium* species and hybrids are stately garden plants, and can be used to create a focal point in the garden. They are effective in small groups, in front of a hedge, fence, or evergreen border, in the perennial border, or naturalized. The cultivars are generally superior to the species. The plant provides beautiful flowers for fresh flower arrangements.

CULTURE: Some lilies are not difficult to grow. They grow best in a site sheltered from wind and heat. These plants need a well-drained soil that is slightly acid and contains plenty of humus. Although unable to tolerate wet soil, they can still be grown, in raised beds, in areas where the water does not drain quickly. The species generally prefer semi-shaded sites; however, most of the hybrids grow well in full sun. If midday shade is provided in southern regions, the flowering period is extended and fading of flower colors is prevented.

It is best to plant in October. Because the bulbs should be transplanted with some of the roots intact, only bulbs that are firm should be purchased. Before planting, dust the bulbs with a powder disinfectant to discourage bulb rot. Plant immediately upon purchase. Those that produce roots only from the bottom of the bulb should be planted shallowly; those that produce both basal and stem roots should be planted with the top of the bulb at least 4 inches deep. The size of the bulb also determines depth. Place the bulbs 9 to 18 inches apart.

The tall stems often require staking prior to flowering, when the tops are quite heavy, to reduce damage from wind and rain.

Apply a mulch to the soil to keep it cool and moist and to reduce weed infestation. The mulch also helps to prevent alternate freezing and thawing of the soil, which causes the bulbs to heave and to become exposed or damaged.

During dry periods, lilies may need supplemental watering. Apply the water to the ground. Avoid wetting the foliage because it can increase disease problems.

Lilies respond well to the application of a complete fertilizer such as 5-10-5 at the rate of 2 pounds per 100 square feet, in very early spring and just prior to flowering. Too much fertilizer, especially too much nitrogen, encourages vigorous vegetative growth and greater susceptibility to disease.

Remove faded flowers to promote stronger plants the following year. Allow all leaves to remain on the plants to manufacture food during the remainder of the growing season. When the flower stalks have died in the fall, they should be cut off just at

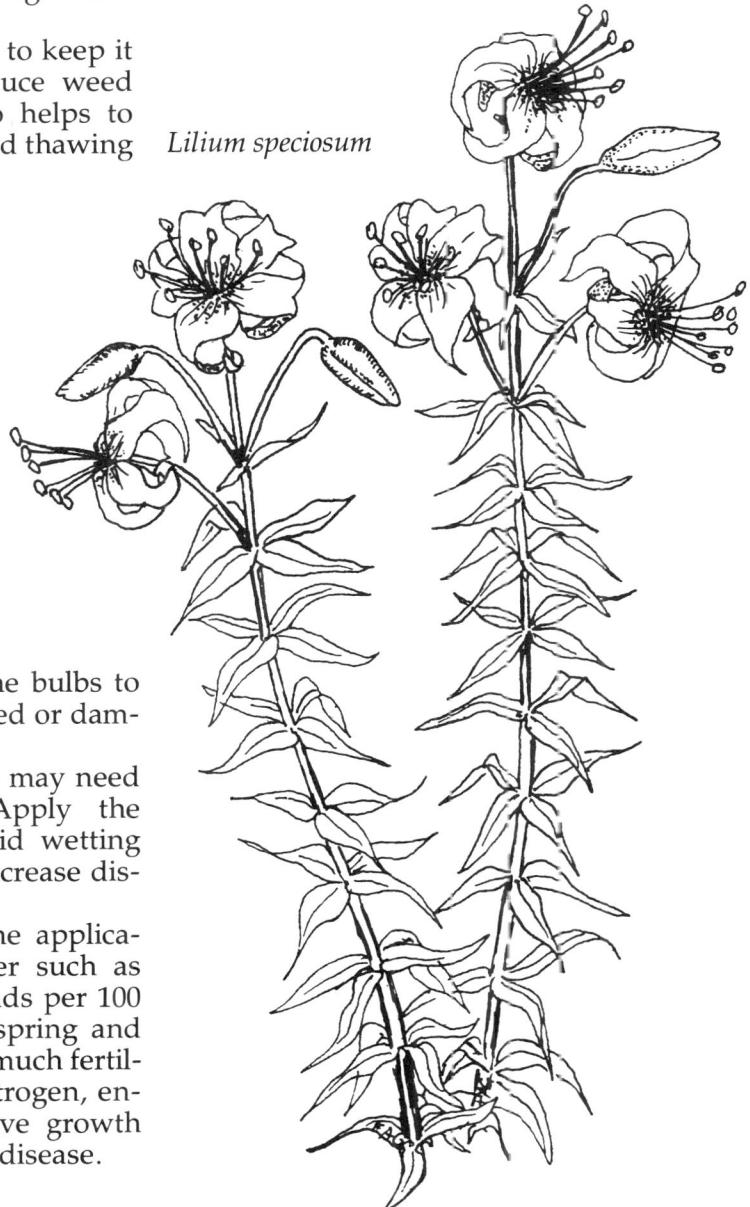

Lilium speciosum

ground level and discarded to reduce the possibility of overwintering disease organisms.

Propagate by division of the offsets, bulb scales, or aerial bulblets in early fall. These will produce flowering-sized plants in 2 or 3 years. Seeds may be sown, but they show variability and some require 4 years to produce a flowering-sized plant.

DISEASE PESTS: Lily mosaic is a virus transmitted by aphids, which infects all parts of the plant except the seed. Some species and cultivars are extremely susceptible to basal bulb rot if placed in a poorly drained soil.

SPECIES:

Lilium candidum: Madonna Lily; also known as Lent Lily, Bourbon Lily, Annunciation Lily. The fragrant, waxy, pure white flowers are borne, 9 to 12 or more flowers in a raceme, in late June. The flowers are campanulate, horizontally borne, and up to 3 inches long. The segments are slightly recurved. The basal leaves last through the winter. The stem leaves are alternate, oblanceolate, and become shorter and narrower at the top. The plant grows 3 or 4 feet high; it is an old-fashioned favorite. It should be planted only 1 inch below soil level and responds well to the addition of lime to the soil. An important oil used in perfume is extracted from the flowers. The species is extremely susceptible to *Botrytis* blight; however, some of the new strains appear to be more resistant. Its native habitat is in the Balkans.

Lilium lancifolium (Lilium tigrinum): Tiger Lily. Orange- or salmon-red flowers with purple-black spots are borne, 1 to 25 in a raceme. The nodding 3- to 5-inch-wide flowers are borne in August. The segments are strongly reflexed. The anthers are red. The pollen is brownish-purple. The dark green leaves are alternate, range from broadly linear to lanceolate, and grow 2 to 4 inches long and $\frac{1}{4}$ to $\frac{1}{2}$ inch across. The stout, purplish stems grow 2 to 5 feet high and are covered with a whitish down. Bulbils are produced in the upper leaf axils. The spherical bulb is 2 to 4 inches in diameter. This popular lily is very hardy. The bulbs, tasting similar to artichokes, are cooked and eaten in the Orient. Their native habitat is Japan, China, and Korea.

◊ 'Flore-pleno': Double-flowering form. ◊ 'Splendens': Larger, more numerous flowers which are deep red with bolder spots.

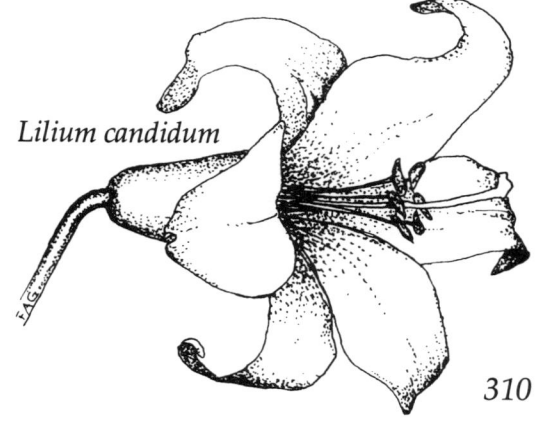

Lilium candidum

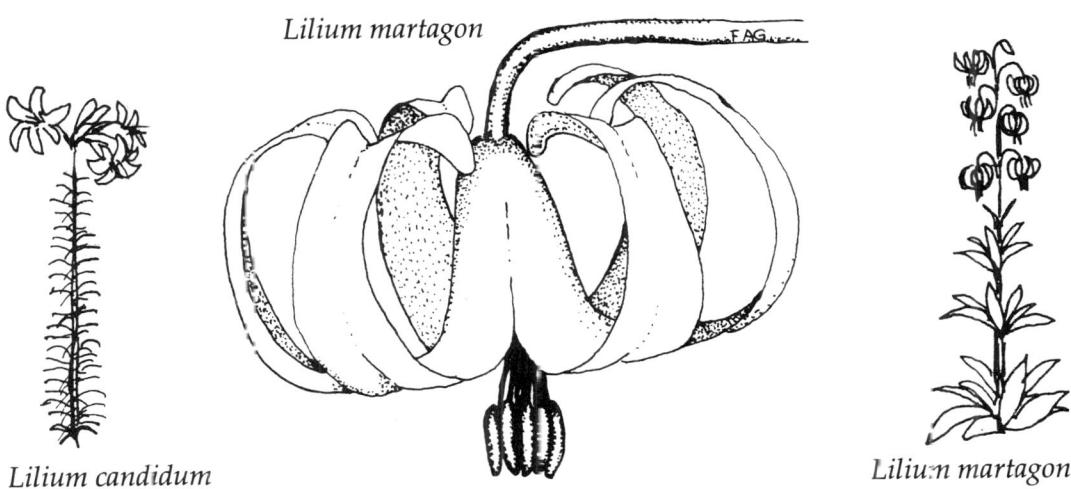

Lilium martagon

Lilium candidum

Lilium martagon

Lilium martagon: Martagon Lily; also known as Turk's Cap Lily, Turk's Cap, Turban Lily. The nodding flowers are borne, 3 to 20 in a raceme, in late June and July. Odorous, they are dull claret-purple with black spots and grow 2 or 3 inches in diameter. The perianth segments are thick, waxy, and strongly recurved. The leaves are usually in whorls of 6 to 9, horizontal, usually oblanceolate, and 3 to 6 inches long. The green stems grow 3 to 4 feet high and are often spotted purple. The bright yellow bulb is oval, 2 or 3 inches in diameter. The plant is hardy, vigorous, and easy to grow. Its native habitat is Europe and Western Asia. The cultivars and varieties vary from white to pink to dull red to nearly black.
◊ 'Album' White flowers, superior to the species.

Lilium pumilum: Coral Lily; also known as Fern-leaved Lily, Tom Thumb Lily, Tiny Lily. Nodding, fragrant, scarlet flowers, occasionally with black spots are borne, 1 to 20 in a raceme, in June and early July. The flowers are up to 2 inches across. The waxy segments are strongly reflexed. The leaves are alternate, linear, 1 or 2 inches long, and borne erect or semihorizontal. The smooth, wiry stems grow 18 to 20 inches high. The oblong bulb is 1 or 2 inches long and $\frac{1}{2}$ to 1 inch across. This graceful species is bright in color and is an excellent plant for the rock garden and for containers. Although it is a popular plant, it is not long-lived and must be replaced frequently. This lily grows well in full sun. Its native habitat is Siberia and Eastern China.
◊ 'Golden Gleam': Pure, shiny golden flowers atop a $2\frac{1}{2}$- to 3-foot plant.

Lilium regale: Regal Lily, Royal Lily. The delightfully fragrant flowers are lilac or purple on the outer side and pure white with a bright yellow base on the inner side, and they have 1 to 7 or more flowers in July. The waxy funnelform flowers are 4 to 6 inches long and 3 to 5 inches across and are borne horizontally. The deep green leaves are alternate, 3 to 5 inches long, and recurved, with rough margins. The leaves are borne horizontally. The 3- to 6-foot stem is stout, glabrous, and dark green with purplish spots. Bulblets are formed on the underground portion of the stem. The plant may need to be staked. In northern areas, the plants usually begin growth early in the spring and can be damaged by late spring frosts. *Lilium regale,* one of the most beautiful of all lilies, was introduced by E. H. Wilson in 1903. Its native habitat is Western China.

◇ 'Album': Pure white flowers.

Lilium speciosum: Showy Lily, Japanese Lily, Showy Japanese Lily. The nodding, fragrant flowers 4 to 6 inches long are borne, single- to many-flowered in a leafy panicle, in late August. The large flowers are reflexed and twisted, and are white with rose inside and spotted with deeper red. The leathery leaves are alternate, range from broadly lanceolate to oblong, grow 3 to 6 inches long and $\frac{1}{2}$ to $1\frac{1}{2}$ inches across, and are borne horizontally. The glabrous stem grows 2 to 5 feet, or more, high. The globular bulb is 3 or 4 inches in diameter. It is valued because it is one of the late-flowering lilies and because it has rich colors. The plant prefers semi-shade. Its native habitat is Japan.

◇ 'Album': White flowers and purplish-brown stems. ◇ 'Magnificum': Large flowers and red stems. ◇ 'Melpomene': Deep carmine flowers with white-margined segments. ◇ 'Roseum': Rose flowers with a green stem. ◇ 'Rubrum': Carmine flowers with purplish-brown stems.

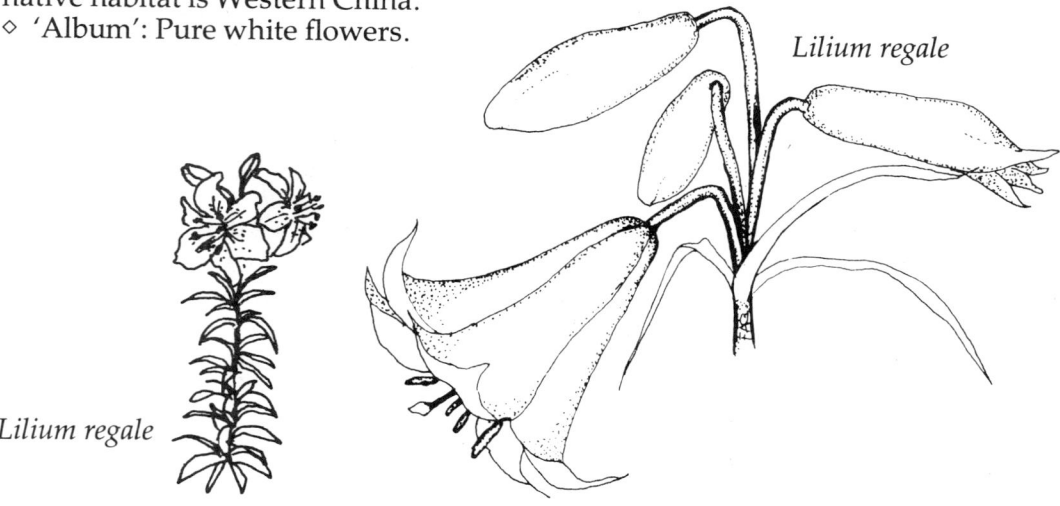

Lilium regale

Lilium regale

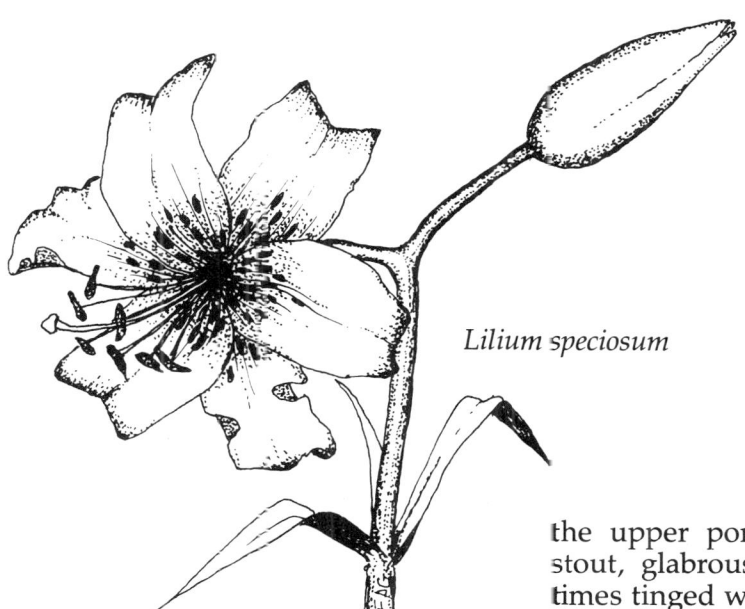

Lilium speciosum

Lilium superbum: Turk's Cap Lily; also known as American Turk's Cap Lily, Lily Royal, and Swamp Lily. The nodding orange-scarlet flowers have purplish-brown spots and a green base, are 3 or 4 inches across, and are borne, in groups of 1 to 40 in a raceme or umbel, from late July to early September. The perianth segments are strongly reflexed. The leaves are lanceolate, and they are 2 to 5 inches long and $\frac{1}{2}$ to $\frac{3}{4}$ inch across. The leaves are borne, horizontally in whorls of 4 to 10 leaves, alternately on the upper portion of the stem. The stout, glabrous stem is green, sometimes tinged with purple, and grows 3 to 8 feet high. The rhizomatous bulbs are borne 1 or 2 inches apart on stout rhizomes and are 1 to 2 inches in diameter. This plant needs an acid soil and plenty of moisture; it prefers a semi-shaded site. This is one of the most magnificent of the native North American species, and it shows considerable variability. Its native habitat is wet areas from New Hampshire to Georgia and Alabama and west to Indiana.

HYBRIDS: Many new hybrids are being introduced each year. These plants are much better adapted to the flower garden. The flower conformation and size have been greatly improved as well. ◇

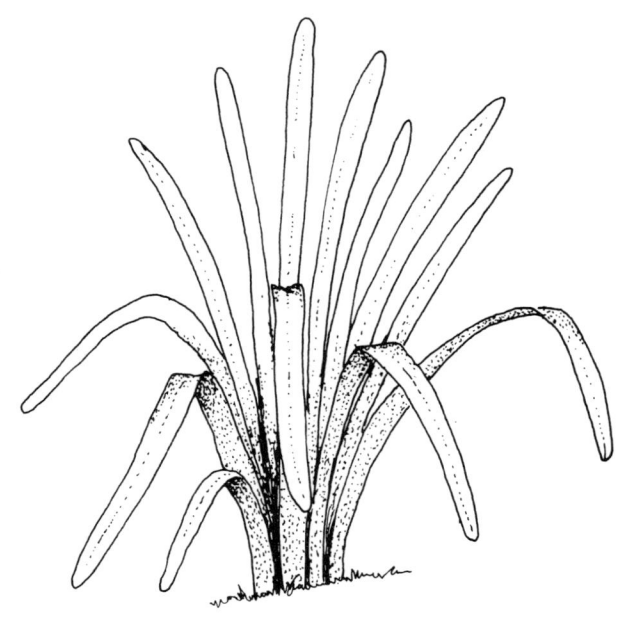

Lycoris

consists of 11 species of bulbous herbs native to China and the area from Japan to Burma.

The name of the genus *Lycoris* probably refers to a Nereid, or mythological daughter of the Greek sea-god Nereus.

Amaryllidaceae
(Amaryllis family)

Lycoris squamigera (Amaryllis hallii)
Magic Lily, Resurrection Lily
Also known as Hardy Amaryllis, Autumn Amaryllis

FLOWERS: The fragrant, rose-lilac or pink flowers 3 or 4 inches long are borne, in a 4- to 12-flowered umbel atop a solid scape, in early August. The flowers appear atop a 2- or 3-foot-high scape without foliage. The perianth is funnelform. The perianth segments are oblanceolate and clawed. The white filaments and yellow anthers are conspicuous.

LEAVES: The narrow, basal leaves are linear or strap-shaped and 15 inches long and 1 inch wide. The leaves are produced in the spring and die back to the ground by late June.

PLANT CHARACTERISTICS: The globose bulb is tunicated.

GARDEN VALUE: *Lycoris squamigera* is usually grown in the perennial border or the wild flower garden. Because the flowers are borne without leaves, the plants look best when placed at the back of the border or interplanted with other shade-tolerant plants that have good late-summer foliage.

CULTURE: *Lycoris squamigera* grows best in light shade or full sun and a well-drained soil.

Plant the bulbs in midsummer or as soon as they become available. Spring-planted bulbs usually do not flower the first year. Place the bulbs 5 to 8 inches apart and 4 to 6 inches deep. Leave the plants undisturbed; they do not respond well to being moved.

It is usually propagated by offsets. Lift the bulbs just after the foliage dies in midsummer and transplant them immediately.

ADDITIONAL NOTES: *Lycoris squamigera* are sometimes listed as *Amaryllis hallii* or as Hardy Amaryllis.

NATIVE HABITAT: Japan. ◊

315

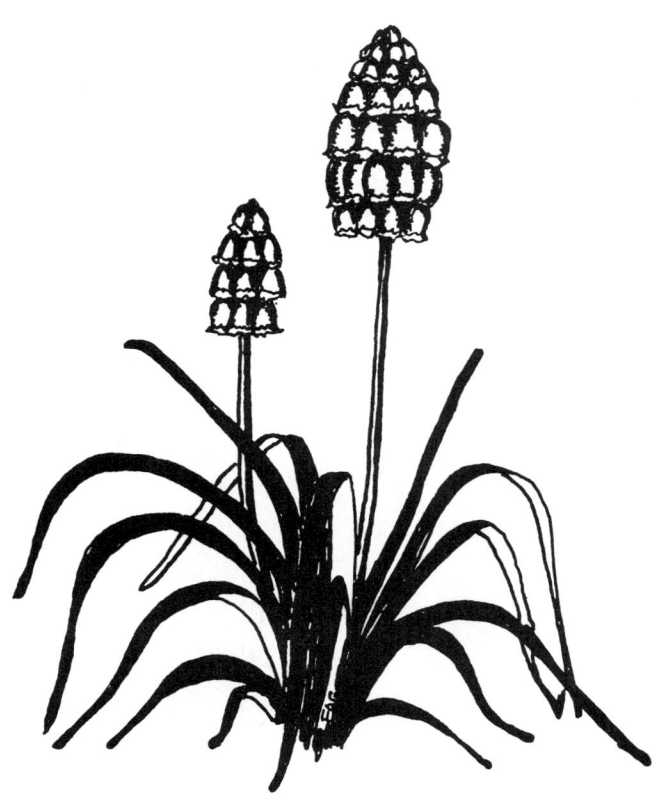

 # Muscari

comprises about 40 species of perennial herb native to the Mediterranean region and Southwestern Asia. The plants are hardy, bulbous, scapose, and spring-flowering.

The genus name *Muscari* is of Latin origin and refers to the musky odor of *Muscari moschatum*.

Liliaceae
(Lily family)

***Muscari* species**
Grape Hyacinth

FLOWERS: The nodding or pendulous, sweetly-scented, blue, violet, white, or, rarely, yellow flowers are borne, in terminal-bracted racemes atop a 6- to 9-inch-high stem from March to June. The perianth ranges from urceolate to subglobose, is usually constricted at the apex, and has 6 tiny, reflexed, dentate lobes. *Muscari* species may have some sterile flowers at the top of the raceme, which may be of a different color.

LEAVES: There are more than 2 basal, narrow, lanceolate leaves. They appear in fall, do not suffer injury from winter temperatures, and die back to the ground in early summer.

PLANT CHARACTERISTICS: The plant grows about 9 inches high from a tunicate bulb.

GARDEN VALUE: *Muscari* species should be planted in every garden. Along with *Scilla* and *Narcissus*, it is one of the best spring-flowering bulbs. The plants are attractive when grown in the rock garden or the perennial border, or naturalized in the lawn under trees and among shrubs. The plants also provide interesting cut flowers.

CULTURE: *Muscari* species are easy to grow. They grow best in full sun or light shade and in a well-drained soil.

Plant in late summer or early fall. Place bulbs 3 inches apart and 3 inches deep. Do not fertilize. The plants persist in the garden if the foliage is allowed to ripen. Leave the bulbs undisturbed indefinitely.

Muscari species are usually propagated by division of the plants in midsummer. They usually freely produce offsets, as well as abundant seeds. The seedlings usually flower in the third year.

SPECIES:

Muscari armeniacum. Armenian Grape Hyacinth. The bright, deep violet flowers with white teeth are borne in a dense, 20- to 40-flowered raceme 2 or more inches long atop a 4- to 6-inch-long scape. The sterile flowers are pale blue. The axis is bright violet. There are 6 to 8 leaves, growing up to 12 inches long and $\frac{1}{4}$ inch wide, and appearing in autumn. *Muscari armeniacum* is the most commonly planted species and the most handsome. It tolerates considerable moisture and shade and can be transplanted when in flower. Its native habitat is Northeastern Asia Minor.

◊ 'Blue Spike': A compact, double-flowering form. ◊ 'Early Giant': Fragrant light blue flowers; one of the best. ◊ 'Heavenly Blue': Light blue flowers.

Muscari botryoides: Common Grape Hyacinth. The pale blue, scentless, glabrous flowers, about $\frac{1}{4}$ inch long and with white teeth, are borne in a dense, short, 12- to 20-flowered raceme. There are white and pink flowering varieties. There are 2 to 4 linear leaves, 9 to 12 inches long and $\frac{1}{3}$ inch across. The scape is 6 to 9 inches long. Its native habitat is from Central and Southern Europe to the Caucasus.

◊ 'Album': White flowers. ◊ 'Caeruleum': Bright blue flowers. ◊ 'Carneum': Flesh-colored flowers. ◊

Narcissus

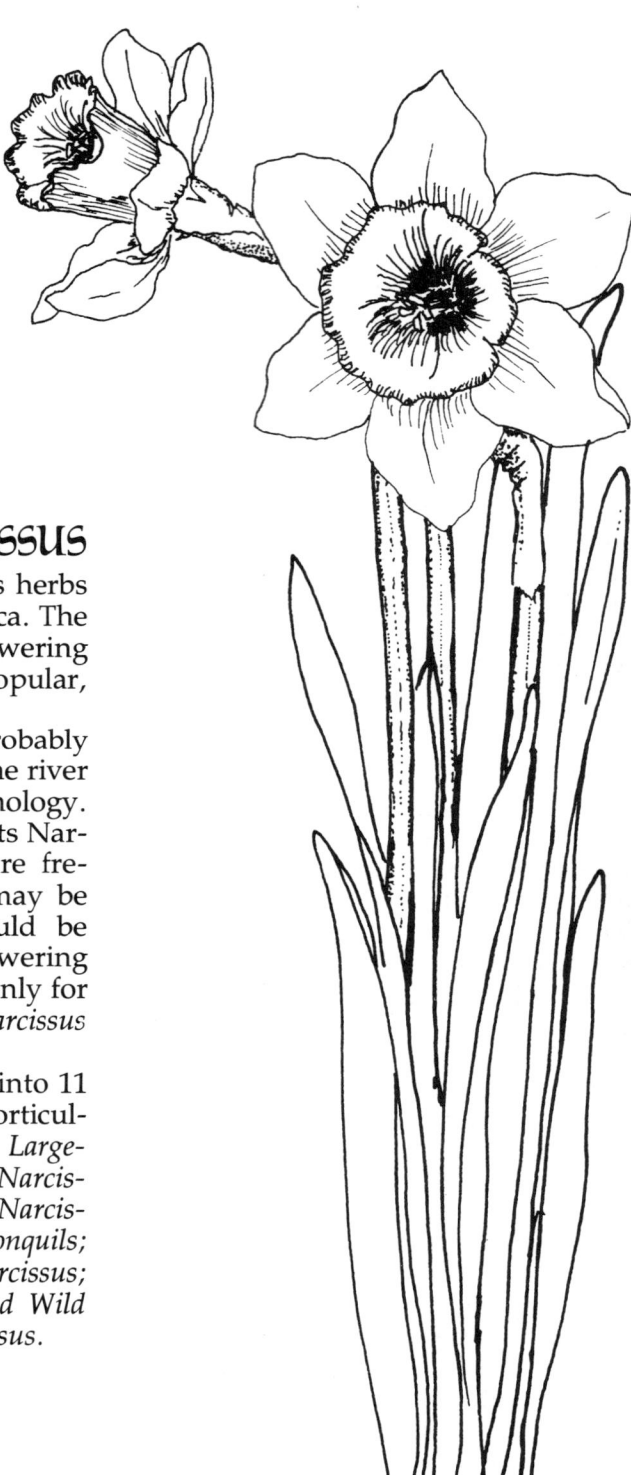

comprises 26 species of bulbous herbs native to Europe and North Africa. The genus contains autumn-flowering species as well as hardy, popular, spring-flowering species.

The genus name *Narcissus* probably refers to Narcissus, the son of the river god Cephisus in Greek mythology. The common names of the plants Narcissus, Daffodil, and Jonquil are frequently used incorrectly. All may be called *Narcissus*; Daffodil should be used only for the trumpet-flowering forms; Jonquil should be used only for the species and hybrids of *Narcissus jonquilla*.

The genus has been divided into 11 classifications by the Royal Horticulture Society: *Trumpet Narcissus; Large-Cupped Narcissus; Small-Cupped Narcissus; Double Narcissus; Triandrus Narcissus; Cyclamineus Narcissus; Jonquils; Tazetta Narcissus; Poeticus Narcissus; Species narcissus: Wild Forms and Wild Hybrids;* and *Miscellaneous Narcissus.*

Amaryllidaceae
(Amaryllis family)

***Narcissus* species**
Daffodil, Narcissus, Jonquil

FLOWERS: The flowers are borne erect or pendant and solitary or umbellate atop a scape subtended by a single-valved spathe. The perianth is yellow or white, occasionally pinkish, or, rarely, green, and is usually salverform with either a long tubular corona (or cup) or a short ringlike corona. The perianth consists of 6 segments that either ascend, spread, or reflex. The 6 stamens are attached in the perianth tube.

LEAVES: The leaves are basal and linear or subulate. The foliage usually dies back to the ground in June or early summer.

PLANT CHARACTERISTICS: The foliage and the scapes arise from tunicated bulbs.

GARDEN VALUE: These hardy, free-flowering plants are among the most popular of the spring-flowering bulbs for color and interest in early spring. The informal growth of the *Narcissus* adapts well to naturalized plantings in the lawn or the wild garden as well as to small groupings in the perennial border, the foundation planting, and in the rock garden. They should be planted in groups of 12 or more to be effective. The plants provide excellent cut flowers.

CULTURE: *Narcissus* grows well in a wide range of conditions but requires a well-drained soil.

Plant the bulbs in October in order to allow the roots time to become established before the ground freezes. Place the large bulbs 4 or 5 inches deep and 6 to 8 inches apart; place smaller bulbs 3 inches deep and 4 to 5 inches apart. They are most effective when planted in clusters.

In a naturalistic setting the bulbs should be planted in masses, in drifts separated by open grass areas. After planting, apply 1 to 3 pounds of 5-10-5 fertilizer per 100 square feet, and water in thoroughly.

Do not remove the foliage until it has turned completely brown and died back. This enables the plant to produce and store food in the bulb for the following year. The plants perform better if lifted every fourth year, separated, and replanted.

Narcissus is easily propagated after the foliage has died by lifting and dividing the offsets or small bulbs that form at the side of the old bulb. Lay the bulbs out to dry in an open shaded area for a few days. Plant immediately or store until early fall. The plants can also be easily propagated by seed, but they require 2 or 3 years to produce flowering-sized plants.

ADDITIONAL NOTES: The bulbs of *Narcissus* are excellent for indoor forcing.

SPECIES:

Trumpet Narcissus: Trumpet Daffodil. 1 flower is borne on each scape and the trumpet or corona is as long as, or longer than, the perianth. This group is divided into 4 subdivisions:
Yellow— ◊ 'Arctic Gold' ◊ 'Flower Carpet' ◊ 'King Alfred'
Bicolor— ◊ 'Foresight' ◊ 'General Patton' ◊ 'Music Hall'
White— ◊ 'Beersheba' ◊ 'Empress of Ireland ◊ 'Mount Hood'
Other colors— ◊ 'Binkie'

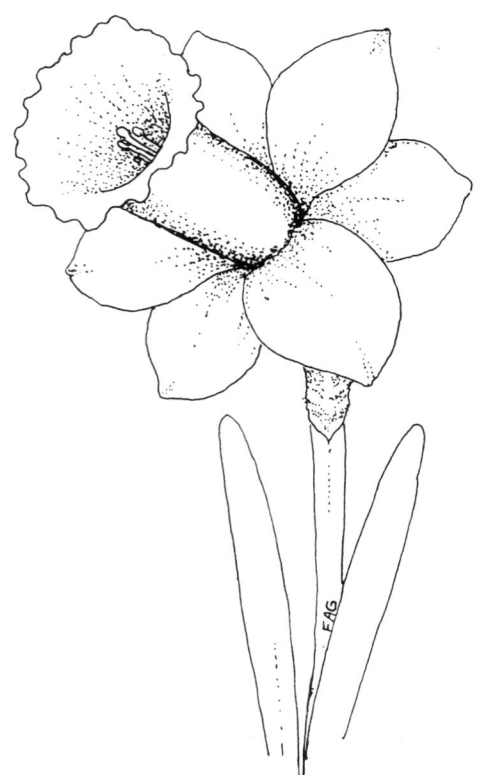

Large-cupped Narcissus: 1 flower is borne on each scape and its corona is more than $\frac{1}{3}$ of, but less than equal to, the length of the perianth segments. It is divided into 4 subdivisions:
Yellow petals and colored cup— ◊ 'Helios Aranjuez' ◊ 'Orange Frilled' ◊ 'Scarlet Leader'
White petals and colored cup— ◊ 'Apricot Sensation' ◊ 'Duke of Windsor' ◊ 'Flower Record'
White petals and white cup— ◊ 'Easter Moon' ◊ 'Ice Follies' ◊ 'White Butterfly'
Other colors, including pink— ◊ 'Chiffon' ◊ 'Debutante' ◊ 'Easter Bonnet' ◊ 'Irish Rose' ◊ 'Mrs. R. O. Backhouse' ◊ 'Passionale' ◊ 'Salmon Trout'

Double Narcissus: This species includes all double-flowering forms. ◊ 'Cheerfulness': White flowers with yellow in the petals. ◊ 'Golden Ducat': All yellow flowers. ◊ 'Snowball': All white flowers. ◊ 'Texas' ◊

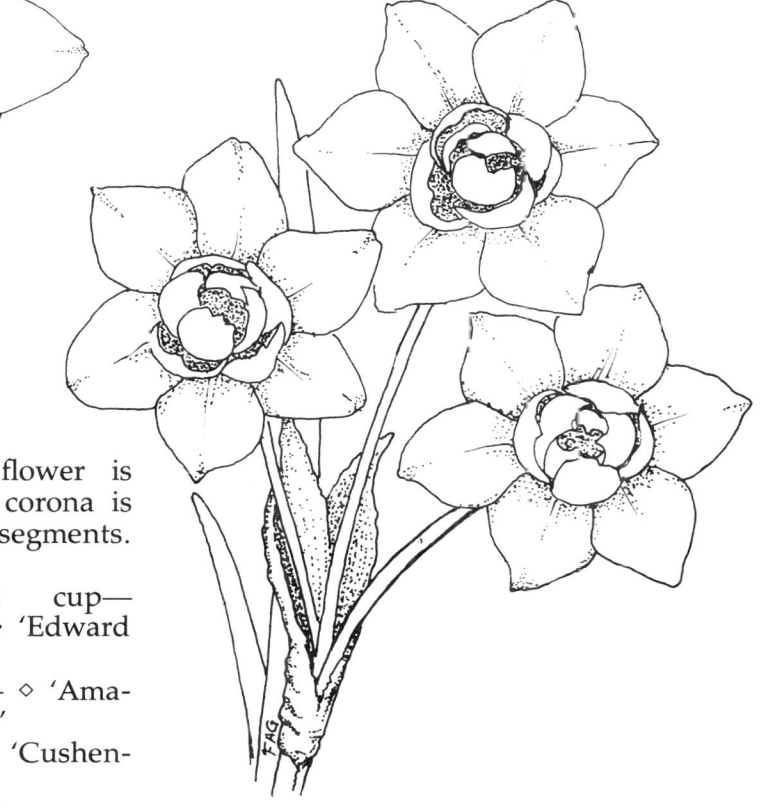

Small-cupped Narcissus: 1 flower is borne in a scape and the corona is shorter than the perianth segments. The 4 subdivisions are:
Yellow petals, colored cup—
◊ 'Burma' ◊ 'Chungking' ◊ 'Edward Buxton'
White petals, colored cup— ◊ 'Amateur' ◊ 'Polar Ice' ◊ 'Verger'
White petals, white cup— ◊ 'Cushendall'
Other colors— ◊ 'Green Elf'

Ornithogalum

comprises about 100 species of perennial herbs native to Africa, Europe, and Southern Asia. The species are bulbous, scapose, and mostly winter- and spring-flowering.

The genus name *Ornithogalum* is derived from the Greek words for bud and milk, but the applications are not obvious. Many of the species are called Star-of-Bethlehem.

Liliaceae
(Lily family)

Ornithogalum umbellatum
Star-of-Bethlehem
Also known as Nap-at-noon, Summer Snowflake, Dove's Dung

FLOWERS: The white star-shaped flowers 1 inch across are borne, in 12- to 20-flowered, corymbose racemes atop a scape 4 to 6 inches high and 6 to 9 inches across, in May and June. The lower pedicels are up to 4 inches long. There are 6 separate perianth segments; they are green with a white margin on the outside and persistent.

LEAVES: There are 6 to 9 smooth, green leaves, basal, narrowly linear, 9 to 12 inches long and $\frac{5}{16}$ inch across, with a broad white midvein. The attractive mound of foliage appears early but dies back to the ground soon after flowering.

PLANT CHARACTERISTICS: The plant grows 9 to 12 inches high. The subglobose bulb is tunicate and 1 inch thick, with many bulbils.

GARDEN VALUE: *Ornithogalum umbellatum* may be a weedy species. It is an excellent summer-flowering bulb for the wild flower garden.

CULTURE: The plant grows well in sun or light shade and in almost any garden soil. Plant the bulbs in the fall, 2 inches deep and 4 to 6 inches apart. Because the plant self-sows freely, removal of fading flowers before seed develops prevents spreading and unwanted seedlings.

The plant is easily propagated by offsets. Lift and replant the bulbs after the flowering period.

ADDITIONAL NOTES: The plant is reported to be poisonous when consumed and should be kept away from small children and pets.

NATIVE HABITAT: Europe and North Africa, naturalized in the Eastern United States. ◇

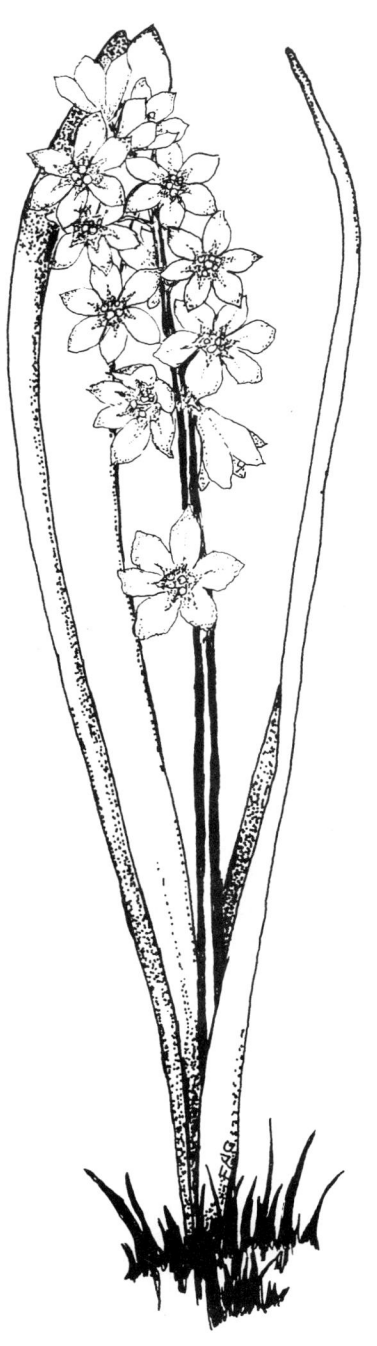

Puschkinia

consists of 2 species of perennial herbs native to Asia Minor and the Caucasus. The species are bulbous, spring-flowering, hardy or half-hardy plants.

The genus was named for Count M. Puschkin.

Liliaceae
(Lily family)

Puschkinia scilloides
Stripped Squill, Lebanon Squill

FLOWERS: The bluish-white flowers $\frac{1}{2}$ to $\frac{3}{4}$ inch across are borne, in a loose raceme of 1 to 10 flowers atop a scape 4 to 8 inches high, in April and May. The pedicels are slender and erect. The perianth is campanulate. There are 6 perianth segments, united in a short tube. Each lobe is white, lined with blue.

LEAVES: The basal leaves range from linear to strap-shaped and grow up to 6 inches long and $\frac{1}{2}$ inch across. The leaves die back to the ground in early summer.

PLANT CHARACTERISTICS: The plant grows 4 to 8 inches high. The bulb is globular and about $\frac{3}{4}$ inch thick.

GARDEN VALUE: *Puschkinia scilloides* is an excellent bulb for the perennial border or the rock garden, or for naturalizing in rough grass. It increases rapidly by seeds and offsets.

CULTURE: The plants grow best in cool climates, where they can be grown in full sun or partial shade. Place in a well-drained, sandy soil.

Plant in bulbs in the fall. Place bulbs 3 or 4 inches deep and 2 or 3 inches apart. Allow the foliage to mature and die back to the ground before removing it.

It is easily propagated by offsets in midsummer. The plant flowers most abundantly when left undisturbed.

NATIVE HABITAT: Asia Minor and the Caucasus.

SELECTED CULTIVARS AND VARIETIES: ◇ 'Alba': White flowers. ◇ var. *libanotica:* Smaller flowers native to Lebanon. ◇

Scilla is a Greek word meaning "I injure," applied by Hippocrates to these poisonous bulbs.

Liliaceae
(Lily family)

Scilla siberica
Siberian Squill

FLOWERS: One or more deep blue flowers $\frac{1}{2}$ inch across are borne, on bracted terminal racemes, in March and early April. The scapes number 1 to 6 and are 3 to 8 inches long. The perianth is rotate, horizontal, or drooping. There are 6 separate perianth segments, with a single prominent nerve.

LEAVES: There are 2 to 5 basal leaves, ranging from linear to lanceolate or oblong, growing 4 to 6 inches long and $\frac{1}{2}$ inch across, and ascending.

PLANT CHARACTERISTICS: The bulbs are tunicate and last for several years. The hardy plant forms an attractive clump and grows up to 6 inches high.

GARDEN VALUE: *Scilla siberica* is a desirable plant for the perennial border or the rock garden, for naturalizing in the wild flower garden, or for massing under and among spring-flowering trees and shrubs. It is one of the bluest of the hardy spring-flowering plants. Its color contrasts well with *Narcissus*, with early species and hybrids of *Tulipa*, and with other early-spring-flowering plants.

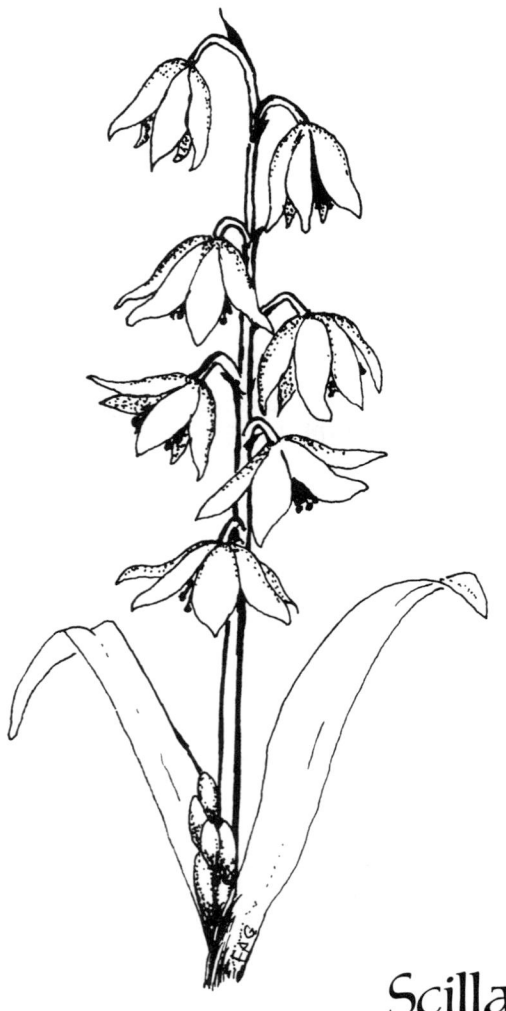

Scilla comprises nearly 90 species of perennial herbs native to Africa, Asia, and Europe. The plants are bulbous and scapose.

CULTURE: *Scilla siberica* is easily cultivated. It grows well in full sun or deep shade in a well-drained soil.

Plant in early autumn. Place bulbs 3 to 6 inches apart and 2 or 3 inches deep. Fertilize occasionally. Once planted, leave the plants undisturbed indefinitely.

They are usually propagated by separation of the offsets in early autumn. The plants may also be propagated by seeds but the seedlings take about 3 years to reach flowering size.

Scilla hispanica has been renamed *Endymion hispanicus;* it is a very delicate-

looking plant with ½-inch-wide and 6- to 10-inch-long leaves. The bell-shaped flowers are borne on 12-inch-long spikes. The colors most commonly seen are deep blue and white.

NATIVE HABITAT: Russia and Asia Minor.

SELECTED CULTIVARS: ◊ 'Alba': White flowers. ◊ 'Azurea': Bright blue flowers. ◊ 'Spring Beauty': Large delphinium-blue flowers. ◊ 'Taurica': Light blue flowers with dark midveins, flowering earlier than the species. ◊

Tulipa

comprises nearly 100 species of bulbous perennials that are native to the temperate areas of the Old World, especially Central Asia. Among the species are popular, hardy, spring-flowering plants.

The genus name *Tulipa* is derived from the Persian word *toliban*, meaning "turban," because the inverted flower resembles a turban.

Tulips have been divided into the following classes: Single Early; Double Early; Mendel; Triumph; Darwin Hybrid; Darwin; Lily-flowered; Cottage (Single Late Tulips); Rembrandt; Parrot; Double Late (Peony-flowered); and the species: *T. kaufmanniana*; *T. fosteriana*; *T. greigii*; and other species.

Liliaceae
(Lily family)

***Tulipa* species**
Tulip

FLOWERS: The showy, brightly colored flowers are usually borne erect and solitary or, sometimes in a group of 2 to 5, on a scape or a scape-like peduncle which is up to 30 inches high and arises directly from the bulb. Solid as well as multi-colored flowers have a wide range of colors, excluding true blue. The perianth ranges from campanulate to slightly funnel-shaped and has 6 separate segments that do not have nectaries and that are often spotted or blotched at the base. There are single, semi-double, and double flowers as well as flowers with large fringed petals.

LEAVES: The leaves are basal or are borne on the stem and range from linear to broad.

PLANT CHARACTERISTICS: The tulip is the most showy of the spring-flowering bulbs. Its growth habit lends itself well to formal plantings in rows, as well as in little clumps in the shrub, perennial, or mixed borders. The dwarf bulbs make attractive accent plants in the rock garden; they look best when planted in clumps or beds of one color. By careful selection of the species and hybrids, a succession of flowers can be on display in the garden for nearly 2 months.

CULTURE: Tulips grow in full sun and in most soils, but they prefer a rich, well-drained soil. Tulip bulbs in poorly drained soils diminish in vigor, and both life span and blooming period become shorter. It is advisable to keep tulip beds fertilized and well drained and to lift the bulbs every few years to inspect them and to make it possible to rework the beds.

Plant in early fall. Before planting, incorporate 5 or 6 pounds of bonemeal per 100 square feet into the soil. In the far South, the bulbs require a cold treatment (4 weeks at 40°F) before fall planting. In areas where rodents eat the bulbs, the bulbs should be planted in wire baskets made of small-mesh wire screening.

Large, showy plantings are most effective when replaced every year. When this is done, place the bulbs 5 or 6 inches deep and 6 to 10 inches apart. The tulips decline each year until they fail to produce flowers or disappear completely because each bulb tends to multiply.

If the soil is dry around the time the buds begin to show, the plants require additional water in order to produce the best flowers. After flowering, allow the foliage to mature and turn completely brown before removing it. Remove the faded flowers to prevent the tulips from setting seeds. These two cultural practices allow the bulb to store food reserves in order to produce the following year's plant.

In northern areas, mulch the plantings after the first frost to provide winter protection.

ADDITIONAL NOTES: The most popularly grown tulips are the result of hybridization, which began in Europe over 3 centuries ago.

DISEASE PESTS: Tulips are subject to *Botrytis*, basal rot, and breaking.

SPECIES:

Tulipa kaufmanniana: This species is occasionally listed as the "botanical tulips." It is popularly called the Waterlily Tulip. It is a very early-flowering tulip, sometimes flowering in March. The large, open flowers have pointed petals and are cream-colored and light yellow, with a yellow center and red stripes on the outside of the petals. The leaves of its cultivars may have brown stripes. The plant grows 5 to 10 inches high and may be used as an individual specimen in the rock garden, or for massing. This plant usually lasts longer as a bulb in the garden than the other species, and it sometimes flowers for many years. Its native habitat is Turkestan.

◊ 'Anchilla': White flowers with red centers. ◊ 'Berlioz': Yellow flowers. ◊ 'Daylight': Scarlet flowers with black bases. ◊ 'Heart's Delight': Red flowers with white edges on the petals. ◊ 'Gaiety': Creamy, short-stemmed flowers with an orange base. ◊ 'Shakespeare': A blend of apricot, orange, and salmon flowers. ◊ 'Stressa': Yellow flowers with blood-red blotches at the base of the petal and a broad red stripe on the outer side.

Tulipa kaufmanniana

Single Early Tulips: These tulips flower early along with *Primula* x *polyantha*. The flowers are 6-petaled and occasionally fragrant. The plants grow 9 to 16 inches high.
◇ 'Bellona': Golden yellow flowers.
◇ 'Christmas Marvel': Bright cherry-red flowers. ◇ 'DeWet': Fragrant, golden-orange flowers. ◇ 'Pink Perfection': Soft pink flowers with a white base. ◇ 'White Hawk': White flowers.

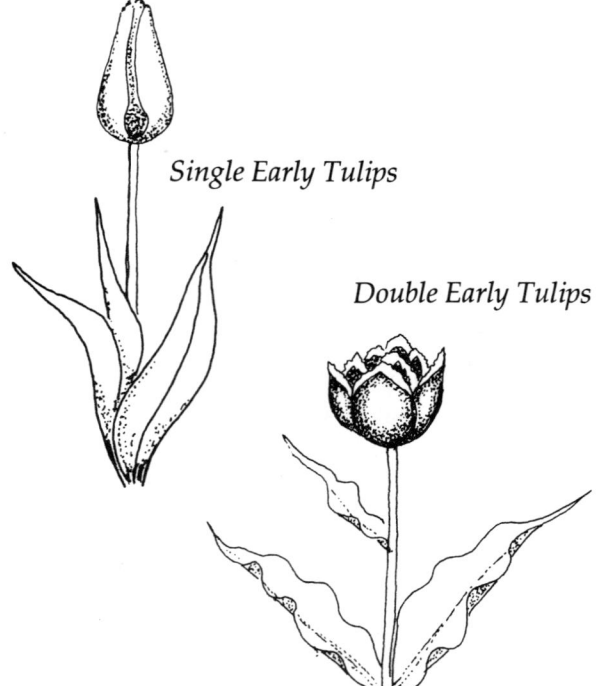

Single Early Tulips

Double Early Tulips

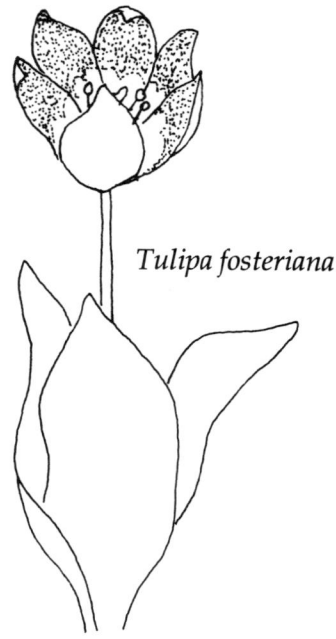

Tulipa fosteriana

Double Early Tulips: These tulips grow 9 to 16 inches high, and produce many-petaled, longer-lasting flowers on stout stems, about the same time as the single early tulips.
◇ 'Electra': Carmine pink flowers.
◇ 'Peach Blossom': Rosy pink flowers.
◇ 'Schoonoord': White flowers.
◇ 'Buurbaak': Fiery scarlet flowers.

Tulipa fosteriana: Foster Tulip. The large flowers are crimson with darker-colored bases; the plants grow up to 12 inches high. Its native habitat is Turkestan. The cultivars grow 8 to 20 inches high and produce flowers up to 4 inches across.
◇ 'Easter Glory': The outer petals are scarlet edged with buttercup yellow; the inner petals are deeper yellow with a red ring at the base. ◇ 'Golden Emperor': Golden flowers. ◇ 'Mme Lefeber' or 'Red Emperor': Vivid red flowers with a black base. ◇ 'White Emperor': White flowers. ◇ 'Yellow Emperor' or 'Summit': Pale yellow flowers.

Darwins: The single- or bi-colored flowers are large and squarish. These late-flowering tulips are among the most popular and grow 22 to 30 inches high.
◇ 'Ace of Spades': Deep purple flowers, tinted black. ◇ 'Aristocrat': Violet-rose flowers. ◇ 'Charles Needham': Brilliant red flowers. ◇ 'Glacier': White flowers. ◇ 'Golden Age': Deep buttercup-yellow flowers. ◇ 'La Tulipe Noire': Maroon-black flowers. ◇ 'Niphetos': Deep cream flowers. ◇ 'The Bishop': Deep violet flowers with a blue base inside and a white halo.
◇ 'Gudoshnik': Creamy peach flowers with a flush of rose. ◇ 'Jewel of Spring': Sulphur yellow flowers with red edges. ◇ 'President Kennedy': Golden yellow flowers with a flush of soft pink.

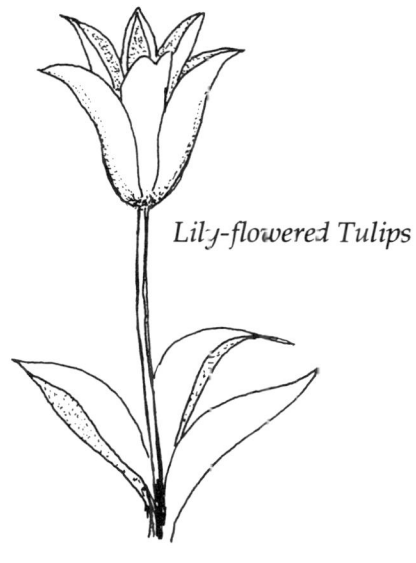

Lily-flowered Tulips

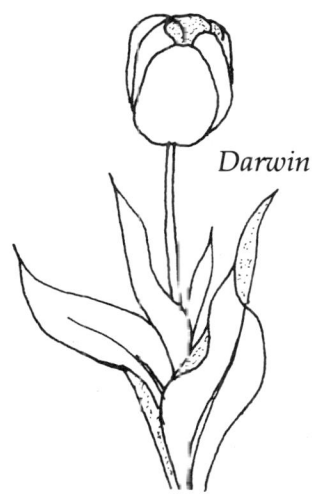

Darwin

Darwin Hybrids: These are a cross of the Darwin varieties and *Tulipa fosteriana*. The flowers are quite large and weather resistant and are borne in midseason. The plants grow 22 to 30 inches high.
◇ 'Apeldoorn': Orange red flowers with a purple-black base. ◇ 'Cream Jewel': Large, long-lasting white flowers. ◇ 'General Eisenhower': Scarlet red flowers with a black and white base on the inside of the petals.

Lily-flowered Tulips: The flowers of the lily-flowering tulips are distinctive because the long petals point and arch outward at the tip. These late-flowering tulips grow 18 to 25 inches high.
◇ 'Mariette': Salmon pink flowers. ◇ 'Maytime': Purplish violet flowers with white edges. ◇ 'Queen of Sheba': Scarlet flowers, brownish-tinged, with a broad yellow margin. ◇ 'Red Shine': Shiny red flowers. ◇ 'West Point': Large primrose-yellow flowers.

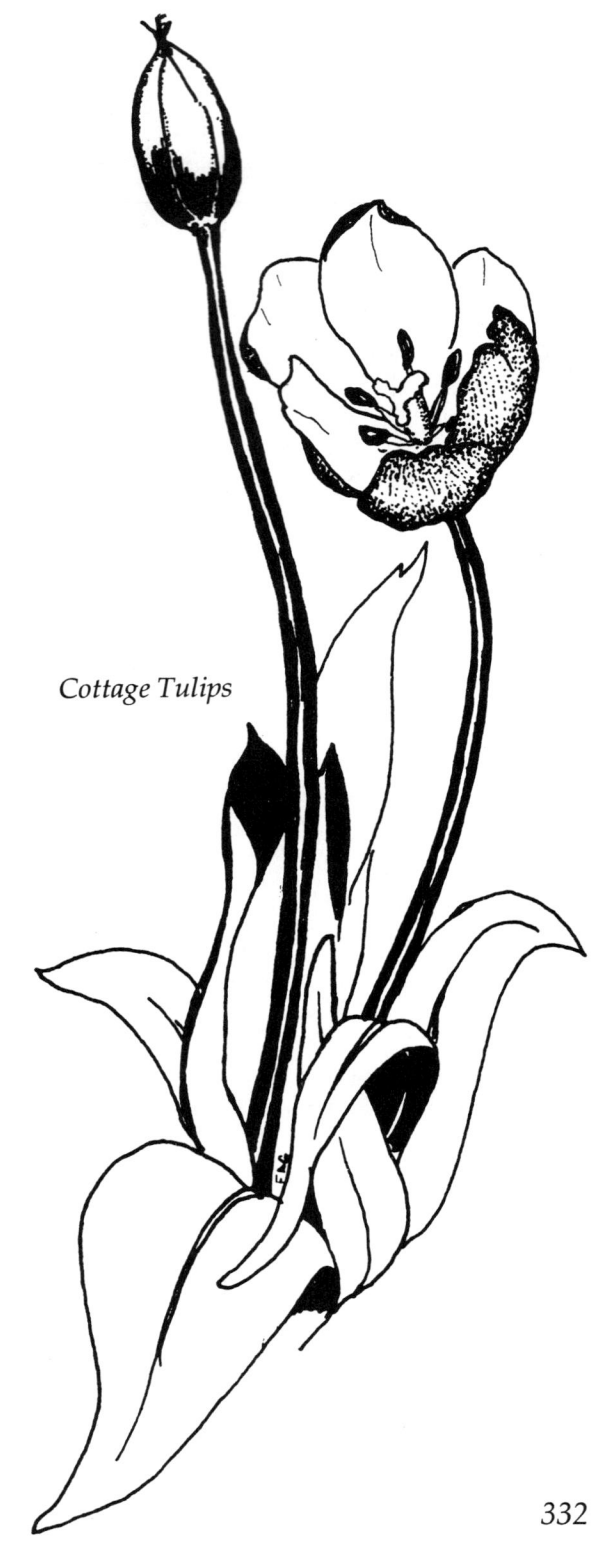

Parrot Tulips

Cottage Tulips: Many of these late-flowering tulips were popularly grown in the cottage gardens in England. The large flowers are usually ovate, and the plants grow 16 to 30 inches high.
◇ 'Blushing Bride': Creamy flowers with a flush of deep rose at the upper edge of the petals. ◇ 'Halcro': Carmine-red flowers. ◇ 'Mrs. John T. Scheepers': Large soft yellow flowers. ◇ 'Palestrina': Salmon-pink flowers tinged with rose. ◇ 'Reknown': Soft carmine-rose flowers. ◇ 'Rosy Wings': Pink flowers, shading to white at the base.

Parrot Tulips: These large, late-flowering tulips vary greatly in color and grow 20 to 28 inches high. The petals are twisted, and the edges of the petals are fringed. They originated as "sports" of other tulips.
◇ 'Black Parrot': Maroon-black flowers. ◇ 'Blue Parrot': Lavender-blue flowers. ◇ 'Fantasy': Green tint on soft rose-pink flowers. ◇ 'Firebird': Vermillion scarlet flowers. ◇ 'Gay Presto': Blood red on white flowers with finely cut petals. ◇ 'Orange Favorite': Orange and green flowers. ◇ 'Texas Gold': Golden-yellow flowers. ◇ 'White Parrot': White flowers. ◇

Glossary

ACAULESCENT. Stemless or apparently so; or stem subterranean, leaves radical.

ACHENE. A small, dry, 1-seeded, indehiscent fruit.

ACUMINATE. Tapering to an acute point at the apex, with the sides somewhat concave.

ACUTE. Tapering to a point at the apex, with the sides straight or nearly so.

ADNATE. The union of dissimilar parts or organs.

ALTERNATE. An arrangement of leaves, buds, and other organs borne singly at different heights on either side of the stem or axis.

ANTHER. The pollen-bearing part of a stamen.

APETALOUS. Without petals.

APEX. The tip or distal end.

APOMITIC. Characterized by apomixis.

APOMIXIS. Sexual reproduction in which a seed is produced without fertilization and in which the resultant seedling is identical to its mother.

APPENDAGE. An attached subsidiary or secondary part to a main structure.

ARISTATE. Bearing a stiff, bristle-like awn; or tapering to a very narrow, stiff apex.

AURICLE. An ear-shaped lobe or appendage found at the base of some leaves and petals.

AXIL. The upper angle between a petiole or peduncle and the axis or stem that bears it.

AXILLARY. In an axil.

BANNER. The upper, usually larger, petal in a papilionaceous corolla; also called a standard or vexillum.

BASAL. At the base; pertains to leaves that are only at the base of the plant.

BILABIATE. 2-lipped; divided into an upper and lower part; applied to a calyx or corolla—each lip may be entire, lobed, or toothed.

BISEXUAL FLOWER. Male and female reproductive organs—stamen(s) and pistil(s)—present and functional in the same flower.

BITERNATE. Twice ternate; in a biternate leaf, the primary divisions are again separated into 3 parts.

BLADE. The expanded portion of a leaf.

BRACT. A modified leaf usually associated with a flower or inflorescence.

BRACTEOLE. A secondary bract or very small bract, a bractlet.

BULB. A modified, shortened underground stem surrounded by thick fleshy food-storing leaf scales.

BULBIL. A small bulb usually borne in a leaf axil.

CALCAREOUS SOIL. A soil that is alkaline because of the presence of calcium carbonate.

CALYX. The outer set of the perianth or floral envelope, composed of separate or united sepals.

CAMPANULATE. Bell-shaped.

CAULESCENT. Having a distinct, well-developed, leaf-bearing stem above the ground.

CAULINE. Pertaining to or attached to the stem.

CESPITOSE. Growing in tufts or small dense clumps to form a mat.

CHAFFY. Covered with small, thin, dry scale bracts; refers to the bracts between the individual flowers in the flower heads of the *Compositae*.

CILIATE. Having a margin fringed with hairs.

CINCINNI (pl.), CINCINNUS (sing.) See Scorpioid Cyme.

CLASPING. A leaf without a petiole and whose base partly or completely surrounds the stem.

CLAW. In some flowers, the long, narrow, petiole-like base of a petal or a sepal.

CLEFT. Divided to or nearly to the midvein or into lobes.

CLEISTOGAMOUS. The production of seeds by self-pollination in the unopened flower.

COLCHICINE. An alkaloid derived from *Colchicum* that, when applied to a plant, usually doubles the chromosome number.

COMA. A tuft of hairs at the tips of seeds.

COMPOUND LEAF. A leaf completely separated into 2 or more leaflets; however, through the evolutionary process, only the terminal leaflet may remain.

CORDATE. Heart-shaped, usually applied to the base of leaves and bracts.

CORM. A short, underground, globose, thickened, vertical, solid, bulblike stem with scalelike buds on the surface.

COROLLA. The inner set of the perianth or floral envelope composed of separate or united petals.

CORONA. Crown, or encircling, garland; an appendage on the inner side of the corolla.

CORYMB. A short, broad, flat-topped or convex inflorescence whose outer flowers open first.

CORYMBOSE. Borne in corymbs or corymblike.

CRENATE. Having rounded teeth on the margin; scalloped.

CULTIVAR (a contraction of "cultivated variety"). A group of plants within a particular species that is distinguished by one or more characteristics (morphological, physiological, chemical, etc.) and that, when reproduced sexually or asexually, retains these characteristics.

CUNEATE. Wedge-shaped, narrowly triangular; the narrow end at the point of attachment, as in the bases of some leafs and petals.

CUSPIDATE. An abrupt sharp point at the apex.

CYATHIUM (sing.), CYATHIA (pl.). An inflorescence in which several male flowers (reduced to a stalked pistil) are clustered in a cuplike involucre; the involucre has 1 or more glands and may have petaloid appendages; characteristic of *Euphorbia*.

CYME. An inflorescene, usually convex or flat-topped, in which the central, or terminal flower opens earliest.

DECIDUOUS. Falling off; not persistent.

DECOMPOUND. Compound, with the divisions compound once to several times again.

DECUMBENT. Reclining on the ground, with the tip ascending.

DEFLEXED. Reflexed; turned abruptly downward or backward.

DEHISCENT. Splitting open (some dry fruits split open to scatter their seeds).

DENTATE. Sharp, coarse, spreading teeth directed outward on the margin.

DENTICULATE. Slightly dentate.

DETERMINATE. An inflorescence whose terminal flower opens first, thereby arresting prolongation of the flower axis.

DIOECIOUS. Having unisexual flowers; the staminate and pistillate flowers borne on separate plants.

DIPLOID. Having 2 basic sets of chromosomes, the usual condition for most organisms.

DISC FLOWER. The tubular flowers in the center of the flower head in most *Compositae*.

DISCOID. Refers to the flower head in the *Compositae* when there are no ray flowers present.

DIURNAL. Opening or occuring only during the day.

ELLIPTIC. Narrowed to rounded ends but broadest at or about the middle.

EMARGINATE. With a sharp notch at the apex.

ENSIFORM. Sword-shaped.

ENTIRE. With a continuous unbroken margin; not toothed or lobed.

EPICALYX. A calyxlike involucre of bracts outside and below the true calyx.

ERICACEOUS PLANTS. Refers to *Ericaceae*, the Heath family, which includes rhododendrons, laurels, azaleas, bearberry, etc., which require an acid soil for normal growth.

EROSE. A margin or apex that appears irregularly jagged or gnawed.

EVERGREEN. A plant whose foliage remains green and functional for more than one growing season.

EXSERTED. Projecting beyond a surrounding organ.

FALCATE. Strongly curved; sickle-shaped.

FALL. One of the parts of the outer perianth in *Iris* and related genera; often broader than the inner and often drooping or reflexed.

FASCIATE. In a bundle or bundled together, such as branches growing parallel and abnormally together.

FASICLE. A close cluster of stems, leaves, flowers, or other parts.

FIBROUS ROOT SYSTEM. A root system composed of profusely branched roots with many lateral rootlets and usually lacking a main or taproot development.

FILIFORM. Long, slender, thread-like.

FLORIFEROUS. Flower-bearing.

FLOWER. The reproductive organ of a seedbearing plant. It is an axis bearing one or more pistils or one or more stamens or both: if only the former, it is a pistillate flower; if only the latter, a staminate flower; if both, it is a perfect (bisexual) flower.

FOLIAGE. Leaves.

FOLLICLE. A dry, dehiscent fruit, usually more than one seed, opening only along one side and arising from a single pistil.

FRUIT. The ripened ovary with its adnate parts; the seed-bearing organ.

FUNNELFORM. A tube gradually widening upward and passing into the limb.

FUSIFORM. Spindle-shaped; broadest at the middle and tapering to both ends.

GENUS (sing.), GENERA (pl.). May be defined as a more or less closely related and definable group of plants comprising one or more species. The unifying characteristic of a genus is a similarity of flowers and fruits.

GLABRESCENT. Nearly glabrous or becoming so with maturity.

GLABROUS. Not hairy.

GLAUCOUS. Covered with a whitish, grayish, or bluish waxy covering that is easily rubbed off.

GLOBOSE. Having a round or spherical shape.

GRAFT. A grafted plant; the point of insertion of two plant parts, usually stems, so that their tissues grow together.

HEAD. A short dense cluster of flowers, as in the *Compositae*, having no persistent woody stem above ground and dying back to the ground each year.

HISPID. With stiff or bristly hairs.

IMBRICATE. Overlapping, as shingles on a roof.

IMPERFECT FLOWER. A flower that lacks either stamen(s) or pistil(s).

INCISED. Cut more or less deeply by sharp and irregular incisions; intermediate between toothed and lobed.

INDEHISCENT. Remaining persistently closed; not opening by definite lines or pores.

INDETERMINATE. Refers to an inflorscence whose terminal flowers open last so that the elongation of the axis is not arrested by the opening of the first flowers.

INFLORESCENCE. The manner of the flower arrangement on the plant; the flowering part of the plant.

INVOLUCRAL. Of the involucre.
INVOLUCRE. One or more whorls of small leaves or bracts subtending a flower or an inflorescence.
IRREGULAR FLOWER. An asymmetrical flower that can be cut longitudinally at only one place, with unequal size, form, or union of its similar parts.
JUVENILE. The vegetative stage in growth and development of a plant that ends when the flowering or reproductive stage is initiated.
KEEL. The 2 lowest petals of a papilionaceous flower united into a boat-shaped structure.
KEELED. Ridged, like the bottom of a boat.
LACINIATE. Slashed into narrow, pointed incisions.
LAMINA. A blade or expanded portion of a leaf or petal.
LANCEOLATE. Lance-shaped, much longer than broad, widest below the middle and tapering to the apex.
LEAF. Consisting of a leaf blade and usually attached to the stem by a petiole; it is the plant organ that is the primary site of photosynthesis.
LEAFLET. One of the divisions of a compound leaf.
LIGULE. A strap-shaped organ; the strap-shaped corolla in the ray flowers of *Compositae*.
LINEAR. Long, narrow, with sides parallel or nearly so.
LOBE. The projected part of an organ; usually a division of a leaf, calyx, or petal cut to the middle of the organ.
MEMBRANOUS. Thin, soft, and translucent, like a membrane and pliable.
MERISTEM. Undifferentiated tissue capable of developing into various organs or tissues.
—MEROUS. Referring to the number of parts; e.g., "5-merous," in which there are 5 (or multiples of 5) sepals, petals, stamens, etc.
MIDRIB. The main rib of a leaf or leaflet.
MONOCOT, MONOCOTYLEDON. An angiosperm whose seeds contain only one cotyledon.
MONOECIOUS. A species with unisexual flowers, with both the staminate and pistillate flowers borne on the same plant.
MUCRONATE. Terminated by a short, sharp, spiny tip.
NECTARY. A nectar-secreting gland or tissue.
OBCORDATE. Inversely heart-shaped, with the notch at the apex; the reverse of cordate.
OBLANCEOLATE. Inversely lanceolate, with the broadest width above the middle and tapering to the base.
OBLONG. Longer than broad, rectangular; the sides parallel or nearly so most of their length.
OBOVATE. Inversely ovate, broader above the middle.
OBTUSE. Blunt, rounded at the apex.
OPPOSITE. Two at a node, on opposite sides of an axis.
ORBICULAR. Circular, or nearly so.
OVAL. Twice as long as broad, widest at the middle, rounded at both ends.
OVATE. Egg-shaped, more or less rounded at both ends and broadest below the middle.
PALMATE. With three or more leaflets, lobes, or nerves radiating fanwise from a common basal point of attachment.
PANICLE. An indeterminate, branched inflorescence; the branches usually racemes or corymbs, the flowers usually pedicelled.
PANICULATE. Borne in a panicle; panicle-like.

PAPILIONACEOUS. A butterfly-like corolla; applied to members of a subfamily of *Fabaceae*. There are 5 petals; the top petal (standard) is outside and usually the largest; the 2 lateral petals (wings) are paired and usually clawed; the 2 lower petals are united to form a pouch or keel and enclose the stamens and pistil.

PAPILLOSE. Bearing tiny, pimple-like protuberances.

PEDICEL. The stalk of a single flower.

PEDICELLED. Borne on a pedicel.

PEDUNCLE. The stalk of a flower cluster or of a solitary flower when the inflorescence contains only one flower.

PELLUCID. Transparent, or nearly so.

PENDENT. Drooping; hanging downwards.

PERFECT FLOWER. A flower with both functional stamen(s) and pistil(s).

PERIANTH. A collective term for the floral envelope (calyx and corolla).

PETAL. A unit of the corolla or inner floral envelope of a many-petalled flower, usually colored and more or less showy.

PETALOID. A petal-like structure other than a petal; resembling a petal.

PETIOLE. The stalk of a leaf.

PILOSE. Bearing long, soft, spreading, straight hairs.

PINNATE. Constructed with the parts (branches, leaflets, veins, and lobes) arranged along both sides of an axis.

PINNATELY COMPOUND LEAF. With the leaflets arranged along both sides of the rachis.

PINNATIFID. Pinnately cleft or divided.

PISTIL. The seed-producing organ, which usually consists of an ovary, style, and stigma.

PISTILLATE. Female; having functional pistils and lacking functional stamens.

POD. A dry, dehiscent fruit.

POLYGAMODIOECIOUS. Essentially dioecious, but with some or all plants bearing bisexual flowers.

PUBESCENT. Covered with short, soft hairs.

RACEME. An elongated, unbranched, indeterminate inflorescence whose flowers are pedicelled.

RACEMOSE. Bearing flowers in racemes; raceme-like.

RACHIS. The axis of an inflorescence or of a compound leaf.

RADIATE. Spreading from or arranged around a common center; bearing radiate flowers as in the *Compositae*.

RADICAL. Arising from the root or crown; refers to leaves that are borne basal or in a rosette.

RAY FLOWER. The ligulate or strap-shaped flower in the *Compositae*; in many species (of the *Compositae*), the ray flowers are usually present on the margin of the flower head.

RECEPTACLE. Usually a more or less enlarged, flattened, or cup-like end of the flower axis upon which some or all flower parts are borne.

RECURVED. Bent or curved backward or downward.

REFLEXED. Abruptly bent backward or downward.

REGULAR FLOWER. An asymmetrical flower that can be divided longitudinally into two equal halves along any radius.

RENIFORM. Kidney-shaped.

REPAND. With a weak, wavy margin.

REVOLUTE. Rolled toward the back, as a margin rolled upon the lower side.

RHIZOMATOUS. Bearing rhizomes.

Rhizome. A prostrate horizontal stem, usually underground, with nodes, buds, or scale-like leaves usually rooting at the nodes and curving upward at the apex.

Root. The descending axis of the plant, usually underground, without nodes, internodes, or leaves.

Rootstock. Subterranean stem; rhizome.

Rosette. A dense basal cluster of leaves radiating from the crown or center, usually at or close to the earth.

Rotate. Wheel-shaped or saucer-shaped; a corolla with a short or inconspicuous tube and with a flat circular limb at a right angle to the flower axis.

Rugose. Covered with wrinkles.

Sagittate. Shaped like an arrowhead, with the basal lobes pointing downward or concavely toward the stalk.

Salverform. A corolla with a slender tube abruptly expanding into a flat circular limb that extends at right angles to the tube.

Scape. A leafless peduncle arising from the ground. It may bear scales or bracts and may be one- to many-flowered.

Scapose. Bearing flowers or an inflorescence in a scape.

Scarious. Dry, thin, membraneous, usually translucent but not green.

Scorpioid Cyme. A determinate, coiled inflorescence bearing the flowers or branches in an alternate arrangement; also called cincinni.

Seed. A ripened, fertile, ovule containing an embryonic plant.

Sepal. One of the separate parts of the calyx, usually green and leafy, that subtends the corolla.

Septum. A partition.

Serrate. Saw-toothed, the teeth pointing forward toward the apex of the organ.

Serrulate. Minutely serrate.

Sessile. Without a stalk.

Silicle. A short fruit of some species of the *Cruciferae* that are usually less than two times as long as wide.

Silique. The elongated fruit of some species of the *Cruciferae* that is usually three times as long as wide.

Simple. A leaf that is not compound; a non-branched inflorescence.

Sinuate. With a strongly wavy margin.

Sinus. An identation or recess in a margin between two lobes or divisions of a leaf, perianth, or other expanded organ.

Smooth. Without roughness; without hairs.

Solitary. Occurring or borne singly.

Spathe. A bract or modified leaf subtending or surrounding an inflorescence.

Spatulate. Spatula-shaped; oblong, with the basal end narrowed and the apical end rounded.

Species (sing. & pl.). The basic unit in a classification system, whose members are structurally similar, have common ancestors, and maintain their characteristic features in nature through innumerable generations.

Spicate. Borne in a spike; spike-like.

Spike. A usually unbranched, elongated, simple, indeterminant inflorescence in which the flowers are sessile.

Spine. A strong, stiff, sharply pointed outgrowth on a stem, leaf, etc.

Spinous. Bearing spines.

SPINULOSE. Bearing small spines.
STAMEN. The pollen-bearing organ of a seed plant, usually consisting of an anther and filament, sometimes reduced to only an anther.
STAMINATE FLOWER. Male, having functional stamens and lacking functional pistils.
STELLATE. Star-like or star-shaped; applied to hairs with radiating branches, to separate hairs clustered in a star-like pattern, or to forked hairs.
STEM. The primary leaf-bearing and flower-bearing axis of a plant.
STIPULE. A basal appendage of a petiole—usually occurring in pairs when present and varying in form from foliar to glandular; sometimes falling off early.
STOLON. A horizontal stem that bends to (or runs along) the ground, roots, and gives rise to new plants at the nodes.
STOLONIFEROUS. Producing stolons.
SUBORBICULAR. Nearly orbicular.
SUBSESSILE. Nearly sessile.
SUBULATE. Awl-shaped, linear or narrowly triangular, tapering to a sharp point.
SUCCULENT. Juicy, fleshy, rather thick.
TENDRIL. A modified stem or leaf, usually long and thread-like, that twines about an object for support.
TERMINAL. Apical; at the tip.
TERNATE. In 3s or separated into 3 parts.
TETRAPLOID. Having 4 (rather than the usual 2) basic sets of chromosomes.
TOMENTOSE. Covered with short, woolly hairs; densely matted.
TUBER. A short, thickened, usually (but not necessarily) subterranean stem bearing buds or "eyes" and serving as a storage organ.
TUBEROUS. Producing tubers.
TUNICATED. With a series of concentric, membranous layers, such as the onion bulb.
UMBEL. An indeterminate, usually convex or flat-topped inflorescence, with the flower pedicels and peduncles arising from a common point; resembling an umbrella.
UMBELLATE. Umbel-like; borne in an umbel.
UNDULATE. Having a wavy surface or margin.
UNISEXUAL FLOWER. Having either the male or the female reproductive organs—stamen(s) and pistil(s)—present and functional in the same flower.
VALVATE. Opening by valves or meeting at the edges without overlapping, as leaves or petals in a bud.
VALVE. One of the sections of a dehiscent fruit into which it splits at maturity.
VARIETY. A subdivision of a species that exhibits various inheritable morphological characteristics (form and structure) that are perpetuated through both sexual and asexual propagation.
VERTICILLASTER. A verticillate inflorescence bearing flowers in a false whorl-like arrangement around the axis; the flowers are borne in sessile cymes positioned oppositely in axils of leaves or bracts.
VILLOSE. Covered with long, shaggy, soft hairs that are not matted.
VINE. A slender-stemmed trailing or climbing plant.
VISCID. Sticky.
WHORLED. Having 3 or more leaves, flowers, or other organs at a node.

Index to Botanical Names

HERBACEOUS PERENNIALS

Acanthus:
  spinosissimus (Acanthus spinosus), 2
  SPINY BEAR'S-BREECHES
Achillea:
  filipendulina (Achillea eupatorium), 4
  millefolium, 6
    nana, 6
    ptarmica, 7
    tomentosa, 7
  YARROW
Aconitum:
  carmichaelii (Aconitum fischeri), 8
  napellus, 10
    henri, 11
    pyramidale, 11
  MONKSHOOD
Aegopodium:
  podagraria, 12
  GOUTWEED

Agrostemma coronaria. See *Lychnis coronaria*
Ajuga:
    reptans, 14
        variegata, 15
        genevensis, 15
        pyramidalis, 15
            metallica crispa, 15
    BUGLEWEED
Alcea:
    rosea (Althaea rosea), 16
    HOLLYHOCK
Alchemilla:
    vulgaris, 18
    LADY'S-MANTLE
Althaea rosea. See *Alcea rosea*
Alyssum. See *Aurinia*
Anaphalis:
    margaritacea, 20
    PEARLY EVERLASTING
Anchusa:
    azurea (Anchusa italica), 22
    SUMMER FORGET-ME-NOT
Anthemis:
    tinctoria, 24
    GOLDEN MARGUERITE
Aquilegia:
    X hybrida, 26
        alpina, 28
        caerula, 28
        canadensis, 27, 28
        flabellata, 28, 29
        longissima, 29
            chrysantha, 29
        vulgaris, 27
    COLUMBINE
Arabis:
    caucasica (Arabis albida), 30
        alpina, 31
    WALL ROCK CRESS
Armeria:
    maritima (Armeria vulgaris), 32
    SEA PINK
Artemisia:
    schmidtiana, 34
        dracunculus (Artemisia redowskii), 35
        ludoviciana, 35
    SILVER MOUND
Asarum:
    europaeum, 36
        canadense, 37
    WILD GINGER
Asclepias:
    tuberosa, 38
    BUTTERFLY WEED

Asperula odoratum. See *Galium odoratum*
Aster:
    alpinus, 40
    novae-angliae, 42
        X *friktarii,* 43
        amellus, 43
        thomsonii, 43
    novae-belgii, 44
    ASTER
Astilbe:
    X *arendsii,* 46
        astilboides, 48
        japonica, 48
        thunbergii, 48
        chinensis, 49
        davidii, 48, 49
    MEADOWSWEET
Aubrieta:
    deltoidea, 50
    PURPLE ROCK-CRESS
Aurinia:
    saxatilis (Alyssum arduini, Alyssum orientale,
        Allysum saxatile), 52
    BASKET-OF-GOLD

Baptisia:
    australis, 54
        bracteata, 56
        leucantha, 56
        tinctoria, 57
    FALSE INDIGO
Belamcanda:
    chinensis (Pardanthus chinensis), 58
    BLACKBERRY LILY
Bellis:
    perennis, 60
    ENGLISH DAISY
Bergenia:
    cordifolia (Saxifraga cordifolia), 62
    PIG SQUEAK
Betonica grandiflora. See *Stachys grandiflora*
Bocconia cordata. See *Macleaya cordata*

Campanula:
    carpatica, 64
        raineri, 65
    persicifolia, 66
        glomerata, 68
        medium, 68
        portenschlagiana (Campanula muralis), 69
        poscharskyana, 69
        rapunculoides, 69
    BELLFLOWER

Centaurea:
    montana, 70
        BACHELOR'S BUTTON
Cerastium:
    tomentosum, 72
        SNOW-IN-SUMMER
Chrysanthemum:
    coccineum, 74
        PAINTED DAISY
    maximum, 76
        lacustre, 76
        leucanthemum, 76
        nipponicum, 76
        X superbum, 76
        SHASTA DAISY
    parthenium, 78
        FEVERFEW
    morifolium, 79
        indicum, 81
        japonense, 81
        makinoi, 81
        ornatum, 81
        GARDEN MUM, CUSHION MUM
Cimicifuga:
    simplex, 82
        racemosa, 83
        BUGBANE
Clematis:
    X hybrida, 84
        florida, 86
        lanuginosa, 86, 87
        patens, 87
        vitifolia, 86
        X jackmanii, 86
        integrifolia, 87
        tangutica, 87
        CLEMATIS
Convallaria:
    majalis, 88
        LILY-OF-THE-VALLEY
Coreopsis:
    lanceolata, 90
        verticillata, 91
        COREOPSIS

Delphinium:
    elatum, 92
        decorum, 94
        X belladonna (Delphinium bellamosum, Delphinium formosum), 95
        LARKSPUR
Dianthus:
    barbatus, 96
        SWEET WILLIAM

Dianthus (cont.)
    deltoides, 98
        PINK
    plumarius, 100
        X alwoodii, 101
        caryophyllus, 101
        ALLWOOD'S PINK
Dicentra:
    eximia, 102
    spectabilis, 104
        Dielytra spectabilis, 105
        cucullaria, 105
        BLEEDING HEART
Dictamnus:
    albus (Dictamnus fraxinella), 106
        GAS PLANT
Dielytra spectabilis. See Dicentra spectabilis
Digitalis:
    purpurea, 108
        FOXGLOVE
Dodecatheon:
    meadia, 110
        SHOOTING-STAR
Doronicum:
    cordatum (Doronicum caucasicum), 112
        LEOPARD'S BANE

Echinacea:
    purpurea (Rudbeckia purpurea), 114
        PURPLE CONEFLOWER
Echinops:
    ritro, 116
        GLOBETHISTLE
Epimedium:
    X rubrum (Epimedium alpinum var. rubrum), 118
        ALPINE EPIMEDIUM
Eremurus:
    X isabellinus (Eremurus X shelfordii), 120
        olgae, 121
        stenophyllus, 121
        SHELFORD FOXTAIL LILY
Erigeron:
    compositus, 122
        FERNLEAF FLEABANE
Eryngium:
    amethystinum, 124
        planum, 125
        SEA HOLLY
Euphorbia:
    epithymoides (Euphorbia polychroma), 126
    myrsinites, 128
        cyparissias, 129
        EUPHORBIA

Funkia. See Hosta

Gaillardia:
   X grandiflora, **130**
      aristata, 131
      pulchella, 131
   Blanketflower

Galium:
   odoratum (Asperula odorata), **132**
   Sweet Woodruff

Geranium:
   himalayense (Geranium grandiflorum), **134**
      ibericum, 135
      sanguineum, 134
   Crane's Bill

Gypsophila:
   paniculata, **136**
      repens, 138
   Baby's Breath

Helenium:
   autumnale, **140**
   Sneezeweed

Helianthemum:
   nummularium, **142**
   Sunrose

Helianthus:
   decapetalus, **144**
   Wild Sunflower

Heliopsis:
   helianthoides, **146**
   Sunflower Heliopsis

Helleborus:
   niger, **148**
      antiquorum, 149
      orientalis (Helleborus caucasicus), 149
   Christmas Rose

Hemerocallis (species): **150**
   fulva, 153
   lilioasphodelus (Hemerocallis lilioasphodelus var.
      flava, Hemerocallis flava), 153
   Daylily

Hesperis:
   matronalis, **154**
   Sweet Rocket

Heuchera:
   sanguinea, **156**
   Coral Bells

Hibiscus:
   moscheutos, **158**
   Rose Mallow

Hosta:
   plantaginea (Hosta subcordata), **160**
      fortunei, 162
      lancifolia, 162

Hosta (cont.)
      sieboldiana (Hosta glauca), 163
      decorata, 163
      lancifolia, 163
   Plantain Lily

Iberis:
   sempervirens, **164**
   Candytuft

Iris (bearded cultivars): **166**
      germanica, 167
      cristata, 168
      kaempferi, 168
      siberica, 169
   Iris

Kniphofia:
   X pfitzeri, **170**
      uvaria, 171
   Red-hot Poker

Lathyrus:
   latifolius, **172**
   Sweet Pea

Lavandula:
   angustifolia, **174**
      officinalis, 175
      spica, 175
      vera, 175
   Lavender

Liatris:
   spicata, **176**
   Gayfeather

Limonium:
   latifolium (Statice latifolia), **178**
   Sea Lavender

Linum:
   perenne, **180**
   Blue Flax

Liriope:
   spicata, **182**
      muscari, 183
      majestica, 183
   Lily-turf

Lobelia:
   cardinalis, **184**
      siphilitica, 186
   Cardinal Flower

Lunaria:
   annua (Lunaria biennis), **188**
   Honesty

Lupinus:
   polyphyllus, **190**
   Lupine

Lychnis:
   chalcedonica, 192
      MALTESE CROSS
   coronaria (Agrostemma coronaria), 194
      ROSE CAMPION
   viscaria (Viscaria viscosa, Viscaria vulgaris), 195
      GERMAN CATCHFLY
Lysimachia:
   nummularia, 196
      clethroides, 197
      punctata, 197
   LOOSESTRIFE
Lythrum:
   salicaria, 198
      virgatum, 199
   PURPLE LOOSESTRIFE

Macleaya:
   cordata (Bocconia cordata), 201
   PLUME POPPY
Mertensia:
   virginica, 202
   BLUE BELL
Monarda:
   didyma (Monarda coccinea), 204
   BEE BALM
Myosotis:
   sylvatica (Myosotis oblongata), 206
      dissitiflora, 207
   FORGET-ME-NOT

Oenothera:
   missouriensis, 208
      tetragona (Oenothera fruticosa var. youngii), 209
   SUNDROPS

Paeonia:
   lactiflora (Paeonia albiflora), 210
   suffruticosa (Paeonia moutan, Paeonia arborea), 214
      lutea, 215
      tenuifolia, 215
   PEONY
Papaver:
   orientale, 216
      somniferum, 219
   ORIENTAL POPPY
   ***Pardanthus chinensis.** See Belamcanda chinensis*
Phlox:
   divaricata (Phlox canadensis), 220
   WILD SWEET WILLIAM
   paniculata (Phlox decussata), 222
   GARDEN PHLOX
   subulata, 224
   MOSS PHLOX

Physalis:
   alkekengi, 226
   CHINESE LANTERN PLANT
Physostegia:
   virginiana, 228
   FALSE DRAGONHEAD
Platycodon:
   grandiflorus, 230
   BALLOONFLOWER
Polemonium:
   caeruleum, 232
   JACOB'S LADDER
Polygonatum:
   biflorum, 234
      canaliculatum, 235
   SOLOMON'S SEAL
Primula:
   X polyantha, 236
      elatior, 237
      veris, 237
      vulgaris, 237
   POLYANTHA PRIMROSE
Pulmonaria:
   angustifolia (Pulmonaria azurea), 238
   LUNGWORT

Rudbeckia:
   hirta, 240
   BLACK-EYED SUSAN
   purpurea. See Echinea purpurea

Saponaria:
   ocymoides, 242
   ROCK SOAPWORT
***Saxifraga cordifolia.** See Bergenia cordifolia*
Scabiosa:
   caucasica, 244
   PINCUSHION FLOWER
Sedum:
   spectabile, 246
   SHOWY SEDUM
   spurium, 248
   TWO-ROW STONECROP
      acre, 249
Sempervivum:
   tectorum, 250
   HEN AND CHICKENS
Stachys:
   byzantina (Stachys lanata, Stachys olympica), 252
      betonica, 252
      grandiflora (Betonica grandiflora), 253
   LAMB'S EARS
***Statice latifolia.** See Limonium latifolium*

Thalictrum:
   rochebrunianum, 254
   speciosissimum (Thalictrum glaucum), 255
      LAVENDER MIST
Thermopsis:
   caroliniana, 256
      CAROLINA LUPINE
Thymus:
   serpyllum, 258
      MOTHER-OF-THYME
Tradescantia:
   virginiana, 260
         X andersonii, 261
      SPIDERWORT
Trollius:
   europaeus, 262
      GLOBEFLOWER

Verbena:
   canadensis, 264
      ROSE VERBENA

Veronica:
   longifolia (Veronica maritima), 266
      incana, 268
      spicata, 269
      VERONICA
Viola:
   cornuta, 270
      TUFTED PANSY
   odorata, 272
      VIOLET
Viscaria. See *Lychnis viscaria*

Waldsteinia:
   ternata, 274
         fragarioides, 274
      BARREN STRAWBERRY

Yucca:
   smalliana, 276
      filimentosa, 277
      flaccida, 277
      ADAM'S NEEDLE

BULBS

Allium:
   christophii (Allium albopilosum), 280
      STAR-OF-PERSIA
   Giganteum, 282
      GIANT ONION
   karataviense, 283
      TURKESTAN ONION
   moly, 284
      LILY LEEK
   schoenoprasum, 285
      CHIVES
Amaryllis hallii. See *Lycoris squamigera*
Anemone:
   blanda, 286
   coronaria, 288
   X hybrida (Anemone hupehensis japonica), 289
      japonica, 289
      ANEMONE
   pulsatilla (Pulsatilla amoena, Pulsatilla vulgaris), 290
      PASQUE-FLOWER
   vitifolia, 291

Colchicum:
   autumnale, 292
      AUTUMN CROCUS
      sativus, 295

Crocus (species): **294**
   'Dutch Hybrids,' 296
      maesiacus, 296
      angustifolius, 296
      korolkowii, 296
      sieberi, 297
      vernus, 298
      versicolor, 297
   CROCUS

Eranthis:
   hyemalis, 298
      ACONITE

Fritillaria:
   imperalis, 300
      IMPERIAL FRITILLARY
      meleagris, 301
      CHECKERED LILY

Galanthus:
   nivalia, 302
      SNOWDROP

Hyacinthus:
   orientalis, 304
      HYACINTH

Leucojum:
   aestivum, 306
      Giant Snowflake
Lilium (species): *308*
      candidum, 310
      lancifolium (Lilium tigrinum), 310
      martagon, 311
      pumilum, 311
      regale, 312
      speciosum, 312
      superbum, 313
   Lily
Lycoris:
   squamigera (Amaryllis hallii), **314**
     Magic Lily

Muscari (species): **316**
      moschatum, 316
      armeniacum, 317
      botryoides, 317
     Grape Hyacinth

Narcissus (species): **318**
      jonquilla, 318
   Daffodil

Ornithogalum:
   umbellatum, 322
     Star-of-bethlehem

Pulsatilla. See *Anemone pulsatilla*
Puschkinia:
   scilloides, **324**
     Squill

Scilla:
   siberica, **326**
       hispanica (Endymion hispanicus), 327
     Siberian Squill

Tulipa (species): **328**
      kaufmanniana, 329
      Single Early Tulips, 330
      Double Early Tulips, 330
      fosteriana, 330
      Darwins, 331
      Darwin Hybrids, 331
      Lily-flowered Tulips, 331
      Cottage Tulips, 333
      Parrot Tulips, 333
     Tulips

Index to Common Names

Aaron's Rod, 256
Adam's Needle, 276
Alkekengi, 227
Alpine Aster, 40
Alpine Columbine, 28
Alum Root, 156
American Columbine, 28
American Cowslip, 110
American Turk's Cap Lily, 313
Amethyst Eryngium, 124
Annunciation Lily, 310
Armenian Grape Hyacinth, 317
Autumn Amaryllis, 314
Autumn Crocus, 293
Azure Monkshood, 8

Baby's Breath, 136

Balloonflower, 230
Barren Strawberry, 274
Basket-of-gold, 52
Beach Speedwell, 266
Bear Grass, 276
Bear's-foot, 10
Bedding Pansy, 270
Bee Balm, 204
Bee Larkspur, 92
Bergamot, 204
Big Blue Lobelia, 186
Blackberry Lily, 58
Black Blood, 198
Black-eyed Susan, 240
Black Hellebore, 148
Black Sampson, 114
Bladder Cherry, 227
Blanketflower, 130
Blazing Star, 176
Blood-red Crane's Bill, 134
Blood-red Geranium, 134
Blue Bells, 202
Blue Cardinal-flower, 186
Blue False Indigo, 54
Blue-leaved Plantain-lily, 163
Blue Lungwort, 238
Blue Phlox, 220
Blue Wild Indigo, 54
Bolbonac, 188
Bourbon Lily, 310
Brown-eyed Susan, 240
Bugleweed, 14
Burning Bush, 106
Bush-pea, 256
Butterfly Milkweed, 38
Butterfly Weed, 38

Canada Snakeroot, 37
Canadian Phlox, 220
Candle Larkspur, 92
Candytuft, 164
Canterbury-bells, 68
Cardinal-flower, 184
Carolina Lupine, 256
Carolina Thermopsis, 256
Carpathian Bellflower, 64
Carpathian Harebell, 64
Carpet Bugle, 14
Caucasian Leopard's Bane, 112
Caucasian Scabious, 244
Celandine Crocus, 296
Chalk Plant, 136
Chamomile, 24
Charity, 232

Checkered Lily, 301
Chigger Flower, 38
Chinese Astilbe, 49
Chinese Bellflower, 230
Chinese Lantern Plant, 227
Chinese Peony, 210
Chives, 285
Christmas Rose, 148
Cloth-of-gold Crocus, 296
Cloth-of-silver Crocus, 297
Clover Broom, 57
Clump Speedwell, 266
Clump Verbena, 264
Clustered Bellflower, 68
Colorado Columbine, 28
Columbine, 26
Common Bleeding-heart, 104
Common Blue Flax, 180
Common Crocus, 297
Common Delphinium, 92
Common Foxglove, 108
Common Garden Peony, 210
Common Globeflower, 262
Common Grape Hyacinth, 317
Common Grass Pink, 100
Common Houseleek, 250
Common Hyacinth, 304
Common Lady's-mantle, 18
Common Monkshood, 10
Common Pearly Everlasting, 20
Common Rose Mallow, 158
Common Shooting-star, 110
Common Sneezeweed, 140
Common Snowdrop, 303
Common Spiderwort, 260
Common Sunrose, 142
Common Thrift, 32
Common Yarrow, 6
Corn Daylily, 153
Coral Bells, 156
Coral Lily, 311
Cottage Pink, 100
Cottage Tulips, 333
Cowslip, 202
Cowslip Lungwort, 238
Creeping Bellflower, 69
Creeping Charlie, 196
Creeping Gypsophila, 138
Creeping Jenny, 196
Creeping Lily-turf, 182
Creeping Thyme, 258
Crested Dwarf Iris, 168
Crested Iris, 168
Crimson Bells, 156

Crown Imperial, 300
Cudweed, 35
Cushion Euphorbia, 126
Cypress Spurge, 129

Daffodil, 318
Dalmatian Bellflower, 69
Damask Violet, 155
Dame's Rocket, 155
Dame's Violet, 155
Danes-blood Bellflower, 63
Darwin Hybrids, 331
Darwins, 331
Daylily, 150
Dittany, 106
Dollar Plant, 188
Double Early Tulips, 330
Double Narcissus, 321
Dove's Dung, 322
Dusty Meadow Rue, 255
Dusty Miller, 194
Dutch Crocus, 297
Dutch Hyacinth, 304
Dutchman's Breeches, 105
Dwarf Crested Iris, 168
Dwarf Yarrow, 5

Edging Candytuft, 164
English Bull's Eye, 240
English Daisy, 60
English Monkshood, 10
English Violet, 272
Erect Bugle, 15
Estragon, 35
Evergreen Candytuft, 164
Everlasting Pea, 172
European Globeflower, 262
European Pasque-flower, 290
European Wild Ginger, 36

Fairy Glove, 108
Fall Crocus, 293
False Dragonhead, 228
False Rampion, 69
False Spirea, 46
False Sunflower (*Helenium*), 140
False Sunflower (*Heliopsis*), 146
Fan Columbine, 29
Fernleaf Fleabane, 122
Fernleaf Peony, 215
Fern-leaf Yarrow, 4
Fern-leaved Lily, 311
Feverfew, 78
Finger Flower, 108

Florist's Violet, 272
Flowering Moss, 224
Fortune's Plantain-lily, 162
Foster Tulip, 330
Fragrant Balm, 204
Fragrant Plantain-lily, 160
Fraxinella, 106
Friar's-cap, 10
Fringed Bleeding-heart, 102
Fringed Peony, 215
Fulvous Daylily, 153

Garden Forget-me-not, 206
Garden Hyacinth, 304
Garden Larkspur, 95
Garden Loosestrife, 197
Garden Monkshood, 10
Garden Phlox, 222
Garden Pink, 100
Garden Rocket, 155
Garden Violet, 272
Garden Wolfsbane, 10
Gas Plant, 106
Geneva Bugle, 15
German Catchfly, 195
German Iris, 167
Giant Onion, 282
Giant Snowflake, 307
Globeflower, 262
Goatsbeard, 46
Gold Dust, 249
Golden Alyssum, 52
Golden-carpet, 249
Golden Clematis, 87
Golden Garlic, 284
Golden Marguerite, 24
Golden-pea, 256
Goldentuft, 52
Goldentuft Alyssum, 52
Gold Moss, 249
Goldmoss Stonecrop, 249
Gooseneck Loosestrife, 197
Grape Hyacinth, 316
Grass Pink, 100
Great Blue Lobelia, 186
Great Lobelia, 186
Greek Anemone, 286
Greek Valerian, 232
Ground Pink, 224
Guinea Hen Tulip, 301
Gypsum Pink, 136

Hardy Amaryllis, 314
Hardy Statice, 178

Heartleaf Bergenia, 62
Heavenly Candles, 276
Hedgehog, 114
Helen's Flower, 140
Helmet Flower, 10
Hen and Chickens, 250
Hollyhock, 16
Honesty, 188
Horned Violet, 270
Horsefly, 57
Horsefly Weed, 57
Horse-mint, 204
Hybrid Astilbe, 46
Hybrid Clematis, 84

Iberian Crane's Bill, 135
Immortelle, 20
Imperial Fritillary, 300
Indian Paintbrush, 38
Indian Pink, 184
Iris, 166
Italian Alkanet, 22
Italian Bugloss, 22

Jacob's-ladder, 232
Japanese Anemone, 289
Japanese Bellflower, 230
Japanese Iris, 168
Japanese Lantern, 227
Japanese Lily, 312
Japanese Loosestrife, 197
Jerusalem Cross, 192
Jonquil, 318

Kamchatka Bugbane, 82
Knyghten Milfoil, 6

Lamb's Ears, 253
Lance Coreopsis, 90
Large-cupped Narcissus, 320
Large-flowered Everlasting, 20
Lavender, 174
Lavender Mist, 254
Lebanon Squill, 325
Leek Lily, 284
Lemon Thyme, 258
Lent Lily, 310
Lenten Rose, 149
Leopard Flower, 58
Leopard Lily, 58
Life-everlasting, 20
Lilac Crane's Bill, 134
Lily-flowered Tulips, 331
Lily Leek, 284

Lily Royal, 313
Lily-of-the-valley, 88
Live-forever, 246
London Pride, 192
Long-spurred Columbine, 29
Love Entangle, 249
Lupine, 190

Madonna Lily, 310
Madwort, 52
Magic Lily, 314
Maiden Pink, 98
Mallow Rose, 158
Maltese Cross, 192
Martagon Lily, 311
May Phlox, 220
Meadow Pink, 98
Meadow Saffron, 293
Meadowsweet, 46
Meeting-house, 28
Milfoil, 6
Missouri Primrose, 208
Mist, 136
Monarda, 204
Money Plant, 188
Moneywort *Lunaria*, 188
Moneywort *(Lysimachia)*, 196
Moonwort, 188
Moss Phlox, 224
Moss Pink, 224
Mossy Stonecrop, 249
Mother-of-thyme, 258
Mountain Bluet, 71
Mountain Knapweed, 71
Mountain Pink, 224
Mullein Pink, 194
Myrtle Euphorbia, 128
Mysteria, 293

Nap-at-noon, 322
Narcissus, 318
Needle Palm, 276
New England Aster, 42
New York Aster, 44
Nose-bleed, 6

Obedient Plant, 228
Officinal Aconite, 10
Old Man and Woman, 250
Old Man's Pepper, 6
Orange Daylily, 153
Orange Sunflower, 146
Oriental Poppy, 216
Oswego Tea, 204

Ox-eye Chamomile, 24
Ozark Sundrops, 208

Painted Daisy, 74
Paper Bellflower, 66
Parrot Tulips, 333
Pasque-flower, 290
Peach-bells, 66
Peach-leaved Bellflower, 66
Penny Flower, 188
Peony, 210
Perennial Bachelor's Button, 71
Perennial Coreopsis, 90
Perennial Flax, 180
Perennial Pea Vine, 172
Perennial Phlox, 222
Perennial Sweet Pea, 172
Persian Insect Flower, 74
Pheasant's-eye Pink, 100
Phlox, 222
Pig Squeak, 62
Pincushion Flower, 244
Pink, 98
Pink Plume Polly, 201
Plains False Indigo, 54
Pleurisy Root, 38
Plume Bleeding-heart, 102
Poker Plant, 170
Polyantha Primrose, 236
Poppy-flowered Anemone, 288
Pot-of-gold, 91
Prairie False Indigo, 56
Prairie Pointers, 110
Purple Coneflower, 114
Purple Echinacea, 114
Purple Foxglove, 108
Purple Loosestrife, 198
Purple Rock-cress, 50
Purple Rudbeckia, 114
Purple Willow Herb, 198
Pyrethrum, 74

Rattleweed, 57
Red Alpine Epimedium, 119
Red Balm, 204
Red-birds, 184
Red-hot Poker, 170
Red Lobelia, 184
Red Sally, 198
Regal Lily, 312
Resurrection Lily, 314
Roanoke Bells, 202
Rock Aster, 40
Rock Madwort, 52

Rock Soapwort, 242
Roof Houseleek, 250
Rose Campion, 194
Rose Verbena, 264
Rose Vervain, 264
Rover Bellflower, 69
Rover Sunflower, 144
Royal Lily, 312

Sanguinary, 6
Satiny Wormwood, 34
Scarlet-lightning, 192
Scarlet Lobelia, 184
Scarlet Lychnis, 192
Scotch Pink, 100
Sea Holly, 124
Sea-lavender, 178
Sea Pink, 32
Serbian Bellflower, 69
Shasta Daisy, 76
Shelford Desert Candle, 120
Shelford Foxtail Lily, 120
Shoofly, 57
Showy Japanese Lily, 312
Showy Lily, 312
Showy Sedum, 246
Showy Stonecrop, 246
Siberian Iris, 169
Siberian Squill, 326
Sieber Crocus, 297
Siebold's Plantain-lily, 163
Silver Dollar, 188
Silveredge Bishop's-weed, 12
Silveredge Goutweed, 12
Silvermound Artemisia, 34
Single Early Tulips, 330
Small-cupped Narcissus, 321
Small Globe-thistle, 116
Small Solomon's Seal, 235
Snake's Head, 301
Sneezeweed *(Achillea)*, 7
Sneezeweed *(Helenium)*, 140
Sneezewort, 7
Snow-in-summer, 72
Soapweed, 276
Soldier's-cap, 10
Soldier's Wound-wort, 6
Solitary Clematis, 87
Spanish Bayonet, 276
Spanish Dagger, 276
Spiderwort, 260
Spiked Loosestrife, 198
Spike Gayfeather, 176
Spike Speedwell, 269

355

Spiny Bear's-breeches, 2
Spring-flowering Crocus, 294
Spring Phlox, 220
Staggerweed, 102
Star-of-Bethlehem, 322
Star-of-Persia, 280
Steel Globe-thistle, 116
Strawberry Ground Cherry, 227
Strawberry Tomato, 227
Stripped Squill, 325
Summer Forget-me-not, 22
Summer Phlox, 222
Summer Snowflake *(Leucojum)*, 307
Summer Snowflake *(Ornithogalum)*, 322
Sundrops, 208
Sunflower Heliopsis, 146
Sun Glory, 146
Swamp Lily, 313
Swamp Rose Mallow, 158
Swamp Sunflower, 140
Sweet Rocket, 155
Sweet Violet, 272
Sweet William, 96
Sweet Woodruff, 132

Tall Cluster Plantain-lily, 162
Tall Phlox, 222
Tarragon, 35
Tawny Daylily, 153
Thinleaf Sunflower, 144
Thomas Hogg Blunt-leaved Plantain-lily, 163
Thousandseal, 6
Threadlead Coreopsis, 91
Tiger Lily, 310
Tiny Lily, 311
Tom Thumb Lily, 311
Torch Lily, 170
Tree Celandine, 201
Tree Peony, 214
Tritoma, 170
True Daisy, 60
True Monkshood, 10
Trumpet Daffodil, 320
Trumpet Narcissus, 320
Tuberroot, 38
Tufted Pansy, 270
Tulip, 328
Turban Lily, 311
Turkestan Onion, 283
Turkey Corn, 102
Turk's Cap, *(Aconitum)*, 10
Turk's Cap *(Lilium martagon)*, 311
Turk's Cap Lily, 311
Tussock Bellflower, 64

Two-row Stonecrop, 248

Veronica, 266
Viola, 270
Violet, 272
Virginia Bluebells, 202
Virginia Cowslip, 202
Virginia Lion's-head, 228

Wall Cress, 30
Wall Pepper, 249
Wall Rock Cress, 30
Wandering Jenny, 196
Wandering Sally, 196
Waterlily Tulip, 329
Western Mugwort, 35
White Eardrops, 104
White False Indigo, 56
White Sage, 35
White Tansy, 7
Whorled Tickseed, 91
Wideleaf Sea-lavender, 178
Widow's-tears, 260
Wild Bleeding-heart, 102
Wild Blue Indigo, 54
Wild Columbine, 28
Wild Cotton, 158
Wild Ginger, 37
Wild Indigo, 57
Wild Sweet William, 220
Wild Sunflower, 144
Wild Thyme, 258
Willow Bellflower, 66
Winter Aconite, 299
Winter Cherry, 227
Winter Rose, 148
Wonder Bulb, 293
Woodland Forget-me-not, 206
Woodland Phlox, 220
Woodroof, 132
Woodruff, 132
Woolly Betony, 253
Woolly Speedwell, 268
Woolly Woundwort, 253
Woolly Yarrow, 7

Yellow Chamomile, 24
Yellow Loosestrife, 197
Yellow Milkweed, 38
Yellow Oxeye Daisy, 240
Yellow Star, 140
Yellow Strawberry, 274
Young's Sundrops, 209
Yucca, 276